1986

Roman Coins

ROMAN COINS

FROM THE EARLIEST TIMES

TO THE FALL

OF THE WESTERN EMPIRE

By

HAROLD MATTINGLY

*Late Assistant Keeper, Department
of Coins and Medals, British Museum*

CHICAGO
QUADRANGLE BOOKS

First published January 12, 1928
Second edition, revised and reset, 1960
Printed and bound in Great Britain
by Butler & Tanner Ltd, Frome and London
Collotype plates printed by
L. Van Leer & Co Ltd, Amsterdam, Holland

Library of Congress Catalog Card No. 60–12823

Contents

v

Contents

Book II

THE EMPIRE. AUGUSTUS TO DIOCLETIAN

Contents

Book III

THE EMPIRE – DIOCLETIAN TO
ROMULUS AUGUSTULUS

Contents

Preface

After thirty years the call comes for a second edition of this work, and my publishers have very kindly, and, as I think, wisely, allowed me to undertake a real revision, not merely to tinker with the text of the first edition. Much that I said in the Preface to it can be repeated today – the need of such a work, the difficulties in the way of writing it, my apologies for any shortcomings on my part. A few remarks may be added.

I have thought it advisable to retain the general plan of the book and the Plates. If I were now writing for the first time I might adopt a slightly different plan and choose a rather different range of illustrations. But there is something to be said for a reasonable degree of conservatism and the first edition seems to be adequate in these points.

On some points, as I am well aware, a new and fuller treatment might reasonably be asked for. Some critics may even say that the opportunity should have been taken to re-write the whole book. My answer is a simple one. To have done that would have meant an indefinitely long delay, and to avoid that it has seemed better to offer something that, however imperfect, will yet be of immediate use.

Progress in the study of Roman coins, especially those of the early Republic, has been so rapid during these years that a good deal of re-writing has become absolutely necessary. In some cases it seems advisable to proceed more cautiously than I did in the first edition. Countermarks and the money-systems of the late Empire are cases in point. Where there is serious doubt about facts positive statements can only mislead. Plate references to the text have been added, but do not claim to be exhaustive. The Bibliography is not meant to be more than illustrative; it contains only a selection of the most important works and such as have been of particular service to me. I refer to works where complete bibliographies may be found.

I have tried to do justice to the great advances in numismatic studies made during the last generation. I must acknowledge here my great debt to many scholars – Professor Alfoeldi of Princeton, Signorina Breglia of Naples, Professor Grant of Belfast, Miss Anne

Preface

Robertson of Glasgow, Dr Pink of Vienna, Dr Sutherland and Dr Colin Kraay of the Ashmolean Museum, Oxford, Messrs Carson and Kent of the British Museum – to mention only a few. I shall have omitted some, especially among the younger scholars, who have a claim to be mentioned; for any such omissions I apologize at once; they are inevitable, unless I strain to leave out no possible name.

Modern research has been developing along a number of new lines – such as the study of anniversary issues, the study of dies, that of certain classes of Roman coins which lie a little apart from the main series and have often been overlooked. I shall try to do justice to these new studies in the proper places. This second edition, like the first, is a great adventure. I trust that it will give its readers a real sense of the fresh interest and hope of our numismatic studies. At the risk of being tiresome I shall emphasize the value that coins have for history and other studies. Until that value is more fully appreciated, we numismatists still need to keep on repeating our claims. My special thanks are due to many who, directly or indirectly, have helped me in my work; if I select for special mention Messrs Carson and Kent of the British Museum let that be put down to my 'pietas' towards my old Department.

Introduction

To trace the origin of Greek coinage we have to go back to the very edge of the historical period, to the twilight in which history and myth are blended in indistinguishable confusion. Roman coinage, on the contrary, is a late development – not far short of 400 years later than the first experiments of Greeks and Lydians. From prehistoric times Rome, in common with the other tribes of Italy, had been accustomed to the use of metal as a convenient instrument of payment. But gold and silver were as yet rare commodities, instruments of luxury and art rather than of commercial life, and bronze, the one metal in general use, circulated in the form of rough lumps (*Aes rude*), of varying weights, shapes and sizes, and bore no stamp of official guarantee. It is probable, however, that the *As* or pound of bronze was known as a measure of value some time before it was actually cast as a coin. A more primitive method of reckoning, which has left its traces down to historical times, was that in sheep and oxen, the ox being valued at ten sheep.

We can hardly be wrong in deducing from these facts a very primitive condition of economic life. That an advanced civilization can exist without a coinage in the precious metals seems to be proved by the examples of early Babylon, Assyria and Egypt. But in those early days coinage had not yet been invented. Rome, had she experienced any real need for a coinage, had not far to look to find a model. As long, then, as we find her contented with her cumbrous native methods of exchange we may reckon her as an undeveloped – in Greek language, as a barbarian – people.

We may reserve for Chapter III of the first part the discussion of the relations of Roman coinage to other coinage of the West. All we need here is a general knowledge of the conditions prevailing at the time when Rome first adopted metallic currency. In Spain and Gaul the only earlier coinages are those of the Greek cities of Emporiae, Rhoda, and Massalia. In Italy, Etruria has a coinage of her own, going back to the fifth century B.C., based in its earliest stages on a silver unit of almost exactly the weight of two scruples, later of one scruple, and also on the Syracusan unit, the litra (13·5 gr. – 0·87 gm.). In its latest development the coinage returns to a scruple standard (harmonized, it appears, with the litra standard), closely akin to the earliest Roman (Plate XXII, 9–14). Not till the third century can there be any possible question of Etruscan influence on Rome here. It appears that, in spite of their immediate proximity, the two States had no great commercial intercourse. In Campania and districts near it there is a cluster of Greek cities, chief among them Neapolis, issuing didrachms of Phocaic standard (Plate XXIII, 5–9). In the extreme South we find Tarentum with gold and silver staters, the former of full, the latter of something less than Attic weight, and Croton, Heraclea, Locri, Metapontum, Thurii and Velia with silver staters only. Rhegium prefers the tetradrachm and maintains it at full weight. In Sicily, Syracuse is the only power coining on a large scale (Plate XXII, 1–3). Under Agathocles we find gold drachms and silver tetradrachms of Attic standard, later under Hiero a silver coinage in many denominations based perhaps on the litra of 13·5 gr. (0·87 gm.). Carthage, at this period, was striking electrum pieces of about 146 gr. (9·46 gm.) and 73 gr. (4·73 gm.) and silver tetradrachms of Attic weight (Plate XXII, 4, 5). It was among these coinages that the Roman coinage grew and developed.

To sum up, we find Rome at first confined to a peculiar system, in which precious metal is hardly known and bronze in rough lumps is the one metal used for exchange. As there is no serious evidence in favour of an extensive early commerce in Rome, we accept this fact as proof of primitive economic conditions. The commercial treaties with Carthage, so far as we really know anything of them, do not very long precede the introduction of coinage at Rome. As soon as Rome, having begun to coin in bronze, felt the need of a more valuable medium of exchange, she had models to guide her choice near at hand.

We have now revised our ideas about the first Roman coinage, have brought down its date to 269 B.C. and made the didrachm and As begin at the same time. If this new view is correct, it has important results for the tempo of the whole of Roman development; that tempo will have been rather faster than has hitherto been supposed. Another question that presses for answer is that of the coinage of the Latin and Italian allies of Rome. At what dates did they cast or strike their coins? And why did some issue coins, others not? We are still quite uncertain of the reasons that led some States to issue, while others abstained. If it is true, as we shall suggest, that the first, ROMANO, coinage was meant for all who followed the Roman interest in Italy, a new possibility comes into view. Were the allies satisfied with this coinage in the first instance?

Introduction

Only then, when the Roman coinage was more centralized and standardized, with more emphasis on Rome herself (note the new signature ROMA), did they begin to want coinage of their own? There seems to be a chance of real advance along these lines.

BOOK I

The Roman Republic

CHAPTER I

The External History of the Coinage:
Money-Systems, Mints, etc.

I. HISTORICAL SKETCH

So much work has been done in the last thirty years on the early Republican coinage that an entirely new treatment is now required. References will be given in the Bibliography to works that give the whole story of modern controversy. In the text it will be necessary to choose one clear line and follow that consistently.

The Romans themselves were inclined to carry back coinage to the period of the Kings, to Numa Pompilius and Servius Tullius.[1] In the history of the early Republic coins are mentioned by name on a number of occasions. Some great scholars, like the Baron D'Ailly, for example, followed this tradition. But all of these early stories may be dismissed out of hand. Coinage, as a necessary adjunct of city life, is innocently thrown back on periods when it was still unknown. There was presumably a time when oxen and sheep were used as measures of value. Our tradition is positive on the point; the Latin word for 'money' ('pecunia') seems to be related to 'pecus' – 'herd'. Whether the custom really lasted down to the age of the Decemvirs, c. 450 B.C., may be doubted. The currency of bronze, not as coin but as metal, passing by weight ('Aes Rude', 'rough bronze') is recorded in our tradition, confirmed by hoards and finally proved by such words as 'expendere', 'weigh out', for 'pay'.

Since D'Ailly's time dates have been brought down step by step, as scholars have attempted to discover just when Rome proceeded to the Greek device of coinage. Mommsen thought of the age of the Decemvirs, Haeberlin and Bahrfeldt of about 340, Sydenham of 308, Mattingly, in his earlier work, of the Pyrrhic War.[2] The most forward view,

[1] For the earliest period see H. Mattingly, 'Aes and Pecunia', *Num. Chron.*, 1943, pp. 1 ff.

[2] Detailed references will be found in Rudi Thomsen, *Early Roman Coinage*, Vol. I, 1957: Mommsen, *Geschichte des Römischen Münzwesens*: Eckhel, *Doctrina Numorum*

which we shall adopt here, is that the tradition of the first Roman silver coinage in 269 is strictly true, but that we have been too long misled by the blunder of Pliny the Elder, who thought that this silver was the denarius and its parts. Our view has been accepted in the main by many scholars, but many modifications have been suggested – none of them, as we think, for the better. But it is fiercely contested by most scholars of the Italian school, who stand firmly by an old tradition which in large measure has been disproved; patriotic pride seems to play its part in insisting in every detail on the early greatness of Rome. The whole complicated tale may now be read in Rudi Thomsen's invaluable book.

It has sometimes been thought that we can discover for ourselves from general considerations just when the Romans must have begun to issue coins. That very lively scholar, Tenney Frank, was convinced that Rome must at least have coined as soon as she came into touch with Campania. We might surely have expected such a coinage, but the only trace of such that survives is the rare bronze coin with Neapolitan types, but the name *PΩMAIΩN*, probably struck just after Rome's alliance with Naples in 327. The fact is that all arguments from supposed probabilities may mislead us; we cannot assess probabilities with any real accuracy. In setting out from the established date of 269 for the first Roman silver we shall have the inestimable advantage of a firm foundation on fact, not theory. We shall have to part – at times, reluctantly – with some time-honoured views, with that of Eckhel, for example, about a 'Romano-Campanian' coinage. That great scholar thought, very strangely, that all the early Roman didrachms were struck in south Italy and were hardly strictly Roman at all; 'were it not for the name, no one would take them for Roman coins'. Haeberlin's majestic 'Systematik' can no longer stand in its original form if the new dating is adopted, but it surely represents a vital insight – that the first Roman coinage is not unitary, but multiple, based on an elaborate system. Had Haeberlin ever been converted to the new dating, he might well have produced a system, not unlike that which we shall offer.

Early in the third century there may have been an advance from the currency of bronze, quite rough or in primitive bars, to something more developed – bars with types on both sides – what we, rather oddly, call 'Aes Signatum'. There is a suggestion, not a certainty, that

Veterum, Vol. V: Samwer and Bahrfeldt, *Geschichte des Älteren Römischen Münzwesens*, 1883: Haeberlin, *Die Systematik des Älteren Römischen Münzwesens*, 1905: Mattingly, 'The Romano-Campanian Coinage and the Pyrrhic War' (*Num. Chron.*, 1924): Sydenham, *The Coinage of the Roman Republic*, 1952.

4

the Roman moneyers were first appointed about 289; the date is often contested today, but it may still be near the truth.[1] These bars may reasonably be called 'medallic' in character and certainly served as currency, if not precisely as coin; they may have had a theoretical weight, not strictly observed, of six pounds. They are immensely rare today, but they were not always so, for many broken fragments have been found in some hoards. As one of the bars refers to the Indian elephants of Pyrrhus and another to a naval victory, they may be dated to the period before and after 269. With the introduction of regular coinage they probably began to lose their position.[2]

The date of 269[3] for the first Roman silver is given by Pliny and Livy and confirmed by many later writers. The one big correction that we must make in Pliny's tradition is to reject his denarius of 269 and let 'the first silver' mean what it naturally should – the ROMANO didrachms. It has always been seen that Pliny's statement contained conflicting elements – that the denarius could never have equalled ten libral Asses, as he says. The old solution – to reject the didrachms as not really Roman coins at all – has failed to provide a satisfactory chronology. But try the other solution – put the didrachms in their proper place as the first Roman silver and let the denarius find its true level in the second century, and the horizon at once clears. New problems of course arise, but the worst of the old ones disappear.

The arguments for the late date of the denarius are given in the paper by Mattingly and Robinson[4] and, with slight modifications, hold good today. The Roman bronze, on which the coins of the rebel Capua, Calatia and Atella are overstruck, are of heavier standard than the bronze that goes with the first denarii; that bronze – and with it the denarius – were not yet in existence in 215 B.C. Livy[5] in 197 records that the Attic tetradrachm was about equal in weight to three denarii. These denarii cannot be our X denarii, weighing about 72 gr.; they must be earlier coins, called by the same name, reduced quadrigati of c. 90 gr., such as we find freely in our trays. Plautus with his 'Trinummus' of about the same date, clinches the point; 'trinummus' is the popular name for the big foreign coin. 'Denarius nummus', we must remember, is the exact translation of the Greek δεκάλιτρος στάτηρ a standard silver coin, containing ten pounds of bronze – and that goes

[1] Pomponius, *Digest*, I, 2.2.30.
[2] On these bars, see Mattingly, *Aes Signatum, Serta Hoffilleriana*, 1940.
[3] Pliny, *Nat. Hist.*, XXXIII, 3, 13; Livy, *Epit.*, XV.
[4] 'The Date of the Roman Denarius, etc.' (*Proceedings of the British Academy*, 1932).
[5] Livy, XXXIV, 52.

far back behind any Roman coinage. To complete the argument, we may add that the style of the denarius belongs to the second century, not the third, and that the history of the denarius itself confirms this dating. From about 100 B.C. – I think we may now say from Gaius Gracchus, 123 B.C. – we can date our denarii closely; if we work back from these datable denarii, we simply have not enough to fill the century and a half demanded by the old dating. Half a century would be nearer the mark. Pliny dates the denarius of sixteen Asses to 217 B.C.; we see now that it is as late as Gaius Gracchus. Scholars have long recognized that it must be much later than 217 and have tacitly corrected the date to 140 or 130. But why did they not apply the same correction to the date of the first denarius?

Rome, then, first struck silver in 269 B.C. A careful comparison of that silver with the Roman libral *Aes* leads us to conclude that the latter are of about the same date. A close study of this coinage in all its details leads to an arrangement in four series, with a silver 'nummus' and an As in each. We will first set out our results in this form and then add some explanations and justifications.[1]

Series A

Didrachm, obv. Mars: oak-leaf, rev. Horse's head: corn-ear. ROMANO.
   There is a very rare litra, a tenth, with the same types, but no corn-ear.

As – obv. 'Young Janus', rev. Mercury.
Semis – obv. Mars, rev. Female head.
Triens – obv. Thunderbolt, rev. Dolphin.
Quadrans – obv. Two barley-corns, rev. Open hand.
Sextans – obv. Head of Dioscuri, rev. ·
Uncia – obv. Knucklebone, rev. ·
Semuncia – obv. Acorn, rev. ⟩

Series B

Didrachm, obv. Apollo, rev. Free horse: star. ROMANO.

As – obv. Apollo, rev. Apollo.
Semis – obv. Pegasus, rev. Pegasus.
Triens – obv. Horse's head, rev. Horse's head.
Quadrans – obv. Boar, rev. Boar.
Sextans – obv. Head of Dioscure, rev. Head of Dioscure.
Uncia – obv. Barley-corn, rev. Barley-corn.

[1] Mattingly, 'The First Age of Roman Coinage', *J.R.S.*, 1929 and 1945.

The types are to r. on the obv., to l. on the rev., except on the Uncia, where the barley-corns are to front.

Series C

Didrachm, obv. Hercules, rev. She-wolf and twins. ROMANO.

> As – obv. Diana, rev. Wheel.

and so on, for all denominations.

> Semis, obv. Bull, triens, obv. Free Horse, quadrans, obv. Hound, sextans, obv. Tortoise.

There are also pieces of three and two Asses, with obv. Diana. There is no uncia.

Series D

Didrachm, obv. Diana: varying symbol, rev. Victory crowning palm: Greek single or double letters. ROMANO.

> As – obv. Diana, rev. Diana.
> Semis – obv. Mars, rev. Mars.
> Triens – obv. Thunderbolt, rev. Thunderbolt.
> Quadrans – obv. Open hand, rev. Open hand.
> Sextans – obv. Shell, rev. Shell.
> Uncia – obv. Knucklebone, rev. Knucklebone.
> Semuncia – obv. Acorn, rev. Acorn.

As in Series B obv. types are repeated, reversed for the reverse. The hands shown are r. and l. respectively. The shell is shown convex and concave.

Associated with the didrachms are small bronze coins, of token character, but of uncertain denominations.

There is a large piece, c. 236 gr., with obv. Minerva, ROMANO, rev. Eagle on thunderbolt, sword. κ. ROMANO: smaller pieces c. 180 gr., with obv. Apollo, rev. Lion. ROMANO, and c. 90 gr., with obv. Minerva, rev. Horse's head. ROMANO.

The silver and token As are all signed ROMANO, the heavy bronze has no signature. This lack of signature led to the bronze being placed apart as 'Latin Aes Grave' – something not strictly Roman. It is certain today that it belongs with the silver. No marks of value appear on the silver. On the heavy bronze III stands for three As piece ('tressis'), II for two As piece ('dupondius'), I for As, S for Semis, · · · · for Triens, · · · for Quadrans, · · for Sextans, · for Uncia and Ƹ for Semuncia.[1] The silver and token bronze are all struck, the As and its multiples and parts are all cast. The weights vary from series to series. In Series A the didrachm weighs c. 112 gr., the As c. 5,057: in Series B the didrachm weighs c. 112 gr., the As 5,260: in Series C the didrachm weighs c. 109·9 gr., the As 4,216: in Series D the didrachm weighs c. 102·5 gr., the As c. 4,216. In contrast to the light token bronze the heavy *Aes* obviously represents true metal value: the system is bimetallic. We think of the silver and token bronze as intended for city use, the heavy *Aes* for the country. We are not sure of the relation of As to didrachm: it may have been its sixth part.

It will be useful at this point – though it means drawing a little on what has still to be said about the later, ROMA, coinage – to note the many interlinkings and cross-references which prove that we really have to do with a 'Systematik', a coinage planned and organized in all its parts:

(1) The didrachm, Mars – Horse's head, ROMANO, is continued, varied, with the ROMA series, as also is the didrachm Apollo – Free horse.

(2) The 'Young Janus' – Mercury As passes on from a heavy to a light series. The same is true of the As 'Apollo' – 'Apollo'.

(3) Of the reverses of the ROMANO silver, the horse's head of Series A appears on the triens of Series B, the free horse of Series B on the triens of Series C.

(4) The wheel series of *Aes Grave* in the ROMANO period is like the prow series in the ROMA period, in having the same reverse types for all denominations.

(5) The 'Young Janus' – Mercury series, for all denominations below the As, borrows a type from the Diana – Diana series. This phenomenon is to be observed in both groups, ROMANO and ROMA.

(6) The Diana – Diana series of *Aes Grave* is like the Apollo – Apollo series in reversing the obverse types to form the reverse. This again is true of both groups, ROMANO and ROMA.

Apollo and Diana, of course, are twins.

(7) Diana is found on the ROMANO didrachm, on the *Aes* attached to it and on the following *Aes* in the ROMA group (with symbol, club).

---

[1] Triens, quadrans and sextans are all *active* in meaning – not pieces of three, four and six, but dividers by those numbers: twelve, divided by three, four and six, gives four, three and two.

(8) The 'Young Janus' of the *Aes Grave* of Series A (in both groups, ROMANO and ROMA) appears on the quadrigatus in the ROMA group.

The exact significance of all these relations cannot at once be guessed: it may indeed continue to elude us. But there is surely evidence enough that, when Haeberlin spoke of a 'Systematik', he was most happily inspired. Many scholars refuse to accept our plan of four series in two successive periods. They place the lighter coins later than the heavier and incline to think of sequences within a single mint. One can only say: try it out and see if you can really believe in the arrangements that result.

Some justifications may now be offered for our dating and arrangement. Three of the didrachms can at once be linked to the date 269 – the date of the first silver. The Apollo didrachm is identical in style with the small bronze of Beneventum, which was probably struck when the city became a Latin colony – and could not have been struck before, as its old name had been Maleventum. The Diana didrachm shares its system of Greek letters as mint-marks with the Alexandrine decadrachms of the deified Arsinoe (270 B.C.).[1] This system of mint-marking is never very common on coins: only in these two series, the Roman and Alexandrine, are such long runs known – two complete alphabets plus the first letter of a third for Rome, the same, but two letters in the third alphabet for Alexandria. What seems to be implied is not borrowing on either side, but concurrent issue. The letters must, in some way or another, indicate periods of sequence. They might be calendar years – but, in that case, the comparative rarity of the coins today would be surprising in so long an issue. But, if we take the letters to denote other periods of time in the mint or 'quota' of work, the concurrence implies an even closer connexion of Rome and Alexandria than we have assumed. The types of the Hercules didrachm refer to the two Consuls of 269 – C. Fabius and Cn. Ogulnius. Hercules was the legendary founder of the Fabian 'gens', Ogulnius aedile with his brother in 295 had set up a group of the she-wolf and twins. The Mars didrachm at first sight looks a little earlier: we might have been tempted to date it to 280 or even 290 B.C. But the token bronze that goes with it has been found overstruck on Syracusan bronze of c. 280 – so the 269 date probably holds good for this didrachm too. The four series are seen to be parallel, not successive. The argument from the falling weights is in no way decisive. If the coins were issued, as we shall suggest, for different areas of circulation, some variation in weights and

[1] Cp. Svoronos, *Tὰ νομίσματα τοῦ κράτους τῶν Πτολεμαιῶν*; Nos. 419 ff. and 937 ff.

9

in the relation of silver to bronze has nothing in it to surprise us. Concurrence, not succession, is suggested by the independence of the sets of types and by their variation of style, to which we now come.

There is one style (in Series A) which shows an obvious borrowing from Metapontum, a second (in Series B) which is that of Beneventum – close, too, as I think, to Nuceria. There is a third style (Series C and D) – I think one style, not two – which cannot be paralleled in any mint of Italy or Sicily. As Rome is not likely to have produced such highly competent artists from nowhere, we have to ask where they came from. The obvious answer is 'from Alexandria', which had formed an alliance with Rome in 273 B.C. Four distinct series should mean four distinct mints, and as Rome, near this date (265), created her 'Italian' provinces, we think of a mint for Rome herself and three such mints in Italy. Series C (Hercules didrachm) will belong to Rome; Series A (Mars didrachm) perhaps to Ostia; Series B (Apollo didrachm) to Beneventum or a neighbouring mint for the 'calles', the rough uplands of south-east Italy; Series D perhaps to the citadel of Tarentum, which remained in Roman hands after the Pyrrhic War. Little is known about the Italian provinces: they were administered by 'quaestores classici' ('quaestors of the fleet'?). They were four in number: a 'Gallic province' – seat unknown: Ostia: the 'calles' and a fourth of unknown position. From our coins we can provide a probable series for Ostia and the 'calles': Tarentum may represent the unknown fourth. The 'Gallic province' was perhaps not created till later.[1]

The heavy *Aes* was, it seems, issued for the same districts as the silver – not necessarily from the same mints. The allotment of Asses to 'nummi' is reasonably certain. In Series A didrachm and As are linked by symbol, sickle, in period II; we carry back the connexion to period I, when the symbol does not yet occur. In Series B the obverse of Apollo

---

[1] The difficulty of relating our mints with close accuracy to the Italian 'provinces' must not cause us to forget that such a relation is inherently probable. The fixing of the mints at definite places is obviously difficult and uncertain. The mint of Rome (Series C) is fairly clearly marked in the second period by the 'quadrigatus' and 'Janus – Prow' As. 'Ostia' (Series A) is a rather probable guess, despite the Metapontine flavour of its style. It was the seat of an Italian 'province'. Its coins were copied by the Latin colony of Cosa in Etruria and tend to be common in Etruscan hoards. One great hoard of Asses of this mint was found near Ostia. The sickle in the second period of the mint suggests Latium – being the special attribute of Saturn, Latium's old god-king. 'Beneventum' (Series B) cannot be far wrong, even if the mint was not necessarily in that one city. The same artist made the Roman silver and the Beneventan bronze. 'Tarentum' (Series D) is just a reasonable guess. The Greek mint-marks running parallel to the Alexandrian series certainly point to south Italy. The club symbol in the second series is proper to Hercules, one of the great gods of Tarentum. For convenience, we shall use the names 'Ostia', 'Beneventum', 'Tarentum', in inverted commas, to denote the separate series.

links didrachm and As in both periods. In Series C the Janus – Prow As is certainly of Rome: the Diana – Wheel As is its obvious predecessor in period I. In Series D didrachm and As are linked in period II by the symbol, club: in the ROMANO period there is no symbol to link them, but the same goddess, Diana, supplies the obverse to both didrachm and As.

The first coinage of Rome, then, was not planned for 'urbs Roma' only but for Roman interests in Italy. This is perhaps suggested by the use of ROMANO instead of ROMA in the first period – probably the old genitive plural, with the final M dropped – 'coinage of the Romans'. In the second period, ROMA might seem to lay more stress on the supremacy of Rome. Something more will be said of this when we speak of the coinage of Rome's allies in Italy. It is natural to raise the question 'What States influenced Rome in her first coinage?' First, let us look at the negative evidence. There is no real trace of Etruscan influence, or, what is stranger, of Neapolitan. Traces of Metapontine style have been found in Series A, of Beneventan in Series B; there is nothing else, either from south Italy or from Sicily. The types of horse's head and free horse were, in a sense, borrowed from Carthage; but the borrowing was, so to say, external – the types have their own Roman meanings. The influence of Alexandria must be admitted as very strong: she may have supplied both artists and metal. In view of the alliance with Rome of 273 this is not really strange. Some modern scholars have unnecessarily questioned the reality of this alliance, because, as the First Punic War showed, it was not a military one. It presumably regulated the relations of the two powers where their commercial interests might cross – in south Italy and Sicily.[1]

This first system of Roman coinage seems to have lasted without change during the First Punic War. The fact, though it seems strange,

---

[1] A note on some names of coins may be acceptable. 'Nummus', didrachm, is the Latin word for the Greek στάτηρ standard coin.

'Litra' is the tiny silver coin, a tenth of the 'nummus', representing a theoretical pound of bronze.

'Moneta', 'mint', later 'money', was originally an epithet of Juno, the 'adviser'. Juno seems to have given her name to the mint, which was in her temple. A Carthaginian origin of the epithet 'moneta' has been suggested – it is best left as, at best, a curious possibility (Assmann, *Klio*, VI, pp. 477 ff.: cf. *Num. Chron.*, 1910, pp. 1 ff.).

As means unity, as well as bronze coin of pound weight. Whatever its derivation – from asser', 'bar' or 'axis', 'assis', 'wheel' (?) – it has certainly been assimilated to the Greek εἶς 'one'. Forcellini, in his great Lexicon, gives variant forms of εἶς – αἶς – Doric, ἆς – Tarentine. No evidence for these forms can be found today. But how could Forcellini have imagined Tarentum, before anyone had ever thought of Tarentum as a possible mint for early Roman coins? It certainly looks as if he had before him some evidence that has since been lost.

stands fast. No reduction of weight can be seen in any of the heavy bronze of the period. Debased silver is found occasionally in Series A ('Ostia'), but in none of the other series. The burden of the war, fought largely in Sicily, may have fallen on Hiero of Syracuse. But the war will have been fought also on credit ('fides'), the State, as is recorded for the Second Punic War, not paying its debts cash down, but booking them for future repayments. We are expressly told that the last fleet, which ended the war by the battle of the Aegatian Isles, was built out of private subscriptions.

The second stage of Roman coinage followed about 235 B.C. The date can only be guessed at, but it seems to be after the war, but not long after. The closing of the temple of Janus in 238, when hostilities with Carthage had been finally concluded, would help to account for the Janus head on the obverse of the As. The ROMANO and ROMA periods between them account for the years 269–218: we shall see that a new period began with the Hannibalic War. The reform of the coinage, represented in the ROMA series, seems more probable after the war than in its later, dragging years, when Roman enterprise was at a low ebb. But, to give a reasonable duration to that issue, we must not delay its inception much later.

Again, we find four series, with didrachm and As in each.

Series *A* ('Ostia')

Didrachm, obv. Mars, rev. Horse's head: sickle, ROMA.

> As – obv. 'Young Janus' – Mercury. Other denominations as in period I, but all with symbol, sickle.

Series *B* ('Beneventum')

Didrachm, obv. Apollo, rev. Free horse, ROMA.

> As – obv. Apollo, rev. Apollo. Other denominations as in period I: but the series is, for some reason unknown to us, very rare, and one or two denominations are hardly, if at all, represented.

Series *C* (Rome)

Didrachm, obv. 'Young Janus', rev. Jupiter with Victory in quadriga, ROMA (the 'quadrigatus').

> As – obv. Janus, rev. Prow. This reverse runs through all denominations.

The other obv. are: Semis – Saturn: triens – Mars; quadrans – Hercules: sextans – Mercury: uncia – Virtus.

Series *D* ('Tarentum')

Didrachm, obv. Mars, rev. Free horse: club, ROMA.

As – obv. Diana, rev. Diana: club. Other denominations as in period I, all with club.

The signature on the silver and token bronze is always ROMA; there is no signature on the *Aes*. Marks of value occur on the heavy bronze as in period I; there are no marks on the silver. There are half-pieces, drachms, in Series A, B and C, but not in D. There is also token bronze – Hercules – Pegasus: club, ROMA, c. 6·2 gr.: Mars – Free horse, c. 3·3 gr.: club, ROMA (Series D): Diana – hound, ROMA (Series D), c. 1·8 gr.: Mars – Horse's head: sickle (Series A), c. 3·1 gr.: Apollo – Free horse, ROMA (Series B), c. 3·4 gr. The silver and token bronze are all struck, the heavy bronze is cast.

The succession from the ROMANO period is fairly clear. In Series A and B the types are carried on with slight modifications. In Series C the *Aes* with prow is the natural successor of the *Aes* with wheel: the didrachm is linked to the As by its obverse 'Young Janus' – Janus. In Series D the succession is shown by the As, Diana – Diana, with club added as symbol. The club links the didrachm to the As. Of the symbols the sickle ('harpa') of Saturn suggests Latium: the club of Hercules is very suitable for Tarentum.

The weights are now standardized – that of the didrachm at c. 102·5 gr., that of the As at c. 4,216. Standardized too is the style. The Metapontine style vanishes from Series A, the Beneventan from Series B. What now takes their place is a style similar to that of Series C and D. One might conjecture that Alexandrian workmen replaced the previous staffs in Series A and B.[1]

There is a considerable coinage of Latin and other allies of Rome and other Italian States running parallel to the ROMANO and ROMA coinages: a consideration of this will best be deferred to our third chapter.

The ROMA period ended with the Second Punic War. That three of

---

[1] We have set out our system in a perfectly regular form, such as consistency seems to demand. But one possibility should not be disregarded. If the letter signatures of Series D (period I) represent years, that series would run for 49 years, from 269 to 221 B.C. The ROMA series, then, would have to be a resumption after the Second Punic War. The didrachm is remarkably like some early denarii.

the four mints suspended issue is certain: reductions in the weight of
the *Aes* occur in Series C (Rome) only – not in A, B or D. It is impossible not to connect this break with the disruption of communications by the invasion of Hannibal. The whole burden of the coinage
now fell on Rome. Quadrigati[1] were certainly struck at several mints
outside the capital, but the planning was from the centre and such
mints were no more than branches of the Roman.

Gold appeared as an emergency issue in 217 and 209: it was struck
in two denominations, stater and half-stater[2] (c. 102·5 and 51·25 gr.)
– probably equal to twelve and six quadrigati respectively.[2] The types
are 'Young Janus' (as on the quadrigatus) rev. Oath-scene, ROMA. The
silver, we read in Zonaras, was debased.[3] But the debased quadrigati,
which occur in some quantity, look like irregular issues (of forgers?)
of later date. The weight of the heavy *Aes* was twice reduced – the As
from ten to six ounces in 217,[4] from six to three c. 209. In the first
reduction, the As to the triens are cast, triens to uncia struck: in the
second reduction, the As and semis are cast, semis to uncia struck: here,
there are also cast pieces of ten, three and two Asses. The signature,
ROMA, appears on the struck pieces only. The change of standard is
clearly seen only on the struck coins: on the cast the decline in weight
proceeds in slight, almost imperceptible stages. The quadrigatus perhaps equalled ten Asses of the first reduction, twenty of the second. It
seems probable, if not certain, that struck pieces of the first reduction
had been issued for convenience, as a part token coinage, before 217. It
was on these pieces that the Capuan rebels overstruck their bronze in
215, and one wonders whether, between 217 and 215, these coins had
had time to get far into general circulation.

The quadrigatus had its half-piece – its drachm – with similar types.
At some date as yet uncertain (c. 218, 209 or 205?) a new half-piece was
introduced – the victoriate, with Jupiter on obv. and Victory crowning
trophy on rev. Small bronze coins with obv. Mercury, rev. Prow and
obv. Virtus, same rev., are sometimes considered to be half and quarter
ounces of the Prow series. It is possibly that they were originally token
Aes, like that of the ROMANO and ROMA periods.

In the first reduction, there is a struck series signed ROMA, but bear-

---

[1] It is possible that the Janus – Prow series had also its branch mints, but, here, the
roughness of the style makes judgement difficult.

[2] For the piece of 4 scruples, marked XXX, see below, p. 17.

[3] Zonaras, VIII, 26.

[4] Festus, *De Verb. Sig.*, s.v. *Grave* and *Sextantarii*. Pliny, *Nat. Hist.*, XXXIII, 3, 13,
puts the reduction in the First Punic War and makes it a reduction to two Asses!

ing divergent types. The triens has obv. Diademed Goddess, rev. Hercules and Centaur, the quadrans obv. Head in boar-skin, rev. Bull and snake, the sextans obv. Large bird, rev. She-wolf and twins, the uncia, obv. Sol, rev. Crescent and two stars. A coin, often assigned to this series as a semuncia, has on obv. the head of a towered goddess, on rev. a horseman. If, as seems probable, the goddess is Cybele, the date must be near the end of the Second Punic War. This series is something of a mystery. It is not of Rome itself – the divergent types prove that. The she-wolf and twins of the sextans suggest a Latin colony. If, as seems probable, the mint was in Apulia rather than Campania, the mint might well be Venusia – the goddess of the obv. of the triens, Venus. As one piece, the quadrans, is found in reduced weights, with mint-mark corn-ear and seems from hoards to be Sicilian, we might conjecture that coins of this class were taken to Sicily by the survivors of Cannae who were sent for a punishment to serve in the island.

If the view that we are taking is correct, Rome during the Hannibalic War assumed a complete leadership in coinage, which she never again relinquished. The Italian mints, once closed, did not reopen, with the possible exception of D (see above, p. 13, n. 1). We look in vain for quadrigati resembling them in style, such as we might expect had Rome used them as branch mints.[1]

Conditions after the war must have been chaotic. The victoriate, struck at a number of mints, denoted by letters or symbols, dominated the silver coinage. The quadrigatus was still struck, but only at a very few mints: in circulation it may have fallen apart from the victoriate. Asses of several sizes, ten ounces, six ounces, three ounces, jostled one another in circulation: the market will have assigned suitable values to them. There is rather strong evidence that the ten-ounce standard of the As was for a time restored.[2] For

(1) The As has now its prow on rev. to r., while on the original libral series and on the reductions, down to the very end of the second, the prow was always to l.

[1] We append here a short list of the coinages, struck in Italy on the side of Hannibal:
(a) Electrum, with obv. female Janiform head, rev. Jupiter in quadriga: struck at Capua (?).
(b) Silver of Tarentum in revolt against Rome.
(c) Bronze of Capua, Calatia and Atella, similarly in revolt – very rare silver of Capua.
(d) Cast *Aes*, of reduced weight, of Velecha and 'Mel'.
(e) Token bronze of a few cities such as Arpi and Salapia.
(f) Part, at least, of the coinage of the Brettii, in gold, silver and bronze.
[2] If, as we have argued, the 'denarius' in 197 meant a reduced quadrigatus, that coin would at that time equal ten Asses. If these were libral Asses, the price of silver must have risen. As far as it goes, this tells against the theory of a restored libral As.

15

(2) In several details of type the reductions take a position intermediate between the ten-ounce prow l. and the ten-ounce prow r.

(3) Some libral Asses with prow r. are very like late quadrigati. The As, too, has mark of value on both obv. and rev., like the As that accompanies the denarius.

Our literary authorities record the coming to Rome in quantity of foreign coins from the East – Macedonian gold staters and Athenian tetradrachms. The evidence is too strong to doubt, though confirmation from Italian hoards is lacking.

After the strain of the Hannibalic War reorganization, in coinage as elsewhere, might appear a prime necessity. Here, however, it was delayed – partly, perhaps, because of the Eastern Wars – till about 169 B.C. A new 'nummus' the 'denarius', marked X, replaced the quadrigatus. Beside it were struck the quinarius, its half (v) and the sestertius, its fourth (II s). The quadrigatus only survived in a very few rare issues: the victoriate was struck for some years beside the denarius, but still bore no mark of value. The Asses that accompany the first denarii are usually called 'sextantal',[1] two-ounce Asses; as a matter of fact they are often over that weight. In some series a lighter As may have been struck. All the bronze is now cast and, like the silver, signed ROMA. It may now have become a part token coinage, tariffed above its metal value.

Close to the first denarii there is a series of gold coins, with obv. Mars, rev. Eagle on thunderbolt, in three denominations, marked LX, XXXX and XX – weighing three, two and one scruple respectively. Pliny tells us that the marks stand for sestertii: this would give a very high value to gold against silver, 1–20. Surely the marks denote Asses, as on the silver. The resulting rate of gold to silver, 1–8, is abnormally low, but an explanation is at once to hand in the Aquileia gold rush, when the price of gold for a short time fell by a third. The exact date is not recorded by Polybius,[2] but it must have been near 169.

The new system has one notable peculiarity; it has four 'nummi', standard silver coins, whereas only one is normally required. The clear suggestion is that the system was composite, designed to cover different areas of circulation. The mysterious 'little talents' of the West come at once to our minds – each divided into 12 nummi and 120 litrae; the three metals, gold, silver and bronze, are here correlated, gold

[1] The term 'sextantarii' in our ancient authorities possibly means 'Asses overstruck on sextantes': we find such not uncommonly: the sextantes are of the first reduction, so the As weighs about an ounce.
[2] Quoted by Strabo, IV, 6, 12.

in the talent, silver in the nummus, bronze in the litra. It is quite unlikely that there is any question here of the divisions of the 'great' talent – 60 minae and 6,000 drachms – with drachms of bronze instead of silver. The Alexandrian talent has as its nummus the denarius, the Neapolitan the quinarius, the Sicilian the sestertius; the Rhegine talent was itself a victoriate.[1] Here we have the four nummi of the Roman system; the victoriate treated, as Pliny tells us, 'loco mercis', as bullion, bears no mark of value.

The first denarii were struck at a large number of mints, signing with letters or symbols. So too were the victoriates; but, except in Rome itself, they seem to be associated with the quinarius, not with the denarius. Rome for a time seems to have allowed the small concession to local pride that the signature of the coins represented. The types of the denarius and its parts are Bellona Victrix on obv., the Dioscuri on horseback, charging, on rev. The gold piece of the old types 'Young Janus' – Oath scene, marked XXX, weight about four scruples, should be of about the date of the first denarii. If XXX stands for sestertii, the value of gold to silver comes out as $1:7\frac{1}{2}$ – very near the value suggested above for the Mars gold. The coin used to be considered false, but, as it is exactly in the style of some quadrigati that are certainly genuine, we have no choice but to accept it.

What was the date of this reform? Mattingly and Robinson in their first paper suggested 187 B.C. as a probable date; but some of the arguments then advanced seem today to have less cogency and other indications point rather to about 169. The Prologue to the revival of the Casina of Plautus speaks of new plays being as bad as the new 'nummi', and 'nummus', as we have seen, should mean not 'coin' simply, but standard silver coin – the denarius, in fact, in place of the quadrigatus. The date of this revival seems likely to be near 169, for Prologue says that the play will still be remembered by the older men in the audience, and the original may have been not far from 200. If we work back from closely dated denarii of c. 123 B.C. onwards, we arrive at about 169 as a probable date of origin. Sydenham has put out a theory that the denarius began as an experimental issue in Bruttium, before it came to Rome as the Roman 'nummus'. If this should prove to be correct – at present it is only a theory – the date of 187 B.C. might still be nearly right for the first denarii.

Many scholars, while recognizing the need to bring the denarius

[1] Cp. Mattingly, 'The Little Talents of Sicily and the West', *Num. Chron.*, 1943, pp. 4 ff.

down from 269, still refuse to descend as late as 169 and experiment with dates in the Second Punic War. The evidence of Livy and Plautus for a denarius, heavier than our X piece, in 197 (see above), is decisive against this; it gives us a certain date 'post quem'.

The first period of the denarii with its many mints did not last very long. The quinarius and sestertius soon ceased to be issued; the victoriate survived them till about the end of the period. Apart from a few outlying denarii, the coinage now runs in three clear channels. A central issue, presumably of Rome, has two styles, very close but yet distinguishable – the same moneyers often striking in both: perhaps they represent two 'officinae' of the Roman mint. Victory in a biga appears as a variant for the Dioscuri. The other two mints are distinguishable in style, both from Rome and from one another. Instead of the Victory in biga both have Diana in biga as a new variant of reverse; but the goddess is shown in two very distinct poses – in one, leaning forward over the horses, in the other, leaning back, tugging at the reins. The Diana reverse occurs only once at Rome and then with a slight difference of type. The argument from distinct styles might not be decisive for distinct mints; but it becomes so, when reinforced by the different use of reverse types.[1] There are, then, two mints besides Rome – but, for all their differences, not far from her in style and plan. The obvious thing to do is to assign them to two mints in Italy, supervised from Rome – one, perhaps, in the North, one in the South. The As was steadily falling in weight to something like an ounce. It was perhaps standardized for a time at an ounce and a half. We are not sure whether this was more than an economy measure of the mint: the theoretical standard may have remained the same. Close dates for the period are not available.[2] If we allot some twenty years to period I, c.169–150 B.C., we can allow about the same to period II, 150–130 B.C., or a little later.

The third period, c. 130 or later to 117, may be called that of the charioteer deities. Beside the reverses of the Dioscuri, Victory in biga and Diana in biga, we meet a number of other gods and goddesses, driving chariots – Jupiter, Juno, Mars, Hercules and the rest. On the obverse Bellona still reigns unchallenged.[3] The period is a short one but

---

[1] Cp. Mattingly, *Num. Chron.*, 1949, pp. 57 ff.

[2] De Salis, it seems, worked on the hypothesis of two Italian mints, one in the North, the other in the South. They might represent two of the 'Italian' provinces. An issue in Sicily – considered almost as a part of Italy – is, perhaps, not quite out of the question.

[3] H. Mattingly, 'Some New Studies of the Roman Republican Coinage', *Proc. Brit. Acad.*, XXXIX, pp. 239 ff.

it was one of intense interest and excitement – the age of the Gracchi – and this is mirrored in the coinage. The central part of the coinage, which we naturally assign to Rome, has one very curious feature. It falls into two distinct parts, with only occasional points of contact. As one issue contains a very high proportion of famous optimate names we think of a second officina of the Roman mint or even of a second mint in Rome, established by the optimate party for their own use. The two 'Italian' mints of the last period cannot be traced: they seem to have suspended issue. In their place comes a coinage, intended, it seems, for the wars in Narbonese Gaul. Pisa might be a mint for part, at least, of this coinage. One or two issues fall a little apart – for example that of Ti. Veturius, certainly of this period, but with revolutionary types of Mars and Oath-scene: despite the signature ROMA it seems to belong to Fregellae in revolt in 126 B.C. An issue of Cn. Baebius Tampilus, which only diverges mildly from the Roman norm, may have been struck for L. Opimius, the praetor who destroyed Fregellae: its reverse, Apollo in chariot – a rare type – is nearly the same as that of M. Opimius, a cadet of the Opimian house a few years later. The last issue of the period was for the foundation of Narbo Martius in 117 B.C. It is signed by the two commissioners of the colony and, with them, by five moneyers: all the coins are serrated, but those of three bear the mark of value X, the other two ✷ – ✷ for Rome, X for Narbo, it seems.

The denarius was now retariffed at sixteen, instead of ten Asses. For a moment, the mark XVI appears; it is soon followed by a crossed ✷, which certainly means 'sixteen', whether or no it contains the elements x, v and I; the old mark x persisted here and there in some mints outside Rome.[1] The new victoriate – with the old types, but now equal to half a denarius – has usually been assigned to a later date, c. 105 B.C.,

---

[1] A lucky chance enables us to date this change. The poet Statius (reign of Domitian), mocking at a patron who for his book of verse sent him back a dreary old law-book ('Bruti senis oscitationes'), complains that his own book 'praeter me mihi constitit decussi', 'cost me a decussis – to say nothing of my work on it', while the old law-book was 'emptum plus minus Asse Gaiano', 'cost an As of Gaius more or less'. 'Decussis' and 'As Gaianus' have no meaning in the reign of Domitian: they are obviously quotations from the old law-book. We are thus taken back to Republican times and we find a suitable Brutus, who wrote a little before Gaius Gracchus and may have lived to see his tribunate. 'As Gaianus', then, must be the As of Gaius Gracchus, one of the few Gaius's illustrious enough to give their name to a coin. The decussis is the old denarius of ten Asses. H. Mattingly, *Proc. Brit. Acad.*, XXXIX, p. 242.

The change of tariff from ten to sixteen was probably meant to link Rome more closely to Italy. The victoriate, which was the Rhegine talent, contained twelve nummi: the denarius, about four-thirds of the victoriate, would contain sixteen of these.

but it, too, was perhaps a creation of Gaius Gracchus.[1] Debasement of the silver in the form of plated coins may have occurred in the tribunate of M. Livius Drusus, 122 B.C.[2] The As was, it seems, now definitely rated at an ounce, but only subdivisions of it were struck.

The fourth period runs from 117 B.C. to the Social War. The fixed types of the denarius give way to 'free' types, constantly changing, usually relating to the families of the moneyers. The mark of value is usually ✶, though X still lingers on beside it: as the period goes on, it is frequently omitted. Now, if not earlier, the victoriate – quinarius appears. The As continued to be on the uncial standard. That coin itself, after a long intermission, was again struck for some years near 100 B.C.

The history of the mint of Rome in this period is obscure. There is an apparent break after the Narbo issue of 117; we look in vain for denarii of the old pattern to follow it. Sydenham fills in the gap by moving down the date of the Narbo issue to c. 112 and placing part of my double issue of Rome (c. 123–118) after 117.[3] This is a gallant attempt to save a difficult situation – but the Narbo issue should surely be anchored firmly to the foundation of the colony in 117. When we *can* trace Rome clearly again she is striking in a much changed style and with 'free' types. From somewhere near 107 to 91 the mint can be traced with some sureness. Mints in the North continue to operate at intervals. There is much variation of style and several mints may be involved – Pisa one of them. Somewhere about 104 a mint opens, which strikes its denarii on peculiarly small thick flans: it is linked by two moneyers to one of the Northern issues, but is quite distinct in style and fabric. Its coins remind one of the silver of Massalia and that city may, in fact, be the mint. A small serrate issue, in a style which we should be inclined to call Roman, was possibly made at Narbo for the war against the Teutoni by a mission from the Roman mint. About 110 a new mint opens in south Italy – in Rhegium, to be precise – for the Jugurthine Wars. The types are all 'free', the style is fluent and graceful (what we might call 'Greek'), the flans are large and spread. There is a little issue of c. 101, which seems to belong to the campaign against the

---

[1] The new victoriate was introduced by a 'lex Clodia', of which we know only the name. In hoards the new victoriate only appears c. 105 B.C., but, as so many hoards contain denarii only, the absence of victoriates in earlier hoards is not decisive. A T. Cloulius, whose denarii are certainly to be dated near 123, has also victoriates. It is not very satisfactory to make two men of him. The reduction of the victoriate to half a denarius may have been to the advantage of Romans in dealing with Italy.

[2] So Pliny, *Nat., Hist.* XXXIV, 9, 46. There has been a tendency to refer his statement to the younger Drusus, 91 B.C.: but the earlier date is at least open.

[3] *The Coinage of the Roman Republic*, pp. 60 ff.

Cimbri and should belong to a mint in north-east Italy – Verona, for example. One other issue, fairly distinct as a group, evades our inquiry. Its types are mostly of the old pattern – Bellona on obverse, charioteer deities on reverse. But a later date, near 100 B.C., is indicated both by the appearance of the denarii in hoards and by the issue of an As of good ounce weight – a phenomenon noted on other coins certainly of about that date. The issue was perhaps connected with the scheme of settlement for the veterans of the wars against Jugurtha and the Cimbri and Teutoni.

The fifth period runs from the Social War to c. 70 B.C. Silver was now so seriously debased that no one knew what he was really worth. Serration of the edge had failed to check the forger. Now a new device was invented – the stamping of coins to show what lay below the outer envelope of silver. M. Marius Gratidianus, the praetor who announced the new invention to the public, received extravagant honours at the moment, but was murdered later by the Sullans for his pains.[1] The legislation of Sulla seems to have confirmed the circulation of any coins issued by the State. The quinarius continued to be struck and the sestertius now came in beside it. The As was reduced to half an ounce by the Lex Plautia Papiria of 90 B.C. A few years later the issue of bronze in Rome ceased. A certain 'lex Valeria' of the period reduced debts to a fourth of their amount – almost a realization of the debtor's dream of 'novae tabulae'. The meaning of these changes will be discussed below.

The main burden of coinage now fell on two mints, Rome and a mint in northern Italy, perhaps Pisa. From 82 B.C. onwards the issues of this Northern mint are all serrate. They were not, as I once suggested, struck by the Marian party in exile: they are too closely attached to the main body of coinage for that. But they *do* cover the period of the Sertorian War in Spain and were probably struck for the use of the Government troops in Spain. Apart from Rome and Pisa (?) we find quite a few other isssues. C. Annius, proconsul in Spain 81 B.C., has a coinage struck by two quaestors, C. Fabius and C. Tarquitius, in two or, possibly, three mints. They were certainly struck for Spain – probably at ports of embarkation and not in the province itself. One mint may be Tarracina, a second Northern (Livorno?). A little issue of Q. Metellus belongs to this second mint – not to his Spanish governorship.[2] There is an issue of L. Papius, serrate, possibly struck

[1] Cf. Sydenham, *The Roman Republic*, pp. xliii ff.
[2] This is almost proved by the 'Imperator' title: in Spain he should be 'Procos'.

at Lanuvium, and several other small issues, perhaps of south Italian mints. The coinage now becomes much more varied. Curule and plebeian aediles, as well as quaestors, issue coins. Quite a number of issues are specially marked s.c. or EX s.c., as due to special authorization by the senate.[1] Other issues are marked by such formulae as P ('publice') as coming from metal supplied by the treasury. A coinage of the 'imperator' now appears for almost the first time. Sulla and his friends, in their struggle to win back Rome, lacking senatorial authority had to fall back on their military command. Sulla has two such issues in the East in Greece and Asia Minor. Q. Metellus has his little issue in north Italy, C. Valerius Flaccus has his in Gaul: quite exceptionally, this bears the senate's stamp, s.c. Gold was struck by Sulla and in one very rare issue, by Cn. Lentulus, in south Italy (?).

The sixth period carries us from 70 to 49, the outbreak of the great Civil War. Rome produces the bulk of the coinage, but Pisa strikes intermittently – at first, serrate denarii, then, from 56 onwards, non-serrate. In Rome the coinage falls into three clear divisions: (1) coinage of the III viri-aaaff., (2) coinage of the curule aediles, authorized by the senate (s.c., EX s.c.), (3) a coinage, similarly authorized, issued by men who do not name their office. Issues of this third type had begun in the last period and continue to be prominent in this. Some of them at least were struck by quaestors. My son, Harold B. Mattingly, has recently shown that Roman quaestors gave Games of Victory at Praeneste. Some of these coins were issued for those games – possibly in Praeneste itself.[2] A serrate issue of L. Roscius Fabatus – very like that of L. Papius in the last period – was perhaps struck at Lanuvium. There seems to be no Eastern coinage, though some of the fine coins produced in the period may be due to artists from the East. The very rare aureus of Pompey, struck for his triumph, cannot be definitely placed. Apart from this one coin gold was not issued, and there was still no bronze.

Finally, we reach the period of the Civil Wars, 49–31 B.C. On the one hand we have what may be called the normal issues of Rome and Pisa, the latter striking intermittently: on the other, special issues, occasioned by the wars. Rome can be seen at work; first for Julius Caesar, then, after his death, on the old pattern, then for the Second Triumvirs – down to 41 B.C., when it ceased all regular issue. In silver,

---

[1] Cp. Sydenham, *The Roman Republic*, pp. 95 ff.

[2] H. B. Mattingly, 'The Denarius of Sufenas and the Ludi Victoriae', *Num. Chron.*, 1956, pp. 189 ff.

quinarius and sestertius were again issued and gold was struck for Caesar at a special mint of its own. Some experiments in bronze coinage were made – one for Caesar at Milan (?). In the provinces there were issues for Caesar in Gaul, Spain, Sicily, Africa and the East, for the Pompeians in Sicily, Greece, Asia Minor, Africa and Spain. The second series of Civil Wars, from 43 B.C. onwards, threw up a whole series of new provincial mints. The 'Liberators', Brutus and Cassius, struck at several mints in Greece, Thrace and Asia Minor. Isolated 'imperatores' like Ahenobarbus and Murcus have their little issues, and the traitor, Q. Labienus, has the impertinence to style himself 'Parthicus imperator'. Q. Cornuficius strikes in Africa, Sextus Pompey for several years in Sicily. Antony has a number of issues of bronze at various Eastern mints and an issue of silver, signed by his governor, Scarpus, in Cyrenaica. The second triumvirs struck down to 41 B.C. in Rome – after it, at mints outside it. These mints have often been assigned to the provinces – to Gaul for Octavian, to Africa for Lepidus, to the East for Antony. But all three retained Italy in their common possession, and that surely implies the right to raise and pay troops. In that case, each triumvir had his headquarters somewhere in Italy, and there, among other things, he struck his coins. In practice, Octavian, being in Italy while his colleagues were away, could make things easy for himself and hard for them: in theory, all three had equal rights. The position must have been much like that of Russia and the other Great Powers in Berlin. The mint of Antony was at Anagnia. Servius, commenting on Virgil's Seventh Aeneid, tells us that Antony struck coins at 'dives Anagnia', first for Octavia and then for Cleopatra. We have the coins, and they are of Antony's main series. Since Liegle discovered Praeneste as a mint of L. Antonius in 41 B.C.,[1] we should have been prepared for other Italian mints. The sites of the mints of Octavian and Lepidus are not known; we conjecture that they were in Italy.

Gold was struck freely in the provinces as well as in Rome. There was still no regular coinage of bronze, but there were a number of experiments at mints outside Rome – for Octavian in north Italy or Gaul, for Antony in the East. Most remarkable is Antony's 'Fleet' coinage, struck in connexion with the naval aid supplied by him to Octavian.[2] In it, the sestertius makes its first appearance as a bronze coin. There are two standards of weight – one of a quarter ounce, the

[1] Josef Liegle, 'Pietas', Z.f.N., 1932, pp. 59 ff. (esp. pp. 81 ff.).
[2] M. Grant, From Imperium to Auctoritas, pp. 43 ff.: he attributes the issue to Tarentum.

other much lighter. It was left to Augustus to set the *Aes* coinage on a firm and lasting basis. The Civil Wars meant the end of Republican coinage of the old pattern; the way was open for the new imperial coinage to develop.

2. MONEY-SYSTEMS – DENOMINATIONS, METALS, ETC.

In view of the changes in our historical sketch much of this section has had to be rewritten. There is bound to be some repetition from section I, but we will keep it as far as possible within limits. A few preliminary remarks will help the rest of our inquiry. Silver was the precious metal preferred by Rome, as by most Greek States. Gold, until the late Republic, occurred only in a few emergency issues. Bronze was at first issued at its metal value. Later, it may have been in part token coin. Silver was at times debased – not by an intermixture of bronze with the silver, but by the placing of a thin silver envelope over a bronze core. Originally a device of the forger, it was later taken over at times by the State. It was, of course, a measure of inflation. Inflationary too were the first reductions of the bronze – not merely adjustments of the bronze to changing values in terms of silver. The original unit of account was the As. By the close of the Republic the sestertius had taken its place. Some confusion between these two units is not infrequently found in our authorities: the As and the sestertius might be equated. When the change from As to sestertius took place is quite uncertain – perhaps, not before the time of Sulla.

Of the period before coinage proper, 269 B.C., all that need be said is that the bars with types on both sides were something like currency bars. Their weights vary considerably, but there may have been a theoretical standard of six pounds. The ROMANO series (269–c. 235 B.C.) has its standard silver didrachm, its 'nummus', containing ten litrae – in theory, pounds of bronze – very rarely represented here by a tiny silver coin. The token bronze was probably tariffed in litrae – perhaps litra, half and quarter litra for the three sizes. As for the weights of the didrachm, the heavy weight in Series A and B (c. 112) is more or less that of Naples; the middle weight in Series C (c. 109) appears to be a reduction of this; the light weight in Series D (c. 102·5 gr.) is near to the reduced standard of Tarentum. Here and in the *Aes Grave* the variations in weight may be attributed to differences in areas of circulation. The *Aes Grave* centres round the As, cast at a variety of weights – c. 5,057 gr. – the later Roman pound – in Series

A: c. 5,260 gr., a heavy Apulian[1] pound in Series B: a lighter pound c. 4,216 gr., the so-called 'Oscan', in Series C and D.[1]

The system is obviously bimetallic, but the relations of silver and bronze, varying a little from series to series, cannot be exactly determined. If the As was the tenth of the 'nummus' (its 'litra'), the ratio of silver would be about 1 : 400 – an improbably high figure. At a guess, we would make the As the sixth of the didrachm, its diobol, and arrive at a ratio of 1 : 240. Round the question of the different pounds endless controversy has raged, and we must leave it unsettled for the time. The 'Oscan' pound was, in fact, equal to ten ounces of the later Roman pound, the 'Apulian' to about twelve and a half ounces of the same. Haeberlin deduced, from the weights of some of the smaller denominations of his 'Oscan' pound, that it was divided into ten, not twelve, ounces. But the half-piece is marked s, semis, not • • • • •, quincunx, as should be the case if the division were in fact decimal and not duodecimal.[2]

That the first Punic War made no mark on the coinage seems to be certain – unless the plated didrachms that are found in Series A mean an official debasement of the silver. There are no reductions of weight in the *Aes Grave*. The main reason must have been that the war was fought largely on credit. So far as the war was fought in Sicily, the burden may have fallen largely on Hiero of Syracuse.

The second, the ROMA period, shows a co-ordination of silver and bronze in all mints, with a didrachm of c. 102·5 gr., an As of c. 4,216; silver to bronze, probably, at 1 : 240. The irregularities of the ROMANO series are now ironed out; one system is imposed on all areas of circulation. Rome is seen to be tightening her grip on a coinage, destined, in the first place, for all Roman interests in Italy.

The second Punic War brings new problems. Debasement of the silver is, indeed, recorded; but the debased quadrigati which we find look later and more like the work of forgers than official issues. The emergency issues of gold, in two denominations, the stater of six scruples and its half, were probably regarded as 'talents' and 'half-talents', containing twelve and six didrachms respectively. The As was reduced from ten to six ounces in 217, from six to three in c. 209; in both cases, the two stages of reduction are only clearly defined in the struck issues, not in the cast. If struck pieces of the first reduction

[1] There has been much discussion about these different pounds. It seems sufficient here to state the weights observed, without attempting to dogmatize about origins and relations of one to other.

[2] E. J. Haeberlin, *Aes Grave*, 1910, *passim*.

were, as we have suggested, possibly issued before 217, they will have been in the first place part token coin, still struck as fractions of an As of ten ounces, but struck light for convenience. The reduced Asses were presumably retariffed in terms of the didrachm – ten Asses in place of six, in the first reduction, twenty in place of ten in the second. The didrachm of ten Asses would thus be the first Roman 'denarius nummus', standard silver coin, containing ten pounds of bronze, the 'δεκάλιτρος στάτηρ' of the Greeks.

In the period following the Hannibalic War the Asses of various weights must have found their appropriate values in the market – six, ten or twenty to the didrachm. The Eastern coins that now reached Rome were presumably treated as merchandise rather than as coin. The tetradrachm was regarded as about equal to three denarii – quadrigati of reduced weight. The gold Philippus should have been rated at something like sixteen quadrigati. The victoriate was the half of the quadrigatus.

When the denarius was introduced, it was equal to ten Asses of more or less two ounces. If the bronze represented full value, silver to bronze was about as 1 : 120; but, if it was part token, the ratio will have been higher. The victoriate bore no mark of value and was treated as merchandise not as coin. Equal at first to about three-fourths of a denarius, it steadily fell away in weight. The denarius was for a short time struck heavy – at over 70 gr. – but it soon fell to 84 to the pound – just over 60 gr. The As was possibly standardized for a time at one and a half ounces, but fell away towards one ounce. It is possible that in theory the standard remained the same and that the reduction in weight was simply a measure of economy in the mint. Ten of the reduced Asses still went to the denarius. The Mars gold of 3, 2 and 1 scruple was tariffed in Asses, and the ratio of gold to silver was abnormally low; the reason will have been the gold-rush near Aquileia which brought the price of gold down by a third. The rare gold piece, with 'Young Janus' – Oath-scene type, marked xxx, is apparently tariffed in sestertii. If so, the ratio of gold to silver is $1 : 7\frac{1}{2}$ – very near the figure arrived at for the Mars gold. The date should be very close to it and the cause of the cheapness of the gold the same. We have already seen that the four silver denominations – denarius, quinarius, sestertius and victoriate – are all related to the 'little talents' of the West and were intended especially for different areas of circulation.

When the denarius was retariffed at sixteen Asses, the As seems to have been fixed at a one-ounce standard. If the silver was now debased

to the extent of an eighth – by the issue of plated denarii in that proportion – we can see how the new ratio was arrived at. A denarius,
originally reckoned as equal to ten Asses of two ounces, would naturally equal twenty Asses of one ounce. The debasement of the silver
would reduce the twenty to seventeen and a half, and the change in the
ratio of silver to bronze would be quite slight. The denarius, equal in
weight to about four-thirds of the victoriate, would equal about sixteen of the 'nummi', into which the latter, as Rhegine talent, was
divided. That may be the real meaning of the retariffing – the bringing
of the denarius into closer relations with those areas in which the
Rhegine talent prevailed. When the new victoriate, equal to a quinarius,
came in (in 123 or, later, in c. 105 B.C.), the Romans probably gained at
the expense of Italians in exchange. On one occasion, two very rare
denominations of bronze were struck, the dodrans (nine ounces,
s · · ·) and the bes (eight ounces, s · ·).

The reduction of the As to half an ounce was a measure of inflation,
due to the great Social War. Was the debasement of the denarius so
extreme that it only equalled sixteen of the reduced Asses? Or was it
held to be theoretically of the old value and, therefore, worth more of
the reduced Asses – perhaps as many as forty? At any rate, bronze soon
ceased to be issued – perhaps because of vexatious disputes about its
value, and the denarius, when the Empire came in, is still found equal
to sixteen Asses. The gold of the Sullan period is still rare and may have
been treated as bullion rather than coin and allowed to vary in value in
the market. The debasement of the silver was now so extreme that no
one could tell what he was worth. Once again, the only form of debasement to which we can point is the issue of plated denarii. Stamping the
silver to detect the core of bronze was introduced by the praetor, M.
Marius Gratidianus, in 85 B.C. He won great immediate popularity, but
subsequently paid for it with his life when the Sullans came into power.
They took the view that all money issued by the State must be taken at
its nominal value.

The 'Lex Valeria', of uncertain date in this period, which reduced all
debts to one fourth, cannot be definitely related to the coinage. If the
'argentum aere solutum est' (Sallust, *Catiline*, XXXIII) refers to this
law, we are uncertain of what was implied: does it mean that for a
sestertius of four Asses only one As had to be paid? As inflation took
the form of reduction of the weight of the As, we are inclined to think
that the As was still the unit of reckoning – even if the sestertius was
beginning to be used beside

The gold of Julius Caesar was struck at about forty to the pound. Was it definitely related to the silver (at 25 denarii)? Or was it left to find its market value? When Caesar was in Gaul, we know that gold became so plentiful that the gold pound sold for 3,000 sestertii. That would mean that the aureus equalled seventy-five sestertii or 18¾ths denarii. Of the standards of the experimental issue of bronze by Julius Caesar and his successors, we know as good as nothing. Traces of an As of a quarter of an ounce are found in the 'Fleet' coinage of Mark Antony. The cistophoric tetradrachm of Antony was an Eastern denomination: it was equal to about three denarii.

Looking back, we see that Rome began with a bimetallic system in silver and *Aes Grave*: that silver then became the dominant metal, with bronze perhaps part token: that towards the end of the Republic regular issues of bronze had ceased: that gold coin, until Julius Caesar, was only issued rarely and in times of emergency. Inflation, when it took place, usually took the form of reduction of weight of the As. Debasement of the silver by the issue of plated denarii only began about 122 at earliest. Silver and gold were, as a rule, struck very pure. The bronze of the Republic was an alloy of copper and tin, with a small admixture of lead. Brass (orichalcum), with four parts of copper to one of zinc, was first used by Julius Caesar. Something more about the policies that underlay these manipulations of the coinage will need to be said in our third chapter.

3. FINANCIAL ADMINISTRATION, MINT OFFICIALS, ETC.

The finances of the Republic, as a whole, were in the hands of the Senate, which was responsible for general policy. Their special financial officers, in Rome and the provinces, were the quaestors. The censors only came into account, in so far as they leased out State contracts and State revenues. As the quaestors had charge of the Treasury, the 'aerarium Saturni', they could not be unconcerned for the coinage, but special officials, the III viri-aaaff., were in actual charge of the mint. When no mere matter of administration was involved, but a change of principle, the rights of the sovereign people came into play and the change was made by a law (cp. the 'Lex Flaminia', or the 'Lex Plautia Papiria'). For a long time the control of the Senate seems to have been effective, not only in Rome, but also in Italy and the provinces: coinage in the provinces, divorced from senatorial control, is the distinguishing feature of the age of confusion, the Civil Wars.

Before we discuss in detail the various officials who issued coins, it will be convenient to glance briefly at the historical development. In the period of the didrachms there are no signatures by name: even the symbols seem to stand for mints and work in the mints rather than moneyers. We can only guess who issued the coins. All the early issues that bore no names used once to be called 'consular', on the theory that coinage fell within the general competence of the consul: despite the great authority of Mommsen, this view seems to be unsupported by any substantial evidence. When we come to the denarius, we at once find symbols – which seem to represent moneyers as well as mints – and then actual names, at first in very abbreviated form, then more and more full. It is most natural to assign them to the regular moneyers. Other minting authorities appear in the age of the Gracchi – quaestors or commissioners for colonies. Later still, in the Sullan age, come plebeian and curule aediles, a praetor (once), 'imperatores', a commissioner 'denariis flandis'. Some issues are marked as 'from public money' (EX A.P., etc.), others EX S.C. or S.C. ('by decree of the Senate') – issues made with special authorization by men who do not specify their office. In the period from c. 70–49 B.C. the coinage of Rome flows in three clear channels – coinage of the III viri-aaaff., coinage of curule aediles, coinage marked EX S.C. or S.C., with name of issue, but no office. The Civil Wars produced a cleavage in the coinage. Quite apart from the old coinage under senatorial control there is, we find, a vast development of coinage in Italy and the provinces, controlled not by the Senate, but by 'imperatores' and their subordinates. The way was opening up to the coinage of the Empire.

We come now to the officials who issued coins:

(a) The III viri-aaff. – 'aere argento auro flando feriundo' (occasionally 'auro, aere, argento') – or III viri monetales.[1] The reference to all three metals and to casting as well as striking shows that their duties extended beyond the actual issue of coin. The office was one of the minor offices that composed the 'vigintisexvirate' and was held by young senators at the beginning of their careers; the minimum age – after military service – would be about twenty-seven. The office came immediately before the quaestorship – we know of one instance in which it succeeded it. The office was annual; re-election, if it ever occurred, was abnormal. Not all III viri struck coins: we have not nearly enough moneyers to supply a coinage for each year and Cicero mentions one, Vettienus, who is unknown on the coins. One might

---

[1] Cp. Karl Pink, *The Triumviri Monetales*, etc., 1952.

hold, with Mommsen, that III viri were appointed intermittently, not every year. It is perhaps easier to suppose that the office was filled annually – after all, there were routine duties to be fulfilled apart from coinage – but that, when there was no special demand for coinage, none was issued – except, possibly, a mere shadow issue for the benefit of the moneyers and his friends – such as would normally vanish without leaving a trace.

The date of introduction of the office is much disputed. Pomponius certainly suggests a date in the early third century, though we must not press his evidence too far. If Rome began to issue coins then the date has a certain inherent probability. The first definite mention of the office is in the 'elogium' of C. Claudius Pulcher, consul of 92 B.C. (*C.I.L.*, I, p. 279). Mommsen thought that the office was only an exceptional one till about 90 B.C., because it is not mentioned, with other minor offices, in certain laws (*C.I.L.*, I, pp. 197 and 198): but this negative evidence is not decisive, and Cicero *does* mention the office in his survey of the Constitution (*De Legibus*, III, 3, 7). Pink conjectured that the III viri were introduced in the late third century under the influence of Athens. The evidence seems to be insufficient to justify any positive conclusion, but we are still, I hold, at liberty to believe that the office may be about as old as the Roman mint itself. Caesar appointed IIII viri in place of III viri in 44 B.C. – L. Flaminius Chilo expressly notes that he 'IIII vir pri(mus) fla(vit)', but under Augustus we find the III viri restored.

Signatures of III viri do not occur till late in the Republic – c. 70 B.C onwards – and, as Pink has most happily demonstrated, it was only the President of the college who signed them. But, when a man signs a coin, without naming his office or appending the special authority of the Senate (s.c.), it is reasonable to assume that he is a regular moneyer. These coins, presumably of the moneyers, begin with the early denarii and continue to the end of the Republic. They have often been called 'family' coins, because references to the history of the great families is written large on them. But these issues, of course, always belonged to the Roman State; the great families had no private right to issue coin.

The III viri normally struck individually. But the college certainly contained three members, and the three often struck concurrently. The coins of M. Atilius Serranus, L. Sempronius Pitio and Q. Marcius Libo (c. 140 B.C.) agree so closely in all details that we may be sure that the three formed a college. Other colleges can often be surmised, if seldom demonstrated. In the Northern coinage of the Gracchan age and after

The External History of the Coinage

we find several groups of three, striking together (M. Domitius, Q. Curtius and M. Silanus, for example): it seems to be more probable that they were moneyers than that they were commissioners for colonies. It is curious that they are more evident at mints outside Rome than in the capital itself. After 70 B.C. we find several examples of collegiate striking – the President signing himself III vir, his second and third striking coins singly and together. (Cp. M. Aquillius III vir – Kalenus – Cordus, sharing a denarius; Longinus III vir – Libo and Paullus Lepidus striking separately and together.)

In a number of cases moneyers struck at more than one mint. In the period from c. 150 to 125 many names occur in both the slightly differentiated series of the Roman mint. In the Gracchan age C. Valerius Flaccus strikes in both the series that seem to run concurrently in Rome. In the Sullan age several moneyers seem to have struck both at Rome and at the Northern mint (Pisa?). C. Hosidius Geta (c. 71 B.C.) certainly struck at both these mints: one set of his coins is serrate, the other is not and the styles and fabrics are distinct; hoards show that both series belong to about the same date. These facts certainly confirm Pink's view that the control of the coinage was unitary – but they do not compel us to go as far as he does and deny the existence of more than one mint.

The III viri, being specially appointed to issue coins, need no special authorization from the Senate. This principle, enunciated by Mommsen, stands on its merits and hardly needs further qualification. In the few cases where the name of a moneyer is accompanied by s.c., we must conjecture that he was required to undertake some exceptional commission outside the normal scope or, perhaps, beyond his normal term of office.

We conclude then that the III viri were responsible for most of the Republican coinage: that they were certainly at work in the second century B.C. and may have been so already in the third: that they struck as a matter of routine and needed no special authorization: that they were probably appointed annually and that intermissions mean intermissions of coinage, not of office.

(b) Quaestors. As the quaestor was certainly closely concerned with finance – the III viri probably worked under his general supervision – it is only natural to find him occasionally striking coins himself. This does not happen before the Gracchan age. Urban quaestors are found striking, c. 105 T. Mallius and Appius Claudius, in 100 B.C. (Piso – Caepio), c. 85 B.C. the two Memmii. In the Narbo issue of 117 the two men who sign ✕ may have been urban quaestors. A few other denarii with obverse head of Saturn seem to belong to quaestors. Other quaestors seem to be provincial – for example, the two who strike for C. Annius as proconsul of Spain, the A. Manlius who strikes for Sulla: there is also a pro-quaestor, L. Manlius, also striking for him.

When the quaestor marks his office with a Q, we are sure of our ground: the head of Saturn on obverse is almost as definite an indication. But, where neither of these is present, we are often in doubt. Is the issuer of the coins a quaestor or a special commissioner of coinage? Some of the s.c. issues, as we shall see below, were probably due to quaestors. These issues of quaestors seem to be, in general, exceptional in character. They struck on special occasions, often by special commission of the Senate. In the provinces, a quaestor might strike when coinage was required and no III viri were immediately available. For quaestors in the Civil Wars, see below.

(*c*) The two commissioners for the colony of Narbo Martius (117) signed the whole issue, with five men under them, two (quaestors ?) for Rome, three (III viri ?) for Narbo. It is possible, but far from certain, that some other groups of three were likewise commissioners for colonies.

(*d*) Plebeian aediles struck once on a special occasion, c. 86 B.C.

(*e*) Curule aediles struck about the same time and, more or less regularly, in the period from c. 70–50 under special authority of the Senate (EX. S.C., S.C.).

(*f*) A special 'curator ✕ flandis' is recorded c. 73 B.C. Other such special commissioners may perhaps be looked for in men who strike in close company with quaestors, but without the signature Q.

(*g*) The coinage of Q. Antonius Balbus as praetor, 82 B.C., is quite exceptional. His coinage has often been assigned to his governorship of Sardinia, but it is possible that he issued it as praetor in Rome. The praetors in that period had concerned themselves seriously with the bad state of the silver coinage. Q. Antonius inaugurated a new series of 'serrate' and may have aimed, once again, at using the cutting of the edge to guarantee the purity of the silver.

(*h*) 'Imperatores.' [1] Mommsen laid down the principle that the 'imperator' always had the right to issue coinage for his troops in the field. Some scholars have thought that the early Roman didrachms were thus issued. All we can say is that if such a coinage of the 'imperator' existed,

[1] H. Mattingly, 'The Imperator in the Coinage of the Roman Republic', *Proc. Brit. Acad.*, XXXIX, pp. 261 ff.

it has vanished without a trace. The only clear example is the gold stater of the great Ti. Flamininus, the 'Liberator' of Greece. But it is a Greek rather than a Roman coin and may have been struck *for* rather than *by* the great man. The coin today is exceedingly rare. The issue, we may be certain, was not approved by the Senate: it is a not unlikely guess that it was called in.[1] In general, the 'imperator' issues belong to two periods:

(i) the age of Sulla: he himself struck twice as 'imperator' in the East, while his lieutenants, Q. Metellus and C. Valerius Flaccus, struck in north Italy and Narbonese Gaul respectively. The s.c. on coins of Flaccus is quite exceptional: the coinage of the 'imperator' essentially fell outside the Senate's sphere of control. A precedent had been set, curiously enough, by the C. Papius Mutilus, who was one of the chief allied commanders in the great Social War. The exceptional conditions of the time explain these issues. Sulla and his lieutenants, lacking the authority of the Senate, had to fall back on their military command as a sanction for their issues.

(ii) the age of the great Civil Wars, c. 49–31. Between Sulla and Caesar there is no coinage of the 'imperator'. It is revived in the turbulent conditions of the struggles between Caesarians and Pompeians and between the second triumvirs and the 'Liberators'. The 'imperatores' sometimes struck by themselves, sometimes through the agency of subordinates, legates, quaestors and the like. The Second Triumvirs – at all mints but Rome – like to call themselves IMP III VIR RPC. We are clearly on the way to the imperial coinage; for it was as 'imperator' that Augustus undertook the issue of coins in the precious metals.

(*i*) Proconsuls. In the last period of the Republic, the provincial coinage is issued by proconsuls, as well as by 'imperatores'. Sometimes, the same man uses the titles alternatively (e.g. Brutus). The rare aureus of Pompey (mint unknown, date c. 63 B.C.) is signed PROCOS.

Something has already been said about the coinage, marked EX S.C. or S.C. (there seems to be little difference in meaning). In every case, special authorization of an issue by the Senate is implied – whether it is made by quaestors, aediles or special commissioners. Issues of this kind begin near 120 B.C. and continue to be struck at intervals: they

[1] R. A. C. Carson, 'The Gold Stater of Flamininus', *Brit. Mus. Quar.*, 1955, pp. 11 ff.

are unusually plentiful between c. 85 and 49 B.C. We have already seen that some of these S.C. issues, on which no office is mentioned, were struck by quaestors for games of Victory at Praeneste. Similar explanations may be found to apply to other issues. We have here a fascinating, only half-solved, problem of the later coinage. The regular moneyer – just because he is regular – does not use the mark S.C.: there are very few exceptions to this rule.

Other marks, such as ARG. PVB, EX A.P., P., fairly common in the period from a little before 100 to c. 85, mark an issue as exceptional in another way: the metal necessary for it is drawn from the public treasury. Such issues naturally belong to times of emergency, when an issue was immediately called for. In the ordinary course of things, we gather that silver was bought in the market.

Something has already been said about the chaotic coinage of the late Republic. A few words may be added to fill in details and define its exact character. In the provinces, the 'imperator' or 'proconsul' plays the most prominent part. Julius Caesar chose to use his own name, without mark of office, as full justification for coinage. In Rome he strikes as DICT. QVAT. DICT PERPETVVS and as IMPERATOR. He appointed special 'praefecti urbis' to issue his gold. Antony's 'Fleet' coinage was issued by 'praefecti classis'. Among the subordinate officers who strike for the generals we find legates, quaestors, pro-quaestors and others. Very curious are the titles Q.P. PROQ. P, even Q. PROCOS. which we now find. The quaestor or pro-quaestor seems to be invested with the powers of a praetor or even a proconsul. Such financial officers, temporarily invested with 'imperium', might be thought of as employed at the Italian headquarters of the three III viri RPC. Sometimes, it is not clear whether a title on a coin has anything to do with the issue or is merely descriptive: we think, for example, of the coin of Octavian and M. Agrippa cos.

Of the work of the mint in detail we know little beyond what we may guess or deduce from the later usage of the Empire. Labour in the mint – probably mainly slave labour – was freely spent on such things as the serration of the denarius which was regularly done by hand-made cuts of the chisel. The blanks of the coins were produced by casting. The coins – except the heavy *Aes* of the third century – were all struck.

For the inner working of the mint we have an ample material in the various mint-marks – numbers, fractions, letters, symbols – which begin to appear c. 124 B.C. and continue at intervals down to about 56:

they are very rare after c. 70. The object of these marks must have been to define the work of particular periods and groups of workmen in the mint. As we come to know more of the various series, we shall surely deepen and extend our knowledge of the detailed workings of the mint. In some cases – but by no means invariably – the mark denotes a die – all coins bearing it being from the same one.

It is an interesting subject of speculation, what part of the work of the mint was directly performed under State management and what part was left to private enterprise. On general analogies it is probable that the task of supplying bullion was let out on contract. A private company would undertake to furnish a given amount of gold, silver or bronze at a rate fixed by tender. The contracting out of such duties would naturally fall to the censor. The preparation of the dies and the striking of the coins were probably done by a staff of public slaves, with freedmen in charge – the whole staff being answerable to the masters of the mint.

The cutting of the dies was the work of trained workmen, who will often have been of Greek origin. The number of these workmen will never have been very large and the style of a mint is often so uniform over a period of years that we may recognize the individual work of an artist or his school. By 'art' or 'style' in coins we generally denote this individual quality, and in it we have an important criterion for questions of mintage. By 'fabric' we denote rather the subordinate features of the make of a coin – the particular method of striking, the size of the flan and die; and with 'fabric' rather than with 'art' we may class such details as particular forms of lettering, which depend less on individual gift and more on the local customs of a mint. Fabric is an even better criterion than art for mintage; an individual artist may easily move from mint to mint – local peculiarities of fabric tend to change but slowly. On art and fabric considered together we have to rely for the first step of our determination of mints – the dividing off of different series of coins. A few examples must suffice here. The earliest *Aes Grave* is clearly distinct in style and fabric from the reduced series that follow it. The local issues of the second century B.C., distinguished by mint letters or symbols, show a great variety of distinct styles. The main series of denarii, which we may assume to be of Roman mintage, shows a development of artistic treatment which helps us to fix the dates. The treatment of the helmet of Bellona, of her hair, of her ear-ring varies, the Dioscuri on horseback on the reverse are rendered in a variety of styles. A little later, when we have no longer mint signatures to help us, style and fabric enable us to separate off series of denarii, so unlike the ordinary Roman, that we may safely attribute them to outside mints, probably in Italy. One set of denarii, struck round about 102 B.C., is distinguished by a very peculiar fabric, small dies and very neat and small figures. In the last century of the Republic the art reaches a very high level, particularly on the denarii of L. Torquatus (Plate X, 13), M. Piso (Plate VIII, 18) and M. Lepidus. It seems possible that Lucullus and Pompey brought back with them from the East Greek artists who made a permanent mark on the style of the Roman mint. The serration of the edge is a striking point of fabric which enables us to draw important conclusions about date and mintage (Plate VIII, 11-15).

Roman art, we know, was at no stage of its development free from Greek tradition, and the inspiration of the finest products of the Roman mint is undoubtedly Greek. We find, however, elements that must be put down to other sources. The hard, dry and precise style which is seen on many denarii of the late Republic seems to be peculiarly Italian, and peculiarities noted on coins of provincial mintage may reasonably be attributed to local influence. In the main, the influence of Rome and her provinces is seen more in the direction given to art, for instance in the choice of portraits and actual events for illustration, than in the art itself.

Questions of epigraphy are chiefly interesting in their bearing on dates and will be reserved for the section that deals with them. The discussion of the occasions on which coinage was issued will find its natural place, when we consider the part played by coinage in the life of the Roman State.

4. CHRONOLOGY AND MINTS

As long as coins of the Roman Republic are classed under the names of the magistrates who issue them and arranged in alphabetical order of names, a serious study of the coinage is impossible. Dates and mints must be considered.

With the most important form of scientific classification, dating, much progress has been made and the main outlines have been approximately drawn. Much still remains to be done in the way of correcting and making more precise current attributions. The question of mints was fully treated for the first time in Grueber's Catalogue of the Coins of the Roman Republic in the British Museum: but much still remains to be done. We will first review in succession the main criteria which bear on the date of a Roman coin, then give some examples of the methods of classification by mints.

We begin with the tests of date:

(*a*) *Weights*

The bronze coins can invariably be assigned to their appropriate periods by their weight alone; but, as we have seen above, coins of the one-ounce standard were struck over quite a long period. The denarii of the four-scruple standard are all early; those of the reduced standard of three and a half scruples begin c. 160 B.C.

(*b*) *Types*

As we shall see in Chapter II, Republican types develop according to certain ascertainable laws. The earlier denarii, characterized by Bellona on obverse and Dioscuri on reverse or charioteer deity, fall at once into their approximate periods – first Dioscuri alone, then Diana or Victory in biga added; then other charioteer deities added. A type like that of the Dioscuri with a long run can be assigned to periods according to the other reverses that accompany it. The later 'free' types after c. 112 B.C. must be judged on their individual merits.

(*c*) *Symbols, etc.*

The symbol as the sole signature on a coin is early – we find club and sickle on the ROMA didrachms, corn-ear on the quadrigati, many varying symbols on the denarius and victoriate. The symbols on the ROMANO didrachm Diana – Victory probably mark periods of time. Symbols may stand for mints or moneyers – changing symbols rather for the latter. The symbol, as a subsidiary signature beside the name of a moneyer, begins in the second period of the denarius; it is often of a punning nature. Symbols as mint-marks, denoting periods of time or groups of workers in the mint, belong to a later period, c. 125 to 55 B.C.

(*d*) *Marks of Value*

On the bronze, marks of value for the different denominations are normal throughout, mostly on both sides of the coin. On the denarius the original mark X is universal for many years after 169 B.C.; its omission is exceedingly rare. When the denarius was retariffed at sixteen Asses, the mark XVI appeared on a small group of coins; the mark, crossed ✖, follows, but ✕ still occurs sporadically at mints out-side Rome. After c. 110 B.C. the mark is usually omitted.

(e) *Epigraphy and other details*

The word ROMA appears first on the reverse of the denarius. It is usually in a sort of oblong cartouche and, in the early issues, is some-times almost incuse, i.e. the letters are not raised, but are sunk below the surface of the coin. For the detailed study of form of letters and numbers we must refer to the particulars given in a good catalogue. The form ᐱ for A and Ⱳ for L are decidedly archaic. Ꮐ, with the square top, is earlier than г: the closed P is quite abnormal. Other curious features, such as the use of K for C before A, (cp. Kalenus), of EI for long I (cp. PREIVERNVM), of XS for X (cp. MAXSVMVS), of V for Greek Υ (cp. SIBVLLA), the dropping of the double consonant (cp. CINA, PILIPVS), or of the aspirate (cp. PILIPVS, CETEGVS) are of interest, but throw no special light on chronology. Among numerals, we may note the forms for 50, ↓ early and also, chiefly in a modified form ↓, later, ⊥ from about 88 B.C. on.

(f) *Names of Moneyers*

In general, the most abbreviated forms, with initial letters, monograms or curtailed forms of one name only, are the oldest. The full form with three names only appears c. 140 B.C. The name of the father is often given, that of the grandfather rarely, the tribe quite exceptionally.

(g) *Careers of Moneyers*

The moneyer could not hold office before the age of twenty-seven, and a period of years, more or less fixed by custom, must intervene before he could reach the highest offices of the State. When, therefore, we can find reason for identifying a moneyer with a praetor or consul of known date, we can reckon back to within a little his actual year of office as moneyer. Unfortunately certain identifications are not very easy to find. A particular case will help to make the point clear. A cer-tain C. Pulcher strikes denarii, which, on general grounds, must be assigned to a date near 100 B.C. We have an inscription (*C.I.L.*, I², p. 200) of a C. Claudius Pulcher, who was consul in 92 B.C., after having previously held the offices of quaestor, triumvir of the mint, curule aedile in 99 B.C., and praetor in 95 B.C. Evidently the two men are the same: the year of the coins must be a little before 100 B.C., not

91, the date to which Grueber (*B.M.C. Rep.*, I, p. 198 f.) assigns them. It is becoming clear that moneyers were often cadets of families that stood high in the State, with praetors or consuls to their credit. Messalla, who struck as quaestor in 53 B.C., 'patre cos.', is our best example – certainly not the only one. The two Opimii, L. and M., were cadets of the family of the L. Opimius who was consul in 122 B.C. Here we have a new possibility of checking dates – not very close, but useful in connexion with other considerations.

(h) Style and Fabric

These are primarily useful as criteria of mint, but they can help towards dating also. Certain sequences in time can be observed, but they are too complicated to be studied except in detail. The serrati fall mainly after 117 B.C.

(j) Definite References to Contemporary Events

For full illustration of this we must refer to Chapter II. It is only quite late in the Republic that such reference becomes explicit. In 100 B.C. there is a clear reference to a distribution of corn by the quaestors, Piso and Caepio. Sufenas, c. 63 B.C., celebrates the first giving of the games of Victory at Praeneste; he may be referring back to 81, when such games of Victory were first held, but it is possible that the games were first held at Praeneste in his actual year of office as quaestor. Scaurus in 58 B.C. referred to the surrender of the Arab sheik Aretas a few years earlier. The first portrait of a living man was that of Julius Caesar in 44 B.C. In the many references to the history of the great families on the coins of the moneyers side references to current events may often be suspected. We are still engaged in sorting these out; a few may be taken as certain, rather more as probable, very many as possible.

(k) The Use of a Number of Criteria in Combination

This is, of course, the most promising line of study; what is at first a mere possibility may finally be raised to something near certainty. Let us take one or two examples. The denarii of Ti. Veturius have the old mark of value X, and the line border on reverse (the border of dots replaces it c. 120 B.C.). Hoards show that they are earlier than the Narbo issue of 118 B.C. Yet the coins have the 'free' types, only common some years later, in place of the Bellona of the obverse and the Dioscuri or

39

charioteer deity of the reverse. The conflict here between criteria of different kinds points to something quite exceptional in the issue. The coins were struck, it seems, by Fregellae in revolt, in 126. Again, a set of three moneyers strike in 121 B.C. with their appropriate reverses and obverse of Bellona; coins of the same three moneyers, with the same reverses, but head of Apollo in place of Bellona, occur, as hoards show, some forty years later. There is obviously a deliberate restoration of the first issue.[1] Examples might easily be multiplied. The application of a number of criteria will undoubtedly finally lead to a close dating of almost all coins.

(*l*) *Hoards*[2]

We come to the most objective, and, therefore, the most valuable of all evidences of date, that of hoards. In ancient times, when no highly developed system of banking existed, the concealment of money in the earth was a normal feature in life. But naturally the practice was very much commoner in times of danger than in times of peace; and, as only a very small proportion of ancient hoards actually come to our knowledge, times of profound peace hardly figure in our records of finds. The Republican hoards that have come down to us are mainly of silver; for the dating of the bronze practically no evidence of this kind is available. Often denarii only occur, occasionally quinarii or victoriates are intermixed with them. The great value of a hoard as evidence is just this, that, when once we have determined the date of burial, we have a limiting date for all issues contained in it: all must obviously have been prior to the burial. In practice, of course, the case is not always quite simple. Records of the find may never have been complete or may have been lost. 'Stragglers' may have intruded – that is to say, coins of a date certainly later than the main hoard, but confounded with the hoard either by sheer accident or by the carelessness of some untrained observer. And, again, there is never any certainty that a hoard gives us a complete picture of the coinage up to its burial: even among the late issues there are likely to be chance omissions. But, when a number of hoards of the same period are available for study, we can more or less eliminate these sources of error and place our chronology on a sure foundation.

Hoards of the first period are not common and few have been

---

[1] H. Mattingly, 'Some Historical Coins of the Late Republic, The Sullan Restoration', *J.R.S.*, 1922, pp. 236 ff.
[2] A selection of recent hoards is given in an Appendix.

recorded with sufficient accuracy. Hoards of *Aes Grave* have not yet thrown much light on dates. Hoards of quadrigati are rather rare, hoards of victoriates comparatively plentiful. Hoards of early denarii have not been accurately recorded. Denarii and victoriates are sometimes found mixed in hoards, but the rule is that a hoard concentrates on one denomination. From a date a little after 123 we have a long series of hoards of silver which place our dating on a fairly sure basis. For the study of hoards Grueber, *B.M.C. Rep.*, III, pp. 2 ff., will be found invaluable: it has only one serious blemish – the issues of L. LIC. CN. DOM. are erroneously assigned to 92 B.C. (the year in which the two men were censors), not to 117, and the chronology of the period has been warped to correspond. Three hoards seem to be clearly connected with the revolt of Fregellae in 126 B.C., though a little later than that date. This is intelligible enough, for the discontents of the Italians and the reaction on the part of the Roman conservatives lasted on beyond that year. Then follows a large group of hoards, associated with different periods of the great Cimbrian War. Most hoards of which we know are Italian. A number of hoards in Spain, round the year 100 B.C., seem to be connected with revolts in that province. After a short interval the Social War in Italy, followed by the Civil War between Sulla and Marius and the revolt of Spartacus, produce a new crop. After c. 70 B.C. Italy had peace for nearly a generation: the short crisis of the Catilinarian conspiracy seems to have left no numismatic record. With the great Civil War between Caesar and Pompey our hoards recommence; very few years but are represented by such evidence.

A glance at a single find will give a good idea of the use that can be made of this class of evidence. The *Monte Codruzzo* hoard consisted of some 5,000 pieces, and as many as 4,734 of them were examined by Borghesi and described by Cavedoni (*Ripostigli*, p. 19 f.). It represents, then, an extensive piece of evidence, reported by highly competent observers. The presence of a number of coins in mint condition enables us to detect the latest issues included in it. Among these are thirteen coins of Q. Antonius Balbus, appointed praetor of Sardinia by the Marians in 82 B.C. There are also coins of C. Annius, who was sent by Sulla to Spain to oppose Sertorius in the same year. These are the latest issues that we can trace, and we may date the hoard with high probability to the end of 82 B.C. As a very high percentage of all earlier Republican denarii were included in this hoard, its evidence for dating is obviously very great.

Mints

On this subject in general see H. Mattingly, *Proceedings of the British Academy*, 1957: 'Roman Numismatics': Miscellaneous Notes I and II.

This is a very important but very vexed question. Some scholars are quick to see differences of style and fabric that strongly suggest different mints. Other scholars find nothing that might not fall within the framework of a single mint. On the whole, the positive evidence must here be held to outweigh the negative. If two or three scholars steadily agree on what they see, they obviously are seeing something that is really there, even if other scholars fail to see it. Our close study of mints really begins with Grueber's B.M. Catalogue, founded on the pioneer work of Count de Salis. It shows signs of a painstaking study almost certainly left incomplete by the Count and marred by accidental changes between his time and that of Grueber. If I insist here on the importance of mints and on the possibility of distinguishing them, it will only be with one or two important reserves. Style by itself can hardly prove mintage, widely different styles might exist together in the same mint. But, when differences of fabric reinforce differences of style, the case can become much stronger; for a mint is unlikely to vary its detailed treatment of the coinage at one and the same period. When to this we can add a different choice of the obverse and reverse types and some general historical probabilities we come to something like certainty. Unless a mint betrays itself by signature, we are usually left to guess at its site; even if it signs with a letter, uncertainty often remains. To this we may add that the mints that we find are often only semi-independent. There is every probability that they were directed from Rome: the same moneyers are quite often found striking at more than one mint. The mints of the second period of the denarius, which we call 'Italian', have been much criticized, but the case for them is strong. There are slight but perceptible differences of style, to mark them off from the central Roman issues. When we find that in place of Victory in biga they use Diana in biga on reverse, in two distinct styles, we are reasonably certain of two extra mints. Their closeness to Rome, taken together with the general historical position, makes us think of Italy rather than of the provinces. We know that Italy had her 'provinces', with their quaestors, and surely coinage for these 'provinces' is by no means surprising. Later, especially in the Civil Wars, we find mints that diverge far more widely from the Roman and must be regarded as Italian or provincial, outside the effective control of the Senate.

To sum up: we distinguish a mint

(*a*) by style and fabric, which mark it off as something special;

(*b*) by choice and allusion of types and general historical probabilities;

(*c*) by the names and titles of the minting authority, which, especially in the later period, help to decide mint;

(*d*) occasionally by mark of value: when the mark x persists after 123 it is a sure sign of mintage outside Rome.

I propose here to sketch the mint history very briefly from period to period. Something has already been said about the mints in the Historical sketch.

Period I (c. 269–235 B.C.). The style of the Mars didrachm certainly owes something to Metapontum. But its *Aes* types are copied at Cosa in Etruria and its mint was probably on the east coast, perhaps at Ostia, the seat of one of the Italian provinces. The style of the Apollo didrachm is identical with that of the little bronze of Beneventum – certainly struck after 268, when the city, becoming a Latin colony, changed its name from Maleventum, probably on that very occasion. A style, the same or very similar, is found at Nuceria in Campania. We think of a mint at Beneventum or not far from it. If struck for one of the Italian provinces, this would be for the 'calles', the rough uplands of central to east southern Italy. The style of the other two didrachms, Hercules and Diana, is, I think, the same; as the subjects are so different it is hard to be positive; similar they certainly are. For this new style (or styles) we may search the western mints in vain; nowhere can we trace any sign of it. It is probably borrowed from Alexandria, which had formed an alliance with Rome in 273. An Alexandrian touch has already been noted by some scholars on the quadrigati, which continue this style into the next period. Hercules belongs to Rome, Diana to a south Italian mint, perhaps Tarentum.

Period II (c. 235–218 B.C.). The special styles of mints A and B disappear. The style that takes their place is probably just that of Alexandria, which continues to rule in mints C and D. This is a part of the standardization of the coinage, which now seems to be centrally directed, even if struck at a number of mints.

Period III (c. 218–204 B.C.). The Second Punic War. The three Italian mints cease to operate; coinage is centred on Rome. Whether the *Aes* was issued from mints other than Rome is not certain. The only certain example is that of the semi-libral series, struck with divergent types at a south Italian mint, Venusia in Apulia (?). The quadrigatus was certainly issued from other centres than Rome; but these were not independent mints, only branches of the capital. One issue, with symbol corn-ear, seems to be Sicilian. Other mints – there are likely to be two at least – cannot yet be placed. We wait for some evidence from hoards that may help us in our quest.

Period IV (c. 204–169 (?) B.C.). The quadrigatus seems to continue in two main styles, one Roman, the other possibly Sicilian. The victoriate was struck at a number of mints – some unascertained, some reasonably sure, Croton, Vibo, Corcyra, Nola (N). The distribution of these mint-marks over this period and the next is not yet complete.

After these periods of pre-denarius coinage we come to the denarius itself.

Period I. The denarius is struck in a considerable number of mints, signing with mint-letters or symbols. Few of them are known for certain; thus, H may stand for Hatria, B for Beneventum; but we are not sure. A Sardinian issue is determined by overstrikes of corresponding bronze on Sardinian coins of Carthage. The victoriate continues to be struck at a number of mints, sometimes with a quinarius beside it; it is not yet certain whether the two coins were struck side by side or in succession. It seems probable that the denarii of what we call the first style, with a very large, round bowl of the helmet, were mainly struck outside the capital and that the Roman issues already used a style more like that which followed in the next period. Symbols may be used either for moneyers or for mints. When the symbol changes in the same series we think of moneyers; when it does not change, of mints.

Period II. The many mints cease to function; it is possible that a few with mint-marks such as griffin, female head, GR, D, butting bull, owl, continue into this period. One main style, presumably that of Rome, now emerges. There is a subdivision of style inside this mint, which probably marks a special 'officina'; if it should prove to be of another mint, it must be very close to Rome; it has many of the same moneyers and the same choice of reverse types. Two other mints can be distinguished; both have a predilection for the new reverse of Diana in biga; but the type is rendered in two distinct ways; in one, the horses are galloping and Diana is leaning forward over them, in the other the horses are cantering and Diana leans back. The styles are not very far from that of the capital; there is no likelihood of provincial issues yet; so we shall regard the mints as Italian.[1] One of them might conceivably

---

[1] H. Mattingly, 'The Different Styles of the Roman Republican Coinage', *Num. Chron.*, 1952, pp. 67 ff.

be Sicilian. De Salis thought of two Italian mints – one Northern, one Southern – a reasonable guess, if no more. It would be premature to guess at mint cities. Hoards might throw some light on this difficult question, but hoards of this early period are rare – at any rate, they seem not to get recorded.

Period III. The main issue, of Rome, follows on fairly directly from the last period. About 123 B.C. a second series appears beside the first; it seems to have claims to be Roman and may have been a temporary creation of the optimate party, as famous optimate names are prominent among its moneyers. This double series is hardly parallel to that noted in the last period; there, the distinction of style was slight and many moneyers struck in both; here the styles are quite distinct and the moneyers, in almost all cases, different. The new mints, which seem to belong to the North and the Gallic wars, show several clear distinctions of style and do not look like successive products of one mint. For some issues Pisa may be considered as a probable mint; Pisa was the chief port of embarkation for Sardinia and two rare types of those issues have been found in a Sardinian hoard, one in great numbers. The two Italian mints of the last period seem to vanish without a trace. The coins of Ti. Veturius, certainly of this period, but lying outside the main Roman tradition, should be an issue of rebel Fregellae; the types are defiantly revolutionary, but the signature is Roman; the malcontents are not proposing to found a new state, but to continue in a reformed Roman system. One coin, of Tampilus, diverging, but not so notably, from the Roman norms, may have been struck for Opimius on his campaign against Fregellae. The issue struck for Narbo Martius is marked both crossed ✴ and X; the two parts were struck for Rome and Narbo; all were signed by the commissioners of the colony, L. Licinius and Cn. Domitius; two officers sign for Rome (quaestors?), three for Narbo (moneyers?).[1]

Period IV. It is hard to find any coins to continue the last issue of Rome in 117 B.C. From about 106 B.C. we can find a coinage of Rome, with the new 'free' types; what happened in the interval is quite obscure. Some intermission of coinage there may have been, but hardly for so long a term of years. Sydenham diminishes the gap by placing after 117 a number of coins which seem to me to belong unquestionably before that date. The Northern issues continue; Pisa may now be the chief, if not the only, mint. Branching out from these Northern mints is a

[1] H. Mattingly, 'Some Historical Coins of the Late Republic', *J.R.S.*, 1922, pp. 230 ff.

special one, with small, thick flans of the denarius; its coins resemble in their general appearance the coins of Massalia and that may well have been the mint. A little series of coins, serrate, but otherwise in something like Roman style, may be provisionally assigned to Narbo – a special mission from the capital to strike for the war against the Teutoni. A mint in south Italy – it seems to mark itself Rhegine on one coin – belongs to the period of the war against Jugurtha. The flans are broad and spread and the style is fine, if florid, and suggests Greek influence. It is very possible that this style was copied a few years later on coins of Rome. A short issue is tied by its types to the war against the Cimbri in the north-east of Italy; the mint city is unknown. One last issue – which looks earlier, but cannot be before c. 101 B.C. – is as yet quite unplaced. One single issue – of M. Cato – might possibly be African (Utica?) in the Jugurthine War. There are a few odd coins that do not readily fit into any of these classes; they may belong to mints unidentified as yet.

Period V. Rome, the main mint, is assisted by a second mint, presumably in the North and very probably at Pisa. The earlier coins of Pisa are hard to distinguish clearly from the Roman. Its later issues can be distinguished by their serration. These serrate issues used often to be assigned to Spain; it seems more probable now that they were struck at Pisa, a port of embarkation for Sardinia and Spain. They can hardly be a coinage of the Sertorians; they are too closely connected with the Roman coinage for that. Other coins may also have been struck at ports of embarkation, e.g. the coins of C. Annius, struck by two quaestors at two (or possibly three) mints. One mint, a rare one, is shared with Q. Metellus; Metellus, it is true, *did* command in Spain, against Sertorius; but his title of 'imperator' seems to belong to the Sullan period; the coins were probably struck at a northern port (Livorno?). The second (and third?) mint for Annius seems to be more southerly; Tarracina, perhaps. To this same mint may belong a few later issues of C. Egnatius Maxsumus and others. There are a few odd coins, not exactly placed, but probably south Italian – those of Cn. Lentulus, for example. A serrate issue of L. Papius has very definite reference to Lanuvium and was perhaps struck in that city. Provincial issues, for the first time, are manifest. Sulla strikes twice in the East – once for the war in Greece, then for that in Asia. This latter issue was assigned by de Salis to south Italy, but the evidence seems to point rather to the East. Quite exceptional is the issue of C. Valerius Flaccus in Gaul; he strikes as 'imperator' in the Sullan interest, but signs, quite exceptionally, s.c. The issue is isolated and does not connect clearly with any predecessor or lead to any immediate successor.

Period VI. Rome is the main mint; Pisa strikes intermittently. Of the s.c. coins which we tend to assign to Rome, some may have been struck at mints near the capital; quaestors certainly struck for games at Praeneste – may have struck in that city. The issue of L. Roscius Fabatus, closely copying that of L. Papius, may, like his, belong to Lanuvium. Provincial issues are not to be traced; there is a large issue, which may belong to the war against the pirates, but it seems to be centred on Rome. Issues of Pompey in the East seem not to exist.

Period VII. The issues of Rome can be traced with some certainty, till they cease in 41. Many provincial issues can be determined from their allusions and the course of history. In most cases, the province is sure, the mint city quite uncertain. Thus, we are sure of issues of Caesar and his enemies in Sicily, of Caesar in Spain, Africa and the East, of the Pompeians in Asia Minor and Greece, in Africa and Spain. Part of the African issue, at least, is of Utica. Later, we find coins of Sextus Pompey in Sicily, of Q. Cornuficius in Africa, of Q. Labienus in the East, of Ahenobarbus and Murcus also in the East, as also of the 'Liberators', Brutus and Cassius. The issues of the Second Triumvirs, which we used to assign to their provinces – Gaul, Africa and the East – now seem to belong rather to their mints in Italy. All three had Italy in common; this presumably implied that all three could levy troops and pay them there. Servius was right in naming Anagnia as the mint where Antony struck coins for Octavia and Cleopatra. Since Liegle demonstrated that Praeneste struck coins for L. Antonius and his brother in the Perusine War the possibility of Italian mints has been wide open. There was another mint in the North, Pisa (?), where L. Antonius and also P. Ventidius struck in the interest of Mark Antony. This period is very fruitful for mint study; for mints are many and they can be clearly distinguished by their varying styles and by their selection of types. The fullness of our knowledge of the history enables us to pronounce with much more certainty than usual where these coins were struck; but the whole of this study should encourage us to be sure of our distinctions of mint, even where there is much more doubt about the exact location.

CHAPTER II

The Content of the Republican Coinage. Types and Legends[1]

I. GENERAL PRINCIPLES

We have been looking, up to the present, at what may be called the externals of Republican coinage; it is time to turn to its content, to its types and legends and the information that they give us. Coins may be said, with hardly a suggestion of metaphor, to have a language of their own; but it is a language that is only partially expressed in words and depends more on pictures to convey its meanings. The pictorial part of this language needs much study and something of imagination before it can be understood. We have to learn the symbolism of an age other than our own, and, although much is revealed to the first serious glance, the impression gains on the student that a life-time of study must leave much still unknown.

With the origin of coin-types we have, fortunately, not to deal. Rome begins with the system in vogue in Greek States in the third century B.C., in which types of a general character, mainly religious, relating to the life and traditions of the community, predominate. For some hundred and fifty years Rome does not move far outside the circle of this tradition. After that time, however, an extraordinary prominence is given to the ancient history of the State, chiefly in con-nexion with the families of the moneyers. It is not until the Empire that the Roman coin assumes the role of the modern medal and offers a full commentary on contemporary events. But, even under the Republic, the strong taste of the Roman for actuality did not lack expression in coinage, and comment on events of the day, under certain conventional disguises, became common.

---

[1] It has seemed impossible in this chapter, without over-burdening the text, to give full references for all the types quoted, or to note every case in which a coin discussed in the text is shown in the plates. The student who wishes to go fully into the subject is advised to turn to the *British Museum Catalogue of Republican Coins*, or to one of the other general works noted in the Bibliography. The Key to the plates, with its general references to the text, will help to remedy any deficiencies here.

2. TYPES OF THE AES

It will be convenient to begin with a discussion of the types of the bronze, which throughout follow laws of their own, then to consider the types of the silver and much rarer gold issues in their chronological development.

The types of the bars are of a general medallic character.[1] Only one is marked ROMANOM, but all seem to belong to Rome. Attributes of the gods take a prominent place among the types – the eagle and thunderbolt of Jupiter, the anchor of Neptune, the tripod of Apollo, the caduceus of Mercury, the corn-ear of Ceres, the sword and shield of Mars (?). The bar with rostra and dolphins and feeding hens (or fighting cocks?) seems to refer to naval victory. The bar with elephant and sow refers to the rout of Pyrrhus's great beasts by the grunting of swine. The bar with an ox on both sides may refer to Italy – Viteliu, the land of the young oxen.

As the so-called 'Latin Aes Grave' is now known to be true Roman coinage, its types can no longer be relegated to a footnote. In the ROMANO series the goddess of the tressis, dupondius and As has been variously interpreted; she is probably Diana of Aricia, the patroness of the Latin League. Professor Alfoeldi thinks that she is Rhome, the mythical foundress of Rome.[2] As Diana was closely associated with Virtus and as Virtus might be thought of as a kind of Roma ($\dot{\alpha}\varrho\varepsilon\tau\acute{\eta}$, $\varrho\acute{\omega}\mu\eta$) his idea may not be quite incompatible with ours. The other obverse types of the 'wheel' series can all be associated with the worship of Diana at Aricia. The bull is a common attribute of the goddess (Artemis Tauropolos). The horse may refer to the taboo on horses – because of the sad fate of Virbius, who had once been Hippolytus, torn by his maddened steeds. The hound is proper to Diana, the huntress. The tortoise is specially common in Latium. The wheel seems to symbolize communications by road. With its spokes uniting in one it may also speak of alliance, the Latin League. The same goddess supplies the obverse of the 'Tarentum' series. It is a peculiarity of this series that the obverse is repeated, reversed, on the reverse. The semis has the head of a young warrior (or young Mars?), the triens a thunderbolt, the quadrans an open hand, the sextans a shell, the uncia a knucklebone. The meaning of these deceptively simple types is not clear. The thunderbolt stands for Jupiter, the shell for Venus (?). 'Ostia' has on

[1] Mattingly, *Aes Signatum, Serta Hoffilleriana*, 1940.
[2] A. Alfoeldi, *Die Trojanischen Urahnen der Römer*, 1937, pp. 5 ff.

its obverse a 'Young Janus', probably the god Fontus, on its reverse Mercury. On the other denominations it takes the obverses of 'Tarentum' and pairs them with new types of its own. On the semis a goddess (Venus?) goes with the young warrior; on the triens a dolphin is paired with the thunderbolt; on the quadrans two barley-corns go with the open hand; on the sextans a caduceus goes with the shell; on the uncia a plain dot, as mark of value, accompanies the knucklebone; on the semuncia the mark of value, Σ goes with the acorn. Again the symbolism is deceptively plain. The dolphin suggests Neptune, the caduceus Mercury. The deliberate linking of the two series of 'Tarentum' and 'Ostia' is as yet unexplained; the one thing that it proves is that the two series were planned together. The series of 'Beneventum' is closely parallel to that of 'Tarentum'; the types of the obverse are again reversed on the reverses. The god of the As is Apollo, brother of Diana. On the semis is a Pegasus, a symbol of Apollo as sun-god, perhaps. The triens has a horse's head, an attribute of Mars (?). The quadrans has a boar, perhaps the famous Calydonian boar; legends of the west coast of Greece were common in Apulia. The sextans has a head in a pointed cap, perhaps one of the Dioscuri. The uncia has a barley-corn. Further study may perhaps reveal new meanings, hidden under their cloak of simplicity.

In the ROMA series 'Tarentum', 'Ostia' and 'Beneventum' carry on the same types. 'Ostia' again shares types with 'Tarentum'; 'Tarentum' and 'Beneventum' again reverse the obverses for their reverses. Symbols now occur, sickle for 'Ostia', club for 'Tarentum', vine-leaf for 'Beneventum'; it is not apparent why this series is so rare and why the symbol does not appear on the accompanying silver. Rome has a new series of great interest. The same reverse type occurs on all denominations, but it is now prow in place of wheel. Just as the wheel suggested communications by land, so does the prow communications by sea. The thought of the First Punic War at once comes to the mind, when Rome had had to conquer a new element. But there is also elaborate reference to the old mythical history of Latium, perhaps especially to visitors who had come by sea. Janus of the As is the old god-king of Latium. Saturn of the semis had been welcomed by Janus to Latium when he fled there, escaping from the wrath of Jupiter. That it is Saturn, not Jupiter, is proved by a late series of bronze, in which the god of the obverse has his attribute on the reverse; the attribute of this god is the sickle, not the thunderbolt. As we seem to be moving in the realm of early myth, we may think of the god of the triens as

Mars, god of the Aborigenes; of Hercules of the quadrans as the god of the Great Altar, the slayer of Cacus; of Mercury of the sextans as the god of the Arcadian Evander, founder of the old Pallanteum, on the site that was to be Rome. The goddess of the uncia will be Virtus (ῥώμη).

The token bronze, associated with the silver of the ROMANO and ROMA series, shows deities and their attributes—Diana, Jupiter, Apollo, Hercules, Minerva – hound, eagle and thunderbolt, horse's head and free horse, the Nemean lion. A series, running parallel to the Janus-Prow issues of the first reduction, has strange and puzzling types – a goddess on the triens, perhaps Venus, rather than Juno; Hercules fighting a Centaur on the reverse; a head in boar-skin on the quadrans, with a bull and snake on the reverse, perhaps for the river-god Achelous, who could take both these shapes. The she-wolf and twins of the sextans, as they cannot here stand for Rome herself, suggest a Latin colony. Is the bird of the reverse one of the ravens that fed the twins? The sun and crescent and stars of the uncia are unexplained, apart from their very general astrological meaning. The types of the semuncia, Cybele and horseman, suggest a later date, when the goddess had been brought to Rome; the coin need not belong to this series, though it has usually been assigned to it.

In the reductions of the Janus-Prow series, Diana appears on decussis, Minerva on tressis and dupondius, Minerva instead of Mars on the triens, when struck, not cast.

The types of the Janus-Prow series established themselves as standards for the Roman mint. The bronze mainly served the home market and went little abroad. It is not surprising, then, that it resisted change more successfully than the silver with its wider circulation. Minerva, once introduced, holds her place, instead of Mars, on the triens. One rare and solitary As, with obverse goddess in triple crest, reverse bull, is in all respects a puzzle. It is the only heavy As to bear the signature ROMA and it seems to have no subordinate denominations. The goddess may be Bellona, goddess of war, the bull the mark of Italy. The coin looks like a medal struck for some special occasion.

The bronze that accompanies the denarius shows few changes. Two rare denominations of south Italy, dextans and quincunx (ten and five ounces respectively), have as obverse Ceres and Apollo. The dodrans and bes (nine and eight ounces) have, as new obverse types, Vulcan and Liber. L. Opeimius has a club on the reverse of his quadrans. On northern issues of Cn. Domitius, M. Silanus and Q. Curtius Saturn, Minerva, Hercules, Mercury and Apollo (semis to uncia) have, in place of prow, their own attributes on reverse – sickle, aegis, club, caduceus and lyre. The fact that Apollo replaces the goddess (Virtus ?), normal on the uncia, suggests that Virtus was really Diana, his sister. The reverse of the quadrans of Ti. Veturius seems to have a very special reference, in its accessories of the bath, oil-flask and scraper, to the notorious bath of the wife of the Roman consul at Teanum, which led to the flogging of the chief magistrate. Other local types of the period, the Gracchi and after, show interesting variants – Victory erecting trophy on the As of Cn. Blasio, Mars in quadriga on the uncia of C. Fonteius, rudder on the quadrans of M. Cipius, head of Saturn and the dog (or lion?) on the uncia of L. Philippus. But, though change has begun to intrude, uniformity is still the main feature.

The bronze of the semuncial standard, in its short course, showed itself more open to the changes which were re-modelling the Roman coinage. L. Piso has a Victory on prow on his reverse (Plate XII, 4). A head of Apollo appears on the quadrans of L. Piso (Plate XII, 7), sometimes an anchor and rudder crossed on its reverse. Entirely new are the semis, triens and quadrans of Q. Titius, with head of Apollo and Minerva in quadriga, mask of Pan and Ceres with torches, mask of Pan and mask of Silenus. C. Pansa has a triple prow on the reverse of his As (Plate XII, 6), C. Censorinus busts of Ancus Marcius and Numa Pompilius on his obverse, and prow before two arches on the reverse (Plate XII, 5). So, too, L. Rubrius Dossenus has a Janus head of Hercules and Mercury on obverse, a prow behind a temple on reverse of his As. In this series, too, we occasionally find such formulae as EX S.C., D.S.S. ('de senatus sententia') on the bronze. The L.P.D.A.P. refers to the 'lex Papiria de aere publico'. Had the coinage continued, the bronze might have swung entirely into the lines on which the silver coinage was developing.

The remaining bronze issues of the Republic belong chiefly to the provincial coinage and follow no fixed laws of types. C. Clovius has, for obverse, a bust of Victory, for reverse, Minerva advancing, l.; Q. Oppius a head of Venus and a Victory on reverse. The Asses of Gnaeus Pompey the Younger and Sextus Pompey, struck in Spain, have the weight and types of the uncial As; but the Janus head shows curiously realistic features. Octavian's Gallic coins celebrate his deified father. The 'fleet' coinage of Mark Antony is original in types, as in other details. The obverses are given up to portraits of Antony,

Octavia and Octavian: the reverse types are adapted to the denomination – a quadriga of hippocamps for the sestertius, three galleys for the tripondius, two for the dupondius, one for the As. The bronze of Canidius Crassus, struck in Egypt c. 31 B.C., has as types crocodile and rostrum, and head of Apollo and fasces (Plate XII, 8, 9).

The types of Republican bronze, then, only teach us a very moderate amount about the history. With the silver and gold coinage we reach a far more fruitful field of study. Only in the early periods can we satisfactorily deal with the types in one rapid survey. In the last century of the Republic, after a preliminary review, we shall have to consider the context of the coinage under a number of subject-headings – archaeological, historical and the rest. The little that has to be said about legends will be worked into the discussion of the types.

3. TYPES OF EARLY GOLD AND SILVER

In the first ROMANO series the deities represented are Hercules, Mars, Apollo, Diana, Minerva, Mercury – all deities of high rank, but not quite the selection that we might have expected: we miss Jupiter, for example. Hercules is the god of early Roman legend (Cacus, etc.), also the mythical founder of the Fabian gens, to which one of the consuls of 269 belonged. Apollo is especially at home in Campania and the south of Italy. Mars is the war-god of Rome and Italy. Diana is the goddess of the hunt, also the Roman goddess of war, the goddess, too, of Aricia and the Latin League. She is naturally in place beside her brother, Apollo. Minerva is the city goddess, and as such she may be a goddess of war, goddess also of arts and crafts. Of the reverses, the she-wolf and twins refer to the foundation legend of Rome: when, as here, Hercules is their obverse, one wonders whether there was a form of the legend in which he, and not Mars, was the father of the twins. The horse's head and free horse belong to the worship of Mars at Rome;[1] but as coin-types, they were probably borrowed from Carthage. The Victory crowning trophy is a familiar motif: it may have been borrowed from the coinage of Agathocles, tyrant of Syracuse.

In the ROMA series the 'Young Janus' of the quadrigatus must be Fontus, the son of the god; he is used as obverse type by members of the gens Fonteia. Professor Alfoeldi has suggested that the two heads represent Romulus and Remus. They may, indeed, have been

---

[1] Cp. Ridgeway, Cambridge University Report, 12 Nov. 1925.

so interpreted at times by the masses. The Jupiter and Victory in quadriga is a copy of the monument erected on the Capitol by the Ogulnii in 295. Whether Victory was always there or was added subsequently cannot be determined. The young helmeted heads on the series of 'Ostia' and 'Beneventum' may represent heroes rather than gods: that of 'Ostia' might perhaps represent 'pius Aeneas' himself. The other reverses, lion's head and free horse, have already been commented on. Apollo recurs as obverse at 'Beneventum'. The god of the gold obverse is Fontus. The reverse – two warriors swearing loyalty over the body of a pig – is a symbol of 'coniuratio', alliance. It looks back to the treaty made by Romulus with Titus Tatius, but has clear reference also to the confederacy of Italy against Hannibal. The signature ROMANO is the old genitive plural, with final M dropped – not a nominative singular: silver 'of the Romans', not 'Roman silver'. ROMA expresses the sovereignty of the capital. On the victoriate Jupiter appears at last as obverse type; the reverse, Victory crowning a trophy, is used also at rebel Capua; it is a commonplace theme, not so far from the Victory reverse of the ROMANO series.

With the coming of the denarius we meet new types, which soon settle down to be stereotyped. The goddess of the obverse is Bellona (Diana) Victrix – the natural symbol of victorious Rome. The wing on the helmet is for victory; the griffin is the sign of supernal power. The reverse type, Castor and Pollux, the Dioscuri (Heavenly Twins), charging with spears in rest shows the epiphany of the gods, who fought so well for Rome at the battle of Lake Regillus. They are 'saviour gods', who save Rome herself and prompt her to succour the distressed: that was the part that Rome affected to play in her relations with the Greeks in the East. We think of King Nicomedes of Bithynia adoring the Senate as 'his saviour gods'. The same types are used for quinarius and sestertius. On the victoriate, Jupiter and Victory continue to appear. The obverse of the gold is Mars, the god of war, the reverse eagle and thunderbolt. If the issue was connected, as we have suggested, with the Aquileia gold-rush, there will be a double reference of the eagle – to Jupiter and to the city. The obverse long continues unchanged. On the reverse, new types appear c. 150 B.C. – Diana or Victory in a biga. Diana, who only appears at 'Italian' mints, may well be the goddess of the Latin League. Victory is always in place, for Rome is everywhere victorious. There may have been some special occasion for her first appearance in this form, the final victory over Carthage, for example.

The legend ROMA appears regularly on the reverse, as evidence, that is to say, of the authority coining, not as description of the obverse type, and is at first the only legend. Symbols to mark a mint or a moneyer are common from about 167 B.C. We find, for example, a Victory crowning the Dioscuri (Plate XI, 1), or a Victory crowning Rome (Plate XI, 4). Mint signatures occur at about the same time and also names of moneyers, at first in a very abbreviated form, later in greater detail. The earliest forms show abbreviated praenomen and nomen or cognomen, sometimes one of the two latter only.[1] The conjunction of nomen and cognomen (as AV (relius) RVF (us)) is rare. From about 140 B.C. three names often occur, sometimes divided between obverse and reverse. Further descriptions, such as C.F. (Gaii filius), also occur. F. is very occasionally used to distinguish a son from a father of like name. Extra names (*agnomina*), such as 'Asiagenus', are not uncommon. The tribe is very seldom given – A. MANLI. Q.F. SER. (*Sergia*) – c. 115 B.C. – is one of the few cases known.[2] One moneyer, L. Atilius (123 B.C.), places the letters NOM. in the place usually taken by the name ROMA. There can be no question of an engraver's error as all specimens plainly show the letters NOM.; but the interpretation 'Nomentanus', as surname of the moneyer, carries no conviction, as the name is not known in connexion with the Atilian gens. As the coin is of the time of Gaius Gracchus, some reference to the plans of Gaius for extending the citizenship seems to lurk here. Was 'Nomentanus' a term used to describe the new citizens, whom Gaius wished to create in mass? Nomentum was a community of citizens of the 'passive' right ('sine suffragio'); Gaius may have intended his new citizens to begin as such.[3] The mark of value, X, appears regularly behind the head of Roma on the obverse, as do the corresponding v and IIS on the quinarius and sestertius.

About 130 B.C. the traditions of the reverse type suffer further change. Quadrigae, as well as bigae, now appear and are driven by new charioteers. We find Juno in a biga of goats (C. Renius – Plate XI, 7), Diana in a biga of stags (no moneyer), Hercules in a biga of centaurs (M. Aurelius Cotta – Plate XI, 9); Venus crowned by Cupid in biga (Plate XI, 17), Pax in biga (Plate XI, 19). Quadrigae of horses are driven by Apollo (Cn. Baebius Tampilus – Plate XI, 13), Sol (M. Aburius Geminus – Plate XI, 16), Juno (C. Curiatius Trigeminus –

---

[1] Cp. Grueber, *B.M.C. Republic*, I, p. lxxxi f.
[2] Cp. also L. MEMMI GAL. (Galeria), C. MARIVS C.F. TRO. (Tromentina).
[3] H. Mattingly, *Proceedings of the Cambridge Philological Society*, 1950–51, pp. 12 ff.

Plate XI, 8, 14), Mars and Nerio (?) (Cn. Gellius), Libertas (C. Cassius). The Diana above-mentioned is identified as moon-goddess by the torch in her hand and the crescent in field. Particularly common is the type of Jupiter in quadriga (Plate XI, 15) – so common, in fact, that the name 'quadrigatus', originally appropriated to the didrachm, came to be transferred in later use to the denarius. Chariot types are common in so many series of ancient coins that we come to accept them without further explanation. There is, however, something peculiarly Roman in the representation of particular deities as charioteers. The clue to the meaning is given by the prominence of Victory either alone or as companion to some god. What is shown is deity in triumphant action, as typified by the victorious charioteers at the Games. There is no definite reference to games in honour of particular deities.[1] Occasionally, the team is varied, to suit the character of the deity, from horses to goats for Juno (Plate XI, 7), stags for Diana, or centaurs for Hercules (Plate XI, 9).

Variation in the reverse beyond this narrow range is still uncommon. The earliest examples seem to be the shepherd, she-wolf and twins on the reverse of Sex. Pompeius Fostlus and the bronze monument erected to L. Minucius Augurinus, prefect of the corn-market in 439 B.C., on the reverse of C. Augurinus (Plate XI, 12, cp. 20). In both cases there is obvious allusion to the family history of the moneyers – probably also some contemporary reference. Fostlus stresses the importance of 'urbs Roma' in answer to the coinage of rebel Fregellae: Augurinus, in glorifying the Minucius, who thwarted the designs of Spurius Maelius, is hitting at Gaius Gracchus, who seemed to be an evil repetition of the demagogue aiming at tyranny. Other contemporary allusions may be found in the coinage of the age of the Gracchi. C. Serveilius uses, as reverse, a warrior on horseback, with shield inscribed M, spearing another warrior who flees before him. Under cover of a reference to an ancestor, the famous C. Servilius Structus Ahala, who slew Spurius Maelius, the man who, by supplying cheap corn to the Roman people, affected the crown, C. Serveilius applauds the murder of the second Maelius, Gaius Gracchus. Coins of a slightly later date hint, as definitely, at the activities of the younger Gracchus – M. Marcius, with the ears of corn that accompany the Victory in biga of his reverse, M. Porcius Laeca with Libertas in quadriga crowned by Victory, C. Cassius with a similar type. References to family history are, no doubt, present in

[1] H. Mattingly, 'Divine Charioteers, etc.', *Proc. Brit. Acad.*, XXXIX, pp. 282 ff.

each case: but, as we shall often see below, this was the conventional form in which comment on current events was introduced on the Republican coin. But we are now reaching a time when a more detailed and systematic study of types will be needed. The reverse is given up more and more to types of the new kind – reflecting on topical events, whether connected with the moneyer or with the history of the State or with both. When the obverse, too, is released from the old tradition and various divine heads replace the head of Roma, the old conservatism is finally defeated and the coinage enters on its fullest and freest development. We can hardly be wrong if we associate these changes with the stirring events of foreign history and the increasing ferment in political life that began with the age of the Gracchi. The tradition broke down on two sides, on that of the conservatives and the democratic party. The conservatives themselves surrender to the new movement to the extent of allowing free play to the personal ambitions of individuals; to the democrats more particularly we may attribute the new desire to make the coinage reflect more faithfully the active and changing life of the State.

In the use of legends no great changes are to be noted. The signature ROMA is still normal on the reverse: the crowded reverse type of C. Augurinus causes it to be transferred to the obverse and there it occasionally reappears. It begins to be omitted from about 112 B.C. on and after a time only appears very rarely and then as description of type rather than as signature. Further legends, helping to identify the types, occur sporadically from about the same date. They become more and more common and more and more explicit, until at last we get such full legends as 'Sex. Nonius pr(imus) l(udos) V(ictoriae) P(raenestinos) f(ecit)' or 'C. Vpsae(us) cos (consul) cepit Priv(ernum)'. Of the various symbols, letters and numbers that distinguish so many denarii of the period from 125 to 66 B.C. we have spoken above. The mark of value, X, is replaced by XVI about 123 B.C., and later by ✳, though X persists on certain issues. It disappears altogether as a normal feature of the coin at about the same time as the signature of ROMA. Of the forms of moneyers' names little remains to be said except that they tend to become fuller and more explicit, often with all three names given in full and with name of father and even of grandfather added. A not uncommon feature is the genitive case of possession in place of the more obvious nominative.

4. TYPES OF THE LATER REPUBLIC

We have now to review the coinage in its days of full development and draw from it what lessons we can for history and archaeology. It is hardly possible to find any classification that is complete and that does not involve a certain amount of overlapping.

The following will serve our purpose:

(*a*) Religious types.
(*b*) Personal types.
(*c*) Historical types.
(*d*) Animate and inanimate objects.
(*e*) Architecture, art, etc.

(*a*) *Religious Types* (Plates XIII, XIV)

The religious element is always prominent in the Republican coinage. In the early period most of the stock types are more or less definitely religious. This feature is not peculiar to Rome; it is one that she shares with the majority of Greek States. The theory of the religious origin of coin-types is now generally abandoned, but the facts on which it seemed to rest remain. Religion was an integral part of the national life of Greece and Rome, and coinage, reflecting the life of the community, naturally acquires a religious tinge. The earlier coin types of Rome seem to be of a purely religious character: they honour a divinity simply as a permanent part of the religious life of the State. In the later period, which we have now to discuss, this kind of general reference seems, indeed, to occur often enough, but references to the history of the State or the moneyer's family are sometimes involved; if our knowledge were wider, we should probably have few types of the more general character left. A complete treatment of the subject is, of course, impossible here; all we can hope to do is to discover, as we survey the Roman Pantheon on the coins, to what sorts of uses it might be put.

Jupiter, as the chief god of the State, naturally appears freely on the coinage. L. Rubrius Dossenus, with his obverses of Jupiter, Juno (Plate XIII, 12), Minerva and Neptune and triumphal chariots or Victory on the reverse, refers to thanksgiving to the gods for the victory in the Social War. L. Scipio Asiagenus, both of whose types refer to Jupiter, seems to invoke his blessing on the Roman arms against the Cimbri (c. 103 B.C.). A youthful Jupiter, armed with the thunderbolt, seems to represent the god as armed against the national enemy: we meet him on coins of L. Caesius (c. 109 B.C.), L. Licinius Macer and M. Fonteius (c. 88 B.C.) and Gar. Ocul. Ver. (c. 87 B.C. – Plate XIII, 20). L. Volteius Strabo (c. 80 B.C.) associates Jupiter with the myth of Europa and L. Procilius (c. 82 B.C.) refers to him in company with Juno Sospita (Plate XIII, 17).

The long series of divine types of M. Volteius has been well explained as referring to the five chief agonistic festivals of the Romans – the 'ludi Romani' (Jupiter), the 'ludi plebeii' (Hercules), the 'ludi Cereales' (Ceres, Liber and Libera), the 'ludi Megalenses' (Cybele) and the 'ludi Apollinares' (Apollo). The Jupiter of the denarii of L. Lentulus and C. Marcellus (consuls, 49 B.C.) is, perhaps, an African god (cp. Plate XIX, 5). The Capitoline triad, Jupiter, Juno and Minerva, appears on the reverse of Cn. Blasio (Plate XVI, 1). Q. Pomponius Rufus, with his head of Jupiter and eagle, may be referring to his ancestor Numa, the great traditional founder of Roman rites and ceremonies (Plate XIII, 18). Petillius Capitolinus (c. 35 B.C.) seems to have had a family connexion with the worship of Jupiter Capitolinus, whom he honours on his coins (cp. also Plate XXI, 15). C. Vibius Pansa (c. 48 B.C.) alludes to the special cult of Jupiter at Anxur – which may have been the home of his family. A special Spanish and African cult of Jupiter is, it appears, celebrated on the Spanish coins of Varro (c. 49 B.C.), and the African of Q. Metellus Pius Scipio (c. 47–46 B.C.). The Jupiter with ram's horn of Q. Cornuficius (c. 44–42 B.C.) and Scarpus (c. 31 B.C.) is, of course, the famous Jupiter Ammon. On the denarius of Cn. Cornelius Sisenna (Spain (?), c. 130 B.C.), Jupiter in his quadriga hurls a thunderbolt at an anguipede giant. The same giant is seen in the pediment of a temple on the reverse of M. Plaetorius Cestianus and on the reverse of L. Valerius Acisculus, with obverse, head of Jupiter (Plate XIII, 19). The myth of the war of gods and giants is, of course, familiar, but there is some special Roman application of it involved here.

Saturn is distinguished by his emblem, the 'harpa', and is honoured as the guardian of the State treasury, the 'aerarium Saturni'. Piso and Caepio (100 B.C.), who strike as quaestors of the city, place him on their obverses, as does Cn. Nerius in 49 B.C. The issues of L. Memmius (c. 103 B.C.), L. C. Memies, L. F. (c. 87 B.C.), and Sufenas (c. 63 B.C.), all with this obverse, may have been specially provided for out of the 'aerarium'.

The 'Janus' heads of M. Fourius Philus (c. 115 B.C. – Plate XVIII, 6) and C. Fonteius (c. 110 B.C.) have no special meaning for us, unless in the second case the head is that of Fons or Fontus, son of Janus and ancestor of the Fonteian gens. The heads of Dioscuri on coins of M. Fonteius (Plate XIII, 10) and C. Sulpicius (Plate XVII, 17) are perhaps meant to represent the 'Dei Penates Publici' of Rome: can there be a reference to the returning of the troops to their homes after the end of the wars? The cult of the Dioscuri at Tusculum is certainly the occasion of the appearance of the gods on the obverse of L. Servius Rufus (Plate XVII, 8) and perhaps on that of M. Cordius Rufus too (Plate XIII, 11). Pan and Silenus appear, in virtue of the sound of their names, on coins of D. Silanus (c. 90 B.C. – Plate XIV, 9) and the two men named C. Vibius Pansa (c. 88 and 49 B.C. – Plate XIV, 10, 11). Why Pan and panther should appear on the sestertius of T. Carisius (c. 43 B.C.) we cannot say. Mercury, on the coins of C. Mamilius Limetanus (c. 83 B.C. – Plate XVI, 18), is the ancestor of Ulysses, whose grand-daughter Mamilia was the ancestress of the Mamilian family; to such extremes did Roman genealogists run. The terminal bust of Mercury on coins of M. Piso Cn. f. Frugi has been interpreted as that of the 'guardian of the streets'. Mercury and his lyre on the sestertius of L. Papius Celsus is unexplained.

Mars, as the god of war, is a natural type for any issue in time of battle. We find him on coins of Q. Lutatius Cerco (Jugurthine War), Q. Thermus M. f. and C. Malleolus (Cimbrian War), Cn. Lentulus (Civil War, 87 B.C. – Plate XIV, 2), P. Satrienus (Plate XIV, 3), L. Axsius Naso (Plate XIV, 4), L. Rustius, Albinus Bruti f. (Great Civil War – Plate XIV, 5), and L. Mussidius Longus and P. Clodius M. f. (war of second triumvirs against the 'Liberators'). The last two types are standing types of the reverse, not busts of the obverse – far less common, but extending in use towards the close of the Republic.

Nepture, as god of the sea, has for attribute the trident; he is naturally invoked on occasion of wars at sea. The denarii of L. Lucretius Trio, with his head on obverse, possibly belong to the Sertorian War (Plate XIV, 8), when the alliance of Sertorius with the pirates lent a naval aspect to the campaign: the coins of Q. Crepereius Rocus, of about the same date, are full of references to the sea: Amphitrite on obverse, Neptune drawn by hippocamps on reverse, sea-creatures as symbols in the field (Plate XVIII, 20). Brutus honours Neptune for his sea victory off the Lycian coast (denarii of Casca Longus, c. 43–42 B.C.); Murcus expresses, by the use of his portrait, the fact that he was 'praefectus classis' (Asia, c. 43–42 B.C. – Plate XIX, 19). P. Hypsaeus traced his descent from Leuconoe, daughter of Neptune, and places both heads on his coins (c. 61 B.C.). Sextus Pompey, during his time of power in Sicily, struck coins full of reference to the sea-god who gave him his power: the proud title NEPTVNI, 'Son of Neptune' (cp. denarius of Q. Nasidius) was actually claimed by him after a victory over Octavian.

Bacchus or Liber, the god of wine, appears, in connexion with the Lampsacene Priapus, on coins of Q. Titius (c. 87 B.C. – Plate XIV, 12), in connexion with Pan on coins of C. Vibius Pansa (c. 49 B.C.). As 'Liber' the god was regarded as patron of 'Libertas' and this certainly leads to his appearance on coins of the two Cato's (c. 100 B.C. and 47–46 B.C.) and, perhaps, also of L. Cassius (c. 78 B.C. – Plate XIII, 3): in this latter case his female counterpart, Libera, is associated with him.

Apollo, the god of poetry and music, and, in another aspect, the god of the sun, appears in several distinct capacities. On the coinage of Q. Pomponius Musa (c. 64 B.C.) he, with Hercules Musagetes, is associated with the nine Muses. As sun-god he appears on denarii of M'. Aquillius (XIV, 18), L. Lucretius Trio,[1] M. Cordius Rufus and L. Valerius Asisculus, again, on coins of P. Clodius M. f. (c. 42 B.C. – Plate XXI, 7) and coins of Antony struck in the East (Plate XX, 3); in most, if not all these cases, he symbolizes the 'Rising Sun' (Oriens). It is as the patron of Apollonia that he appears on coins of the consuls L. Lentulus and C. Marcellus, struck at that town in 49 B.C., perhaps also on coins of Brutus. As god of prophecy and the Sibylline books he may find his place on the issues of C. Malleolus and his colleagues which are possibly connected with the founding of Eporedia (Plate VII, 6). The Apollo of the coins of L. Piso Frugi, C. Vibius Pansa, C. Marcius Censorinus, P. Crepusius, L. Censorinus (c. 90 – 87 B.C.) and M. Metellus Q.F. (c. 81 B.C. – Plate XIII, 2), may refer to the 'templum Apollinis' outside the 'pomoerium' in which the Senate conferred with generals in the field. The same reason might account for the Apollo head on quinarii of c. 104 B.C. and on the denarii of C. Piso, probably struck for the campaign of Pompey against the pirates (Plate XIII, 1). The Apollo of Ser. Sulpicius is possibly the god of Delos, the great slave-mart (Plate XIX, 1). The Sibyl, the mythical authoress of the Sibylline books which Rome used to consult in time of need under the direction of Apollo, is represented on coins of L. Torquatus, T. Carisius and L. Valerius Asisculus. In the first case, the

---

[1] If the worship of the sun-god was hereditary in the 'gens Lucretia', we should find a special reference in such passages of the poet Lucretius as II, vv. 59 ff.; III, vv. 91 ff.; VII, vv. 39 ff.

consultation of the books on the question of Egypt may be referred to, in the second two the prophecy that Parthia could only be conquered by a king and that Julius Caesar must therefore assume the royal title. The young god of the obverse of L. Iulius Bursio combines attributes of more than one divinity (Plate VIII, 10). The young laureate head suggests Apollo, the wing Mercury, a trident in the field Neptune. No satisfactory explanation of the type has yet been suggested. Such syncretism became common in the third century A.D., but was quite unusual under the Republic.

Hercules, on the obverse of 'Lentulus Marcelli filius' (c. 99 B.C.), is a thin disguise for Marius returning in triumph from the Cimbrian War. The legend of Hercules and the Nemean lion forms the reverse of C. Poblicius (Plate XIV, 16). The Spanish Hercules of Osca appears on coins of P. Lentulus P.f.L.N. and of Domitius, both struck in or for Spain, c. 76 B.C. and 38 B.C. respectively, the African Hercules (Melcarth) on denarii of Q. Metellus Scipio (struck in Africa, c. 47–46 B.C.). The same allusion is, perhaps, to be seen on the issue of Ti. Q., struck during the Jugurthine War. The Hercules of L. Livineius Regulus may refer to the claim of M. Antony to descent from Anteon, the son of the hero.

Vulcan, as the god of smiths, is patron also of the mint, and as such appears on denarii of L. Cotta (c. 102 B.C.).

Juno, the queen of the gods, is honoured under two main forms, as Juno Sospita and as Juno Moneta. As Sospita, she was the special goddess of Lanuvium, wearing goatskin head-dress and armed with spear and shield. Her great function is the protection of men in the grip of danger, as of war. Her earliest appearance is on coins of L. Thorius Balbus[1] (Plate XIII, 13); later we find her on coins of L. Procilius, L. Papius and L. Roscius Fabatus (Plate XIII, 14). The last three moneyers were probably all adherents of the popular party, which seems to have had a special devotion to this goddess. The clearest testimony to the character of the goddess is found on the African denarius of Q. Cornuficius. Cornuficius had been a devoted Caesarian, but, after Caesar's death, espoused the cause of the Senate and, in his province of Africa, gave asylum to fugitives from the proscriptions. His reverse shows him receiving a crown as reward from Juno Sospita, whose work he has been doing (Plate XX, 4). L. Papius Celsus places as reverse to the portrait of Juno Sospita a curious type of eagle and wolf, relating to the foundation of Lavinium which is confused with

---

[1] With legend I.S.M.R., 'Juno Sospita Mater Regina'.

Lanuvium. Juno Moneta (the 'Adviser' in Roman etymology) is the goddess of the mint, which stood in her temple; her origin, just possibly Carthaginian,[1] was certainly forgotten at a later date. We meet her under the name MONETA on coins of L. Plaetorius (Plate XIII, 15) and T. Carisius: perhaps we should also attribute to her some unnamed busts, as, for instance, those of the obverses of Cn. Naevius Balbus, L. Flaminius Chilo, and L. Mussidius Longus. The coins of L. Plaetorius were struck by him as quaestor by decree of the Senate: it is possible that he opened a new mint. T. Carisius places on his reverse implements of minting and undoubtedly refers to the reform of the mint by Julius Caesar.

Minerva, the goddess of wisdom, of city life, and of war, is a rarer type than one might have expected: no doubt her place is often taken by Roma. Her bust, distinguished by aegis, is seen on obverses of P. Servilius Rullus, C. Considius Paetus and C. Vibius Varus. She drives a quadriga on the reverse of C. Vibius Pansa (Plate XIV, 7). Rome herself appears but seldom after about 100 B.C. Most interesting is the reverse of Kalenus and Cordus, which shows the concord of Roma and Italia, probably when Caesar was talking of extending the citizenship to Transpadane Gaul. A later rendering of the 'Roma' head is seen on the aureus of C. Vibius Varus (Plate XIV, 17).

Diana of the Aventine, we have seen, played a notable part in the earlier history of Roman types. Sertorius in Spain worshipped Diana the huntress with exceptional devotion and imposed on the credulous natives as her protégé: to this fact we may perhaps attribute the frequent appearance of the goddess on coins of the period (A. Postumius A. f. S. n. Albinus, Ti. Claudius Ti. f. Ap. n., Plates XIII, 7; XVIII, 18; C. Postumius Tatius – Plate XIII, 8, and L. Axsius L. f. Naso). C. Hosidius Geta refers to her in connexion with the Calydonian boar (Plate XIII, 9). As patroness of the great Sulla she is honoured by his son Faustus in 61 B.C. (Plate XVI, 3). P. Clodius M. f. has a reverse type of Diana Lucifera, in connexion with obverses of Apollo and Sol. The Diana of Ephesus, on the reverse of the consuls L. Lentulus and C. Marcellus, may point to the place of minting of the issue.

Ceres, the goddess of the earth, is naturally associated with distributions of corn, as on the issues of M. Fannius and L. Critonius, the plebeian aediles, and of L. Furius Brocchus. She appears to be connected with the foundations of colonies on coins of L. Cassius Caeicianus (Plate XIII, 4) and C. Marius C. f. Capito; on other issues,

---

[1] This point is still much debated.

such as those of C. Memmius C. f., L. Sestius pro-quaestor, L. Mus-sidius Longus, and P. Clodius M. f., we are less sure of the occasion. On issues of Julius Caesar and Q. Cornuficius – struck in Africa – she represents the great grain-producing province.

Nemesis, the goddess of the divine anger, appears on the reverse of C. Vibius Varus (Plate XIV, 17).

Venus, as the divine ancestress of the Julian 'gens', figures on coins of L. Iulius L. f. Caesar, and, more prominently, on coins of the moneyers of Julius Caesar, M'. Cordius Rufus, C. Considius Paetus, M. Mettius and L. Aemilius Buca; also on Spanish issues of the dictator and on the Sicilian issue of A. Allienus. Venus Victrix was the watchword of the Caesarians at Pharsalia. The reason for her appearance on coins of L. Censorinus and his colleagues (Plate XIV, 19) is uncertain. Sulla, too, claimed to be under the special protection of the goddess ('Epaphroditus'): she appears on the coins of L. Sulla 'Imperator iterum', and on the anonymous aureus with reverse, double cornucopiae. The Memmian 'gens', too, had a special cult of Venus, to which we owe the magnificent address to the goddess in the first book of Lucretius, who thus honoured his patron. C. Considius Nonianus honours the Venus of Eryx and places her temple on his reverse (Plate XXI, 17). Venus Verticordia appears on the reverse of M. Cordius Rufus (Plate XIII, 11). The Venus and Cupid on coins of Cn. Egnatius Maxsumus still await their explanation.[1]

The Cybele of M. Volteius, M. Plaetorius Cestianus (Plate VII, 11) and A. Plautius is probably in the first place the goddess of the 'ludi Megalenses'.[2] Whether the towered goddess of C. Fabius C. f. (Plate XIII, 5) and P. Fourius Crassipes is a Cybele or a towered Roma is open to question. Cybele appears in a chariot drawn by lions on the aureus of C. Norbanus and L. Cestius (Plate XIII, 6).

A veiled Vesta appears on coins of P. Galba as curule aedile (Plate VII, 10) and of Q. Cassius (Plate XIV, 20) and Longinus. In the last two cases a reference to the trial of the Vestal Virgins in 113 B.C. for unchastity is probable.

C. Serveilius C. f., alluding to the first celebration of the games of Flora, places her head on his obverse; and a similar reference to her games is probably implied on the coins of C. Clodius C. f. Vestalis.

It will have become abundantly clear from this short survey that the religious life of the Roman State in the last century of the Republic

---

[1] Was she, perhaps, one of the Fortunae of Antium?
[2] Perhaps compare also Pl. XIX, 3.

found a full record in the coinage and that allusions drawn from it were made to serve a great variety of purposes. At the same time it is not unfair to speak of a decline in true religious feeling. In the older types, religion was dominant and was considered for its own sake. In these latter days, it often serves no higher purpose than the gratification of family pride or the conveyance of an allusion to the events of the day. Of mythological references we have already had occasion to speak in passing; we shall review them in a little more detail, as a preparation for the study of the early history of Rome. Of genuine belief there can be little question; mythology is little more than a picturesque appendage to the history of the great families.

From the divine world we pass to the semi-divine sphere of those minor powers or virtues, who played such a prominent part in Roman religious belief (Plate XV). The Roman tended to see divine activity in every happening of life, however trivial. In course of time whole chains of happenings came to be associated with the powers of the major deities of the State – war with Mars, agriculture with Ceres. But there was still room enough left for the activity of minor powers, conceived of as persons with more or less clearly defined functions and attributes. Thus the great unknown power that turns the wheel of human fate was worshipped as 'Fortuna'. Peace had no presiding major deity, but was placed under the guardianship of the minor goddess Pax. Over the harmonious relationships of public and private life Concordia presided, Pietas over the various manifestations of the peculiarly Roman virtue of 'Loyalty'. The ideal of political freedom is committed to the charge of Libertas, that of honourable dealing to Fides. In the military sphere we meet the two soldier virtues, Virtus and Honos, and above all others the Victory that accompanies step by step the march of Rome. Finally, the Genius or spirit that presides over every person or place is invoked in particular contexts. Under the Empire we shall be astonished at the extent to which these minor cults develop. Under the Republic their place is a restricted one. How old the belief in their powers was may be learned from a cursory reading of such an author as Plautus. But their role was chiefly played in private life, and it is only towards the close of the Republic that they, with so much else of individual interest, make serious encroachments on the coinage of the State.

Concordia appears on issues of Paullus Lepidus, c. 56 B.C., as a woman veiled and diademed. We also meet her on coins of P. Fonteius Capito, L. Vinicius and L. Mussidius Longus (Plate XV, 2). In all cases the thought of harmony in the State is prominent; the shadow of the

Civil Wars hangs over the coinage. Later, Concordia is a sign of the harmonious co-operation of the triumvirs: she appears on a quinarius of M. Antony and Octavian with another expression of the same idea, the clasped hands, on reverse. A personification of Fides appears, once only, on the denarius of A. Licinius Nerva (Plate XV, 6); as the reverse shows a horseman dragging a captive, the allusion seems to be the military devotion of some member of Caesar's forces.

The Fortuna of the people of Rome is very appropriately placed on the obverse of the Pompeian moneyer Q. Sicinius at the outbreak of the great Civil Wars. The same Fortuna is invoked by M. Arrius Secundus in the days of the siege of Mutina. The Fortuna standing with rudder and cornucopiae on the reverse of P. Sepullius Macer will be rather the fortune of Julius Caesar himself, and the same figure is used for Octavian by Ti. Sempronius Graccus (Plate XV, 7).

The Genius of the Roman people appears on the denarius of Cn. Lentulus (Plate XV, 4)[1] and the tutelary Genius of Africa, under the form of the Egyptian goddess Sekhmet, on the denarius of P. Crassus jun., struck for Q. Metellus Scipio in Africa.

Libertas, the spirit of the Republican constitution, is one of the commonest of personifications. On the reverses of M. Porcius Laeca and C. Cassius she is seen driving a quadriga. There are probably double references in each case, to popular measures carried by ancestors of the moneyers and to the present activities of the 'populares', led by C. Gracchus. A large place is assigned to Libertas in the coinage of C. Egnatius Maxsumus – a bust of the goddess on one obverse, the goddess in a biga on one reverse, and a second reverse of a temple of Jupiter and Libertas. Libertas here seems to be Feronia as specially worshipped at Tarracina and there may be a reference to the newly won rights of the Italian peoples. On denarii of Brutus (Plate XVII, 7) and Q. Cassius (Plate XV, 5) Libertas represents the constitution, endangered by the ambition of the first triumvirate. On the denarius of Palikanus she suggests the loyalty of Julius Caesar to the Roman constitution. In the coinage of the Liberators Brutus and Cassius the goddess naturally plays a leading part.

The Pax in a biga on the reverse of the denarii with symbol, an elephant's head, may refer to the foundation of Junonia on the site of Carthage – a final peace now sealing the long series of African Wars. The obverse of the quinarius of L. Aemilius Buca (Plate XV, 10) celebrates the final triumph of Julius Caesar. The kindred goddess,

[1] His family had a special cult of the Genius.

Felicitas, appears on the obverse of the quinarius of Palikanus (Plate XV, 3) and on the reverse of the denarius of L. Flaminius Chilo. She represents the happiness and prosperity which Peace brings in her train.

The Pietas of M. Herennius (Plate XV, 11) is explained by the type of the reverse, the Catanian brothers, as an allusion to family affection – probably in reference to the family of the moneyer. On the obverse of Q. Caecilius Metellus Pius she is identified by her bird, the stork; Metellus won the epithet 'Pius' by the filial devotion which led him to strive to secure the return of his father from exile. The Pietas of the obverse of A. Hirtius, if indeed it is rightly described, denotes 'Piety' in a religious sense and alludes to the chief priesthood of Julius Caesar. On the reverse of denarii of Mark Antony of the Perusine Wars, the reference is to L. Antonius, the consul, brother of the triumvir, who took the title 'Pietas' in token of his devotion to his brother's interests (Plate XX, 8).

Salus on denarii of D. Silanus (Plate XV, 12) looks to the safety of the State, endangered by the outbreak of the great Social War. On the denarius of M. Acilius the two personifications, Salus and Valetudo, look back to the first medical practitioner of Rome, a certain Archagathus, who, in 219 B.C., was given a shop at the public expense in the street Acilia.[1]

Victory is the commonest of all personifications and is a familiar feature of the coinage at all times. She represents the overcoming power of the Roman arms in general rather than any particular triumph. At first standing figure or figures in chariots are the rule: she is seldom without her attributes wreath and palm, and is always winged. The seated Victory of the reverse of M. Cato bears the simple epithet 'Victrix' (Plate XV, 14). Later in the Republic a winged bust appears as, for instance, on coins of L. Valerius Flaccus (Plate XV, 15), Q. Titius, L. Papius Celsus, T. Carisius, L. Plancus praefectus urbi (Plate XV, 16), Q. Oppius and C. Numonius Vaala (Plate XV, 17).[2] We have no space here to describe the variety of ways in which Victory is represented: she crowns a trophy, crowns the drivers of quadrigae, flies with a shield in her arms, or is shown standing or seated with her wreath and palm. The triteness of the conception tends to make us oblivious of the true splendour of this visible expression of the power of the Roman State in action.

---

[1] A secondary allusion to the critical illness of Cn. Pompeius in 50 B.C. is probable.
[2] Cp. also Pls. VII, 7; X, 20; XX, 20.

Virtus, the personification of martial valour, is represented by a helmeted head on denarii of M'. Aquillius M'. f. M'. N.; it is the valour of his grandfather, the conqueror of the slaves in Sicily in 101 B.C. (Plate XVII, 13). Conjoined with Honos, Virtus appears, too, on the denarius of Kalenus and Cordus (Plate XV, 8). Both coins were probably struck by Caesar as governor of Cisalpine Gaul: hence the military allusions are doubly appropriate. Honos on the denarius of Palikanus is probably the type of public office (Plate XV, 9). The spirit of the Triumph is personified on the denarius of L. Papius Celsus (Plate XV, 13), celebrating the triumph of Julius Caesar in 46 B.C.

One last class of personifications remains to be considered – personifications of towns or provinces. With the figure of Roma herself we are already familiar. The rebel Italians of 91–89 B.C. substituted for Rome the figure of Italia, similarly conceived as an armed goddess. Hispania on the denarius of A. Postumius Albinus celebrates the province where the bitter fight with Sertorius was being waged (Plate XVIII, 19). It is doubtful, here, whether the long falling hair is an evidence of mourning: if it is, the province is represented as mourning till her deliverers come to save her. The denarius of Kalenus and Cordus shows on the reverse the reconciliation of Rome and Italy (Plate XV, 8). The Gallic man[1] and woman on the obverses of L. Hostilius Saserna certainly represent the Gallic nation, subdued by Caesar: but, inasmuch as the conquered province is now allied to Caesar against his domestic enemies, the allusion is not an unfriendly one. Of the tutelary genius of Africa we have already spoken. A head of Africa, in her distinctive head-dress of an elephant's trunk and skin, is seen on the rare aureus of Pompey the Great and on the denarius of Eppius, struck for Q. Metellus Scipio, and again on the denarius of Q. Cornuficius. A towered female head on denarii of Crassus jun. probably represents the town of Utica. C. Antonius, as proconsul of Macedon, places on his obverse the spirit of his province, wearing the national broad-brimmed hat (Plate X, 17). Asia is seen on the reverse of L. Murcus as a kneeling figure waiting to be raised to her feet by the Roman general. On denarii of the younger Cn. Pompey, struck in Spain, figures representing Hispania and Baetica welcome the Romans as their deliverer.

(b) Personal Types (Plate XVI)

The reference to the family history of moneyers runs through the

---

[1] The identification as Vercingetorix is attractive.

whole Republican series and will confront us again and again under almost every section. To avoid needless repetitions, we will make no attempt to give a full list of such allusions here. Rather we will content ourselves with a short survey of the various forms that such allusions take at different periods, enforcing our points by a few characteristic examples. To this survey we may aptly append a discussion of the use of portraiture under the Republic and of the emergence of the personal element, as the dominant feature, at the close of its coinage.

The earliest moneyers were content to mark their coins with a badge or device, such as may well have been used for a signet-ring, and these badges continued in use even after signatures by name had become general. Thus the staff (*scipio*) may represent the famous 'Scipio' branch of the Cornelian gens. The elephant's head of the Metellan family was derived from the famous victory of L. Caecilius Metellus at Panormus in 251 B.C., when the war elephants of Carthage were captured. Another family glory of the 'gens Caecilia' was the Macedonian victory of 146 B.C. (Plate XVI, 13, 15). An apex and hammer (*tudes*) may stand for an Apicius Tuditanus, a dog for a member of the Antestian gens (Plate XVI, 11), an ass's head for one of the Silani. Later, allusions to family history assume larger proportions. They may be of various kinds – references to the history of the Republic (cp. Fostlus and the legend of Roma, Plate XVI, 12), or to the mythical history of the Greek world in the misty background, or to the old Roman mythology – Mars and Nerio (Plate XVI, 14), Acca Larentia (Plate XVI, 19). When the Trojan origin of Rome had come to be accepted as an article of faith, it became fashionable for the great Roman houses to develop 'stemmata' running back into the divine and heroic past of Greece. It became a sort of patent of nobility, much like 'coming over with William the Conqueror' here. There was a wide field for misinterpretation of genuine tradition, for embroidery and for plain inventions. Greek hangers-on were no doubt largely responsible for supplying the necessary myths, but the Romans themselves must bear a full responsibility for their fatuous indulgence in this childish form of self-glorification. In the last century of the Republic the abuse, for such it must be called, had gone so far that the glorification of the family almost overlaid the true national character of the coinage. But an emphatic warning must be registered here. It would be a grave mistake to assume that the most obvious references are the only, or even the dominant ones. The convention *did*, indeed, become well established that the moneyer should select his types with an eye to the past glories of his own family. But the Roman world at large must obviously have been more interested in the events of the day than in these mythical splendours; and its interests were so far consulted, that topical allusions were interwoven, often with considerable ingenuity, in the web of family legend. Research on Roman coin-types has aimed mainly at elucidating the history of the 'gentes', and with such success that further explanation has hardly been sought. We must remember that this is but half the case: if few moneyers brought themselves to renounce the right to belaud their ancestors, few were entirely oblivious of the current events of the day.

A few examples will illustrate the forms that family allusions may take. The Mamilian 'gens' celebrates its descent from Mamilia, the grand-daughter of Ulysses (Plate XVI, 18), the Hypsaean 'gens' its descent from Leuconoe, daughter of Neptune. We are all familiar with the Trojan pedigree of the Julian 'gens'; but this special familiarity is simply due to the prominence which Julius Caesar gave to his house and its family legend (Plate XVI, 20). The flatterers of the Empire wanted to provide Vespasian with an ancestry from Hercules, but the Emperor himself laughed the project down. Other houses based their nobility on the Roman kingship. N. Fabius Pictor claims association with Quirinus (Plate XVI, 17). The 'gens Marcia' claimed to derive from Ancus Marcius (Plate XII, 5), the 'gens Calpurnia' from Calpus, son of Numa Pompilius, the 'gens Pomponia' from Pompus, another son of the pious king. More than one family of Sabini boasted descent from the old Sabine king, Titius Tatius. The family of the Pompeii Fostli claimed as ancestor the shepherd Fostlus, who found Romulus and Remus with the she-wolf. Other moneyers boast of great Republican ancestors – Brutus, the murderer of Caesar, of Brutus the first consul, C. Serveilius of the Ahala, who put to death Sp. Maelius; the Metelli had a particularly honourable place in the 'Fasti' – they could boast of the victory of Panormus and the victory in the third Macedonian War. The Aquillian gens could point to the conqueror of Aristonicus and the pacifier of Sicily, the Aemilian gens to L. Aemilius Paullus, conqueror of Perseus (Plate XVII, 10); M. Aemilius Lepidus, the later triumvir, has a gallery of family honours on his coinage – the Aemilius Lepidus who slew a foeman in battle at the age of fifteen, the Lepidus who was guardian to Ptolemy V, the vestal Aemilia, for whom the goddess miraculously re-kindled the sacred fire, which had been suffered to go out, the Aemilius who restored the 'Basilica Aemilia' in 78 B.C. Faustus Sulla, son of the dictator, uses for reverse his father's signet-ring, showing the surrender of Jugurtha by Bocchus (Plate XVII, 14). M. Aemilius Buca, striking in 44 B.C., depicts on one of his reverses the dream of Sulla, who thought that he saw the goddess Bellona, whom the Romans sometimes identified with the moon, standing by him and putting thunder in his hand, with which to destroy his enemies. The sons of the great Pompey naturally write large on their coinage the honours of their father. Other heroes of the coinage were decidedly stars of the second or third magnitude – the Sex. Nonius Sufenas, who first celebrated the games of Victory, the Coelii Caldi of the coinage of Caldus, the C. Plautius Venno Hypsaeus who took Privernum in 341 B.C., the Restio of the coins of C. Antius Restio.

One particular kind of reference is that of the punning or canting badge – Pan for Pansa (Plate XIV, 10), Silenus for Silanus, the Septemtriones for Trio, the jackdaw for Gragulus, the wren for Todillus. Badges of this character were evidently common, and were freely used for coin-types: but it is doubtful whether all the explanations offered of this description can be seriously accepted.

The question of portraiture demands a word to itself. Tradition at first forbade any portrait other than that of a god. The earliest infringements of the rule date from about 105 B.C. Cn. Blasio portrays an ancestor, who recovered Rhegium in 270 B.C., rather than the famous Scipio Africanus the Elder (Plate XVI, 1), and L. Philippus, a Philip of Macedon, perhaps the famous Philip II rather than Philip V, who was defeated at Cynoscephalae (Plate XVI, 2). The helmet with goat's horns and the letter ϕ leave no doubt about its being a king Philip. Philip V, of course, had been an enemy of Rome: but he had died as her ally and it is perhaps not impossible that, two generations later, he might appear on her coins. On the analogy of this coin, the diademed head on the obverse of Faustus Sulla (Plate XVI, 3) has been interpreted as Jugurtha; but is it not rather Bocchus, king of Mauretania, if a human being at all? So, too, we may perhaps recognize in the Gaul on the obverse of L. Hostilius Saserna a portrait of Vercingetorix himself. From about 90 B.C., we meet portraits of early great men of Rome – Numa Pompilius, Titius Tatius, Ancus Marcius, Brutus the first consul (Plates XVI, 5; XVII, 6), Ahala (Plate XVI, 5), the tribune Ser. Sulpicius Rufus, the consul M. Claudius Marcellus (Plate XVI, 6). Then come later personages, Aemilia Lepida the Vestal, the consul C. Coelius Caldus (Plate XVI, 4), the consul Q. Pompeius Rufus, the consul A. Postumius Albinus, the tribune Antius Restio, the praetor L. Regulus (Plate XVI, 10).

The representation of the living man only begins in the year 44 B.C. with the portrait of Julius Caesar, which the Senate ordered to be placed on the coins (Plate XIX, 9, cp. 15). Before that date, allusion to the living had always been subsidiary and indirect, as in the case of Marius, Sulla and Pompey the Great.[1] But the times were ripe for the change. The example of Julius Caesar was readily followed, not only by his successors, the second triumvirs (Plates XIX, 14; XX, 1, 2, etc.), but by the Liberator Brutus – Cassius, however, abstains – henceforth every man who has confidence in his destiny does not hesitate to place his portrait on the coins.[2] Cn. Pompey jun. strikes with his father's portrait (Plate XVI, 9). Sextus Pompey associates with his own portrait those of his father and brother (Plate XVI, 8; cp. XIX, 11, 12). The way was, in fact, open to the full Imperial coinage. Augustus had not to educate the public to accept the appearance of personal types: all he had to do was to concentrate attention on his own person by eliminating rivals.

(c) *Historical Types, etc.* (Plates XVII–XX)

In passing over to our third section, that of mythology and history, we are not wandering far from family history, for, even where we cannot now trace it, family allusion is always to be suspected in reference to the past. Among the Greek myths represented on Republican coins are the story of Medusa, of Bellerophon and Pegasus, the hunt of the Calydonian boar (Plate VIII, 15), the rape of Europa (Plate VIII, 14), Hercules and the Nemean lion, the flaying of Marsyas, the home-return of Ulysses, Apollo and the Muses, Attis and Cybele, Scylla and Charybdis, and Trinacrus, the legendary hero of Sicily. The legend of the Catanaean brothers, Amphinomus and Anapias, who carried their aged parents on their shoulders from an eruption of Etna, is used as a type of 'Pietas' by M. Herennius (Plate XV, 11) and Sex. Pompeius. In a similar way the more famous story of Aeneas and Anchises figures on coins of Julius Caesar. Among Roman legends we may cite the rape of Nerio by Mars, the story of the shepherd Fostulus and his wife Acca Larentia, who cared for the infants, Romulus and Remus. The anguipede giant on coins of Cn. Cornelius Sisenna, M. Plaetorius

[1] The famous gold stater of Flamininus, the Liberator of Greece, was a Greek, not a Roman coin. The placing of a portrait of a living Roman on the coin of another State was no direct concern of Rome.
[2] The heads on coins of M. Arrius Secundus and C. Numonius Vaala (Pl. XVI, 7) perhaps represent living men, as does possibly that on the coin of L. Servius Rufus. Later, even women are allowed to appear; apart from the very doubtful cases of Fulvia and Scribonia, we have certain portraits of Octavia and Cleopatra.

Cestianus and L. Valerius Acisculus has been dubiously taken to represent a mythical deity of Valentia, the oldest name of Rome – conceived of sometimes as a destructive, sometimes as a beneficent and healing power. A further set of allusions to the mythology of the Valerian gens has been very ingeniously traced on coins of L. Valerius Acisculus by Ch. Lenormant: but the types are, in fact, very obscure, and all we can safely say is that some of Lenormant's suggestions are ingenious enough to be true.

From mythology we pass, with little change, to the history, so closely interwoven with mythology, of early Rome. The coins supply us with a pictorial history of much of the tradition of the kingdom and Republic – the foundation legend (Plate XVII, 1), the kings, Romulus (Plate XVII, 2), Numa Pompilius (Plate XVII, 3), Ancus Marcius (Plate XVII, 3), Titius Tatius, the rape of the Sabine women (Plate XVII, 4), the death of the traitress Tarpeia, Brutus the first consul, the battle of Lake Regillus, the treaty with Gabii, Ahala, the slayer of Sp. Maelius, the relief of the siege of Tusculum (Plate XVII, 8), the capture of Privernum, the exploits of the Metelli, of Scipio Africanus and M. Claudius Marcellus (Plate XVII, 6), the Lepidus who was guardian of Ptolemy (Plate XVII, 9), the young hero, M. Lepidus, who killed a foeman at the age of fifteen (Plate XVII, 11), the conquest of Perseus (Plate XVII, 10), the sack of Corinth, the victories of the Aquillii in Asia and Sicily (Plate XVII, 13), the trial of the Vestal Virgins, the surrender of Jugurtha by Bocchus to Sulla (Plate XVII, 14), the triumphs of Pompey (Plate XVII, 15). The motive for such allusions is partly family pride, partly antiquarian interest, intensified by the desire to see the present parallel to the past event. More peaceful events, such as the foundation of the games of Ceres and Flora (Plate XVII, 2, 12) and Victory (Plate XVII, 16) are also recorded. Interesting references to Roman customs are seen in the oath sworn over the body of a pig (Plate XVII, 17), the appeal of a soldier against sentence (Plate XVII, 18), the voting scene (Plate XVII, 19), and the seated Vestal Virgin (Plate XVII, 20).

More interesting, if harder to detect, are the references to contemporary history. Before about 135 B.C. such references as have yet been discovered are few indeed. An occasional symbol seems to have topical point, e.g. Victory flying over the Dioscuri may mark the end of the second Macedonian War – Victory crowning Rome the end of the wars with Carthage: the shield and dragon-trumpet suggests the wars against the Gauls of the land that was to be Narbonensis in the years just before 120 B.C. Behind the introduction of new types in the period after 150 B.C. some historical allusions may lurk; the types of Sex. Pompeius Fostlus and C. Augurinus, in particular, depart so far from the beaten track that we are forced to suspect a very special occasion for the coinage. The coins follow those of Ti. Veturius struck for Fregellae in revolt. Fostlus, with the she-wolf and twins, stresses the importance of 'urbs Roma': Augurinus, glorifying the ancestor who thwarted Sp. Maelius, hits at Gaius Gracchus, the Maelius of a later age.

A little later we find ourselves on surer ground. The three moneyers M. Metellus Q.F., Q. Maximus and C. Serveilius struck coins after the murder of Gaius Gracchus. Serveilius, with his reverse of Ahala slaying Sp. Maelius, expresses the belief, sanctioned by the Senate, that Gracchus had aimed at the kingdom as Maelius had done (Plate XVIII, 1). Some forty years later, when Sulla restored the power of the Senate after the rule of the Marians in Rome, these three coinages were restored (Plate XVIII, 2), a head of Apollo replacing that of Bellona on the obverse. The Senate, safely arrived, as it fondly hoped, at the end of the Civil Wars, looks back to the first blow struck on its side.

Indirect allusions to the legislation of C. Gracchus are seen in the Libertas in quadriga on the reverse of M. Porcius Laeca and C. Cassius and in the ears of corn on the reverse of M. Marcius. A little later comes the revival of the reverse type of Augurinus by his son Tiberius. The anonymous denarius with reverse Pax in biga and symbol, elephant's head (emblematic of Africa), may suggest the foundation of Junonia on the site of Carthage.

The great Gallic Wars, culminating in the foundation of Narbo Martius, have left their record in coinage. The man attacking a dog on the reverse of Cn. Domitius reminds us of the huge dogs of war kept by the Arvernian king Bituitus (Plate XVIII, 3).[1] The reverse of C. Metellus, Jupiter in biga of elephants, makes us think of the victorious general Cn. Domitius, who rode through the province of Narbonensis in a similar car (Plate XVIII, 4). The warrior in biga on the reverse of the L. Licinius – Cn. Domitius issues is certainly a Gaul and relates to the war with Bituitus, whether or no we identify him with the king himself. The issue was certainly struck on the occasion of the foundation of Narbo Martius. Victories in Illyria are perhaps commemorated by M. Fourius Philus (Plate XVIII, 6). A little later we find allusions to the Cimbrian War, the Roman and barbarian fighting (M. Servilius) and the similar type of Q. Thermus (Plate XVIII, 8). The Victory

---

[1] Perhaps compare also coins of L. Torquatus (Pl. XVIII, 7).

types of M. Cato may celebrate the triumphant end of the war. Allusion to the Jugurthine War may be seen in the galley types of C. and M. Fonteius, perhaps also in the Hercules of Ti.Q.

C. Fundanius shows on his reverse Marius triumphing over the Cimbri and Teutoni, and Lentulus Marcelli f. honours the same general by the Hercules of his obverse and by the armed figure crowned by the Genius of the Roman people on his reverse (Plate XVIII, 9). When Saturninus, in 100 B.C., proposed his famous corn-law, Q. Caepio, the urban quaestor, informed the State that the treasury could not bear the financial burden. But the law went through and we have actual coins of Caepio and his colleague Piso struck in the same year, but perhaps rather for some counter-measure of the Senate. The foundation of Eporedia after the war is perhaps glanced at on the reverse of L. Cassius Caeicianus. A special coinage, that of C. Malleolus, A. Albinus, L. Metellus and L. Pomponius Molo was struck for the occasion. The Roma crowned by Victory marks the conclusion of the war; the Dioscuri, while associated with the family history of A. Albinus (A. Postumius Albus was dictator at Lake Regillus), suggest the colony rich in horses; the Apollo of the obverse may be the god of colonies, or, perhaps, rather of the Sibylline books which ordered the foundation. The Social War has left a full record of both sides, Roman and rebel. On the Roman side, we note the 'Salus' type of D. Silanus, the galloping horseman (a despatch-rider) of L. Piso (Plate XVIII, 13),[1] the rape of the Sabines of L. Titurius Sabinus (a reference to a previous war of Rome with her close kindred), the chariots of the great gods (thanksgiving services) of L. Rubrius Dossenus. Corn distributions are celebrated by P. Fourius Crassipes (Plate XVIII, 14), and M. Fannius and L. Critonius (Plate VII, 8). On the Italian side, we find the head of Italia in place of Roma, the swearing of alliance over the body of a pig, Italia crowned by Victory, the bull of Italy trampling the she-wolf of Rome, the visit of envoys of the Italians to King Mithradates. The inscriptions are part Latin, part Oscan, and the names of various generals, among them Q. Silo, C. Papius Mutilus and Numerius Lucilius appear (cp. Plate XVIII, 10–12). Many of the types are adapted from Roman coins of the period of the Cimbrian Wars. The brotherhood in arms of that war had undoubtedly done much to revive the hope of citizenship in the allies, the more so as Marius himself had shown a very liberal attitude towards the question. It is naturally to that brotherhood that the rebels now chose to appeal. It

---

[1] He bears either a torch (a 'fiery cross' (?)) or a palm, as sign of victory.

has been suggested that in the serrate and non-serrate denarii, we see a clash between democrats and optimates, the former preferring 'hard', the latter 'soft' money. But the suggestion must not be pressed too far: a preference for the serrate in some provinces seems to enter into the question. The view that the Sertorians struck serrate denarii in Spain has had to be abandoned. On the Sullan side, we have Sulla's own coinage, struck in the East. The coinage issued by L. Lucullus on Sulla's orders from the 20,000 talents levied on the cities of Asia Minor is probably represented by the aurei and denarii, with obverse, Venus and Cupid, and reverse, jug and lituus between trophies. Other coins show us Sulla in his triumphal chariot (Plate VI, 12) and an equestrian statue raised in his honour. The Sullan restoration was celebrated, as we have seen, by a re-issue of types of the days of Gaius Gracchus. There are also coins of C. Annius, the Sullan governor of Spain, 82–80 B.C., of Q. Metellus Pius, probably struck for his campaign as lieutenant of Sulla in north Italy, rather than for his war against Sertorius, and of C. Valerius Flaccus in Gaul. The triumphal banquet of Metellus, when he was crowned at the feast by a Victory, is shown on the reverse of P. Lentulus P. f. L. n. (Plate XX, 11). Other coins of Roman mintage were probably struck for the war with Sertorius, with such types as Mars, Diana and Neptune.

The coinage of the Marians is more eloquent. Their relations with the Italians are portrayed on a number of types (Plate XVIII, 15–17). C. Mamilius Limetanus, with his reverse of the home-returning Ulysses, suggests the return of the Marians from their exile. The coins of Q. Antonius Balbus may represent the products of the robbing of the temples in 82 B.C. Other coins refer to the war in Spain, but were not struck, as was once thought, for the Sertorians,[1] but by the Roman government at ports of embarkation for Spain. The coins of A. Postumius Albinus show a head of Hispania and his reverses show the sacrifice of a bull on a hill – a reference to an early legend, in which the sacrifice secured Rome's supremacy over Latium – and a togate figure, between fasces and standard (Plate XVIII, 18, 19), showing the return of a general from military to civil life (?). The coinage of Q. Crepereius Rocus, which is full of references to the sea, may refer to the war at sea and the alliance of Sertorius with the pirates (Plate XVIII, 20). The issues of Cn. Egnatius Maxsumus seem to refer to the Feronia – Libertas of Tarracina and the two Fortunae of Antium.

---

[1] H. Mattingly, 'Some Historical Coins of the Late Republic, The Marian Faction', *J.R.S.*, 1922, pp. 234 ff.

The period from 70 to 50 B.C. yields us several striking examples of contemporary allusions and would undoubtedly yield more if we understood more of its detail. A very rare aureus celebrates the triumph of Pompey the Great on his return from the East; the obverse shows the head of Africa, the scene of his earliest triumphs, the reverse the hero in his chariot accompanied by his son on one of the horses. Definite allusions to Pompey's exploits against the pirates[1] and against Mithradates, as also to those of his predecessor, Lucullus, are lacking, so far as we know. M. Aemilius Scaurus, who had served under Pompey in Syria, celebrates the surrender of the Nabathaean king Aretas: the coin was struck in 58 B.C. when Scaurus was curule aedile (Plate XIX, 2). A similar type of A. Plautius showing the submission of 'Bacchius Judaeus', obviously refers to some episode of the Eastern Wars (Plate XIX, 3). There seems to be no authority for identifying this Bacchius with the Jewish prince, Aristobulus, tempting as the suggestion appears, and we are left to suppose that it was some minor prince, whose surrender is here recorded.

The coinage of Brutus, with types of Libertas, Brutus the first consul, and Ahala, is proved by finds to belong to this period, not, as one would have imagined, to the period after Caesar's death. But appropriate to the day it certainly was. It was a piece of Republican propaganda against tyrants and may have been struck just before the great Civil War. The examples of Brutus the first consul and Ahala are invoked to show how tyrants should be dealt with. The coinage of P. Crassus, son of the triumvir, was issued by special permission of the Senate, probably in connexion with the raising of a troop of Gallic horse for the Parthian War in 55 B.C. The consulship of Messalla (53 B.C.) is celebrated on the coinage of his son (Plate XIX, 4). A coinage of Julius Caesar, struck probably in Cisalpine Gaul for circulation there and beyond the Alps, has recently been found in the issues of Kalenus and Cordus, M'. Aquillius M' f. M'. n., Longinus, Scribonius Libo, Paullus Lepidus, and others. The reverse of Kalenus and Cordus, Roma and Italia clasping hands, refers to Caesar's policy of treating the Transpadanes as Roman citizens. The 'Concordia' and 'Bonus Eventus' of Paullus Lepidus and Libo seem to refer to the Conference of Luca.

The outbreak of the great Civil War leads to a great enlivenment of the coinage, which now provides a running comment on the course of events. On the side of the Pompeians, we have the emergency issues

---

[1] But perhaps compare the denarius of Ser. Sulp. (Pl. XIX, 1).

of Q. Sicinius, with the head of the 'Fortune of the Roman people', and of L. Lentulus and Q. Marcellus, the consuls, with the ominous reverse, eagle and standards. The scene now shifts to the provinces. In Spain we have coins issued for Pompey by Cn. Piso and Varro, a second issue of the two consuls in south Italy, a third in Sicily, a fourth at Ephesus, with the reverse of 'Diana of the Ephesians' (Plate XIX, 5).[1] After Pharsalia we have the issues of the Pompeians for the campaign of Thapsus, with definite allusions to Africa. Most interesting is the coinage of M. Cato, struck at Utica, the town that witnessed his death and gave him a name (Plate XIX, 8). In Spain the sons of the great Pompey, Gnaeus and Sextus, strike for the campaign of Munda, with types celebrating their hearty welcome by the provinces (Plate XIX, 11, 12).

On the side of Caesar, we have the denarius with the elephant and the implements of the priesthood, perhaps struck a little before 49 B.C., and the aurei and denarii, with the remarkable legend LII (52) just possibly giving the age of Caesar himself (Plate XIX, 6).[2] References to Gaul are seen in the Gallic arms of the reverse of Albinus Bruti f., and, above all, in the Gallic warrior and Gallic woman on the obverses of L. Hostilius Saserna. A. Licinius Nerva refers to the devotion of Caesar's troops, Palikanus to his regard for the constitution, L. Papius Celsus to his triumph, T. Carisius to his reforms of the mint, L. Valerius Acisculus to the Sibylline prophecy that only a king could conquer the Parthians. Other types probably have topical allusions, Ceres and Bacchus to distributions of corn and wine, Venus to the legendary history of the Julian gens. Finally a group of moneyers strike with the portrait of Caesar.[3] Other issues seem to belong to the provinces, either in the name of Caesar only or of a legate, like A. Allienus, proconsul of Sicily in 48 B.C. It is noteworthy that Eastern issues on both sides are still rare: the Eastern campaigns were fought mainly with Eastern currencies.

Finally, with the last period of the Republic, we find a coinage that wanders further and further from the Republican traditions and, were it not for the number of competing potentates, might almost be called imperial. At Rome, the Senatorial restoration is represented by a group of moneyers who coin on the old lines. L. Servius Rufus, referring to the relief of Tusculum by an ancestor in 374 B.C., hints at the attempts

---

[1] Possibly in Africa, with an African goddess on reverse.
[2] Cp. *Revue Arch.*, 1866, p. 20: article of Count de Salis.
[3] For coins of Caesar, see Pl. XIX, 7, 9, 10.

made by Octavian and the consuls, Hirtius and Pansa, to raise the siege of Mutina. The types of M. Arrius Secundus and C. Numonius Vaala seem to bear on the same campaign. Then comes the second trium-virate and, on the next coinage, the portraits of the triumvirs and references to their family history are interspersed among pure Repub-lican types (Plate XIX, 14, 15). The 'Liberators' and their friends meanwhile struck freely in the East (Plate XIX, 17–19). There is one reference, in the most perfect taste, to the battle of Philippi – the coin of L. Mussidius Longus, with, obverse, head of Concordia and, reverse, statues of Venus Cloacina on a platform (Plate XIX, 16). The Romans and Sabines in early days had purified themselves after their combat on the spot where statues of the goddess were afterwards erected; and, with this reference, the moneyer passes skilfully over a terrible episode of civil war, which must have brought as much sorrow as joy to dwellers in Rome. The coins of Q. Voconius Vitulus and Ti. Sempronius Gracchus, which show Octavian only, to the exclusion of his colleagues, certainly belong to the days of the Perusine War. The reverse of Gracchus, standard, plough and sceptre, points directly to the allotments of land to veterans which were the immediate occasion of the breach.

Here the Republican coinage of the capital closes: the triumvirs agreed for the future to supply their needs of money from provincial or Italian mints. In Spain we have a single issue from the mint of Osca by Cn. Domitius Calvinus, c. 39–37 B.C. In Gaul we have joint issues of Antony and Lepidus at Lugdunum, followed by coinage in the name of all three triumvirs and by coins of Antony, including the interesting quinarii that give his age on two successive birthdays (XL and XLI) (Plate XX, 1). Then comes the coinage of Octavian, for whom Balbus, Q. Salvius, and the famous M. Agrippa issue coins (Plate XX, 9). Several issues of Octavian appear to belong to irregular mints ('Moneta castrensis') of the days when he levied an army in his own name to combat Antony (Plate XX, 2). The side of Antony in the Perusine War is represented by coinage in his name issued by his brother, who alludes to himself by his self-chosen name of 'Pietas' (Plate XX, 8), struck at Praeneste and a mint (Pisa?) in north Italy, and by P. Ventidius Bassus, the later victor over Parthia (Plate XX, 5). In Sicily we have the coinage of Sextus Pompeius, bearing the title 'praefectus classis et orae mari-timae', which he extorted from his unwilling rivals. The proud title 'son of Neptune' on the coinage of Q. Nasidius refers to Sextus's initial success over Octavian's fleets in the decisive campaign (Plate

XX, 10). In Africa, Q. Cornuficius, governor 44–42 B.C., celebrates the refuge that he gave to fugitives from the proscriptions (Plate XX, 4); and in the same province, or perhaps in Sicily, we have coinage of Lepidus and, after him, of Octavian, struck, no doubt, for the campaign against Sextus Pompey, the sequel to which was Lepidus's bid for supreme power and dismissal into private life.

In the East, there is first an ample coinage of the 'Liberators', Brutus and Cassius, boasting of their fight for 'Libertas', of the famous ancestors of Brutus, of their victories in Lycia and over Rhodes (Plate XIX, 17, 18). Murcus, the admiral, who joined their cause, celebrates with a denarius his arrival in Asia (Plate XIX, 19). Cn. Domitius Ahenobarbus, another admiral of the 'Liberators', struck in his own name after his victory over the fleet of Octavian off Brundisium on the day of Philippi, but soon joined Antony and struck for him. A special place of dishonour must be reserved for Q. Labienus, son of the Labienus who deserted Caesar: joining the Parthians to invade Syria, he has the effrontery to boast of himself as 'Parthicus Imperator' (Plate XIX, 20). Finally we come to the extensive coinage of Antony himself. We see his alliance with Octavian (Plate XX, 3, 6), the temporary estrangement over Perusia (Plate XX, 7), his marriage alliance with Octavia (Plate XX, 12), last of all his capitulation to the influence of Cleopatra, 'the queen of kings and of kings who are her sons' (Plate XX, 16). His ill-fated son, Antyllus, shared the honour of a portrait with him (Plate XX, 15). There is the remarkable bronze issue celebrating the naval help sent to Octavian against Sextus Pompey and the references to the conquest of Armenia, notably on the denarius of Cleopatra (Plate XX, 13, 14, 16). Lastly, for the campaign of Actium, Antony struck his famous series, with types complimentary to his army and fleet, proudly setting out by name the full number of his legions (Plate XX, 17–19). To the same occasion belongs the coinage of Scarpus in Cyrenaica (?) in the name of the eighth legion, with which he held Egypt against attack from the West (Plate XX, 20).

Here we may leave the study of Republican times. The war of claimants for the supreme power has forced itself into the foreground and the way is open to the development of a purely imperial coinage.

(d) *Animate and Inanimate Objects* (Plate XXI, 1–14)

The use of various animate and inanimate types to express ideas is an important branch of the language of coins. A few typical examples must suffice us here. The symbolism, we shall see, is sometimes direct and obvious, sometimes, to our minds at least, far from obvious. Firstly, there are types related to the worship of the gods – for Jupiter the eagle and thunderbolt (Plates XIII, 18; XXI, 20), for Juno Sospita the serpent and the griffin (?) (Plate VIII, 13), for Juno Moneta the implements of coinage, for Neptune the dolphin, for Apollo the tripod and patera (Plate VIII, 18), for Diana the stag or hunting dog (Plate XIII, 8), for Hercules the club, bow and arrow and lion-skin, for Mars the wolf (Plate XIV, 3), for Minerva the aegis and helmet, for Mercury the caduceus and the tortoise, for Ceres the modius and corn-ears, for Vesta the priestly vessels. Secondly, there are types relating to moneyers: the calf for Q. Voconius Vitulus, the ram for L. Rustius, the elephant for Q. Metellus Pius (cp. Plate X, 15), the Macedonian shield for M. Metellus. The sphinx of T. Carisius might represent the signet-ring of Julius Caesar. Thirdly, there are types relating to places – the triskelis for Sicily, the lion for Lugdunum, the winged horse for Lampsacus (Plate XIV, 12), the horse for Parthia, the tiara for Armenia. Finally, there remains a mass of types of general symbolic significance.[1] The eagle and standards represent the army (Plate VII, 7), the ship or prow the fleet, trophy and captives stand for victories. The clasped hands denote concord (Plate XXI, 9, 13), the caduceus trade, the palm and wreath victory, the globe world-power, the cornucopiae general prosperity, the fasces the constitution, priestly vessels the sacred offices (Plate XXI, 4, 14), curule chairs curule office (Plate XXI, 5, 6, 10), the sceptre dignity and power, the rudder government. The statue of Marsyas seems to represent the forum as the centre of Roman institutions (Plate XXI, 2). The star over a prow suggests good fortune to the fleet (Plate XXI, 12). The pileus and daggers of Brutus hardly need the legend EID MAR to call to our minds the bloody deed by which Roman liberty was vindicated. Crescent and star or stars (Plate XXI, 7) represent the heavens, the star by itself may be a symbol of consecration.

(e) *Architecture, Art, etc.* (Plate XXI, 15–20)

The Roman passion for building is not unfairly represented on the coins. The representations are often sketchy and inadequate, but, in the absence of better records, have an importance of their own. Apart from temples – the Capitol (Plate XXI, 15, 20), the temple of Neptune, the temple of Vesta (Plate XIV, 20), the temple of Venus Erycina (Plate

[1] See Pls. XXI, 1, 3, 8, 11; VII, 13, 14, 16, 17, 18; X, 10, 11, 14, 16, 17, 18; XII, 7, 8, 9; XIII, 9, 15; XIV, 5; XV, 10, 13, 14.

XXI, 17), the temple of the deified Caesar, the temple of the Clemency of Caesar and a temple of the Sun, and another of Jupiter and Libertas – we have views of the rostra (Plate XXI, 19), the platform from which tribunes addressed the people, of the Villa Publica, the state guest-house in the Campus Martius (Plate XXI, 18), the 'Basilica Aemilia' restored by M. Aemilius Lepidus in 78 B.C. (Plate XXI, 16), and the Aqua Marcia, the famous aqueduct brought to Rome in 144 B.C. by Q. Marcius Rex. Other objects of topographical interest are the corn-memorial of the Augurini by the Porta Trigemina, the statue of Marsyas in the Forum, and the 'puteal', or well-head of Libo, also in the Forum, the resort of money-lenders.

A few special features of Roman life are illustrated on exceptional issues. Piso and Caepio and M. Fannius and L. Critonius show public distributions of corn, C. Serveilius C.f. shows two gladiators measuring swords, L. Regulus a fight between men and wild beasts in the arena (Plate XVI, 10). Caldus offers a view of 'lectisternium' (Plate XVI, 4), the religious banquet to the gods, when their statues were brought out and exhibited on the sacred couches. The 'Sors' type of M. Plaetorius Cestianus alludes to the lots of the 'Fortuna' of Praeneste; the youthful figure, leaning on the balcony, is the boy attendant who brings out the lot. A voting scene appears on the reverse of the denarius of P. Nerva and, in less elaborate form, on that of Longinus. The reverse of P. Laeca (Plate XVII, 18), shows a soldier appealing against the sentence of his general, represented by his lictor, to a togate figure, representing the Roman people. In this case, a contemporary reference to the demand of the allies to a share in the right of 'provocatio' seems to be implied.

The relation of the art of the Roman die-sinker to other contemporary forms of art can only be glanced at here.[1] The portraits on coins probably derive largely from the 'imagines' or waxen masks, kept as part of the family heirlooms of all the great houses. Only in the last period, for contemporary portraiture, is a copying from statues probable. We suspect originals in statuary for a number of divine types, for the Muses of Q. Pomponius Musa, for the Catanaean brothers of Sex. Pompey, the Perseus group of Paullus Lepidus, the group of Marcus Lepidus and Ptolemy V as his ward, the Aeneas and Anchises of Caesar.[2] The surrender of Jugurtha by Bocchus to Sulla was, we know, the subject of a signet-ring of the dictator Sulla. The most

---

[1] For types of special interest or beauty, cp. Pls. VIII, 16–20; X, 13.

[2] The reverse type of Eppius seems to show a representation (or caricature?) of the Hercules of Lysippus.

interesting, because the most certain, example of the copying of a major work of art is seen on the reverse of L. Plautius Plancus. Pliny[1] tells us that L. Munatius Plancus placed in the Capitol a picture by Nicomachus, showing 'Victoria quadrigam in sublime rapiens'. This description so perfectly describes the reverse of the coin that we cannot doubt the identification (Plate VIII, 20).

Here we must leave a subject, which, by its wealth of allusion and detail as well as by the obscurity of many of its references, appears to defy a summary treatment. Even the brief sketch here given will have served a useful purpose if it leads Roman students to exploit the material already available and to provide, by research into outstanding difficulties, further material for the next generation to exploit.

[1] *Nat. Hist.*, XXXV, 10, 36.

Coinage in the General Life
of the Roman Republic

For this, our third chapter, we have reserved some aspects of coinage which bear on the general political life of the State. Our inquiry will lead us over ground already, in part, covered, and will confront us with some problems of great difficulty and obscurity; it will, however, reward us with some light on questions that are as interesting in their present bearings as in their place in the past. We will consider first the general part played by the coinage in the economic life of the Republic; secondly, emergency measures affecting the coinage; thirdly, coinage in relation to policy, that is to say, in relation to Italy, the provinces and foreign powers.

1. OCCASIONS OF ISSUES

Coinage in ancient times was issued far less regularly and uniformly than it is today. A few great commercial States – Athens, Corinth, the Roman Empire – maintained an almost continuous flow of coinage over long periods of time. Most of the ancient world, however, coined only at intervals, as particular necessities dictated. Out of this phase, the Roman Republic, despite the extent of its foreign conquests, never entirely passed. Granted, then, that the issue of money is to be left to the dictation of circumstances, it becomes obvious that war will play a decisive part in deciding when and where money shall be issued. War, for the ancient State, was a normal condition of life – not an exceptional emergency. For a State like Rome, a general peace was a happy ideal seldom realized. The requirements of war, then, were the main deciding factor for the coinage: during the intervals of more or less complete peace its volume diminished. All the great wars of the West – the Second Punic War, the wars in north Italy and Spain, the war with Jugurtha, the war with the Cimbrians and Teutons, the series of civil wars – one and all are represented by great additions to the coinage.

The wars in the East bore a somewhat different character. Rome, still relatively a poor country, found herself fighting in lands where masses of coinage had been accumulating for centuries. She allowed herself to be led by circumstances here and, instead of turning fresh masses of bullion into coin, used her victories to transfer vast quantities of coined money from the defeated countries to herself. The gold Philippus, the Attic and the cistophoric tetradrachm flooded the Roman market and supplemented the deficiencies of the somewhat meagre native system. Only in the last century of the Republic do we find Rome issuing her own denominations in the East.

Roman coins, then, were issued largely to meet the requirements of wars. What more can we add to our knowledge of the occasions of coinage? Regular issues for purposes of trade can hardly be proved. The regular coinage of the State must, of course, have served the purposes of trade as well as war, but special issues prompted by commercial aims can hardly ever be demonstrated. The foundation of new colonies was certainly accompanied at times by special coinages: we are certain of the fact in the case of Narbo Martius; it is possible also for Eporedia in north Italy (99 B.C.). Similar issues probably occur earlier, but cannot yet be identified with certainty, as they are not signed by the founders of the colonies, many of whose names are preserved for us by Livy, but only perhaps by subordinate officials, either the ordinary moneyers or officials specially appointed for the occasion. It was, however, only natural that the colony, often an outpost of Rome in a district as yet remote from her power, should be started in life with a supply of Roman coinage. In the later Republic, we can place our finger on other occasions of a special character – the distributions of cheap corn to the populace or the celebration of games, notably those of the curule aediles in Rome. In the case of the distributions the expense was normally borne by the State. In the case of the shows, the burden fell on the magistrates, who received special permission from the Senate to commemorate their magnificence by special coinage. Probably, if we could trace the occasions of all Republican issues, we should find that the vast majority fall under one or other of these headings. By the time of Cicero, we have evidence of bullion being brought to the mint by private individuals to be stamped as money.[1] We may well doubt whether any serious proportion of Republican coinage was thus issued. In time of emergency, the reserves of precious metal in the 'aerarium Saturni' could be drawn upon. In earlier times,

[1] Cp. Cicero, *Ad. Att.*, VIII, 7, 3.

the State probably depended for its supply of bullion partly on the spoils of war, partly on the existing stocks of metal, struck or unstruck, in the home market; the task of finding the metal for particular issues was, to judge from analogies, let out on tender to private companies. The general tendency throughout the Republic was for the volume of currency especially in the precious metals to increase. As the wealth of the world was drawn more and more steadily towards Rome, money became an ever commoner commodity and prices rose in a steadily soaring curve. Rome experienced, in full measure, the consequences, good and bad, of this economic development: with it we may connect a fact of such political import as the rise of the capitalist class, the 'equites', to power from the days of Gaius Gracchus.

2. GENERAL FINANCIAL POLICY AND THEORY

Such was the general trend of Roman economic policy. Economic theory is little understood today and we can hardly credit the Roman financiers with even our limited knowledge. The immediate need was always their guide. They took such measures as it dictated and had to bear the consequences as best they might. We have now to consider some occasions of special urgency, where reforms of the coinage were definitely used to extricate the State from her financial straits. The great Eastern Wars, we have seen, more than paid for their cost and brought to Rome reserves of coin and bullion. Even the campaigns against Spaniards and Ligurians were not barren of spoils, and Carthage had to pay heavily the price of defeat. But what of the great wars that strained the financial resources of the State and yet brought no immediate reward? We arrive at once at an astonishing conclusion. The Romans never learned how to accept the fact of a permanent war-debt, to be funded and repaid over a long period of time.[1] They preferred the alternative, disastrous to individuals, but not without its conveniences for the State – that of partial repudiation of debt. That this repudiation was not nakedly announced, but was covered under the show of a reform of the coinage, alters nothing of the essence of the case.

The First Punic War, following so close on the introduction of coinage at Rome, did not produce those perturbations in the coinage that we might have expected. Silver of the mint of 'Ostia' is not infrequently debased; if the coins are official, this would mean an inflation. No

[1] But the *tributum* was conceived of as a forced loan, to be paid back as occasion offered.

similar debasement is found at the other mints. None of the series of *Aes Grave* shows any reduction of weight. Hiero of Syracuse may have helped liberally with funds. The great expenses of building the fleets were probably financed on credit; private citizens would advance the money, expecting repayment after the war. Such borrowing is definitely recorded for the fleet that won the battle of the Aegatian Isles.

About the Second Punic War we are better informed. Gold was struck in two emergency issues. The silver is said to have been debased, but it is hard to find any evidence of this in the coinage. The quadrigati and victoriates are for the most part of pure silver. The As was reduced from ten ounces to six in 217 B.C., from six to three in c. 209. There is no doubt that these were measures of inflation, making it easier to pay State debts. The silver was presumably made equal to more of these reduced Asses – to ten instead of six at the first reduction, to twenty instead of ten at the second. Even so, as the vast demands of the war defeated even the most drastic monetary changes, other measures had to be adopted. 'Tributum' was raised in amounts never dreamed of before and citizens in general put their money at the disposal of the State and gave their services free without asking for immediate payment.

After the victory over Carthage Rome entered on a period of rapid political and commercial growth. She had departed once and for all from the simple conditions of the Italian city-State; she was on the road to becoming a world power and must expand her coinage to answer to her new position. The indemnity from Carthage and the spoils of defeated enemies in East and West relieved her of any difficulty about supplies of bullion. Inflation of the coinage was inevitable, but it was inflation of the better kind, the issue of ever-increasing amounts of good money. There was no need for the debasement of the silver or for reduction of the standard. Money, however, became ever cheaper in relation to other articles and there was a steady rise both in prices and in wages. As usual, however, the rise in prices was more automatic and inevitable than the rise in pay. The soldiers seem to have received no rise in pay at all co-ordinate to the rise in prices. Temporary relief was no doubt afforded by handsome donatives after victories. The general result of the increase of money must have been an increasing inequality in possession. The accumulation of capital began and the class of 'equites' came to rank next to the Senate as an aristocracy of money. The causes of the new conditions may not have been very clearly understood, but the conflict of interests was obscurely felt and began to find political expression. The moneyed classes came to stand for pure money and a check to inflation. The impoverished could see no objection to measures which diminished the power of the capitalist, and the Senate, which was an aristocracy of land, not of money, was not always indisposed to foster their interests.

We come to the age of the Gracchi, when so many latent conflicts of the preceding years came at last to an open clash. The policy of the democrats was in no sense a single one. The Gracchi attempted to unite around them many different classes of malcontents and had to try, as best they could, to harmonize interests not always at one. There was first of all the policy of helping the poorer citizens – on the land by restoring agriculture, in the city by cheap doles of corn, abroad by citizen colonies. For all these purposes large issues of coinage were essential.[1] C. Gracchus included in his alliance against the Senate the capitalist class, the knights. They were willing to accept the democratic proposals of Gracchus, but insisted that there must be no tampering with the coinage: the State must pay for its new expenditure either out of its reserves in the treasury or from the new revenues of Asia. The Senate found itself opposed to this demand; the new expenses must be met by inflation of the coinage, i.e. the burden must be shifted on to the shoulders of the moneyed classes. This is evidently the meaning of the enactment of M. Livius Drusus, who, in his tribunate, 'mixed an eighth part of bronze with the silver'. Our authorities do not tell us which Drusus brought in this measure, but the probabilities are in favour of the elder.[2] It now seems possible to guess with some hopefulness at the financial policy of Gaius Gracchus.[3] The new As of sixteen to the denarius was perhaps intended to harmonize the Roman coinage with standards current in Italy; the denarius might be considered as equal to sixteen of the nummi, twelve of which went to the victoriate, the Rhegine talent. The new victoriate of the value of a quinarius may, if of this period, have had the same purpose. The many schemes of Gaius Gracchus required great supplies of money; he seems to have prompted one issue, intended for the use of the new citizens whom he proposed to create – the 'Nomentani'. A protest was not slow in coming. The foundation of Narbo Martius, itself a triumph for the democratic party, was accompanied by a large issue of serrate denarii:

---

[1] In the period from 126 to 118 B.C. we appear to have a double series of coins at Rome, part perhaps issued by the Gracchan party, part by the Senate.
[2] The measure has usually been attributed to the younger Drusus, tribune in 91 B.C.
[3] H. Mattingly, 'Gaius Gracchus and the Coinage', *Proc. Brit. Acad.*, XXXIX, pp. 24 ff.

the cutting of the edge was designed to give palpable evidence that the new coinage was of pure silver. In the following period serration certainly played some part in the party strife; but we cannot relate it as closely as I did in the first edition to definite political events, and the preference of some provinces for serrati enters into the question. With the outbreak of the Social War the need for plated coin became more and more acute. The silver was debased to such an extent that no one knew what he possessed[1] and, to make matters worse, the monetary standard, still based on the As, was again tampered with. The As was reduced to half its weight and 50 per cent. of the State debt was repudiated. Had the silver still been pure a re-tariffing of the As in denarii would have been inevitable. As it was, the reduced As and the debased denarius could be left at the old ratio. Even so, the enormous expenses of the unprofitable war could not be covered.[2] (But see above, p. 21.) The State and the individual were on the verge of bankruptcy and the cry arose for 'novae tabulae' – a clean sheet, with a cancelling of all existing debts. Something very like this was actually decided on, when the Lex Valeria[3] provided that debts should be paid at the rate of quadrans for As – 5*s.* in the pound. This last measure, though not operative for any long time, no doubt wiped out most of the remaining State debt. But the position was intolerable in the long run, and the return of the Marians to power enabled the financial interests to make their voice heard. The cancelling of a large portion of existing debt was a necessary evil that must be endured. But for the future the coinage must be re-established on a firm basis. The As was not restored to its old value, but its issue on the lower standard was suspended[4] and

---

[1] Cp. Pliny, *Nat. Hist.*, XXXIII, 3, 46; XXXIV, 6, 27; 9, 132; Cicero, *De Officiis*, III, 20, 80.

[2] The loss of Asia to Mithradates was, of course, a contributory cause.

[3] The 'Lex Valeria' was a measure of the democratic party. They found themselves on the horns of an awkward dilemma, for, while they stood for a pure currency, they had to face an impossible burden of State debt. They thought no more than did the *optimates* of funding it. The 'Lex Valeria', then, was passed as an emergency measure of repudiation to satisfy malcontents and to extricate the State from its immediate difficulty. The debt once disposed of, coinage was for the future to be pure and trustworthy. Definite repudiation of debt was preferred to indirect repudiation by debasement. The passage in the manifesto of the rebel leader, C. Manlius, in Sallust (*Catiline*, Ch. XXXIII, 3): 'novissime memoria nostra propter magnitudinem aeris alieni volentibus omnibus bonis argentum aere solutum est', might seem to refer to the Lex Valeria, but what then does 'argentum aere solutum est' mean, and did all 'boni' approve that law? A reference to the compulsory circulation of base denarii seems more probable. Mommsen, *Röm. Münzwesen*, pp. 383, 384, applies the passage to the Lex Valeria: he thinks that that law substituted for the old libral As, equal to a sestertius, the As of the coinage only worth a quarter of that amount. For criticism of Mommsen's general view, see *Proceedings of the Cambridge Philological Society*, 1925, pp. 21 ff. The question remains largely in the realm of guess-work. [4] There are no issues of semuncial standard from the Marian moneyers.

the silver, which now had to bear the chief part in currency, was purified. M. Marius Gratidianus the praetor 'invented the art of distinguishing pure money'. 'The art' was probably that of stamping the denarii, to show up any base metal below the silver envelope. Serration too may have been resumed. For the moment the plague of base silver was abated. Sulla, on his return, repealed the Lex Valeria, but reimposed the compulsory currency of base coin. The State was to be allowed to inflate the coinage to just such an extent as seemed advisable,[1] and, fortified with this power, could dispense with the extreme measure of cancelling debts. The savage vengeance wreaked on M. Marius Gratidianus by the Sullans proves that his measures had had far-reaching consequences. He had evidently touched the *optimates* in the tenderest of all spots – the pocket.

The victory in the long conflict rested with the Senate. The Marian faction split into conflicting sections. The 'equites' came to be afraid of the extreme 'populares' and, encountering a more accommodating spirit in the Senate, moved towards that 'concordia ordinum', which Cicero set before him as his ideal. Minor differences of policy between possessors of different kinds sank into insignificance before the essential conflict between the 'haves' and the 'have nots'. The demand for 'novae tabulae' was steadily resisted. The plating of denarii was not abandoned, but, in deference to the knights, the Senate used its powers with some discretion. The awkward question of the bronze was left unsolved. It was not reintroduced at Rome either on the uncial or on the semuncial standard. A return to the uncial standard would have meant a going back on a previous policy. A continuation of semuncial coinage would have led to a difficult question in tariffing the bronze in terms of silver. Serrate issues are still found, but they seem to occur only at the Northern mint (Pisa?). Even there they cease about 56 B.C. They were probably intended to please the Gauls. The victory of Julius Caesar which led on to the Empire was, of course, a victory for the democratic party, and we expect to find its financial policy triumphant. We shall discuss later the question of debasement under the Empire. Here we must only say that the early Emperors appear to have been true to the democratic policy of pure money. The temptations of an easy inflation, however, soon made themselves felt, and later Emperors were drawn into the same baleful courses as the Senate of the Republic.

[1] Cp. *Digest*, XX, 109.

3. COINAGE AND POLICY

Finally we have to consider the coinage in its relation to foreign policy, first in Italy, then in the provinces and abroad. We shall have to consider how far other than economic considerations entered into the account, whether Rome used her coinage as a means of advertising her name in the world and whether she used her military power to secure herself unfair advantages.

We begin with Italy. We must distinguish at once between the various kinds of States in relationship to Rome. On the one hand, there is Rome herself, the colonies of Roman citizens, whether with the full or with the restricted citizenship, the smaller communities of citizens lacking urban organization. For all these Roman coinage is naturally valid: it would be against all constitutional law for a burgess colony to strike in any name than that of Rome. Next come the various allies of Rome, bound to her by treaties of a more or less favourable complexion – prominent among them the great class of Latin colonies, enjoying a privileged position and able to aspire, under given conditions, to the citizenship. For all these, independent coinage is theoretically possible. Finally, we have States bound by no fixed ties to Rome – who would obviously decide for themselves whether to coin or not.

Let us begin with the Latin allies. A few – Cales, Suessa, Paestum, Signia and Alba Fucens – strike silver. There is heavy bronze of Luceria, Asculum, Venusia, Hatria, Ariminum and Firmum, reduced series of Luceria and Venusia. Token *Aes* occurs at Cales, Suessa, and Ariminum. Why some Latin colonies struck or cast, while others did not, is quite uncertain. Perhaps the right to coin was normal; it rested on the will of the community whether or not it exercised it. It seems that the first ROMANO coinage may have served Roman allies as well as Rome, but, that in the second ROMA period, when Rome seemed to be laying more stress on her supremacy, some of the allies were moved to issue for themselves.[1]

In Etruria there is coinage in silver and gold and *Aes Grave* from Volaterrae and a number of unascertained mints. Greek cities like Naples, Heraclea, Tarentum and others strike silver down at least to the Second Punic War. It is unlikely that any of these coinages continued later. Small bronze was issued at a number of mints – Teate,

[1] These Italian coinages may be studied in *B.M.C. Italy* and Giesecke, *Italia Numismatica*, 1928.

Caelia, Graxa and others. Paestum continued to issue down to the early Empire. There is coinage of the Brettii in gold, silver and bronze, coinage of the Lucanians in bronze.

While we are uncertain how far Rome exercised influence on the Italian States in the earlier periods, it appears certain that after the Second Punic War she claimed more and more a monopoly, only tolerating issues of small bronze at a number of communities.

Even before Rome's supremacy in Italy was finally reached she had acquired her first transmarine provinces and had to face the problem of how to provide coinage for them. She came further into close contact with foreign powers and had to decide on what principles to treat their currencies and how to relate them to her own. It will be necessary to treat this question in detail, province by province, but a few introductory comments will help to clear the ground. Rome does not attempt to enforce any one uniform policy – she allows herself to be influenced strongly by local circumstances. She does not to any great extent issue coinage as a means of flying the flag abroad. If in the West she gradually assumes something like a monopoly, it is practical convenience rather than principle that guides her; for in the East, where local money was readily available, she shows no disposition to enforce her own money system and only a very moderate anxiety to coin in her own name.

In Sicily the local coinage was almost restricted to Syracuse (Plate XXII, 1–3), when the Romans first set foot in the island. When, after the death of Rome's faithful ally, Hiero, Syracuse revolted and was re-conquered, Rome stopped the Syracusan issues of silver (cp. Plate XXIII, 14), but allowed small coinage in bronze both at Syracuse (Plate XXIV, 4) and a few other towns. She herself issued bronze, signed by Roman officials, at Panormus (Plate XXIV, 5), and perhaps at other mints. Her treatment of Sicily, in fact, followed the same lines as her treatment of Italy. The Roman silver – first the victoriate and then the denarius – filled the gap, but we can only point to a few probable issues from Sicilian mints. The silver litra seems to have been reckoned as one-fifth of the denarius.

Sardinia and Corsica depended from the first on Rome for coinage. The one bronze issue of Sardinia, with obverse of 'Sardus Pater', signed by M. Atius Balbus, is not earlier than the time of Julius Caesar (Plate XXIV, 9).

In Spain Rome found provincial silver coinage of the Carthaginians and silver issues of the Greek cities of Emporiae and Rhoda (Plate

XXII, 7, 8) – the latter continuing into the second century.[1] Scipio Africanus follows the Barcids with a coinage in Spain but, after him, Roman issues probably do not occur till the first century B.C. Beside this Roman coinage, we find a native silver, the 'argentum Oscense', so named from one of the chief mints, Osca (Plate XXIV, 6), with names of towns or tribes in Celtiberian and such types as obverse, head of Hercules, reverse, horseman. The standard is that of the denarius. A lighter coin of victoriate weight is found early in the series. This coinage has been variously dated – to the period before the fall of Numantia, or to the Sertorian War. Livy attests the existence of the 'Oscan silver' soon after the Second Punic War and, as pieces in mint condition have been found with Republican coins of about 100 B.C., it must have been issued at any rate near the latter date.[2] The lack of development in style and types might lead us to assign it a shorter term of issue: Livy's Oscan money was probably something different from what we today call by that name. In the existence of this native silver, certainly tolerated if not actually instigated by Rome, we have clear evidence of a liberal policy, aiming at making the province of the silver mines self-supporting. The bronze coinage is of less importance. We find issues with Latin legend and types of Roman pattern at Saguntum (Plate XXIV, 8), Segobriga and Valentia (Plate XXIV, 7) in the years following the overthrow of Viriathus. The coinage with Celtiberian types and legends seems to belong mainly to the last century B.C., perhaps after the cessation of the issue of 'Oscan silver'.

In Africa, Carthage, the conquered enemy, and Numidia, the favoured ally of Rome, issue money during the second century. The Carthaginian coinage, of course, ceases with the fall of the city, the Numidian continues to the time of Juba the First, the ally of the Pompeians. The denarius clearly supplied the needs of the Roman province, though we cannot be certain of issues from African mints before the great Civil War. The special coinage for the Jugurthine War may have been issued from a south Italian mint.

In Gaul, Massalia was the one community issuing coins during the early second century (Plate XXII, 6). To harmonize her coinage with the Roman, she replaced her drachm by a lighter coin, corresponding to the Roman victoriate (Plate XXIV, 10).[3] But this was probably the

---

[1] The later drachms are of denarius weight. Early Roman didrachms are rarely found in Spain, 'quadrigati' and victoriates more commonly.
[2] In the later of these issues, the standard of the denarius prevails, and the denarius of Cn. Domitius, c. 37 B.C., imitates the reverse of the 'Argentum Oscense'.
[3] The date of this change is uncertain, probably not far from 200 B.C.

act of enlightened self-interest, rather than of compulsion. Denarii were struck for Narbo Martius, perhaps also for the war preceding its foundation, again in the Cimbrian Wars, then under C. Valerius Flaccus, c. 82 B.C., again by Julius Caesar as governor, and then by the second triumvirate. The native Gallic coinage is difficult to date. The silver, struck on the standard of the half-denarius (the later victoriate), is all late, and the same is true of much of the bronze, which clearly betrays Roman influence. It evidently belongs to the period of Romanization from Julius Caesar to Augustus. The bulk of the gold and part of the coinage in base silver and bronze is earlier in date but certainly not nearly as early as has been suggested. The establishment of the Roman province of Narbonensis may well have been the decisive event. The gold, as is well known, is largely dependent for types on the aureus of Philip of Macedon. But this coin, as we shall see, was well established in circulation at Rome and may well have come to Gaul by way of Rome and Massalia.

Late in the Republic we find the beginnings of a provincial coinage in silver and copper in the town issues of Lugdunum (Plate XXIV, 12), Vienna, Cabellio (Plate XXIV, 11) and Nemausus (Plate XXIV, 13). We shall later find Gaul playing a decisive part in the establishment of the imperial coinage.

Britain hardly concerns us as yet. Suffice it to say that our island follows, at a little distance, a development similar to the Gallic. The purely native coinage, mainly in gold and uninscribed, may date from a little before the middle of the first century: the later inscribed coinage shows traces of Roman influence and is later than Julius Caesar.

In the Adriatic district – Illyricum, Epirus, Acarnania – the Roman victoriate, which corresponded to a local unit of weight long familiar there, played an important part from about the end of the Second Punic War.[1] But it did not oust the local coinage: we continue to find silver issues of the same standard at Apollonia (Plate XXIV, 14), Dyrrhachium, Corcyra and other mints.

Turning from West to East, we find a different policy prevailing. There are no certain issues of coins of Roman standard before the coinage of Lucullus for Sulla. Even after his time, such issues are rare – not till the days of Mark Antony can the Roman aureus and denarius have been really familiar coins. The great Macedonian and Syrian Wars

---

[1] We also find multiples of the victoriate (2 and 4) and coins of denarius weight (e.g. at Corcyra, Pl. XXIV, 15). The introduction of the later victoriate (= a quinarius) at Rome may have led to the reduction here of double victoriates to denarii.

served rather to bring the money of the East to Rome than that of Rome to the East (cp. Plate XXV, 1, 2, 4). When Rome, establishing her provinces, is led to take a part in the coinage, she maintains the local standards. To the end of the Republic silver was struck freely at many Eastern mints and even the Emperors followed the policy of maintaining local standards. Issues by Rome herself are few and far between – the silver tetradrachms of Aesillas (Plate XXV, 3) and Sura for Macedon, the silver tetradrachm of Metellus for Crete, the cistophori of Asia with the names of the Roman governors (Plate XXV, 6).[1] Far from enforcing her own coinage, Rome is chary of any interference with local coinage. Here, as elsewhere, she follows that wise policy of 'laissez aller', which was perhaps the mixed product of a wise self-restraint and embarrassment in face of a very complicated problem. It has been maintained that coinage in gold was considered from the time of Alexander to be a prerogative of the Empire, not of the king or city-State, and that Rome showed herself jealous of this prerogative. The comparative scarcity of gold coinage, however, is probably attributable rather to the well-known preference of the Greeks for silver. It is doubtful whether Roman jealousy has much to do with the matter.

One problem, however, Rome could not entirely evade – the intricate problem of co-ordinating the masses of gold and silver in her Eastern provinces both with one another and with her own denarius. No better evidence of the question is yet available than the powerful sections of Mommsen's great work,[2] to which we must refer the reader who seeks further detail. It is necessary, however, to add the warning that the evidence to be drawn from metrological writers is very obscure and uncertain of interpretation.[3] The first main fact to be grasped is, that the Roman denarius, at first a little heavier, later a little lighter than the Attic drachm, was normally equated with it: this equation was still maintained, even after the reduction of Nero. The tetradrachms of Athens herself (Plate XXV, 9), then, and all other

[1] On Pl. XXV, 5, is shown a rare copper coin, perhaps struck by Brutus in Macedon.
[2] *Geschichte des Römischen Münzwesens*, pp. 661 ff.
[3] We may instance the statements of Festus and Pollux about the different kinds of talents. The Attic equals 6,000 drachms or denarii; the cistophoric accordingly equals 4,500. So far so good. But what of the little talents of the West-Alexandrine which equals twelve denarii, the Neapolitan which equals six, the Sicilian which equals three and the Rhegine which is itself a victoriate? It has been thought that these are ordinary talents, as regards subdivision into minae and drachmae, but that the drachmae are bronze, not silver ones. It is more probable that these little talents have their own proper division into twelve nummi and a hundred and twenty litrae; the litra, in theory, was a pound of bronze, but was subjected to various reductions of weight.

95

pieces of Attic weight were reckoned as equal to four denarii.[1] The Rhodian drachm (Plate XXV, 10), was equated to the old victoriate, $\frac{3}{4}$ of the denarius; the 'cistophorus' (Plate XXV, 6), a tetradrachm of the Rhodian system, was therefore equal to three denarii. In Syria the tetradrachms of Attic weight (Plate XXV, 7), were equated to four denarii, and Mommsen thinks that the same rate was applied to the lighter Tyrian tetradrachms (Plate XXV, 8): such an over-tariffing of foreign money is, however, improbable, and Mommsen's arguments are not strong. So far as the Aeginetan standard still survived (e.g. in Crete and Cilicia), it is probable that the Romans treated the Aeginetan didrachms as equivalent to the cistophoric tetradrachm, i.e. as three denarii. The Attic and the cistophoric were almost the only two Greek standards with which Rome had much to do and we may assume, as a sound working principle, that Rome treated all Greek drachms as equal either to denarii or to victoriates. Of any deliberate attempt to favour the Roman coin unduly we have barely a trace. Bruno Keil[2] has shown some reason to think that the substitution of the new victoriate ($\frac{1}{2}$ denarius) for the old ($\frac{3}{4}$ denarius) may have been fraudulently used to depress the value of Greek currencies equated to the victoriate, but it is best to suspend judgement pending the discovery of decisive evidence. For gold and silver Rome seems to have accepted the standard of 1 to 10, and at that rate would tariff the aureus of Philip at about 20 denarii.

To sum up our results: at home, Roman coinage was always intimately bound up with the political life of the State – its flow was determined by the requirements of war, by the expenditure on corn-distributions and shows, even more than by the more normal requirements of trade. In the absence of a developed banking system, it was probably not easy to put money on the market for general trade purposes: the nearest we get to such commercial issues are probably those issues which were destined for the use of new colonies. In time of emergency the State availed itself of the dangerous right of 'reforming' the coinage to reduce the national debt. The false theory that the State can lower the standard and debase the currency was, indeed, contested, and sometimes defeated – but only to come up again. But it was particularly a theory of the Senate and, when the Senate fell, the Empire started with good chances of building on a sound basis.

[1] Livy, XXXIV, 52, says 'equal to three in weight'. This is no error; he is relating the tetradrachm, not to our x denarius, but to an earlier and heavier denarius, a quadrigatus of reduced weight.

[2] *Z.f.N.*, 1920, pp. 47 ff.

Abroad, Rome does not use her right of coinage in any very aggressive or avaricious spirit. There is clearly something of political choice in her partial monopoly of coinage in the West. In the East, where economic considerations were strongly in favour of another policy, those considerations in the main seem to triumph over the political. Autonomy in coinage is one of the last elements of autonomy to disappear in the Eastern provinces and was, in fact, preserved largely intact into the Empire.

I have not made any very serious changes in this chapter, but I am conscious that it is most imperfect, only touching on some questions, which we should dearly love to answer. The use of coinage as an instrument of policy is only very faintly sketched. It is a subject on which further research is clearly indicated.

Additional Note – The question of the pay of the soldiers is so complicated that it seems best to deal with it in a note. Polybius tells us that it was two obols. As his drachm is heavier than the Roman denarius – equal to twelve and a half Asses, to be precise – two obols means four Asses, more or less. Caesar, we are told, doubled the pay. Under Augustus we find it as ten Asses a day. The original four Asses, then, had been raised to five and afterwards doubled. We might have expected some increase when the As of sixteen to the denarius came in and, again, when the As was reduced to half an ounce. The only increase that we can point to is from four to five. The question is complicated by the other question of how much the soldier had to pay for clothes and food out of what he received. Relief could be given in the form of less demand for these items. Pliny tells us that, when the As became the sixteenth part of the denarius, a denarius continued to be given for ten Asses in the soldiers' pay. Many attempts have been made to make sense of this passage – none of them quite convincing. The mutineers at the beginning of the reign of Tiberius are found to be getting ten Asses and demanding sixteen.

CHAPTER I

The External History of the Coinage: Authorities, Mints, Money-Systems, etc.

I. HISTORICAL SURVEY[1]

Not the least troublesome of the problems which Augustus had to face was that of the coinage. Out of the storms of the Civil Wars, which had wrecked the old system, had, indeed, emerged a new one in its place; but it was not one which had any claim to permanence. The Senate, in losing control of its governors and generals in the provinces, had lost control of the coinage: the mint of Rome was closed and gold and silver were being struck only on a military basis for military needs. With the bronze there was the additional difficulty that the standard was now quite uncertain; since the failure and cessation of the semuncial issues of Rome, no one could say with authority what coin a Roman As ought to be. There were the needs of the provinces as well as Rome to be considered; nor must any serious attempt at reform fail to take account of the great rise in prices that had accompanied the development of Imperial power. The position of Rome as mistress of the world seemed to demand for her the primacy in coinage; at the same time, the urgent needs of the armies in the provinces must receive due consideration. What policy was Augustus to follow? Was he to reinstate the Senate in its old position of control? That would mean a vexatious hampering of his powers as 'Imperator'. Was he to share with the Senate the direction of the Roman mint? That solution had already been tried by Julius Caesar and by Augustus himself, as triumvir with his colleagues, and had been abandoned as unsuccessful. Either the share of the Senate would be a real one and might embarrass the Emperor, or it would be a mere pretence and would simply create bitterness. The Senate could not be expected to abdicate as readily as it abdicated later in the case of the corn-supply and the city-police.

[1] Throughout this section reference should be made to the *B.M.C. Empire* (Vols. I–V) and to *Roman Imperial Coinage*, Mattingly and Sydenham, Vols. I–V.

Nor, as a third choice, could the existing system be allowed to continue without reform. It was on that system, however, that Augustus decided to build.[1] As paymaster of the armies, he must keep in his own hands the issue of the precious metals; the coins in which the troops received their pay must bear his image and superscription. This was the more necessary as the Imperial gold at least was to be a coinage of the Empire; and in the provinces there must be no question as to who was the real master of the Roman world. Augustus decided, however, to avoid the direct challenge to the Senate that the establishment of an Imperial mint in Rome would have implied. Grafting his new coinage on to the coinage of the generals in the provinces, he issued his gold and silver at provincial mints in his capacity of 'Imperator'.

The bronze coinage seems to have been subsidiary to that in the precious metals, designed mainly for circulation in Rome and Italy. Augustus placed it under the control of the Senate, attested by the letters s.c. ('Senatus consulto'), and thus offered a guarantee against possible abuses of a token coinage. But there is no question of a 'dyarchy', joint rule by Emperor and Senate, here. The Senate had no real independence; in signing this coinage it was simply giving its authority to measures devised and proposed by or for the Emperor.

Before we enter on the mint history of the Empire it will help us to decide exactly what we mean by the word 'mint'. A mint, of course, means a place where coins are planned, dies cut, coins struck. Such is the mint in the full sense – fully autonomous, doing everything for itself, not taking orders from any superior mint. But there may also be mints of lower rank – mints that while using their own dies accept a pattern of coinage designed elsewhere or mints that do no more than strike from dies supplied to them from the centre. Mints of the second and third orders may be regarded as something like 'Filiale', branches of the central mint. They are also extremely hard to detect. Even if we are sure from style that some dies deviate from the central pattern, how can we tell where they were made? And when we come to the lowest class of mint – the place that does no more than strike from imported dies – hardly anything but a lucky hoard will reveal their position. Some scholars today are insisting that a number of mints up and down the Empire may be assumed, almost as a matter of course. It is dangerous to be positive in such assertions. The Roman government may have preferred moving about coined money rather than bullion. In the

[1] H. Mattingly, 'Origins of the Imperial Coinage in Republican Times', *Num. Chron.*, 1919, pp. 221 ff.

East, we know, local Eastern denominations continued to be preferred. Much of the controversy about the mints of the early Empire hinges on these distinctions. To make matters plain at the outset, I will say that, when I speak of a mint, I mean a fully autonomous one; if I am thinking of one of the lower order I will make that plain.

In his early years Augustus certainly used a number of mints. They have their distinctive styles and choice of types. Some, at least, of his first issues after Actium are Eastern (Plate XXX, 6, 7). Ephesus was one mint, Pergamum, perhaps, another. Then come three issues which we are inclined to attribute to Spain. One of them is very close to a little issue of P. Carisius at Emerita (Plate XXX, 2) and was struck at that mint (Plate XXX, 3). The sites of the other mints are uncertain. But they are quite unlike coins produced at Rome or in Gaul later. Spain at the time was in the forefront of public interest (Plate XXX, 4, 5) and Augustus spent some time there himself. The styles of these two mints are very frequently copied on bronze coins of Spanish cities. Obviously, as has often been pointed out, an argument like this might mislead. All we mean is that, if these were the imperial coins chiefly circulating in Spain, the Spanish cities would naturally copy their portraits. Some scholars deny this close resemblance of these imperial and Spanish issues. My own judgement affirms it. About the years 21 and 20 there were fresh Eastern issues – perhaps also a few years later (Plate XXX, 8). Augustus also struck the local denomination, the cistophoric tetradrachm, in Asia Minor. From 19 to 12 B.C. he reopened the mint of Rome for gold (Plate XXX, 1) and silver, but the experiment evidently did not work well, for it ceased about the time of the death of Agrippa – perhaps because of it; Agrippa ranked as a true Republican and may have counselled Augustus to take a step that looked constitutional.[1]

So far, all these mints have been mints in the full sense of the word. Those who would throw them, with their varying styles and choices of types, into one mint, would produce a very strange creature indeed. In the latter period of the reign the picture changes completely. From 15 B.C. a new series begins which sets the pattern for the whole Empire for the rest of the reign. From 15 to 12 it has one style; in 12 this style changes to that which continues normal thereafter. If, as we shall suggest, Lugdunum was the seat of this second style the first

[1]In the first edition I tried to associate changes in the coinage with the constitutional settlements of 27 and 23 B.C. in view of uncertainties about mints and dates it is better for the time to suspend judgement.

may have belonged to another Gallic mint – such as Nemausus or Narbo.

Such a planned coinage must be operated from one central mint. Even if some variations in style may point to other mints producing dies, the pattern of coinage remains unchanged. We are fortunate to be able to place this central mint at Lugdunum in Gaul. The arguments are very strong:

(*a*) The main style is emphatically like that of the 'Altar' coins of Lugdunum, unlike the *Aes* of Rome or the gold and silver struck in the capital from 19 to 12 B.C.

(*b*) Strabo tells us that 'the Roman Emperors' (or governors) 'strike their gold and silver' there – at Lugdunum. Strabo probably means that the imperial mint was there, not that it was just a provincial mint. The full meaning is more likely to be correct than the lesser ones sometimes derived from it. Strabo mentions no other such mint anywhere else in the Empire.

(*c*) A number of inscriptions of the early Empire mention a mint at Lugdunum; an urban cohort was stationed there to guard it.

These arguments taken together are really decisive. The silence of Strabo about other mints, the absence of inscriptions cannot be accidental – when set against the unitary character of the coinage itself.

This theory of the primacy of Lugdunum has come in for severe criticism of late.[1] Some of this criticism is really misconceived; it depends on lack of attention to the different meanings of the word 'mint' of which we have spoken. No one will profess to know how exactly the system, centred at Lugdunum, was operated. But those students who object to having any one place selected as a centre for coinage and who do not like Lugdunum for centre, if such a centre there must be, will have, I fear, to swallow their objections. Augustus made the choice; we may not fully understand why he acted as he did – but that is not argument – simply a lack of full understanding on our part. The desire for centralization can be understood at once. But why not at Rome? Perhaps because Augustus wished to avoid taking over completely an old prerogative of the Senate or because he feared that in Rome co-operation with the Senate would be forced on him and he was not prepared for that. Granted once that Rome, the natural

[1] Cp. M. Grant, 'The Mints of Roman Gold and Silver in the Early Principate', *Num. Chron.*, 1935, pp. 39 ff. H. R. W. Smith, *Problems historical and numismatic in the reign of Augustus* (esp. 'The Lugdunum Monopoly', pp. 161 ff.).

centre, was passed over, why should Lugdunum not be chosen? It was the capital of an important province, which was in a very special sense a preserve of the imperial family; it was near the great armies of the Rhine, where a prince often commanded. We tend to think of the rule of Augustus as absolutely safe because he died at an advanced age in his bed. It does not follow that he always felt himself secure. The imperial treasure of gold and silver at Rome might have been a temptation to an adventurer. It might be much safer in Gaul, with an urban cohort to protect it against chance mishap and the German armies near by in case of really serious danger.

Much has been made recently of the finding of coin dies at various sites, especially in Gaul and Spain.[1] We cannot absolutely rule out the possibility that some of these are official. But the great regular mints do not yield us any such dies; they did their duty, kept their dies faithfully and destroyed them when done with. The probability is that these stray dies belong to forgers; they may occasionally have been procured feloniously from the regular mint; more often they will have been the work of the forger himself; his best work will have been almost exactly like that of the official coinage.

In *Aes*[2] Augustus instituted a new coinage in 23 B.C., which continued more or less unbroken to c. 4 B.C. and was resumed just before the end of the reign. Some scholars prefer a later date of origin – 20 B.C. or after.[3] I still find the old argument more convincing than any that has been brought against it; the first moneyers of the series sometimes give, sometimes do not give, Augustus the title TRP which he assumed in 23 B.C. This coinage, like the gold and silver of Rome, was struck by moneyers, III viri-aaaff; on the last issues of the reign their names are omitted. S.C. appears as a main type. The Emperor is always referred to except on the little quadrantes (Plate XXXIII, 13); but his portrait only appears on the As. As we have said, this is no independent coinage of the Senate; it carried out propositions made by the Emperor or his agents. There are Eastern issues of *Aes*, perhaps from a number of mints, on which reference is made to the Emperor rather than to the Senate – AVGVSTVS, CAESAR, C.A. ('Caesaris auctoritate' says Professor Grant). From 12 B.C. on there is the famous 'Altar' series of Lugdunum. Antioch has a bronze coinage bearing the letters S.C. like the Roman; even in an imperial province Augustus could put the

[1] Cf. C. C. Vermeule, *Some Notes on Ancient Dies and Coining Methods*, 1954.
[2] This is a convenient description for the coinage in base metal, which consisted partly of brass, partly of copper.
[3] K. Pink, *The Triumviri Monetales*, 1952.

Senate forward as his partner in coinage – probably to avoid any sus-picion of wilful inflation. Lugdunum had its famous 'Altar' series (Plate XXXIV), Nemausus had a coinage of bronze, which, although in name a local coinage, circulated far beyond the city bounds. Pro-fessor Grant has of recent years unearthed a number of Eastern coinages that were issued by the Roman State, but have hitherto been merged with the local or provincial issues.

The arrangements of Augustus for the provinces really belong to our third chapter. Here we need only say that the gold and silver circulated over the whole Empire (Egypt may have been an exception), but that certain local issues of silver and base silver continued (in Asia, Syria, Egypt) and that token bronze was freely struck at many centres, both in the West and, to a vastly greater extent, in the East.

Tiberius was faithful to the example of Augustus. He continued to issue his gold and silver from Lugdunum. The style is now fairly uniform; differences that might look at first sight differences of mint turn out to be differences of period. The 'Altar' coinage of Lugdunum ceased to appear quite early in the reign – and local coinage in the West began to decline. It is hard not to associate these facts with the revolts of Sacrovir in Gaul and Tacfarinas in Africa. Tiberius will have been led to distrust too much local sentiment. Critics of this view seem to push it to extremes and then ridicule it there. In the East, Commagene, becoming a province, had its own issue of bronze (Plate XXXIV, 3).

In the first year of Caligula the mint was probably moved from Lugdunum to Rome – that is to say, no matter where coins may have actually been struck, they were now planned at that mint. Tiberius had been conservative to an absurd degree; a principle or man once approved could not be changed. During his reign, it had been becoming apparent that Rome, not Lugdunum, was the natural centre for coinage. The change, long deferred, was at once carried out under his grand-nephew. By the beginning of the reign of Nero, when the gold and silver carry the letters EX S.C., it is apparent (but not to all – Professor Grant, for example) that Rome is now the centre. The change has taken place then at some date between Tiberius and Nero; the point that we have chosen seems to be the most appropriate. A slight change in style in the first year of Caligula may attest the change (Plate XXX, 9, 10). Professor Grant has handled these arguments severely like a cross-examining barrister and leaves little of them intact. But delicate attempts like ours to discover the truth in an obscure question must be handled delicately; otherwise, a possible advance towards the truth may simply be thwarted. In the West local issues cease completely. There is no trace in the coinage of the megalomania of the Emperor.

The policy of the mad nephew was carried on by the pedantic uncle who succeeded him; this continuity may have been due to the financial advisers of the Emperor. Scarcity of bronze in the West may have led to extensive imitation of the Roman issues (Plate XXXIV, 2). For Claudius we find one central mint – now, as we think, at Rome. Laffranchi has claimed to detect three distinct styles – and on points of style his eye seldom deceived him.[1] If correct, this view would mean that there were two mints beside Rome, cutting their own dies on her plan. There is a solitary issue of an 'Altar' coin from Lugdunum – probably for the fortieth birthday of the Emperor; he had been born in that city.

The minority of the young Nero,[2] under the guardianship of Seneca and Burrhus, led to a revival of the Senate which became the more marked when Agrippina and her protégé, Pallas, were forced out of public life. On almost all the gold and silver of Rome of Nero's early years the formula EX S.C. appears (Plate XXX, 11). In the first place, it may have referred to the oak-wreath, which formed the type of the reverse; but when we find it still present on the later reverse types of Ceres, Roma and Virtus, we must accept it as applying to the coinage itself. The Senate does not, indeed, go so far as to resume its rights of coinage; the gold and silver is not struck S.C. simply in pursuance of a decree of the Senate. But the right of authorization, expressed by EX S.C., is definitely claimed; the Senate will at least share in the responsibility. This partial return to the old Republican system did not outlast the years of Nero's tutelage. The reform of the coinage of A.D. 64 marks a return to the system of Claudius. The EX S.C. disappears from the gold and silver and the Emperor again monopolizes the coinage in those metals. No *Aes* was struck in the first years of the reign. Perhaps there was no great demand for it, perhaps the countermarking of old money meant that that was being kept in circulation longer than usual. Another possibility now occurs to us; was the issue of S.C. coinage – only nominally controlled by the Senate – offensive to all that was left of independence in that body? Was the intermission of such a coinage in these first years a gesture of friendship – sparing

[1] 'La Monetazione Imperatoria e Senatoria di Claudio I', *Riv. It.*, 1949, pp. 32 ff.
[2] An important dissertation on the *Aes* coinage of Nero by D. E. MacDowall is awaiting publication.

the Senate, for the moment, an unwelcome duty? In A.D. 59 the 'aerarium Saturni' was transferred from the quaestors to 'praefecti' nominated by the Emperor; this may have meant a tightening up of Imperial control of the Treasury. In A.D. 64 Nero resumed the issue of *Aes* on a grand scale; he struck quite a number of pieces without S.C.; the Emperor never relinquished the right to issue *Aes* in his own right, though he only occasionally made use of it. The mint of Lugdunum was reopened to strike *Aes* in A.D. 64 (Plate XXXIII, 14), but was soon closed owing to a disastrous fire. The Lugdunum issues used to be regarded as earlier issues of Rome; it is now quite certain that they run parallel to the Roman. Unlike the 'Altar' issues they now bear the mark S.C.; the Emperor, if he chose, could carry over his joint coinage with the Senate into an imperial province.

The Civil Wars produced a considerable number of little coinages, with no name or portrait of Emperor, but with frequent reference to the 'Senate and people' or 'the people of Rome'.[1] They are not Republican in our modern use of the word; rather, they appeal for a return to a good state, 'res publica', such as had existed under Augustus. Portraits of Augustus, alive or as 'Divus', appear beside the anonymous coins. We can be fairly sure of the provinces of these coins, seldom of their mints. Spain certainly had its issues, two if not more (Plate XXX, 13); one will have been from Tarraco (Plate XXX, 16). Other classes of coin must be assigned to Gaul. The slogan of Vindex, 'Salus generis humani', marks some issues as due to him. Recent research suggests that the series, hitherto assigned to Gaul, actually falls into two distinct parts – the coinage of Vindex (Plate XXX, 14) and a coinage, following after his defeat, struck at Lugdunum for those who, though despairing of Nero, refused to accept Galba.[2] The victorious legions of Vesontio had thrown down the images of Nero. These coins share one feature with those of Vindex. They pay homage to the Senate; but they also refer to the 'Genius P.R.' and Mars Ultor and copy several coin-types of Nero. A series of military character, glorifying the armies and asking for co-operation from the praetorians, is probably to be assigned to Cologne; it has very close links with an early coinage of Vitellius. The exact date is uncertain – perhaps a few months before the end of 69, when there was ferment among the German legions (Plate XXX, 15). Kraay has suggested that the coins were meant to be sent to Rome,

---

[1] Cp. H. Mattingly, 'Coinage of the Civil Wars of A.D. 68–69', *Num. Chron.*, 1914, pp. 1 ff.

[2] H. Mattingly, 'Verginius at Lugdunum', *Num. Chron.*, 1935, pp. 32 ff.

to work as propaganda on the Imperial guard.[1] One small issue seems to be marked as African by the s.c. which occurs on coins of Clodius Macer; he himself has his little issue at Carthage (?) during his short usurpation (Plate XXX, 12). The rebels of the 'imperium Galliarum' have their own coinage, defiantly nationalistic, struck, maybe, at Cologne. There is no mention of Rome or its Emperor in any form. Vindex had never stressed nationalistic aspirations. Coins of Nero are found countermarked s.p.q.r. or p.r. for use by the Gallic insurgents.

Galba, succeeding to the cause of Vindex, shows some connexion with his coinage. Coins with Galba as a figure on horseback, were struck partly in Gaul; on one of these the TRES GALLIAE are represented as imperial personages with little globes below their busts; this is the only evidence of nationalistic spirit below the surface of the movement; but the German legions claimed to be repressing a Gallic 'tumultus'.

Galba strikes, of course, at Rome. He has two if not more Spanish issues, one of Tarraco (Plate XXX, 16); that includes a little bronze beside the gold and silver. In Gaul he has the 'horseman' issues of which we have just spoken, and issues in *Aes* from a Gallic mint (Narbo) and an issue of silver (Plate XXX, 17), possibly one of Lugdunum.

The *Aes* of Galba has recently been the subject of a special study by Kraay.[2] He divides the coinage into a number of blocks, more or less clearly separable from one another, one of which is Gallic; he inclines to assign these blocks to different 'officinae' of the mint. His work, based on a close study of dies, must form the basis of any future work, but his allocation to 'officinae' has not convinced all scholars. One series of Galba, clearly defined and of a notably medallic character, is placed by Kraay at the very end of the reign. I had conjectured that it was posthumous, struck by Vespasian for Galba when he restored his honours. I still incline to this view in spite of Kraay's arguments against it.[3]

---

[1] Cp. H. Mattingly, 'The "Military" class in the Coinage of the Civil Wars of A.D. 68–69', *Num. Chron.*, 1952, pp. 72 ff.: Colin Kraay, 'Revolt and Subversion: the so-called "Military" Coinage of A.D. 69 re-examined', ibid., pp. 78 ff.

[2] 'The *Aes* Coinage of Galba', *Num. Notes and Monographs*, No. 133.

[3] Kraay objects (1) that dies of the Galban series, though admittedly shared with Vespasian, are also shared with Vitellius; (2) that there is no suitable place for the coinage in the first years of Vespasian. But, if Vespasian chose to use a die or two of Vitellius, as he well might, he might also use it for restored Galba; as for occasion of issue, we do not know enough to be as positive as Kraay inclines to be. Some of my arguments based on types are strong and have not been refuted. After all, Vespasian *did* restore Galba's honours; and what is the good of accepting a statement in general and then objecting the moment that it is applied to a particular case?

Otho strikes in one style only – that of Rome. Here we can be really certain of the mint. He did not succeed to any of the mints of the Civil Wars; Spain, which swung over to him for a moment, soon crossed over to Vitellius. There are no *Aes* coins of Otho; all that have been quoted are forgeries. The reason cannot lie in the dislike of the Senate for Otho; it had given him full recognition. Otho made the support of the Senate one of the chief planks in his platform. Had the reign lasted longer, the need for *Aes* would presumably have made itself felt. Was it that Otho refrained from vexing the Senate with a duty that it detested? It was an irritation that might at least be postponed.

Vitellius struck at Rome in three successive issues. He struck at the Spanish mint which we take to be Tarraco; at Cologne (?), following the anonymous military issue; at one other mint that signs with a palm (Lugdunum?). The Spanish portraits are distinguished by a wild, but impressive ferocity (Plate XXX, 18). His *Aes* is mainly of Rome; there are rare coins of Tarraco (Plate XXXIV, 4), perhaps a few of Lugdunum.

The armies of Spain and Gaul and the praetorian guard at Rome had all tried their hands at making Emperors. It was left to the legions of the East to fulfil the prophecy that 'from the East should come one who should rule the world' and to give the Empire in Vespasian a man who could restore to it the stability and rest that it so sorely needed. Vespasian has more mints than any Emperor down to the third century. To begin with his Eastern issues, we find his coins at Antioch (Plate XXXI, 6), Ephesus (Plate XXXI, 4) and Byzantium and one or two other mints in their neighbourhood; at Tyre (Plate XXXI, 5)[1] and, possibly, also, at Alexandria and Cyprus (Plate XXXI, 7). A mint signing o is possibly of Lycia (Olympus?) (Plate XXXI, 8). The Flavian expedition against Italy produces a little coinage at some such city as Aquileia or Verona (Plate XXXI, 3). Most of these mints have their distinctive style and choice of types; but Ephesus, Byzantium and one or two other mints in the same district, though they have their own styles, use the same selection of types with small variations. In the West, Vespasian strikes at Tarraco (Plate XXXI, 1), at Lugdunum (Plate XXXI, 2) and another Gallic mint; he may have a few coins of Cologne. Rome is naturally his most prolific mint. The *Aes* is of Rome and Lugdunum (Plate XXXIV, 7) and, in the East, Commagene (Plate XXXIV, 6). A few early coins seem to belong to Tarraco. A class which I used to consider as Spanish has been shown by Kraay

[1] Obverse of Titus.

to use reverse dies of the mint of Rome. But there is something in the style of the obverses that *does* suggest Tarraco (Plate **XXXIV**, 5); possibly, workers from that mint were transferred to the capital. These provincial mints – with the one exception of Lugdunum for *Aes* – fade out in the course of the reign; they die with the passing of the conditions that gave them birth. Antioch closes in 72, Ephesus in 74, Tarraco in 73 or 74, Lugdunum (for gold and silver) at about the same time. The Emperor had no intention of standardizing the chaotic conditions of the Civil Wars and dividing the imperial coinage over a number of provincial mints.

When Lugdunum struck again towards the close of the reign, it was only, as under Nero, as a subsidiary mint for *Aes*. Vespasian, then, at a time when the course of events rather suggested the creation of provincial mints, deliberately chose to centralize coinage at Rome. There was obviously an immediate wisdom in this policy. The Civil Wars had shaken the Empire to its foundation, the revolt of Civilis and the Empire of the Gauls, which had issued a small treasonable coinage of its own, had shown how imminent was the danger of a cleavage in the Imperial structure. Vespasian's whole endeavour was to repress the dangerous local movements and to do everything possible to restore Rome to her position of power and honour. But, in shunning the more immediate danger, Vespasian steered direct towards a danger, less obviously threatening, but calculated in the long run to defeat the best hopes that the Empire offered. Centralization of government at Rome meant stability and efficiency for the time; but it also meant a severe strain on the resources of government and a discouragement of all that was alive and vigorous in local life. The more liberal and hopeful policy of the best of the later democrats and of Julius Caesar received a fatal setback. The provinces lost all chance of a timely sharing in privilege and power: when, in the inevitable course of development, the prestige of Rome and Italy became obsolete, there was no longer freedom, but only servitude, to be shared.

Titus has one main style in all metals, that of Rome. In *Aes* we find a continuation of the Lugdunum issue and another issue, distinct from it, which might conceivably be British; it falls at the height of the activities of Agricola in Britain and we know that he tried to introduce the Britons to the amenities of Roman city life. Domitian strikes on almost exactly the same plan (Plate **XXXIV**, 8 – British mint?).

Nerva has one main style in all metals, Rome. Trajan has only a few odd gold and silver coins that fall apart from the Roman issues (Plate XXXI, 9). We cannot find any clearly defined mint for his Eastern wars. One little issue of *Aes* is perhaps of Cyprus. At the very beginning of the reign there is one small series which does not fit readily into the mint of Rome; it is just possible that it was struck by a mission sent to Germany for the occasion.

Hadrian breaks away a little from the normal, but not to the extent that we might have expected. His main issues are of Rome. He has a few early coins that look Eastern (Plate XXXI, 10), then a very considerable coinage of denarii, mainly of Asia Minor (Plate XXXI, 11). He also issued cistophoric tetradrachms on a considerable scale in Asia Minor and Bithynia from a number of mints, overstriking many old specimens. A little Eastern issue of *Aes* of the middle of the reign may be of Antioch. He did not, as we might perhaps have anticipated, open mints in the many provinces over which he travelled.

From Antoninus Pius to Didius Julianus the coinage revolves round its one centre, Rome (Plate XXXI, 12). A little issue of silver for Marcus Aurelius and L. Verus (in Greek) was struck in the East for the Parthian War. Avidius Cassius in his revolt struck no coins; none, at least, survive. Had there not been a very firm principle that Rome was the proper place of issue for Imperial coins, the wars of Domitian and Trajan on Rhine and Danube and the Empire-wide wanderings of Hadrian would naturally have called local mints into being. The burden that now fell on the two mints, Imperial and Senatorial, of the capital was an extremely heavy one, and we may conjecture, with much probability, that both were enlarged and subdivided, in order to deal more efficiently with their task. But, although it may have seemed advisable to divide the mints into sections or 'officinae' and to allot to each a special part of the coinage, those 'officinae' were kept within the capital itself; Rome did not send out branch mints into the provinces. If central control was the aim, it could be most efficiently exercised at a single centre. Trajan even seems to have made an attempt to centralize many of the provincial silver coinages of the East at the mint of Caesarea in Cappadocia; but the experiment was abandoned after his death. The regularity of the succession in this period and the scarcity of pretenders in the provinces made it easier to maintain the monopoly of coinage for Rome. I have seen one Egyptian hoard of Antoninus Pius, all in Roman style, but containing quite a number of die identities. Such identities always suggest that the coins have not travelled far from their place of mintage. But the coins may have been sent in mass from Rome; there is no need to assume that they had been struck in Egypt.

The second series of Civil Wars, 193 to 197, produces a crop of coinages not unlike those of the Civil Wars, 69 to 70. Again, the emergence of rival Emperors in the provinces leads to issues from provincial mints. Septimius soon seized Rome and struck there in all metals. He did not strike any coins in Pannonia, for he made a dash straight for the capital. In the East we find three distinct series for him. One was certainly of Laodicea ad Mare, displacing Antioch for the time as capital of Syria; a second, of certain character but uncertain site, may be of Emesa or Samosata (Plate XXXI, 14); the third has been placed by Laffranchi at Alexandria, on a comparison of its style with that of the Alexandrian tetradrachms. I find his evidence quite convincing. Some scholars are sceptical about these mints, and, like Dr Pink, crowd them all into the one mint of Antioch. But Antioch was disgraced for the time by Septimius, and the three mints have their distinguishing styles and also their special choice of obverse and reverse types. Clodius Albinus, as Caesar of Septimius, shares in his coinage at Rome, then strikes for himself at Lugdunum, rare gold, less rare silver (Plate XXXI, 16), very rare *Aes*. Eastern coins are as good as unknown for him; either Septimius disregarded his Caesar's claims in the East or else the coins, never struck in any quantities, were called in after his rebellion. Pescennius Niger has one clearly defined series, presumably of his capital, Antioch (Plate XXXI, 13). But his coins are varied in style and often border on the barbarous. We should guess that they were struck at a number of mints. The same is true of Septimius. Apart from the clearly defined series which we have described, there are occasional coins that look Eastern, but stand isolated by themselves. They may be the products of occasional mints. We might expect one at Byzantium which for several years held out for Pescennius. We know that the Civil War gave vent to many ancient jealousies between cities; what more likely than that many of these cities took the opportunity of issuing a few coins in the name of the Emperor whom they preferred? Who was to blame them for their arrogance? Hardly the man for whom they struck; he had more important things to worry him. As for their enemy, he was that already; the issues of a few coins could not add much to the sin of having chosen the wrong side. Eckhel has spoken of a 'War of types' at these Eastern mints; it should be described rather as a war between cities, using the same coin idiom.[1]

[1] Eckhel in *Doctrina Numorum*, VII, pp. 152 ff.

Septimius, unlike Vespasian, did not return immediately to the policy of centralization. Himself a provincial, he had a full under-standing of the point of view of the provinces and, after the revolt, he found himself out of sympathy with the upper classes in Rome. He had no objection, then, to letting Laodicea continue to strike for the Parthian War, now more or less as a branch of the Roman mint (Plate XXXI, 15). He suspended these issues in A.D. 202 and did not issue coins for his British campaigns. But he had established a precedent which was not to be forgotten.[1]

The period from Septimius to Diocletian was one of transition from the old system to the new. Rome was still the only mint that struck regularly and continuously; but, now and again, a provincial mint would emerge and, once having emerged, might establish itself on a more or less permanent basis.

We note again that, if provincial mints were striking from Roman dies, Antioch and Lugdunum could hardly have failed to show some close connexion with Rome in their first issues – and this is assuredly not the case. Septimius has an issue of light tetradrachms which has not yet been placed; it looks as if it belonged to a mint that was an army centre, perhaps also a Roman colony.

Caracalla shares in his father's mints of Rome and Laodicea. So does Geta, his brother. In his sole reign Caracalla has a great Eastern issue of tetradrachms in Syria and neighbouring provinces. They are not exactly Imperial coins, but they seem to have served the needs of the Eastern wars. It is not clear whether these issues were a con-cession to the pride of the issuing cities or a burden laid on them; in view of what we know of Caracalla, the latter view seems the more probable.

Macrinus spent the whole of his reign in the East, and some Eastern coinage is therefore probable for him. In fact, he has two series, fairly clearly separable – one with a portrait with a short beard, the other – surely the liker to the Macrinus of the time – with a beard allowed to grow long. The short beards are of Rome, the long of Antioch. After the initial issues the two styles influence one another and doubt can arise about the mintage of particular coins. For Diadumenian, son of Macrinus, there is no clear difference of portrait and the allocation of coins to the two mints is difficult. The very rare coins of Diadumenian

---

[1] There is some evidence for local British issues of a semi-barbarous character at Chester, cp. finds in the Deanery Field, Chester. Report, Liverpool, 1924, by Professor R. Newstead.

as Augustus must be of Antioch, as he was only promoted very near the end of the reign and there was not time for such a coinage at Rome.

Elagabalus's main issues at Rome are clearly distinguishable. His Eastern issues are puzzling. There are several classes, apparently from mints that had not been striking before. Nicomedia, where the Emperor wintered on his way to Rome, probably produced some fine aurei (Plate XXXI, 17). Severus Alexander has his main series of Rome. He has a few Eastern issues, mainly at least of the first years. If we assign them to Antioch it is hardly more than a guess.

For the next reigns, Maximin I, the Gordians, Balbinus and Pupienus, there is only one style and mint, Rome. With Gordian III, we find early issues of Antioch (?) then a resumption of issues, perhaps, at the same mint, more or less conformed to the Roman style (Plate XXXI, 18). Philip I continues at the same mint for a year or so (Plate XXXI, 19). He also issues tetradrachms of the pattern of Antioch (Plate XXXII, 1), sometimes with the signature MON. VRB – a clear suggestion that the larger denomination was now introduced into the Roman system. The pretender, Iotapianus, has a very rare Syrian issue (Plate XXXII, 3). Pacatian (Marinus) has a small issue at Viminacium (?) (Plate XXXII, 2), but the idea that that city was a mint for other Roman coins has now been abandoned. Trajan Decius strikes at Rome and Antioch; he has also a third mint, which in style is not far removed from the Roman, but varies the obverse legend and the choice of reverse types.[1] It was probably in north Italy, possibly at Milan, which was certainly to be a vital military centre a little later. Trebonianus Gallus has coins of Rome and Milan (?). The Milan coins of Trebonianus are again close to Rome in style, but again there is a difference in the choice of reverses and in the form of obverse legend. The practice of the mint also varies. At Rome Volusian divides the six 'officinae' with his father, each taking three; at Milan Trebonianus has two 'officinae' to Volusian's one. The Eastern issues of the reign may be of a mint not Antioch (Plate XXXII, 4); it seems that at about this time that city fell into the hands of the Persian, Sapor I. Aemilian has issues of Rome, but not of Milan. This fits in well with what we know of the history; Valerian was busy bringing up troops from Germany to help Trebonianus, and Milan would be his natural base in Italy. A few half-barbarous coins were perhaps struck in Moesia.

[1] It is possible that some reverse dies may have been sent to it in the first place from Rome.

Aemilian has no Eastern issues – it may be because Sapor was over-running the Roman provinces.

With the reign of Valerian we pass into a period of transition, in which the principles that had governed the early Empire one by one decay and the first experiments are made which led on to the new organization of the Empire by Diocletian. Our knowledge of the period is too imperfect to admit of very confident judgements; but we may suspect that, if we knew its details better, we might regard it rather as the preface to the new order than as the last chapter of the old. Decentralization in coinage assumed larger and larger proportions. To the demand of the provinces for equality with Italy, which found its full expression in the emergence of the Gallic Empire, were now added decisive considerations of practical convenience. With the collapse of the Imperial coinage under Gallienus, the local coinage of the cities began to totter to its fall. On the Imperial mints must now fall the burden of supplying the entire needs of the Empire and for such a burden no one mint could possibly suffice. With the multiplication of mints that inevitably ensued went an increasingly severe control of the coinage, by means of signatures identifying mint, 'officina' and issue. The temptations to abuse were now unusually acute, owing to the debasement of the silver, and easier and readier means of control were sought than those which may have sufficed, when only the one mint of Rome demanded supervision.[1]

For the joint reign of Valerian and Gallienus we have plentiful coins of Rome and Milan (?) and at least one Eastern mint, site uncertain (Plate XXXII, 6). In his sole reign Gallienus strikes in not less than three Eastern mints. Professor Alfoeldi has analysed these coinages with great care and made suggestions as to their sites; careful checking is necessary before we can feel any certainty about them.[2] There was probably one mint in Syria, one in Asia Minor (Plate XXXII, 9), a third at Cyzicus. Cyzicus puts SPQR on its coins; why? Perhaps, because the East from c. 260 was virtually under Palmyra, affecting to act for Rome, but moving more and more towards independence. The Eastern mints came under Palmyrene control, and the portrait of an Emperor no longer meant that a coin was really Roman. The addition of SPQR would give this assurance. A mint was opened at Siscia and struck in some quantity for the last years of the reign (Plate XXXII,

[1] For issues of Rome, cp. XXXIII, 4.
[2] A. Alfoeldi, 'Die Hauptereignisse der Jahre 253–261, n. Chr. im Orient, etc.', *Berytus*, 1937, pp. 41 ff.

8).[1] Of the many pretenders we have coins of Regalian and his wife, Dryantilla, struck at Carnuntum (Plate XXXII, 11), the place where they are found; they are often overstruck on old coins and are half-barbarous in character. Macrian II and Quietus (Plate XXXII, 10) have one mint of some size – at their headquarters at Emesa?;[2] they have also a small issue of another mint, much less accomplished in style; one very rare coin of Gallienus in this style has turned up in a recent hoard. But what of the 'thirty tyrants'? Did no others of them issue coins? We should say at a guess that every pretender who lasted more than a few weeks certainly struck his coins; it was one of the most obvious ways of announcing his rule. When such an issue was short-lived and confined to a narrow compass, the coins would be called in before they got into the general body of coinage.

The Gallic Emperors require a word for themselves. Postumus revolted when the news of the captivity of Valerian came West; he drew after him Gaul, Britain, some say part at least of Spain. His successors lasted down to 274. Postumus strikes at a mint, previously used by Valerian and Gallienus (Plate XXXII, 5, 12). It was certainly Gallic and has usually been placed at Lugdunum. But the series of Postumus is admittedly uniform, presumably all of one mint. A few of the later issues bear the mint-mark of Cologne (Plate XXXII, 13). Elmer places the whole series – and the earlier coins of the Roman Emperors – at that mint. It remains possible that Lugdunum was the original site and that the mint was transferred to Cologne at the time when the signature of that city appears. After Postumus, Elmer finds a second mint for Victorinus, Marius, Laelianus, Victorinus as well as the Tetrici, which he places at Treviri.[3] Hitherto it has been placed in south Gaul – at Lugdunum or some other city. I am not convinced about Treviri, though it must be admitted as an interesting possibility. Nor am I satisfied that Marius and Laelianus can be brought into Elmer's scheme. Marius seems to have a mint of his own at which Victorinus struck a few coins. As for Laelianus, why should not his coins be assigned to Mainz, the city where he staged his revolt against Postumus? Victorinus and the Tetrici certainly strike at two mints, Cologne (Plate XXXII, 14) and the uncertain second mint (Plate XXXII, 15). Postumus strikes *Aes* in some quantity, without s.c.

Milan struck for Valerian and Gallienus in their first years. We

[1] A. Alfoeldi, *Siscia*, Budapest, 1931.
[2] H. Mattingly, 'The Coinage of Macrianus II and Quietus', *Num. Chron.*, 1953, pp. 53 ff.
[3] G. Elmer, *Die Münzprägung der Gallischen Kaiser*, 1941.

find what seems to be the same mint striking in mass for Gallienus in his later years (Plate XXXII, 7); it looks as if there had been a short interruption between the earlier and later series. Aureolus, in his revolt against Gallienus, struck for Postumus at Milan. A fact, lost in our literary authorities, has been recovered from the coins; they bear the mint-marks and types, characteristic of Milan, at the time when Aureolus held the city. Aureolus was acting in the commission of the Gallic Emperor. This has been admirably demonstrated in a paper by Professor Alfoeldi in *Z.fN.*, 1927, pp. 195 ff. He has also recovered from Banduri a coin of Aureolus himself with the correct types and mint signature – unlikely, therefore, to have been invented, before the mint of Milan was recognized.

Claudius struck at Rome, Milan, Siscia, Cyzicus and another mint in the East, site unknown. Aurelian struck at these same mints and also at three new mints – Serdica (Plate XXXIII, 2), Tripolis and a mint, using signature dolphin. He has rare coins of the mint that Elmer calls Treviri, possibly also a few coins of Lugdunum. Under him the mint of Milan (Plate XXXIII, 1) changes its site to Ticinum. It signs T or TI (Plate XXXIII, 3). Africa and Spain, both provinces which played little part in the military history of the period, have no mints of their own. The attempt has been made, and is not yet finally abandoned, to attribute the coins above assigned to Ticinum to Tarraco. The arguments against Tarraco are, however, absolutely decisive;

(*a*) We have the signature M under Aurelian, giving place to T and TI.

(*b*) The mint is mainly in the hands of Gallienus, only for a moment in those of Postumus. This is not what we should expect if it were situated in Spain.

(*c*) Coins of the mint are admitted to be especially common in north Italian finds.

(*d*) The style of the mint is allied to that of Rome and Siscia, not to that of Lugdunum.

We have only to realize that the military unimportance of Spain is a full explanation for the absence of a Spanish mint, and we can say good-bye once and for all to an unfortunate misattribution. The picture of the mints does not change much under Tacitus, Florian, Probus (Plate XXXIII, 4 – Rome; Plate XXXIII, 5 – Siscia; Plate XXXIII, 8 – Siscia, 6 – Antioch) and Carus (Plate XXXIII, 9 – Gallic) and his sons. The mint in south Gaul, generally placed at Lugdunum, signs

A under Tacitus; it was possibly at Arelate. Diocletian opens new mints at Heracleia (the old Perinthus) and Treviri (if that mint is indeed new). Of the pretenders of the time, Saturninus has one very rare aureus of an Eastern mint. There are also rare barbarous coins of Bonosus. Supposed coins of Aelianus and Amandus are very doubtful, to say the least. The pretender Julian in Pannonia has some rare silver and gold (Plate XXXIII, 7).

The British Empire of Carausius and Allectus opens a new chapter of mint history. The chief mint of Carausius, London, signing M L (Plate XXXIII, 11), is continued by Allectus. A second mint, signing C or CL (Plate XXXIII, 12), is used by both Emperors. It has usually been placed at Camulodumum. But there is much to be said for assigning the coins to Clausentum (Bitterne, near Southampton), as base for the fleet of the Isle of Wight. Other mints of Carausius were not used by his successor.

One mint which signs RSR may have been at Rutupiae, even if the exact reading of the letters remains uncertain. It has also been regarded as a first stage of the mint of London or as a mint of Boulogne. A couple of coins, marked BRI, one of which was found at Uriconium (Wroxester), may belong to that city; BRI is explicable as an easier form of VRI. It seems at least possible that other coins of Carausius, not barbarous and bearing such signatures as S.P. or S.C. – not mint-marks, but letters denoting periods of work in the mint – may have been struck by other British cities. Carausius may have tolerated, if not encouraged, such auxiliary issues. The really barbarous coins of the Emperor are another matter. They are contemporary with the regular coins, but no clear account of them can yet be given. On the Continent Carausius strikes a number of coins, a few of them marked R, in a style not unlike that of the base silver of Tetricus. R indeed may stand for Rotomagus; but is not the main series more likely to belong to the port of Boulogne (Plate XXXIII, 10)?

We see how in the third century provincial mints, hitherto almost confined to times of civil war, begin to be more or less regular. A system covering the whole Empire is evolving. Mint signatures become more and more regular – M, TI., L, ANT, C, etc. This is a case where we see clearly how the system of the fourth century gradually grows out of the confusions of the third.

In A.D. 296 Diocletian made permanent and regular the new order for all time. Coinage was distributed over a large number of mints, each serving the needs of a limited district, all normally signing their issues with a distinctive mint-mark. Rome was simply one mint among many, no longer even 'prima inter pares'. But, as we have already suggested, this breaking down of the Italian monopoly came too late to foster the independent growth of the provinces. It was still one powerful central Government that held firmly the reins of power; if that government spread itself over a number of local centres it was only to tighten its grip, not to give play to local interests and traditions. The mechanical unity of the Government was still strong enough to hold the Empire together; but the invisible links that go to build up an organic unity were being seriously loosened. Let the Government once give way and there was no spirit living in the Empire to find expression in a new constitution.

Besides the main issues of the Empire, Imperial and Senatorial, a number of provincial issues can be traced. We have already spoken of some of these. There is silver of Asia Minor, Bithynia, Caesarea in Cappadocia, base silver of Antioch and other mints of the district and very base silver of Alexandria. In *Aes* there are issues of Antioch, Commagene, Cyprus, Alexandria, etc. Many of these issues are still almost uncharted. City issues died out in the West under Caligula. In the East they flourished well into the late third century. Alexandria was the last local mint to strike its own coins; they only stop just before the reform of Diocletian, or even overlap it. Something more will be said of these local coinages in our third chapter; much was left to local enterprise, but some degree of control was exercised from the centre.

2. THE MONEY-SYSTEM IN ITS VARIOUS STAGES[1]

The way is now clear for the discussion of the money-system of the Empire in its various developments.[1] Augustus, accepting the facts of the existing system, very cleverly adapted it to his needs. During the last period of the Republic gold had been freely struck at a standard of

[1] We must here mention some few monetiform pieces, which, not being strictly coins, will not concern us further:

(a) Tesserae of brass and lead, used for distributions of corn, for shows, for various private purposes. Among these are the 'spinthriae', tesserae showing 'curious' subjects, perhaps to be explained as the 'lasciva nomismata' of Martial, VIII, 78, 9.
(b) 'Medallions' of *Aes*, used for distribution on special occasions – not struck on any fixed standard. The 'medallions' of gold and silver, though perhaps used for similar purposes, are normally multiples of the aureus and denarius.
(c) Imitations of coins used as ornaments, such as bracts, or thin one-sided pieces of gold.

40 to the pound. Augustus standardized the aureus[1] (Plate XXVI, 1) at 42 to the pound and fixed its value at 25 denarii; the denarius he continued to strike at the later Republican standard of 84 to the pound (Plate XXVI, 4). Half pieces in both metals were struck, in gold fairly frequently, in silver but rarely and, till Vespasian, only at the Eastern mints (Plate XXVI, 2, 3 and 7).[2] A gold coinage was clearly necessary for the Empire, both for the sake of prestige and for the practical necessity of dealing with expanding trade and rising prices. The sequel will show how wisely Augustus acted in maintaining the quality of the silver. But his system could not escape the weakness of all bimetallic systems – the establishment of a fixed relation in coinage of two metals which are naturally liable to fluctuations in the open market. In the base metals, there was more room for innovation. Since the collapse of the half-ounce standard the Republic had had no fixed rules here and Augustus had to create an entirely new system. Instead of one metal, bronze, he made use of two, brass or orichalcum and pure copper – the former for the sestertius and dupondius, the latter for the As and quadrans[3] (Plate XXVIII, 1, 3, 4). There are several points of interest to be noted here: (1) the sestertius is no longer struck in silver; (2) the two metals, brass and copper, are based on different standards – the sestertius, weighing one ounce,[4] presumes a theoretical As of brass weighing a quarter of an ounce, whereas the actual As of copper weighs two-fifths of an ounce; (3) the only division of the As now struck is the quadrans – triens, sextans and uncia disappear. The fact that the sestertius, which still remained the unit of account, was struck in brass has led to the suggestion that Augustus's system was really a trimetallic one – that brass in the coinage bore something like its true market value.[5] This is, on the whole, improbable; the ratio of the metals suggests that all the base coinage was now in some degree token money. But why, then, did Augustus trouble to use two metals, brass and copper, instead of choosing one of them for the whole of the base currency? It is unlikely that it has anything to do with the pay of the soldiers.

[1] Aureus is an abbreviation for 'aureus denarius'. For gold, silver and billon multiple pieces, 'medallions', see Pls. XXVII, 9–11; XXIX, 6.

[2] The silver piece was regularly named 'victoriate' from the normal reverse type, Victory; a similar use for the gold would be natural enough, but it is not definitely attested.

[3] The closest parallel in the Republic is to be found in the 'fleet' coinage of Mark Antony. The 'Triumphal' issues of Augustus in *Aes*, c. 7 B.C., were apparently of two denominations, dupondius (Pl. XXVIII, 2) and As.

[4] The dupondius normally weighs ½ ounce, but, in the early Empire, was sometimes struck at a rather heavier weight.

[5] A. Beanlands, 'The Origin of the Augustan Sestertius', *Num. Chron.*, 1919, pp. 1 ff.

Dupondius and As were both struck carelessly and their weights might even overlap. It was desirable, then, to have a clear distinction in colour, between the yellow of the orichalcum and the red of the copper. Further to distinguish them, the radiate crown was often used for the dupondius, the laureate wreath for the As.

We have then the following system:

- 1 aureus (122·9 gr., 7·96 gm.) = 25 denarii = 100 sestertii = 400 Asses.
- 1 gold quinarius (61·45 gr., 3·98 gm.) = 12½ denarii = 50 sestertii = 200 Asses.
- 1 denarius (61·46 gr., 3·99 gm.) = 4 sestertii = 16 Asses.
- 1 silver quinarius (30·73 gr., 1·995 gm.) = 2 sestertii = 8 Asses.
- 1 sestertius (1 oz., brass) = 4 Asses.
- 1 dupondius (½ oz., brass) = 2 Asses.
- 1 As (⅖ oz., copper) = ¼ sestertius.
- 1 quadrans (1/16 oz., copper) = ¼ As.

The relations of the metals in coinage are:

Gold is to silver as 1 : 12½
Silver is to brass as 1 : 28.
Silver is to copper as 1 : 45.
Brass is to copper as 28 : 45 (5 : 8 nearly).

Gold and silver are both struck almost pure and very true to standard weight. Brass and copper are struck much more carelessly – *a marco*, not *a pezzo* – i.e. not on a carefully adjusted weight for each piece, but at so many to the pound. The quadrans was often struck at a little above its normal weight. The brass contains almost exactly 80 per cent. of copper to 20 per cent. of zinc; it seems to have been a natural alloy, obtained first from the Bergomate territory in Germany, later from the Mons Marianus in Spain.[1] The copper was struck almost pure.

The period from Augustus to Nero saw no change of system. The weight of the aureus was gradually reduced – but only in practice, not by legislative act; a drop in the denarius accompanied it. The weight of the dupondius rose under Caligula and Claudius to nearly five-eighths of an ounce and that of the sestertius to about one ounce and a tenth. We conjecture a drop in the market price of brass as the cause; but, as the change is definitely greater in proportion for the dupondius than the sestertius, we may see also an attempt to make a better distinction between dupondius and As.

[1] Pliny, *Nat. Hist.*, XXXIV, 2.

The reform of Nero has three main features, two permanent and of lasting importance, one of experimental interest only: (1) The aureus and denarius were permanently reduced in weight, the former to one-forty-fifth, the latter to one-ninety-sixth of a pound – their relations in coinage remaining unchanged (Plate XXVI, 5, 6); (2) the silver began to be alloyed to the extent of about 10 per cent.; (3) an orichalcum coinage of sestertius, dupondius, As, semis and quadrans (Plate XXVIII, 5, 7, 8), based on an As of a quarter ounce, was introduced, but was abandoned after a short trial, in favour of the old system. The semis was also struck in copper at the weight of half the copper As (Plate XXVIII, 6). The last reform had no permanence; on its merits it deserved to succeed, but it was unpopular, because it reduced the As to a purely subsidiary position, and was therefore abandoned. The other two reforms had far-reaching results. The reduction of weight, though it brought a certain temporary gain to the exchequer, must not be condemned as the short-sighted act of an embarrassed government. During the first century of the Empire, the depreciation of money values and the rise of prices reached and passed its zenith. Gold and silver were steadily lost to the money market, both through foreign trade, notably with the Far East, and through being immobilized in articles of luxury. The reduction in weight of the standard pieces tended to restore the balance and stabilize prices again. There can be no question of any attempt to secure a better relation of Roman coinage to Eastern currencies, for the provincial silver of the East undergoes a corresponding change of weight. The debasement of the silver was a more serious innovation. For the moment it may have helped to re-establish in the coinage the market relation of gold and silver. In the long run it meant the unavowed abandonment of the bimetallic system and the opening up of a dangerous means of saving to any embarrassed government.

The system of Nero then is:

1 aureus (114·10 gr., 7·39 gm.) = 25 denarii.
1 denarius (52·68 gr., 3·41 gm.) = 4 sestertii.

The relations of the metals now are:

Gold is to silver as 1 : 11·73 (nearly), or, allowing for the debasement, about 1 : 13.
Silver is to brass as 1 : 32.
Silver is to copper as 1 : 51.

E*   123

The relations of brass to copper remained unchanged.

For nearly a century and a half no further change of system is to be recorded.[1] The old heavier aureus was again struck sporadically in the Civil Wars and regularly from about the second year of Domitian to the second year of Trajan. At the same time a slight increase in the weight of the denarius is to be noted. Large silver pieces ('medallions') of Domitian and Hadrian are shown on Plate XXVII, 9, 10. Debasement of the silver was steadily on the increase – about 15 per cent. under Trajan, 25 per cent. under Marcus Aurelius, nearly 40 per cent. under Septimius Severus. The danger lay in the fact that the change of standard was not openly avowed; the silver was still issued as a value, not as a token currency, and debasement was definitely used as a means of easy but unsound inflation. The expenses of government were steadily increasing out of proportion to any increase in receipts and the State was moving slowly in the direction of bankruptcy. The old heavier coinage steadily went to the melting-pot. Finds seldom show any pieces earlier than Nero; and Trajan, in A.D. 107, actually withdrew from circulation such Republican denarii as were still current.[2] Under Trajan we find the semis struck at an Eastern mint, under Hadrian a tiny coin, perhaps the uncia, issued at Rome (?). Small coins (quadrantes) were issued in the second century for limited circulation within the precincts of the mines. Quadrantes without the head of Emperor, but with the signature of the Senate, S.C., were probably issued as coins by the Senate on special occasions in the capital.

Caracalla, in A.D. 215, introduced definite reforms in the monetary system. He reduced the weight of the aureus to one-fiftieth of a pound (Plate XXVI, 9)[3] and struck, beside the denarius, a new piece distinguished by its larger module and the radiate head of the Emperor, weighing about 80 grains (5·18 gm.). This coin, which is known to us from the Augustan history as the 'Antoninianus' (Plate XXVI, 10), has been variously interpreted as the equivalent of 2, $1\frac{1}{2}$ or $1\frac{1}{4}$ denarii. There can be little doubt that 2 is the right figure. The Government was evidently concerned to increase the volume of the coinage; the expenses of the State were steadily mounting and the loss of gold and silver in foreign trade and in articles of luxury was still felt. The debasement of the silver had already attained dangerous proportions. The only alter-

---

[1] The silver quinarius was again struck by Vespasian (Pl. XXVI, 7).
[2] Cp. *Num. Chron.*, 1926, on restored coins of Trajan.
[3] For a double aureus, see Pl. XXVI, 8.

native was to reduce the weight and the Government preferred to make the reduction on a new coin rather than on the one in common use. The denarius was still worth more as a coin than as metal and was thereby saved from the melting pot; but the double denarius brought the Government a larger profit. The sequel confirms this view. The two coins, denarius and 'Antoninianus', were not accurately adjusted to one another; they did not, therefore, settle down into general use side by side. Severus Alexander ceased to strike 'Antoniniani'. Balbinus and Pupienus, driven to issue coin rapidly and in quantity for the war against Maximin, recommenced the issue (Plate XXVI, 11), and from that time on the 'Antoninianus' gradually replaces the denarius as the main silver coin; after the reign of Gordian III (Plate XXVI, 12), the denarius and its half, the quinarius, were hardly struck at all.[1] The weight and fineness of the 'Antoninianus' steadily declined, until finally, at the crisis of the reign of Gallienus, when Valerian fell into Persian captivity and Postumus seceded in the West, the Government took the final plunge and flooded the market with masses of base silver (billon) scarcely distinguishable from copper.[2] It was little less than absolute bankruptcy. Business must have been terribly hampered and the losses of private individuals must have been heart-breaking. The mischief would have been less serious had the gold coinage remained stable. But this prop, too, gave way. The weight of the aureus had been reduced by slow degrees to about 90 gr. (5·83 gm.) under Alexander Severus, falling to about 70 gr. (4·54 gm.) under Philip I and Trajan Decius (Plate XXVI, 13). Serious variations of weight occur in individual specimens and even the metal itself was occasionally debased. A division of the aureus into three became common: under Trebonianus Gallus we find a whole of c. 84 gr. (5·44 gm.), and a two-thirds piece of c. 56 gr. (3·63 gm.). Under Valerian and Gallienus we find the third, the 'triens', commonly called by the Augustan historians the 'triens of Saloninus' (Plate XXVI, 14). In the confusion of the reign of Gallienus[2] the standard is almost completely lost; gold pieces of almost every weight occur and can hardly have passed in commerce except by weight. So far as a standard can be traced, it seems to have been one of about 78 gr. (5·05 gm.) for the whole piece, with subdivisions of one-third and two-thirds and multiples running up to as many as ten aurei.[3] The Gallic Emperors

[1] For a quinarius of Trajan Decius, see Pl. XXVI, 15.
[2] For 'Antoniniani' of Gallienus, see Pl. XXVII, 1, 2.
[3] A multiple aureus of Gallienus is shown on Pl. XXVII, 11.

attempted to maintain a better standard of about 90 gr. (5·83 gm.) (Plate XXVII, 3), but it, too, fell away under Victorinus and Tetricus I to about 70 gr. (4·54 gm.). Our literary tradition cannot be trusted in details, but it records two facts, which are inherently probable: (1) that coins were now frequently named after the Emperor issuing them, so that one could tell exactly what piece of metal was intended in each case; and (2) that the Government tried to collect taxes, not in its own unsatisfactory coin, but in gold and silver bullion. We presume without any certainty that the aureus, as long as it continued to be a clearly defined denomination, was equal to 25 denarii and 12½ 'Antoniniani'. But we have a suspicion that there may have been perturbations in the system, not yet clearly traced. Trajan Decius overstruck 'Antoniniani' on old denarii; the 'Antoninianus' seems now to have stood where the old denarius had stood. He also struck a double sestertius, often called a medallion, and revived the semis. As things moved towards chaos, the actual value of coins may have been determined in a changing market. Orichalcum almost went out of use, the dupondius and As were struck so carelessly that their weights constantly overlapped, and only the radiate crown of the dupondius remained to distinguish it from the As (Plate XXIX, 3). The debasement of the denarius led to a reduction of weight in the base metal, which did not, however, keep pace with it; the Senatorial coinage began to be relatively valuable and was hoarded. The final crash under Gallienus deprived it of its *raison d'être* and it practically ceased to be issued. Again we presume, without certainty, that as before, the denarius contained 4 sestertii, 8 dupondii or 16 Asses. In the confusions of the reign of Valerian and Gallienus debasement went to the extreme limits. Prices soared. Gold was no longer issued except for gifts to the troops; it was probably exchanged against the miserable billon at rates varying in the market.

For gold we cannot be sure of a fixed standard, until Diocletian issues his pieces of one-seventieth of the gold pound, marked with the Greek numer *o* (Plate XXVII, 8). Pure silver was struck only by the British Emperor Carausius at a standard of about 50 gr. (3·24 gm.), and, even here, plated coins are not uncommon. The main coinage is of base billon, containing about 4 per cent. of silver. The only piece that is at all common has the radiate crown and the module of the 'Antoninianus' and weighs about 60 gr. (3·89 gm.). It is frequently marked *XX, XX.I, XXI, KA,K.A*, and it may now be taken as almost certain that all these varied marks have but one meaning; the coin is a unit containing twenty smaller units.[1] A smaller billon coin, occasionally marked *VSV* in exergue under Aurelian and Severina, weighs about 38 gr. (2·46 gm.), and one smaller still, struck by Aurelian's successors, weighs about 25 gr. (1·62 gm.). Copper is struck in three or four denominations – about 300 gr. (?) (19·44 gm.), about 230 gr. (14·9 gm.), about 120 gr. (7·77 gm.), falling to about 90 gr. (5·83 gm.), and about 30 gr. (1·94 gm.).

So much for the coins. The problem that faced Aurelian was the restoration of the coinage from the degradation into which it had sunk under Gallienus.[2] That he honestly attacked it is certain; what is doubtful is, whether he attempted a complete restoration by making his 'Antoninianus' of bad billon pass as the old 'Antoninianus' of Caracalla or whether he was content to assign to it a value, well below its original value but also well in advance of the low value to which it must have fallen in its worst period. We know that the reckoning in sestertii was still in force as late as c. A.D. 295; but the mark of value, *XX*, on Aurelian's 'Antoniniani' shows us that we have now to deal with a decimal system, in place of the division of the denarius into 16 Asses. When we come to Diocletian's reform of A.D. 296, we find that he issues a new coin of about 150 gr. (9·72 gm.) to represent two of his units of account, the 'denarii communes', which represent about 1/50,000th part of the pound of gold, but incorporates the 'Antoninianus' of Aurelian in his system as a subdivision of the larger coin. The 'twenty' piece of Aurelian is no longer the 'twenty' piece under Diocletian, but something smaller; either the value of the coin or the unit of reckoning has been changed. We might have been tempted to select the latter alternative, but the evidence of a papyrus compels us to prefer the former.[3] It probably belongs to the end of the third century and records a reduction of the 'Italian coinage' to the half of a 'nummus'. This, if our date be correct, is definite evidence for a reduction of the value of the piece of Aurelian; if, as seems natural, 'nummus' here means 'sestertius', it records a reduction to a half of its value.[4]

We can now attempt to reconstruct the system of Aurelian. He wished to restore a coinage that would express real values, but lacked the silver necessary for a pure coinage. His new 'Antoninianus', like

---

[1] *XXI* can conceivably mean 'twenty units – one unit'; but *XX.I* could hardly mean 'twenty-one units'. Missong first made this point clear in *N.Z.*, 1869, pp. 105 and especially 112 ff.

[2] Cp. H. Mattingly, 'Sestertius and Denarius under Aurelian', *Num. Chron.*, 1927, pp. 219 1 ff.

[3] Cp. article in ibid., 1927, p. 225, 'Sestertius and Denarius under Aurelian'.

[4] See below, p. 195.

the old one of Caracalla, still contained two denarii[1] but of a value much reduced from the old. It seems probable that the old reckoning in sestertii was still in use and that Aurelian regarded his new coin as a sestertius; the denarius, then, will have declined from being four sestertii to being a half of one. The second billon piece will be the denarius itself; vsv, which is found on it as a mark of value, will mark it as the *denarius communis*, the coin of common account.[2] The values of the bronze coins of Aurelian can only be guessed at. Were the three denominations sestertius, dupondius and As?

We arrive, then, at some system like this:

> 1 lb. AV = c. 60 aurei = c. 3,000 XXI pieces (double denarii) – sestertii = c. 6,000 denarii (vsv pieces) = c. 12,000 smallest billon pieces (Plate XXVII, 7, also Plate XXVIII, 11, Probus) = 60,000 of the little subdivisions of the XXI piece.

Under Tacitus, Carus and Carinus we find on pieces more or less closely resembling the normal XX piece, the marks of value *I.A, X.I, X.I.I, X.ET.I*. These are probably anticipations of the reform of Diocletian: the value of the piece is to be reduced to just a half of its tariff under Aurelian.[3] What value Carausius assigned to his silver coins is unknown, but it must have been something like the one-thousandth part of the gold pound. Diocletian's aurei of one-seventieth of a gold pound will not fit exactly into the system we have proposed. It is possible that, by a slight readjustment,

> 1 AV lb. = 70 aurei = c. 2,800 XXI pieces = c. 5,600 denarii = c. 11,200 smallest billon = c. 56,000 subdivisions of the XXI piece.

The view of Aurelian's reform here presented has no claim to finality, but it is unlikely that it is seriously at fault. Aurelian did not attempt the impossible – to restore a coinage of silver value without the necessary metal. Though he still struck a double denarius, he assigned to it no more than the value of a sestertius. Diocletian, when he restored with the good silver the old value of the denarius, was able

---

[1] Cp. Seeck in *N.Z.*, 1896, pp. 171 ff.: 'Sesterz und Follis'. Whether the unit of the piece was an As of the denarius (restored to its old rate of ten, instead of sixteen Asses), or a 'libella', a tenth of the sestertius, may be left in doubt. Traces of a similar decimal reckoning are to be found in the late Greek bronze of Asia Minor, with marks of value IB (twelve), IA or I (ten): these seem to be described as Asses.

[2] Cp. Babelon, *Note sur quelques Exagia Solidi*, etc., Paris, 1918.

[3] The counter-marking of copper of southern Asia Minor of the size of the I (10) piece with the mark ε (5) would be an exact parallel.

to incorporate the system of Aurelian into his own. Once again we see that the reform of Diocletian, imposing as it is at first sight, does not really represent any very decisive change: it is only the completion of the work of the great restoring Emperors who had preceded him. We can now add one item of considerable interest. The reform coin, the XXI piece, of Aurelian, was steadily resisted in the West of the Empire. The provincials were not content with the surrender value attached to it and clung to the old bad billon of Gallienus, Claudius and the Gallic Emperors. Hence come the many hoards of this billon all over the West. When Carausius made his peace with the Empire he placed the XXI on his coins – only to remove it again when the peace was broken.[1]

3. MINT AUTHORITIES. EMPEROR AND SENATE. ORGANIZATION OF THE MINT

The issue of coins was, as we have seen, divided between the Emperor, issuing gold and silver in his own right, and the Senate, striking *Aes* with mark s.c. on propositions made by him. *Aes* without s.c. could at any time be issued; after Gallienus it was the only *Aes* surviving. Of the circulation of the *Aes* we are not certain; perhaps, originally, it was intended mainly for Rome and Italy; it may then have spread over the West, except so far as the mint of Lugdunum supplied the need; in the East it was always rare. The Senate had never more than a nominal control; the grip of the Emperor on Treasury and coinage seems to have become ever firmer with the lapse of time.

The mint of the Emperor was under the general control of the chief financial minister, the 'a rationibus'. A special procurator of the mint is first met with under Trajan. The provincial mints probably fell to the charge of the provincial procurators; special procurators of the mint in the provinces only appear in the third century.[2] The Senatorial mint must have been under the general oversight of the heads of the Senatorial treasury, the 'aerarium Saturni' – from Nero on, 'praefecti aerarii', nominated by the Emperor. The 'III viri a.a.a.f.f.'[3] are proved by inscriptions to have existed as late as the early third century, and were presumably still employed on the Senatorial – if not on the Imperial – coinage; their names, however, do not appear on gold and silver after 12 B.C. or on 'Aes' after c. 4 B.C. The Senatorial mint of the

[1] H. Mattingly, *Studies in Roman Economic and Social History in Honour of A. C. Johnson*, 1951 ('The Clash of the Coinages', pp. 275 ff.).
[2] Cp. for Treveri, *C.I.L.*, VI, 1641.
[3] The retention of the old title was probably a mere piece of conservatism.

Republic had been housed in the temple of Juno Moneta on the Capitol; the Imperial mint in the reign of Trajan was in the fifth region, near the Baths of Trajan. Beyond this we are left to conjecture. It is best to assume for the time that the Senatorial mint remained under the same roof as before and that the Imperial mint was from the first in the fifth region. It has been suggested, on slight evidence, that Domitian housed the two mints in the same building.[1] The coinage of Nero, Vespasian Titus and Domitian, considered in relation to the Great Fires of Rome, may help to throw light on the matter. The decline in the 'Aes' coinage of Nero in the very last years of his reign, though not directly due to the great fire of A.D. 64, may be connected with a subsequent reorganization of the mint; the gold and silver is not affected. The destruction of the Capitol by fire in December, A.D. 69, must have affected the Senatorial mint, if it was still in the temple of Juno Moneta. As a matter of fact, 'Aes' of the first year of Vespasian is very rare at Rome, whereas gold and silver are plentiful enough. The great fire of A.D. 80 under Titus seems to have affected both mints – at any rate there is little or no coinage at Rome in any metal during the last year of the reign. Domitian in A.D. 81 strikes in all metals, but suspends his 'Aes' issues in A.D. 82, and commences in A.D. 83 with a new selection of reverse types, including the new type of *Moneta Aug*. It looks as if Domitian first restored the Imperial mint to working order and temporarily had 'Aes' issued from it, then, after an interval of a year, reopened the Senatorial mint in a building of its own. The evidence of the coins cannot be considered decisive, but it certainly suggests that the two mints were still separate.[2]

For the internal organization of the mints we depend on a few scattered inscriptions, mainly relating to the Imperial mint under Trajan, and on the evidence of the coins themselves. The Imperial mint was staffed with freedmen and slaves, was organized on military lines, and was under the superintendence of an 'optio et exactor auri argenti et aeris'; this title seems to indicate that the supply of all metals was in the same hands. The workmen fell into four main classes:

(1) The skilled artists, 'scalptores', who engraved the dies.

(2) The 'officinatores', the unskilled workers, including the 'flaturarii' (casters), the 'aequatores' (trimmers), the 'malleatores' (strikers) and the 'suppostores', who held the dies in position under the hammer.

---

[1] Mowat in *N.Z.*, 1909, pp. 87 and especially 95 ff.

[2] All this is interesting but speculative; see what is written on the subject in *B.M.C. Empire*, III. Cp. also D. E. MacDowell in a dissertation on the coinage of Nero, awaiting publication.

From an early date in the Empire, die-position is regular, and we must assume that the adjustment of the dies to one another could be accurately determined. The 'signator' was an important official, connected with the actual striking: he probably superintended operations and may have been responsible for affixing some mark, which would identify the issue to which any coin belonged.

(3) The 'nummularii' – probably State bankers, whose duty it was to bring the new money on to the market. Their duties would include the receipt of obsolete coin or bullion and the issue of new money in its place.

(4) The 'dispensatores', or accountants, who kept the books.

Exaggerated ideas of the numbers of men employed have been founded on the account of the war of the moneyers under Aurelian, which is said to have cost thousands of lives. In point of fact it is doubtful whether more than a couple of hundred men at the outside were employed. It must be remembered that, according to the ancient practice, only a part of the work was directly run by the State. Part was let out on private tender – as, for example, the casting of the blanks for the coinage.[1] General analogies lead us to suppose that direct State management came more and more into force in the second and third centuries. The information we have been considering applies mainly to the Imperial mint under Trajan; it is unlikely, however, that procedure varied very much, either at different periods or in the Senatorial mint.

It was clearly a matter of great importance to establish a firm control over the workers and to ensure that the responsibility for the issue of coin should be brought home to the right quarter. A division of the mints into 'shops' or 'officinae' is certain for the second to third centuries and is inherently probable for the first. Mint-marks of any kind are rare in the first two centuries; they begin to be common under Gallienus and mark not only the mint, but the 'officina' and the particular issue to which each coin belongs. Curiously enough, the gold is less regularly and fully marked than the billon. That the authorities, however, had at all times means of fixing responsibility is made probable (1) by general considerations and analogies, (2) by the existence of a separate officer styled 'signator'. We can hardly resist the conclusion that coins at all times bore certain 'privy marks', which would identify their issues and that all that was done in the third century was to make this control apparent to the general public, particularly in the case of the billon

---

[1] Cp. *B.M.C. Empire*, I, p. lx, and n. 2.

where abuses were most to be feared. Such abuses might take two forms: (1) coins of irregular weight or alloy might be issued from the mint; (2) coins might be issued by the regular moneyers outside the official premises. Both forms of abuse were evidently rampant in the time of Aurelian and the second form, which might involve many who were not regular mint officials, may account for the huge dimensions assured by the 'war of the moneyers' under the dishonest finance minister of Aurelian, Felicissimus.

The temptation to the mint officials to tamper with the weight and title of the coin obviously became acute when the State itself set the evil example. Debasement of the gold was never common; that of the silver began, we have seen, under Nero and went to desperate extremes in the third century. But even the early Empire has not escaped suspicion of dishonesty; the existence of masses of plated coins of the Emperors, from Augustus to Nero, has led to the belief that these formed part of the regular issues, that the Government, in fact, was not true to the standards it had itself set up. The evidence is conflicting and hard to sum up. The plated coins are often irregular in style and in details of type and legend, and thus betray their unofficial origin; often, again, they might pass for official money. We have also to remember that the melting down of pre-Neronian gold and silver would naturally not extend to plated pieces. We shall not be far wrong if we conclude that the plated coins are mainly forgeries, that Augustus and Tiberius did not countenance their official issue, but that Caligula and Claudius, under whom they are particularly common, possibly relaxed their diligence here. After Nero, when the State avowedly debased its silver, we do not expect to find it resorting further to plating; and, as a matter of fact, most plated coins are now obviously forgeries and often combine obverses and reverses that could never occur together on regular issues.

Of the different meanings usually attached to the words 'style' and 'fabric', and of the use of the two as criteria of date and mintage, we have already spoken in our first book. It is remarkable, in view of the immense volume of the Imperial coinage, how uniform the style of a mint can be over considerable periods; we can often trace the individual work of particular artists or schools of artists, almost as clearly as in the case of larger works of art. Good examples may be found in the coinage of Augustus, of Nero, of Hadrian, of Septimius Severus, and of the Emperors from Tacitus to Diocletian in Gaul. The explanation, no doubt, is that a single fine model might be very closely copied by pupils or even multiplied mechanically by the process of 'hubbing'.[1] The most striking feature is the care bestowed on the obverse. It is hardly too much to say that all the best ability of the time went to the rendering of the features of the Emperor; the reverses were treated with much less care and are hardly ever of much artistic value, however interesting their subject-matter may be. But even here there is some advance in conception, if not in execution; the large field of the sestertius, in particular, lent itself to elaborate compositions, which occasionally, as in the 'Annona Augusti Ceres' group of Nero, achieve real distinction. The nationality of Imperial art was undoubtedly mainly Greek; the best work follows the Greek tradition, and is most probably due to Greek artists, drawn to Rome by the prospects of advancement. What Rome contributes is mainly the new direction given to artistic impulse – the concentration on portraiture and the interest in matters of immediate interest rather than in general types and abstractions. The local art of the West, as seen, for example, in the coinages of Gaul, Spain and Africa in the years after A.D. 68, and in the Lugdunum coinage of Albinus, is technically weak, though not wanting in ambitious design. The best coinage of the Gallic Empire reaches a very high level, but we are less certain here of the local character of the art. The coinages of the Illyrican district are frequently rough and uncouth. In the East itself we find occasional work of exceptional beauty, as, for example, on the gold of Augustus, and on the Ephesus coins of Vespasian. In general, the coins bear out the view that the best of Greek artists worked at Rome itself. Fabric is usually fairly uniform for any given period at any one mint and is a very valuable aid to classification. Even where the art ranges from high to low levels, uniformity in lettering, in size of flan, in the exact method of striking, often enables us to determine the issues of a mint.

We have just spoken of the uniformity of style in the different mints. There are, however, variations within the same mint from 'officina' to 'officina', which show differing renderings of the same general model. A large find of coins of the reign of Trajan Decius was very instructive in this respect.[2] It was possible to distinguish varieties of portraiture, which almost certainly correspond to the different 'officinae' of the mint. The lessons of this find were most promising for future work; they suggest the possibility of gradually extending our knowledge of

[1] That is, by the production of a number of identical dies in incuse from one original in relief.

[2] Cp. *Num. Chron.*, 1924, pp. 210 ff. Much further information about officinae was derived from 'The Great Dorchester Hoard', H. Mattingly, ibid., 1939, pp. 1 ff.

the Imperial coinages into details, so that we may be able to state with confidence, not only at what mint, but at what period of the mint and in what sections coins were struck.

4. CHRONOLOGY AND MINTS

Questions of chronology bulk less large here than in the Republican coinage, inasmuch as the reign is usually given by the obverse portrait, while the details of the Imperial title often give an exact date to a year or part of a year. Inside each reign there will be development of portraits, it may be, of obverse legend, which will help to date by periods. A certain number of coins are dated by consulships of the Emperor. The 'imperator' title, with numbers, often gives a close dating, where these titles can be associated with particular victories. Most important are the datings of the tribunician power, which, when numbered, gives a particular year. The one serious drawback is that the power could be reckoned in several different ways: (1) year by year from the date of first conferment ('a die in diem'), (2) from December 9th, the old day on which the tribunes entered on office; the first year would be a broken one up to that date, (3) by calendar years, after a first broken year up to December 31st. It is impossible to give any general solution; detailed research, reign by reign, is needed. Fortunately, the uncertainties that arise are usually of a few months only. Dates can often be obtained from reference to historical events. The 'vota' coins of the Emperor are also valuable for dating.[1] 'Vota V' began to be celebrated at the end of the fourth year of a reign, 'Vota X' from the end of the ninth year and so on. The 'vota' are reckoned from the first day on which the 'imperium' was conferred. Here too a difficulty arises. 'Vota V mult. X' might come at the end of the fourth year, 'vows for five years paid, vows for ten undertaken with increase'; but it could also mean 'vows undertaken at the beginning of a reign for five years, with increase for ten'. The differing use must be studied from period to period. In general, we may say that most imperial coins can be dated, if not to exact years, at least to periods of years not exceeding five. A few cases remain where expert knowledge must be called to our aid.

(a) There are certain coins of the Empire that bear no Imperial portrait. Most of these belong to the Civil Wars of A.D. 68–69. The attribution is determined by weight, style and similarity to contemporary issues of Galba and Vitellius. An anonymous sestertius of c.

---

[1] Cp. H. Mattingly, 'The Imperial "Vota" ', *Proc. Brit. Acad.*, 1950, 1951.

270 has on obverse the portrait of the Genius of the Roman people, on reverse s.c. int. vrb. in wreath (Plate XXIX, 4). The reference certainly is to a ceremonial entry of the Genius into Rome ('introitus'). But is the reference to Gallienus as Genius P.R. (Alfoeldi's view)? Or is it rather to the establishment of the cult of Genius P.R. by Aurelian? The portrait is certainly like Gallienus; but may he not have been popular in Rome, so that the copying of his features might be intentional? There is not, as we used to think, any reference to the 'interregnum' after the death of Aurelian.

(*b*) Issues struck in honour of members of the Imperial family. These are frequently commemorative in character, and have to be dated on grounds of style and historical probability. The As of Agrippa was certainly struck long after his death – almost certainly by Caligula. The memory of Augustus was kept in honour long after his death – by Tiberius, Caligula, Claudius, Galba, Titus and Nerva. The sestertius of Britannicus may not have been issued till the reign of Titus, who had been his intimate friend in boyhood.[1] The dated coinage of Alexandria is often most valuable in supplying probable dates for undated Roman issues.

(*c*) Issues struck in honour of Emperors after their death. The deserving Emperor was in the normal course consecrated, and bears the title 'divus' on his posthumous coinage. The bad Emperor suffered 'damnatio memoriae'. A number of cases remain in which Emperors, though not consecrated, were honoured after their death with coinage bearing the titles of their lifetime. Caligula struck a coin that might represent the deified Tiberius; but he added no identifying legend and, finally yielding to the opposition of the Senate, substituted the portrait of the divine Augustus.[2] Coins of Spain under Galba show Augustus, with his lifetime titles, as well as 'divus'. Galba himself received back his honours from Vespasian, among them perhaps the honour of a posthumous coinage.[3] The theory of a large posthumous issue for Hadrian by Antoninus Pius is now abandoned. It is ruled out by the evidence of hoards. But there *was* a fight over the consecration of Hadrian which was not settled overnight, and, while that fight was on, a few rare coins may have been issued for Hadrian. Other such issues – perhaps for Trajan Decius under Trebonianus Gallus – may still await discovery. We must not be misled by a false calculation of probabilities

[1] H. Mattingly, 'Britannicus and Titus', *Num. Chron.*, 1930, pp. 2 ff.
[2] Cp. *J.R.S.*, 1920, p. 37.
[3] Cp. *Num. Chron.*, 1922, pp. 186 ff. Kraay has recently contested this view; see above, p. 109, n. 3.

here. Wherever we have a case of doubt as to whether an Emperor was definitely consecrated or condemned, the possibility of posthumous coinage, without the title 'divus', must be carefully considered.[1]

(*d*) Issues struck in honour of the deified Emperors and Empresses and their kindred. Such coins are normally issued by the immediate successor and can be readily dated. But here, too, exceptions occur. 'Divus Augustus' is honoured by Caligula, Claudius, Galba, Titus, Domitian and Nerva. 'Diva Augusta' (Livia) by Claudius and Galba. Trajan has a gallery of his divine predecessors, in which Tiberius, though not a god, is allowed a place. A series of coins of the 'divi' of about the middle of the third century, long attributed to Philip I or Gallienus, may now be assigned with confidence to Trajan Decius and may be regarded as a part of the religious policy which involved the first general persecution of the Christians.

Even these few examples will show that, even in the Empire, the scientific study of chronological detail cannot safely be neglected.

The evidence of finds[2] has already been used at various points of the argument, but there may be room for a summary of it here. Pre-Neronian gold and silver very rarely occur after the reform of Nero; Republican denarii are occasionally found, but very seldom after this same date. The one exception consists in the legionary coinage of Mark Antony, which, by its very baseness, escaped the melting-pot, and occurs in hoards as late as the middle of the third century. With hoards of the very early Empire Gallic coins are occasionally interspersed, and later, provincial or local silver, as of Lycia or Amisus, is not infrequently found with the Imperial. From Nero to Gallienus the silver is hoarded as a single series – coins of Domitian and Nerva, which seem to have represented an improvement on the Neronian standard, are seldom found. Denarii and 'Antoniniani' are often found in quantity in the same hoards. Finds of gold often cover considerable periods of time and show progressive degrees of wear: they do not, on the whole, bear out Mommsen's view that gold went out of circulation very rapidly. The aurei of Domitian and Nerva, which revert to something like the pre-Neronian standard, are absent. 'Aes' was not very much hoarded until the third century, when the debasement of the silver enhanced its relative value. The debased billon of Gallienus and his successors is, on the whole, clearly separated in hoards, both from the

---

[1] I allow this to stand as an innocent guess; but the quest for posthumous coinages must not be pressed too far.
[2] For finds see also Appendix.

earlier silver and from the later 'reformed' billon of Aurelian. The debased billon of the Gallic Empire is often associated with masses of similar Roman coins in Gallic hoards; the two currencies, being of about equal badness, ran side by side, but Gallic money was apparently not very willingly accepted by the Empire. It seems that the basest billon lived on in circulation in the West for a generation, while the reform coin of Aurelian was steadily resisted. The reformed coins of Aurelian and his successors are usually found by themselves with only slight admixtures from earlier times.

The general question of classification by mints was fully treated in the first chapter of Book I; we have here to consider it in its special application to the Empire. Is classification by mints really desirable here, or should the chronological order have the supremacy throughout and should attributions to mints be relegated to the notes? To this question we must return an emphatic answer in the negative. The mints of the Empire are, in the great majority of cases, not simply subordinate branches of the central mint of Rome, but independent organizations with traditions of their own. If the issues of provincial mints are scattered over the mass of the coinage, we gain no true conception of these smaller bodies; all that happens is that our picture of the mint of Rome becomes somewhat blurred or distorted. It is only with the closer attribution to mints that the coinage of Augustus has become intelligible. The issues of the Civil Wars of A.D. 68 to 69 are partly meaningless, partly misleading, until we can distribute them locally. The determination of the mints of Vespasian illustrates the political history and throws light on his general policy. In the period after Severus, the tracing of the issues of Antioch and Milan throws a flood of light on the direction in which coinage was moving. Unless we are content to remain in permanent ignorance of many facts of historical value and to run the risk of drawing entirely erroneous conclusions from details of types, it is essential that we should determine not only when but where each coin was struck.

But, granting the necessity of such a classification, how are we to arrive at it? There is no short cut to success; long practice in distinguishing differences of style and fabric and discovering which of these are characteristic of different mints is essential; only in this way can the various local groups be separated off. History, then, comes to our assistance. In the early Empire we are led first by a consideration of the conditions prevailing at the end of the Republic and by the general policy of Augustus. Later, after Nero, we have to study the history of the movements in the provinces that led to the elevation of new Emperors. Later again, after Septimius Severus, when provincial coinage had come to stay, we have to follow the trend of the campaigns, trace the movements and consider the needs of the armies. The study of types is valuable as a confirmation of our results, and comparison with local issues in copper will often supply useful clues. But here a word of warning is needed. Similarity of style to local issues does not prove local striking; at the most it suggests the probability that the area of circulation was the same. The evidence of types again can be positively misleading. The central mint of Rome must obviously often have had occasion to celebrate events of particular local interest in the provinces, and, conversely, the provincial mints cannot be entirely indifferent to the course of events in the capital. Some critics have absolutely refused to countenance the attribution of a large series of coins of Augustus to Spain on the one ground that reference to events in the capital is writ large on them. The objection is really irrelevant. Augustus had definite reasons for issuing his coins in the provinces, but he had no reason for eliminating from them the reference to the seat of his Empire. The Spanish origin of the coins is adequately attested by historical considerations, as well as by style, and should not be doubted on *a priori* grounds, which take no account of the real facts of the case. It is unfortunately true that, in spite of all the labour that has been expended on them, our knowledge of Imperial mints is still far from satisfactory. Even where we can identify groups of coins not struck in Rome, we are often at a loss for an exact attribution to their locality. But sufficient ground has already been won to justify the highest hopes; and here, as often, it will be found that the path of greatest difficulty is also the path of highest promise.[1]

[1] This is a highly controversial subject: I do not wish to inflame controversy further by too positive a taking of sides. But let us hold fast to a couple of points:

(1) Differences on which a number of observers can agree must clearly exist. They are there, even if some scholars fail to see them. They can be seen, when the eye is sufficiently trained.

(2) Where differences of style, fabric, and choice of types are found together the only reasonable explanation is difference of mint. It is quite absurd to assume differences in all these points inside one mint at one and the same time.

CHAPTER II

The Content of the Early Imperial Coinage.[1]
Types and Legends

1. TRANSITION FROM THE REPUBLIC

By the end of the Republic we found that the coinage was fast out-growing the stereotyped and conventional forms in which it had begun. The official religion of the State still played an important part; but more often than not religious forms conveyed definite topical allusions and the minor deities or 'Virtues' were beginning to appear beside the greater gods. A great part of the space was allotted to mythological and antiquarian allusions, in which the families of the moneyers played an important role, while, beside the family allusions, reference to contemporary history was becoming increasingly common. Above all, interest in the individual was steadily on the increase; the portraits of great men of old are soon succeeded by the portraits of living statesmen and generals, and, even before the Empire, the coinage was assuming an Imperial tinge. The coming of the Empire marks no violent breach in the development, though, in the natural course of events, some features received new emphasis, while others fell into abeyance. With the dis-appearance of the moneyers from the coins, the glorification of the great families ceases; Augustus, indeed, allowed the moneyers of gold and silver to follow to some extent the old practice, but he had no intention of making it permanent. The interest in the individual was to be focused on the Emperor and the members of his family.

2. GENERAL PRINCIPLES

The movement of the later Republic had been all away from the stereotyped form to the free illustration of the life of the State, and the Empire, in the long run, only accelerated this movement. There was a

---

[1] Cp. C. H. V. Sutherland, 1951, on 'Early Imperial Coins'; P. L. Strack, 'Unter-suchungen, etc., Trajan to Antoninus Pius'. Introductions to *B.M.C.* and *R.I.C.*

moment in the early Empire, however, when a new set of conventions appeared likely to settle down on the coinage. The *Aes* of Augustus hardly varied from one or two fixed patterns. On the gold and silver the type of the two princes, C. and L. Caesar, remained in use for a long term of years, and Tiberius used the one reverse type of Pax Augusta during the greater part of his reign. With Caligula the tradition begins to give way. More and more freedom is introduced into the choice of types and by the reign of Vespasian we find ourselves in the full development of the Imperial coinage. Only on the half-piece of aureus and denarius, the quinarius or victoriate, was the standard type of Victory normally retained. The Imperial coinage, in fact, served not only the end of currency, but most of the uses of the modern medal. The accession of a new Emperor, the adoption of a successor, important concessions to Senate or people, building of temples, roads or harbours, journeys in the provinces or victories over the foreign foe – one and all are brought to the public notice on the coins. In this use of the coin as a means of publicity is implied its use as an agency of propaganda. The Emperor ruled by tradition and consent, as much as by force; it was most important for him to have public opinion on his side. He therefore seized the opportunity that the issue of coins presented of showing events in the light in which he wished them to appear and of definitely announcing not only his actual achievements, but also his hopes and policy. A certain reserve is clearly needed in accepting such official bulletins, but their value for history is obvious.

Remembering that one branch of the coinage, the gold and silver, was directly in the hands of the Emperor, while another, the *Aes*, was run by him through the Senate, we look hopefully to find some distinctive differences between the two branches of coinage. At no time do we fail to note some difference in choice of types; certain events were specially chosen for representation on the *Aes*, sometimes because the large flan of the sestertius offered a better field for large scenes than the smaller denominations. But it is only in the first days of the Empire that the two branches fall really wide apart. The head of the Emperor appears on one denomination only of the *Aes*, on the As. Reference to him takes the form of laying stress on honours paid to him and on his position as 'tribunicia potestate' and 'pontifex maximus'. Great prominence is given to the mark s.c., which may be used as a main type. From the reign of Caligula we become conscious of an underlying unity of direction, which grows almost reign by reign. Even down into the third century slight evidences can be found which point to some difference in administration of the two branches, though they were now closely harmonized. We have already made it clear that, even in the early Empire, the Senate had no real independence; the Emperor could not risk having propaganda put out in a sense different from his own.

No clear picture of the varied wealth of allusion in the Imperial coinage can be given, except by a detailed study under various heads; but, before we proceed to this, we must clear the ground by stating some general guiding principles.

The obverse is normally given up to the 'image and superscription' of the reigning Emperor; only on the smaller denominations of 'Aes' are other obverses commonly found. The right of portraiture could, however, be extended either to a colleague in the Imperial power (e.g. Agrippa, Plate XXXV, 3), to the Empress or to a prince or princess of the house, or to some deified Emperor or other Imperial personage after death. Portraiture on the reverse, as a less important honour, was more freely delegated. Of the importance of this privilege there can be no question. The Emperor replaces the goddess Bellona of the Republic as the visible head of the Roman State; he is chary in the first place of sharing his right with others; when he begins to allow it freely to other members of his house, it clearly marks the fact that the Empire was gradually being transformed from an elective office into an hereditary monarchy. The illustrious dead of the Imperial house receive the honour at first more freely than the living; they were not to be feared as rivals. Obverses other than portraits hardly occur except on the 'Republican' issues of the Civil Wars of A.D. 68–69.

The legend of the obverse is normally in the nominative, marking the Emperor as the issuer of the coin. A dative, of dedication, is much less commonly found. The genitive of Republican tradition hardly occurs except on the issues of L. Clodius Macer in Africa. In the form of the Imperial name and in the choice of Imperial titles the greatest variety prevails. The praenomen is frequently omitted, the gentile name commonly, the family name seldom, if ever. The title 'Augustus', the most common designation of the reigning Emperor, is normally present; the family name of the first Emperors, 'Caesar', came to be associated with the successors of the Julio-Claudian line, and was frequently combined at the beginning of the title with the praenomen of imperator. That praenomen, which marked the Emperor as the one holder of supreme military power, was only occasionally used at first; later, it became more and more the common form. The use of the same title 'imperator' as cognomen, often with a numeral to denote the number of times that the Emperor had been acclaimed for victories won by himself or his legates, is particularly common in some reigns.[1] The consulship, the tribunician power, the chief priesthood, often figure in the title, and with them such titles of honour as 'Germanicus', 'Dacicus' 'Britannicus', conferred in honour of particular victories. The title of 'Pater patriae', the most distinguished that an Emperor could bear, was often added as a particular compliment. The kinship of the Emperor to his predecessors in office is often indicated by such titles as 'Divi F.', 'Divi Augusti F.', 'Divi Nervae Nepos', or by the use of the dead Emperor's name as part of the new Imperial title.[2] Other titles, such as censor (Vespasian, Titus, Domitian) or proconsul (Nero (?), Dio-cletian), are far less common. In the third century the epithets 'Pius Felix' (*P.F.*) were freely embodied in the official style. The Empress or princess is regularly 'Augusta', the prince, who is not actually a colleague, 'Caesar'; the use of this family title to mark the prince of the blood can be traced as early as Titus and Domitian. The epithets, 'Divus', 'Diva', mark the consecrated Emperor or Empress.

The legend of the reverse is sometimes a mere continuation of the obverse; it completes the Imperial title, without reference to the type. Normally, the legend is direct and descriptive, defining the deity or 'Virtue' or event portrayed in the type. Frequently we have a deictic nominative – simply pointing to the type. Less commonly we have a dative of dedication or a genitive of possession; the ablative of attendant circumstances is excessively rare.[3] An occasional accusative without government must be understood as governed by a verb implied. The Emperor of the obverse, for instance, erects a statue of Mars and expresses the fact by the accusative 'Martem' on the reverse.[4] Often legends are formed by complete phrases, or even sentences, describing an elaborate type; we need only instance Nero's 'Pace P.R. terra marique parta Ianum clusit' or Trajan's 'Regna adsignata' or 'Armenia et Mesopotamia in potestatem P.R. redactae'. The types demand a fuller and more classified treatment, to which we can now proceed.

Imperial coins occasionally make a fresh contribution to history in periods where the literary tradition is scanty. All along the line they supply interesting illustrations of facts already known. In their continuity they help a little towards correcting the broken character of most of our records.

[1] e.g. under Claudius I, Domitian and Septimius Severus.
[2] Cp. Nerva Traianus, Traianus Hadrianus, Hadr. Antoninus, etc.
[3] Cp. coins of the Civil Wars of A.D. 68, 'florente fortuna P.R.'.
[4] So Caracalla.

The obverses present a remarkable gallery of portraits; we can know the Emperors as well as if we had met them personally. Variations of obverse type supply some idea of the way in which the Emperors wished to be regarded, The bare head suggests the 'princeps', the laureate wreath the 'imperator', the radiate crown the sun-god as type of the Emperor. An occasional divine attribute assimilates the Emperor to a deity – the aegis to Minerva, the club to Hercules. The cuirass and paludamentum on the bust suggest the general; the bare bust seems to suggest the hero.

But it is to the reverses that we must look for closer information. In nearly every reign we find some events passed over in silence, others brought into great prominence. Augustus lays emphasis on his honours as restorer of the Republic and as the author of triumphs over Parthia and Armenia, not so much is said of the campaigns in Germany – not a word, of course, about the disaster of Varus. The types, IMPER. RECEPT. and PRAETOR RECEPT. of Claudius I do not add to our historical knowledge; but they *do* show that the Emperor chose to insist on the way in which he had come to the throne.

But what are we to say of the great masses of coins of general character? The historian is tempted to dismiss them lightly as too general to be of much service. It must be admitted that the task of making sense of them is a difficult and uncertain one. But we have only to compare the coinage of successive reigns to see that there is not mere caprice, but method in the selection. The pattern is woven deliberately and must have a meaning. We may begin by reminding ourselves that gods and virtues carry definite meanings, if of a general kind; Jupiter denotes the lord of the Roman world, the protector of the Emperor; Mars stands for the risks and triumphs of war, Neptune for comings and goings by sea. Ceres, the goddess of the corn, represents the imperial corn-supply, Venus the love of Emperor and Empress, Minerva the arts, Diana war and the chase. The Virtues have their own range of meanings. Pax refers to peace in the world, in the State, in religion. Felicitas is the blessedness that radiates out from the Emperor to his subjects, Salus shows his salvation and his power to save, Providentia his divine wisdom – in provision for the succession, or for the corn-supply or, maybe, for defence against a pretender. Out of these diverse deities and Virtues mosaics are constructed with well-defined patterns. A picture of the Government is built up, as it wished itself to be seen.

What we really gain, then, is some knowledge of the views that successive Emperors took of themselves. The general shape of a reign is known from history; the coins give the added colouring that was chosen by the Emperor. The numismatist can lead the historian to a position from which he can gain some new views to enrich his historical outlook.

3. TYPES CLASSIFIED

(a) Types of the Emperor and his Family

A very large part of the whole Imperial coinage might be brought under this heading; for convenience, however, we will confine ourselves here to types having a more special reference to the Imperial family, leaving to the separate sections on religion, the State, the provinces, the army, those types in which the interest is divided between the Emperor and such other themes.

The mere fact of striking a coin with one's portrait constituted as definite a claim to Empire as can well be imagined.[1] Special honours would often be commemorated (cp. Plate XXXV, 1, 2), but there was no one special reverse type that represented a claim to Empire. Such a one has been seen in the oak-wreath, presented by the Senate to the Emperor as 'Saviour of his country' (Plate XXXV, 4); but this type was only struck for some Emperors, and not always at the beginning of the reign. Each Emperor celebrated his accession by such choice of types as seemed to answer the immediate needs of the time. The most distinctive Imperial title, 'Augustus', is regularly assumed by the claimant to Empire; reference to the component parts of the Imperial power, the 'imperium' and the 'tribunicia potestas', though common, is by no means universal.

A certain number of types present the Emperor in a variety of formal aspects, as 'rector orbis' with rudder on globe (Plate XXXV, 8), as priest sacrificing, as general armed or haranguing the troops, as guardian of the Empire, with spear and globe, or globe and sceptre (Plate XXXV, 15), or as maintainer of peace with branch and sceptre. We see him as a warrior riding, sometimes hunting wild beasts, some-

---

[1] The pretender in the provinces – e.g. Pescennius Niger, Albinus, Pacatian – regularly issues coin. It was unusual, however, for an Emperor to take the trouble to suppress such issues. History records usurpation of right of portraiture in a number of cases where the coins are silent – e.g. for Perennis under Commodus (*Herodian*, I, 9, 7), Valerius Paetus under Elagabalus (*Dio Cassius*, LXXIX, 4). Many of the 'Thirty Tyrants' of Gallienus's day have left no record on coins: perhaps in some cases the usurper only knew of his usurpation when the order for his execution arrived: we remember that Gallienus was responsible for excluding senators from provincial governorships.

times riding down a foeman. Similarly, the Empress appears as priestess, as 'mother of the camp', as 'mother of the Senate' (Plate XXXV, 12), as goddess (Vesta, Venus, Ceres, Cybele) or as 'Virtue' (Constantia, Pax Augusta). The harmony in the Imperial family, particularly the wedded bliss of Emperor and Empress, is represented by types of Concordia or by figures clasping hands, sometimes presided over by Concordia (cp. Plate XXXV, 13). Other types are more definitely dynastic. The 'Aeternitas Imperi', of Septimius Severus, with the heads of the Emperor and his family (Plate XXXV, 11, cp. also 17), the later 'Felicitas Saeculi', 'Felicitas Temporum', all point to the members of the Imperial house as the surety for the continuance of the prosperity of the Empire and its Golden Age. The 'Pietas Augusti' of Titus (Plate XXXV, 6), that shows him clasping hands with Domitian, represents a pious hope of fraternal concord that was only imperfectly realized. The vital question of the succession was always to the fore. Apart from adoption types of a formal nature, as, for instance, that of Hadrian adopted by Trajan (Plate XXXV, 5) or Trajan adopted by Nerva, we find the type of Providentia used with special reference to the wisdom that leads the Emperor to arrange for the succession (cp. Plate XXXV, 7). The 'Providence' is usually that of the Emperor himself; occasionally the thought of the Divine Providence, which is behind him, received emphasis. The same idea, regarded rather from the point of view of the successor, is conveyed by the types of Spes, either alone or presiding over a group of Emperor and heir. The 'Concordia' of L. Aelius, who rests her arm on a statue of Spes, represents the harmony existing between the Emperor and his chosen successor. The idea of Providence implies some thought of conscious selection and is specially appropriate to the period in which the Emperor was succeeded by an adopted, rather than by a natural son. It is less to the fore when the dynastic principle gains strength and the Empire passes from father to son; the 'dynastic' types of which we spoke above then tend to take its place.

The princes of the Imperial house, and particularly the heir apparent, regularly bear the title 'Caesar' and are honoured as 'Principes Iuventutis', or 'Chiefs of the Knights' (cp. Plate XXXV, 14, 16). The Knights, the second order of the State, were organized in 'turmae' under leaders called 'severi'; they bestowed the title of 'Princeps Iuventutis' by acclamation on princes, who were certainly, as a rule, 'severi' of the first troop. Gaius and Lucius, the young grandsons of Augustus, were the first to be so acclaimed; then followed Nero and

Domitian and most of the princes of the Imperial house. It is note-worthy, however, that the title was felt to be suitable only for a young man: Tiberius as Caesar never held it, nor did L. Aelius Caesar – even the young Marcus Aurelius, though he has a type of 'Iuventus', is never directly honoured as 'Princeps Iuventutis'. The insignia of the office, as shown on coins, are naturally of a military character – shields, spears, standards, trophies – most characteristic of all, a small wand or baton. Often, naturally enough, the prince is represented on horseback. In the third century, the original use of the term was to some extent forgotten, its types are confused with those of the Emperor (Philip II, for example, carries the globe of Empire) and finally the title is occasion-ally borne by the Emperor himself.[1]

The Emperor who had deserved well of the State regularly received divine worship after death. He was consecrated, bore the title of 'Divus' and was worshipped as a god, with a *flamen* and *sodales* of his own. Temples were erected in his honour and sacrifices were offered at his altars. The bad Emperor suffered condemnation of his memory and had his acts annulled, except in so far as considerations of equity and expedience restricted so extreme a measure. A few Emperors – such as Tiberius and Galba – were left in a limbo between the imperial heaven and hell; though not consecrated, they were not condemned and might in some cases receive honours of coinage after death. Consecration was at first strictly reserved for the Emperor himself. The idea was certainly borrowed from the Eastern kingdoms of Syria and Egypt, where the king, even in his lifetime, ranked as a god. The consecration of Julius Caesar[2] was a powerful weapon in the hands of his avengers. The precedent once set was naturally repeated for Augustus and became a fixed part of the imperial tradition. The first woman to receive conse-cration was Livia – not, however, immediately after her death from Tiberius, but some years later under her grandson Claudius. Nero consecrated his baby daughter, and Domitian, not content with conse-crating his father and brother, extended the honour to his own infant son (Plate XXXVI, 3) and to Julia, daughter of Titus. He built a special temple to the 'Flavian house' and seems to have claimed divinity as an hereditary right of the family. Trajan himself consecrated his sister Marciana and his father, Trajan senior, as well as his pre-decessor Nerva. In the long run, however, the honour was usually con-

[1] e.g. by Probus, probably as a compliment to the great cavalry corps at Ticinum.
[2] Cp. Pl. XXXVI, 1, for the star which was taken to be the soul of the divine Julius. Pl. XXXVI, 2, shows a sort of unofficial consecration of Agrippa, if my interpretation of the somewhat mysterious type is correct.

fined to Emperor and Empress, and, when we reach the third century, mainly to the Emperor alone (but note exceptions, Paulina, Maziniana, Nigrinianus). Towards the close of that century, consecrations became few, whether because the violent successions precluded such honour of predecessors or because the popular interest in the cult was on the decline. The series of coins of the 'Divi' struck by Trajan Decius (Plate XXXVI, 11, 12) is probably the sign of a general endeavour to revive interest in religion, especially in the religion of the State, and has a definite relation to the persecution of the Christians in that reign. The symbolism of consecration is varied and picturesque (Plate XXXVI, 1–10).[1] There are such obvious types as the pyre, the altar, the temple, the statue of the new god. The soul of the dead Emperor was conceived of as borne skywards by an eagle (cp. the eagle of Divus Augustus, the eagle carrying Emperor, e.g. Hadrian, to the heaven of stars, which was to be his future home). Prominent therefore are the symbols of the sky and the sky-gods – the star, the rays of the sun, the thunderbolt of Jupiter. Particularly, in the case of the Empress, the new deity was assimilated to the divine powers, and we find as consecration types, Diana Lucifera with her torches, Ceres with her corn-ears and torch, Juno with her peacock, or the peacock as her emblem. The consecration of Faustina I was celebrated by a gallery of types of 'Aeternitas' (cp. Plate XXXVI, 9) and 'Augusta' represented with the attributes of goddesses, with the immortal bird, the phoenix, or with the mantle of the starry sky. A charming fancy of a moneyer of Domitian shows us the baby Caesar, the infant Zeus of Crete,[2] seated on the globe of the earth and stretching up his hands to the stars. Finally, to return from heaven to earth, a favourite theme of consecration types was the appearance of an effigy of the dead Emperor borne by a quadriga of elephants, the imperial beasts, in the 'circensis pompa' or solemn procession before the games in the circus.

The travels of the Emperor were a matter of direct public concern; apart from the importance of the duties, military or civil, that demanded his presence in the provinces, his coming or going had an interest for the people of Rome; did not their material wants and their pleasures depend largely on him? The arrival or departure of the Emperor is usually represented by a type on horseback – the prancing horse usually suggesting the riding abroad, the pacing horse the slow and solemn entry in procession (Plate XXXVI, 14, 17). In 'profectio' types the

---

[1] Pl. XXXVI, 4, consecration of Vespasian; the 'divus' is placed under the special protection of Jupiter and Mercury.   [2] Cp. A. B. Cook, *Zeus*, I, p. 51 f.

Emperor often holds a spear in rest, in 'adventus' types he often raises his right hand in acknowledgement of the plaudits of the crowd. More elaborate groups sometimes show the Emperor accompanied on his way by soldiers. Journeys by sea are represented by types of galleys (Plate XXXVI, 15, 16). Septimius Severus and Gordian actually use the legend 'traiectus', 'crossing'.

Of great importance in the social and economic life of Rome were the imperial largesses or 'liberalitates'. The custom of supplying the poor of Rome with necessaries such as corn or wine at reduced prices had been common under the Republic – partly as a form of private display, partly as a measure of State relief. The corn-doles of the Republic were constantly referred to under the symbolism of Ceres, goddess of corn, and Annona and Abundantia, the presiding spirits of the corn-supply. Above and beyond this the Emperors proceeded to distributions of money to the Roman poor, on the analogy of the donatives given to the troops. These 'congiaria' or 'liberalitates' (Plate XXXVII, 1, 2), as they came later to be called, were in the first century only sparingly given. Trajan increased the sums distributed and Hadrian and his successors made the distribution a prominent feature of their policy. These 'liberalitates', given at accession, at the return from travel, at the adoption of a successor, constituted a serious burden on the exchequer and contributed their share towards State bankruptcy. Necessary they may have been, popular they necessarily were and figure to a corresponding extent on the coinage. The most direct form of celebration is a distribution scene in which the Emperor, seated on a platform, presides over the distribution to citizens. Liberalitas, the spirit of the bounty, a normal subsidiary feature of these scenes, is often used as an independent type and to the attached legend, 'Liberalitas Augusti', a number denoting the particular bounty is often added. The type of Spes has sometimes a similar reference: here it is not 'Spes Augusta' but 'Spes P.R.' that is represented, the hopes of the people for the rising generation, who are to profit by the imperial generosity. The sister types of Aequitas and Moneta refer to the fairness of the Emperor in handling the general question of supply ('Annona') and of the mint. Aequitas normally holds rod, Moneta cornucopiae, but exchanges of attributes sometimes take place. In the third century a Moneta or Aequitas type, with three figures holding scales and cornucopiae and having beside them small piles of metal, becomes normal for the medallions of base silver (Plate XXIX, 6). Were these pieces standards, to show exactly what alloy was being used at the mint?

At the beginning of every year vows were undertaken and paid for the health and well-being of the Emperor – with special ceremony and solemnity at intervals of five or ten years; the Empire had at first been conferred not for life, but for terms of years, and some memory of this may survive in the Imperial vows. As occasions of public rejoicings and merry-making these vows figure largely on the coinage – sometimes with general types such as 'Pietas', sometimes with more specialized 'vota' types, explained by the legend, 'Vota P.R.', 'Vota Soluta V', Vota Suscepta X', etc. (Plates XXXV, 9; XXXVII, 8, 9). The usual type is a sacrifice scene,[1] with the Emperor sacrificing over an altar or in front of a temple, sometimes accompanied by other figures, a prince, attendants at the sacrifice, flute-players. Beside the regularly recurring 'vota', special vows were undertaken for particular occasions – for the recovery of the Emperor from illness, for his safe return from travelling abroad. The Roman State, which undertakes these vows, is sometimes represented by the Genius of the Senate and the Genius of the Roman people sacrificing together.

The triumphs of the Emperor, though springing from his connexion with the army, belong rather to his activities in Rome. They were celebrated with great pomp not only for victories won by the Emperor, but also at times for victories won by his lieutenants in the field. The normal type to celebrate them is the triumphal quadriga, in which stands the Emperor, holding the laurel-branch of victory and the eagle-tipped sceptre; sometimes more elaborate scenes, such as the 'Triump. Aug.' of Vespasian (Plate XXXVI, 13), offer some picture of the accompanying procession. An empty quadriga seems sometimes to stand for a triumph offered to the Emperor by the Senate, but not accepted by him. A more permanent record of Imperial victories is seen in the triumphal arches which were usually erected after successful campaigns, and appear on coins, inscribed with the name of the defeated enemy ('De Brit.', 'De Germ.').

(b) Types relating to the Senate and People of Rome

The management of the *Aes* coinage by the Senate is regularly attested by the *S.C.* of the reverse. On the gold and silver the Senate appears only indirectly, as the voter of honours, which the Emperor thinks fit to commemorate on his coinage; among such honours are the oak-wreath given to the 'Saviour of the State' or the posthumous

---

[1] Where the vows are 'soluta' a sacrificial beast normally appears—not when the vows are undertaken.

honours of a quadriga in the 'circensis pompa', voted to the deified Emperor. The more constitutional Emperors took pains to emphasize the harmony existing between them and the Senate. Galba celebrates the restoration of constitutional government (Plate XXXVII, 3). Vespasian won the goodwill of the body by restoring to honour the Senate's favourite, Galba; the occasion is commemorated by sestertii of Vespasian – one with posthumous portrait of Galba – with the legends 'Concordia Senatui' and 'Senatus Pietati Augusti' [1] and the type, a Senator crowning the Emperor. Trajan for years placed on his reverses the legend 'S.P.Q.R. Optimo Principi', in joyful recognition of the grateful acceptance that his wise government found. The personified Senate, represented by its Genius, a venerable elder, appears both on coins of Trajan and Antoninus Pius (Plate XXXVII, 7; cp. XXXV, 10, Hadrian). In the third century the Senate naturally falls into the background.

Consideration for the people of Rome was never far from the minds of the Emperor's advisers. The bad Emperor might neglect or flout the Senate; some respect for the people was essential unless he was to be exposed to constant unpleasantness and danger. Apart from the many types, such as the 'liberalitates', which directly concern the citizens of Rome, the Roman people finds direct mention on coins either under the guise of the 'Genius P.R.' (Plate XXXVII, 5) or in those personifications which are directly related to it, 'Spes P.R.', 'Felicitas P.R.', 'Hilaritas P.R.'; to these we may add 'Salus Publica', 'Fides Publica', 'Libertas Publica', and others. In all these cases the Government is at pains to show that the interests and needs of its people are not forgotten by it; the tradition of the Empire, which began as the defender and inheritor of the rights of the people, is steadily maintained.

(c) *Types relating to Rome, Italy, and the Provinces*

If in many points the cautious policy of Augustus commands more respect than the bold innovations of Julius Caesar, this can hardly be claimed for his treatment of the provinces. Julius Caesar, carrying out the policy of the democrats, seemed ready to hasten on the equalization of privilege and the broadening of the base of Empire. Augustus drew

---

[1] These two coins form a very strong argument for a posthumous coinage of Galba. The two legends that attend the one rare reverse type seem to complement one another: Concordia (the Emperor himself) pays tribute to the Senate, the Senate pays tribute to the piety of the Emperor – in honouring Galba. Kraay has claimed as a fatal objection that, on the coin of Galba, 'Augustus' would now have one meaning on the obverse, another on the reverse. But, if one Emperor were known to be paying honour to a predecessor, the references would be intelligible enough.

back on to the old conservative basis and initiated a policy of cautious reserve, which remained in force long after his death and fatally cramped and confined the possibilities of the Empire. The inevitable equalization of the provinces with Rome and Italy was delayed, until it was too late to bear much fruit.

The coinage faithfully mirrors this development. In the first century, the provinces hardly appear on coins, except as defeated subjects of Rome – represented by captive figures seated under trophies with bound hands and dejected mien (cp. Plate XXXVIII, 2, 3). The making of Emperors in Gaul and Spain brought these provinces to the fore; Gallia and Hispania appear as warrior goddesses, armed in defence of their claimant (cp. Plate XXXVIII, 1). Trajan devotes a peaceful type to his new province of Arabia, with her aromatic canes and her camel, and, after the multitude of Victory types showing the crushing of Dacia, presents Dacia as a new member of the Roman Commonwealth of nations (cp. the Danuvius type, for the province). Only under Hadrian, however, do the provinces really come into their own – and Hadrian was an isolated genius, whose ideas for the Empire found no successor to carry them out. Hadrian was the first of the Emperors to regard his Empire from any but a purely Roman point of view. His provincial birth, his natural curiosity, his far-sighted ability, combined to give him a wide outlook. He spent a large part of his reign in personally visiting the provinces, learning their problems at first hand, winning their confidence and satisfying their material needs. His magnificent series of types, struck in A.D. 134 to 135 as the crown of his life's work, shows the arrival of the Emperor in the various provinces (Plate XXXVIII, 16) – a scene of sacrifice – the restoration of the provinces – the Emperor raising a kneeling figure to her feet – the provinces themselves, represented as women in peaceful or warlike guise, with native dress and attributes (Plate XXXVIII, 6–11, 15, 17–19). Emphasis is deliberately laid on the local characteristic – the ibis of Egypt, the games of Achaea, the cities of Asia, the curved sword of Dacia. It is the peaceful provinces that are 'restored'; the warlike provinces have their army types instead. The Empire according to Hadrian was to be keenly alive not only at its centre but in all its parts. But Hadrian, as we have said, found no true successor. Antoninus Pius has, indeed, a series of provincial types, struck in connexion with the offering of crowns at his succession; but he was at heart a Roman and, with all his nobility of character, lacked something of understanding of what the Empire required. The series of later provincial types mainly refers, as before, to victories over rebels. The one great exception is the sudden rise of the Balkan provinces to Imperial importance with the accession of Trajan Decius; he introduces the types of Dacia, the two Pannoniae, and the Genius of the army of Illyricum (Plate XXXVIII, 12, 13) – a break with custom and no doubt no small shock to the civilians of Rome.

Direct reference to Italy, in spite of her privileged position, is not very common – we naturally think first of the 'alimentary' institutions of Trajan and his successors. Roma, the Amazon goddess, who typifies in some aspects the Roman State, was probably felt to stand for Italy as well.[1] She is commonly represented as a goddess armed, with short tunic, spear or parazonium and shield – occasionally with a Victory or inscribing a shield. Italy, as queen of the world, is represented on a sestertius of Antoninus Pius. An extension of the pomoerium finds its records in Trajan's type of colonist ploughing[2] (Plate XXXVII, 4).

The province is normally represented as a woman, sometimes in a long dress, with attributes of peace, sometimes as an Amazon armed, sometimes as an earth-goddess reclining: her character is defined by the attributes which she holds, by her head-dress and costume and by such adjuncts as camel, rabbit, or corn-ears in the field. To the same order of types belongs Oriens, the rising sun, radiate, as representative of the East, and the river and Ocean gods of the coinage of Hadrian.

(d) *Types relating to the Army*

The Empire was not from the first a military despotism. It began by performing the very necessary duty of reducing the army to its right position in the State, that is to say, of recognizing its just needs and demands, but of shutting it off from any serious influence on politics. The presence of the praetorian guard in Rome and the revolts of rival Emperors in the provinces led at last to the complete breakdown of the sound old tradition and to a reign of military lawlessness. Some trace of this development may be seen on the coinage, where reference to the army becomes more and more insistent as the Empire advances and culminates in the period of Aurelian, in the third century, where the army may be said to dwarf the State in importance. Even in that period, however, some facts were allowed to pass in silence. The Emperor at all times had to purchase the loyalty of the troops with donatives – moderate under most good rulers, excessive under the weak and feck-

---

[1] For Rome of the seven hills, cp. Pl. XXXVIII, 14.
[2] For Trajan's new road, cp. Pl. XXXVIII, 5.

less. Every one has heard of the auction of the Empire held by the praetorians, when Didius Julianus was the highest bidder. It is remarkable that these donatives do not figure on coins; they were a matter between the commander-in-chief and his men and were not considered to interest the general public at all, but the type of 'Moneta Aug.', which shows the Emperor as paymaster, has obvious reference to the pay of the troops. Domitian, who raised the pay, is very fond of the type.

Despite the firm pacific policy, which characterized the Empire as a whole, the military tradition was strong. Even when all was quiet within the Empire, the guard on the frontiers could never be relaxed; and, although after a time separatist movements in the provinces are rare, wars of succession were disastrously common. The military element in the coinage is always, then, an important one. One important class of types celebrates victories in the field; we find Victory inscribing a shield with the record of triumph, Victory crowning the Emperor, Trajan presenting a Dacian captive to the Senate, the troops acclaiming their victorious commander (cp. Plate XXXIX, 16). Another series of types, characterized often by the legend 'Virtus Aug.', lays stress on the valiant achievement that has led to victory; the Emperor is represented on horseback in the field or surrounded by a group of soldiers. A favourite theme for representation is the harangue given to the soldiers by the Emperor – whether to the guard in Rome, or to the armies in the provinces. Hadrian has a fine series of types, which show him haranguing his troops, not only from a platform in the camp, but also on horseback in the field after the completion of their manœuvres (Plate XXXIX, 15, 16). Claudius strikes the type of 'Imper(ator) recep(tus)', the praetorian camp, and 'Praetor(ianus) Recept(us),' a praetorian clasping hands with the Emperor, in honour of the guard who gave him the throne (Plate XXXIX, 1). Nero on his 'Decursio' type is seen sharing in the military exercises of the praetorians (Plate XXXIX, 13). Domitian, who relied so largely on the loyalty of his army, represents the taking of the military oath or 'sacramentum' (Plate XXXIX, 14). Hadrian's 'Disciplina', which shows him leading a file of soldiers, attests the fact of the excellent spirit and discipline which he induced in his troops (Plate XXXIX, 5, cp. 6). The class of types represented by such legends as 'Concordia', 'Fides Exercituum' – whether simple figures of Fides and Concordia with standards or more elaborate groups – hides a wealth of meaning under a simple form. Coin types have often to be interpreted on the theory of opposites – the type expresses a desired result which is quite different from the actual reality. These types first become common in the Civil Wars of A.D. 68 to 69 (Plate XXXIX, 3), where everything hung on the adhesion of the guard and main legions to the Emperor's cause. The 'Concordia' types of Nerva are the one comment in coinage on the fierce discontent of the guard, which forced Nerva against his will to surrender Domitian's murderers to execution (Plate XXXIX, 4). A 'Concordia Exercituum' of Hadrian in A.D. 119 suggests fears of trouble in the army after the execution of the rebel marshals. A 'Concordia Militum' type of Commodus marks the end of a bitter and dangerous quarrel between the armies of Gaul and Spain (Plate XXXIX, 7). The almost uninterrupted sequence of similar types in the third century tells a clear story of anxiety and insecurity; military loyalty, the basic virtue of a soldier, was chiefly conspicuous by its absence in a period when more Emperors perished by the hands of their friends than by those of their enemies. Of the triumph types we have spoken above. One remarkable type of Gallienus, showing Victory in a biga of mules, with the astounding legend, 'Ubique pax', has been claimed as the one example of satire on an Imperial coin. The 'Gallienae Aug.' of the obverse and the 'Ubique Pax' of the reverse sound like gibes at the effeminate Emperor and his strange 'universal peace', when the East was half lost, when the West had seceded and when there were risings in half the provinces. But Alfoeldi is probably right in insisting that the coin is serious after all. As 'Galliena' the Emperor is assimilated to the goddess of the mysteries, Proserpina. In the only part of the world that mattered – that part which adhered to him – Gallienus claims to be a 'Prince of Peace' indeed.

The most distinctive class of military coins remains to be discussed. Mark Antony had been the first to strike coins with types of eagle and standards and galley and the names of his individual legions. The practice was revived by Clodius Macer in A.D. 68, by Septimius Severus in his fight for the throne in A.D. 193, and repeated by Gallienus in A.D. 261–2, by Victorinus in A.D. 268 or 269, and by Carausius in A.D. 288–9 (Plate XXXIX, 2, 8–12).[1] On all these occasions the Emperor was particularly dependent on the support of the army and was led to give it an importance above what was usually considered fit. Septimius strikes with one unaltering reverse, eagle and standards, varying only the name of the legion; he strikes for the legions which espoused his cause against Pescennius Niger. Gallienus varies his type from legion to legion, employing one form or another of regimental

---

[1] C. Oman, 'The Legionary Coins of Victorinus', etc., *Num. Chron.*, 1924, pp. 1 ff.

badge. His coinage was evidently designed mainly to appeal to the loyalty of the Western legions during his wars with Postumus. Victorinus[1] follows the practice of Gallienus in using legionary badges as types. Among the legions named are several which could never by any possibility have been under his command. It seems certain that the coins record an event, unknown in the scraps of history that have come down to us – an abortive attempt by the Gallic Emperor, in alliance with Palmyra in the East, to overcome the Roman centre of the Empire.[2] Carausius seems to have copied the policy of Victorinus, striking coins for a number of legions, on whose allegiance he could only base the most shadowy of hopes. It is highly probable that these legionary coins were largely used in the pay of the particular legions whose names they bear. Gold coins of these series are always excessively rare if they are struck at all – they were perhaps meant only for presentation to senior officers. Victorinus's legionary coins are all of gold and are very rare – a fact that would suggest that he may have been intriguing rather with the commanders of armies than tampering with the loyalty of the rank and file.

We have now made some attempt to survey the Imperial coinage in its relation to the different parts of the State – the Emperor, the Senate, the People, the army, the provinces. To complete our study we must adopt a more formal classification and consider types in their classes as religious, historical, animate and inanimate, and buildings. Some of these formal types will be found to bear on the subjects we have already discussed.

(e) *Religious Types* (Plates XL, XLI, XLII)

Types of this character continue to occupy a large space in the coinage. The Empire opened with a definite revival of old Roman religion: we are in fact impressed with the persistence of the old mythology in days when it was losing its grip on men of all classes alike. The religious symbolism of the coins is still that of the Roman-Greek Olympians – Jupiter[3] with his thunderbolt and eagle, Juno with her sceptre and peacock, Neptune with his trident, Apollo with his lyre and bow, Mars with his spear and trophy, Mercury with his caduceus and purse, Hercules with club and lion-skin, Janus, Minerva, Venus, Vesta and the rest. It is not often, however, that the deity is present in a mere formal

[1] Cp. Oman in *Num. Chron.*, 1924, pp. 53 and especially 56 ff.
[2] Cp. Mattingly in *T.I.N.C.*, 1938, pp. 214 ff.
[3] Cp. Pl. XL, 11, 14.

capacity, without reference to particular functions related to current events. Jupiter appears as Victor (Plate XL, 14), giver of Victory in war (Domitian, Hadrian), as 'Custos' (Nero), or 'Conservator' (Domitian, Valerian I), the deliverer of the Emperor from imminent danger, as 'Fulgerator' (M. Aurelius, Septimius Severus), destroying the rebel enemy, as once the giants. A favourite type shows him sheltering the Emperor under his outstretched arm (Trajan – Plate XL, 11, Marcus Aurelius). Mars[1] may be either 'Pater', the ancestor of the Roman State, or 'Ultor', the god of war in action against the enemy, 'Propugnator', the defender from danger, 'Victor', the giver of victory, or 'Pacator', the giver of peace. Hercules[2] was a natural type of the Emperor, who laboured in the arts of war and peace for the good of mankind, and plays a considerable part in the coinage (cp. Plate XL, 12). His honour culminates under Commodus, who accounted himself a Roman Hercules and dared to identify himself with the god (Plate XL, 16) as founder of a new Rome. Apollo is honoured by Augustus as 'Actius', the giver of the victory that founded the Empire, by Nero as 'Citharoedus', in honour of Nero's own artistic accomplishments (Plate XL, 4), later by Commodus as patron of the Roman mint. On coins of Trebonianus Gallus and Volusian (Plate XLI, 5), he appears as the god of healing. Neptune is sometimes honoured as 'Redux', when he is implored to protect the Emperor travelling by sea (Plate XL, 5). Minerva, the goddess of wisdom, culture, and war, held a place of honour throughout, particularly under Domitian, who placed the whole of his activities under her protection (Plate XL, 9, 10). Juno usually appears as the divine counterpart of the Empress ('Regina'), occasionally as 'Lucina', the giver of easy childbirth (Plate XL, 17). Diana figures either as the goddess of the night-sky ('Lucifera'), often in connexion with 'consecration', or as huntress – patroness of a sport which was taken very seriously by the Romans and which fascinated more than one Emperor. Roma constantly appears as an Amazon goddess, often as giver of victory. From the time of Hadrian on she is worshipped with the epithet 'Aeterna' as the symbol of the eternity of the Empire (Plate XL, 13). Ceres is either a type of the Empress (Plate XL, 15) or the presiding spirit of the corn-supply. Castor is a suitable type for the young prince, as 'princeps iuventutis' (Commodus, Geta). Cybele, as 'Magna Mater', is a type for the Empress (Plate XLI, 2), who comes to be known as 'Mother of the Senate' and 'Mother of the Camp'. Vesta at all times represents the religious side of State life,

---

[1] Cp. Pl. XL, 2.   [2] For types of labours of Hercules, cp. Pl. XLI, 7, 9.

often in close association with the Empress, while Venus, the ancestress of the first Imperial line, remains a natural type for the woman who has won the love of the master of the world. She is represented under various aspects as 'Felix', 'Victrix' (Plate XL, 6), 'Genetrix'. Bacchus appears rarely – but one must not forget his appearance on a coin of Gallienus, with the truly wonderful legend, 'Conservator Exercitus'. The reverence is no doubt to some special occasion, when a timely supply of wine helped to preserve the morale of the army.

The celebration of sacred banquets in honour of the chief gods (*lectisternium*), after the great eruption of Vesuvius, is represented by types showing the 'pulvinaria', or couches on which the attributes of the gods were displayed (Plate XL, 7, 8).

The study of the attributes, which, even where legends are wanting to identify it, indicate the character of the type, is far too intricate to approach here. Its general principles are simple enough – the small Victory held in the hand on a globe marks the 'Victor', the branch the 'Pacator' or 'Pacifer',[1] the spear and trophy the 'Ultor'. Venus is marked out as 'Victrix' by the helmet held in her hand, Ceres as 'Frugifera' by her ears of corn, Diana as 'Lucifera' by her torch. Only a long experience can determine the interpretation in cases where real doubt is possible.[2]

Hitherto we have spoken only of the old Olympian mythology; what of the newer developments, the Eastern religions, including Christianity, and the worship of the man-god, the Emperor? The emotional cults of Syria and Egypt, which were so popular among certain grades of society in Rome, were but slowly admitted to the official world. Serapis and Isis appear once under Hadrian, then again under Commodus and more freely later (Plate XLI, 3). The Dea Caelestis of Carthage comes in with the dynasty of Severus who married into a Syrian priestly family. The special worship of the sun-god of Emesa, Elagabalus, was confined to the reign of the Emperor who bore his name (Plate XLI, 4). The worship of the sun-god in a more general aspect was familiar from the cult of Apollo; the Eastern cults of the god first take root in Rome under Septimius Severus and gradually grow in power, until under Aurelian Sol ranks for a moment as the chief divinity, the 'lord of the Roman world'. There is no single definite

---

[1] Cp. Minerva Pacifera, Pl. XLI, 1.

[2] A full study of the picture language, which is usually only familiar to students of coins and gems, is an urgent necessity. For a very valuable introduction, see J. M. C. Toynbee, 'Picture-Language in Roman Art and Coinage' (*Essays presented to Harold Mattingly*, 1936, pp. 205 ff.).

reference to Mithraism, but the worship of 'Sol Invictus Comes' under the later Emperors (cp. Plate XLI, 8), undoubtedly suggested Mithraic associations to the troops who brought the worship of Mithras westward.

The worship of Cybele, the great mother, became prominent under the Antonines and the Severi, but seems to have fallen into disrepute after the reign of Elagabalus. The type of 'Hilaritas P.R.' may sometimes have a definite reference to the great spring festival, the 'Hilaria', which celebrated the resurrection of Attis. Its reappearance on the coins of the Gallic and British Emperors might be a sign of the importance of the worship of Cybele in those provinces. Curiously enough there are no clear signs on coins of that syncretism, or deliberate blending of several deities in one, which was so marked a feature of the religious thought of the third century.[1] Judaism naturally figures only as a vanquished enemy of the Roman State, not as a religion. Christianity before Diocletian could not claim any place on the coinage; officially, it was at best tolerated. The one possible Christian reference is in the reverse of Salonina, with the distinctly Christian legend, 'Augusta in Pace' (Plate XLI, 6); Salonina ranks in tradition as a Christian, but how much is implied in the legend we cannot say.

The worship of the Emperor is more important. We have already spoken of the highly organized State-cult of the deified Emperors, but the living Emperor too was freely worshipped in the provinces and even in Rome worship might be offered to his spirit or 'Genius'. In the coinage we can trace a growing tendency to bestow divine attributes on the Emperor and to assimilate him to, if not actually to identify him with, particular divinities. The laureate crown, the usual head-dress of the Emperor, is borrowed from Apollo, the radiate crown from the sun-god, the aegis from Jupiter or Minerva; however little the real meaning of this symbolism may be remembered, there is no question as to its origin. So too the Emperor might be assimilated to Jupiter, the lord of the world, or to Hercules, the great benefactor of mankind, whose merits were crowned with immortality. The divine types, in these cases, suggest the Emperor, who is the earthly counterpart of the god. The idea was most at home in the Greek East, where Mark Antony had been acclaimed as a 'νέος Διονῦσος' – an avatar of the wine-god, and Nero as 'νέος Ἀγαθοδαίμων'; in Rome the same idea is implied rather than expressed. Augustus was especially assimilated to Apollo

---

[1] But cp. the medallion of Julia Mammaea, described in Gnecchi, *I Medaglioni Romani*, II, p. 83, Pl. 100, 8.

and Mercury, Nero to Apollo, Commodus to Hercules, the Emperors of the late third century to the sun-god. The Empress, even in her life-time, was freely associated with the divine world – particularly with Ceres, with Vesta, and with Venus; the crown of corn-ears, which she so often wears, is borrowed directly from Ceres. When the adjective 'Augustus(a)' is applied to a deity, we seem to have something very like identification, but this use is mainly late and at no time really common.

In estimating the importance of the religious ideas involved in these uses, it is most important not to exaggerate. A large part of the Roman Empire was far more prepared to worship an immanent than a trans-cendent god and found it easy to find divinity in men who were distinguished for exceptional power or virtue; the influence of Euhemer-ism, which saw in the gods of the State only great men of olden times, reinforced this tendency. But in other parts of the Empire, and parti-cularly in Rome, there was a far clearer sense of distinction between the human and the divine. Many Romans regarded even the established practice of 'consecratio' with a certain humorous reserve. General common-sense hung back from the extremes of Eastern religion or court flattery. The megalomania of Caligula has left no trace on his Roman coins. The sculpture of the Arch at Beneventum might repre-sent Jupiter as handing over to Trajan his thunderbolt, in token of abdication: the coins, which must surely come nearer to average popular belief, still show a colossal Jupiter, extending his arm with its thunderbolt in protection over the Emperor. Domitian might be 'dominus et deus' in the language of flattery, starting from his freed-men; but the two titles never appear on coins till the reign of Aurelian and then only on a very rare issue of the small mint of Serdica. The worship of the Emperor, then, marks an important stage in the develop-ment of religious thought; Rome herself contributes little to its development and exercises a salutary check on it, by maintaining beside it the older religious beliefs.

There was, however, one side of Roman religious belief which lent itself to the new tendencies – the worship of minor deities, personified conceptions or virtues, by the side of the major deities. Primitive Roman religion drew an exact parallel between the concrete world of experience and the somewhat shadowy spiritual world. Every occur-rence and act of life was related to a spiritual power or 'numen'. In time certain ranges of activity were attributed to a major deity, who includes in himself a number of potential minor powers. Mars, for example, in his various aspects of 'Propugnator', 'Victor', 'Ultor', may be considered to be a combination of powers associated with the acts of repulsing the enemy, gaining victory and wrecking vengeance on the defeated. Definite traces of this can be seen in the Maia Mercurii, the Heries Junonis, the Moles Martis of primitive Roman religion; the name in the nominative represents one particular aspect of the god, whose name is given in the genitive. Apart from the major deities the Romans worshipped a number of other powers – such as Victoria, Virtus, Salus, Pax, Fortuna – which, though less vividly realized and less potent than the great gods, had something more than a momentary character and presided over well-defined branches of life. The Empire took over the cult of these minor divinities and developed it to an enormous extent in the coinage; in them it had ready to hand a convenient form of symbolical reference to almost every possible activity of the State, which had the extra advantage of possessing a real hold on popular belief. Fortuna, to the Roman, was no mere linguistic abstraction; she was an actual power, influencing human life, to whom sacrifices might be offered and vows made.

Each of these powers might be worshipped under some particular aspect, with reference to some particular branch of its activity; and here the relation to the worship of the Emperor comes in. With the person of the Emperor is associated a wide range of powers, which can be divided over a number of personifications; the 'Victoria Augusti' is his capacity for gaining victory, the 'Virtus Augusti' his spirit of courage in the field, the 'Libertas Augusti' his spirit of constitutionalism at home. Where the genitive 'Augusti' is used we are probably strictly correct in regarding the personification as a definite quality of the Emperor himself; when the adjective 'Augustus(a)' takes its place, the association is a looser one and only relates the personification in a general way to the Imperial system. 'Pax Augusti', as distinguished from 'Pax Augusta', should denote rather the pacific temper of the Emperor than the vaguer idea of 'imperial peace'.

We have now to define more closely the particular ideas associated with these virtues[1] in the coinage and the attributes by which they are defined; a few attributes such as the cornucopiae, representing abundance,[2] and the sceptre, representing dignity, are common to many – but most attributes are proper to particular powers and are only transferred to others by a conscious or unconscious blending of ideas. Let

[1] We usually speak of these powers as Virtues, but it might be more appropriate to call some of them – Spes, for example – 'blessings', 'res exoptandae'.

[2] It is the characteristic sign of the Golden Age; all the powers that bear it are thus associated with that time of primitive bliss.

us start with the more general conceptions and then go on to those that are associated with more limited sides of national life. Concordia (Plate XLI, 14), with her attribute, the patera of sacrifice, represents harmony – in the Imperial family, in the State, in the army ('Concordia Augusta, P.R., Exercituum'). Felicitas (Plate XLI, 17, 19), with her caduceus, suggests prosperity, with particular reference to material welfare; she is closely associated with Mercury, the god of trade. Fides (Plate XLII, 1), usually described as 'Publica', with her dish of fruit and corn-ears, seems to denote 'Public credit' and to be associated particularly with the censorial functions of the Emperor. 'Fides Militum', with distinct attributes, the military standards, has our modern meaning of 'loyalty'. Fortuna[1] (Plate XLII, 2), with her rudder and globe, may be related either to Emperor or State. She is the power that raises or abases men, seen at her height when she raises a man to the pinnacle of Empire. As 'Redux' she is invoked to give the Emperor a safe home-coming from his travellings. Pax (Plate XLII, 12, 13, 14), with her attribute, the olive-branch, is the power who presides over the Augustan peace; the constant reference to her on the coins attests the general pacific policy of the Empire. Pietas (Plate XLII, 15, 16) represents a favourite Roman virtue, in a variety of applications. As piety in a religious sense, she appears sacrificing over an altar; as piety in a family sense, she is specially represented by a woman with children (Plate XLII, 15); with her types are occasionally associated the stork, her bird, or the traditional group of Aeneas, Anchises and Ascanius. Salus (Plate XLII, 19), feeding her snake, is usually related either to the Emperor or to the State; she suggests particularly the deliverance of the Emperor from serious illness or danger or of the State from disaster. A similar conception is conveyed by Securitas (Plate XLII, 20) resting her head on her hand or leaning on her column; she follows after Salus and suggests the peace of mind which comes when danger is past.[2] Victory (Plate XLII, 23, 24), with her wreath and palm, is the commonest of all these Imperial virtues. She represents the victorious quality of the Roman Emperor and State; often she stands on the globe of the world or on a prow, to denote sea-victory – she is associated, by epithet, with particular triumphs (Britannica, Parthica) and often inscribes a shield with the title of the triumph. Specially characteristic

---

[1] Fortuna should perhaps be considered a goddess rather than a Virtue; she was sometimes identified with the Syrian goddess, Atargatis.

[2] Issues of Securitas types suggest serious alarm; the Roman government, if it had been faced with such threats as air-raids, would undoubtedly have reassured the public with types of 'Securitas Publica'.

of her are her wings, which bear her abroad in triumph over the world. Associated with Nemesis, she represents the vengeful and warning aspect of Imperial victory.

Many of the virtues are closely associated with particular events or classes of events. The all-important corn-supply is represented by Annona (Plate XLI, 11). Ubertas, with her purse, is a third-century personification denoting wealth – probably with reference to Imperial largesses. Liberalitas (Plate XLII, 8), with her tessera or, perhaps better, her account-board ('abacus'),[1] represents the bounty of the Emperor in provinding the customary largesses. Aequitas (Plate XLI, 10), with her scales and measuring rod, and Moneta, with her scales and cornucopiae, are kindred conceptions, associated with the giving of due measure in the corn-doles and the coinage. The public games and shows which were frequently given by the Emperors on occasion of public rejoicing and were as much expected of him as the corn-doles, may be represented by Laetitia (Plate XLII, 7), with her wreath and anchor; the anchor expresses the idea often expressed directly in the epithet 'Fundata'. This personification refers directly rather to the joyful occasion than to its celebration; for the latter the term is 'Munificentia Aug.', usually expressed by some type chosen from the show, as for example the elephant of Antoninus Pius. Hilaritas (Plate XLII, 3) might be especially associated with the 'Hilaria', the great spring festival of rejoicing in the cult of the Great Mother, but the reference might be to public rejoicings in general. Aeternitas (Plate XLI, 12), with her heads of sun and moon, her mantle inwrought with stars, or her phoenix, has reference either to the immortality of the blessed dead, the 'divi' and other members of the Imperial house, or to the eternity of Rome. The military virtues are well represented. The commonest after Victory is Virtus (Plate XLII, 26), usually a female, occasionally a male figure, with spear and parazonium – the symbol of the active courage of the soldier – and Honos (Plate XLII, 4), with his sceptre, who stands for the dignity of the military profession. Honos and Virtus together seem to refer especially to the praetorian guard; for, while Virtus might be predicated of any army, Honos, prestige, the 'swagger' of service, applied peculiarly to the praetorians. In type Honos and Virtus are closely assimilated to the divine pair, Apollo and Diana; Diana could be identified with Virtus. Concordia and Fides, when definitely related to the army, express the idea of comradeship and loyalty and bear standards as attributes. The Constantia of Claudius (Plate XLI, 15) represents

[1] Cp. Dodd in *Num. Chron.*, 1911, p. 246.

rather the idea of steadfast endurance. The important question of the succession is represented by Providentia, the wise foresight of the Emperor, with her wand and globe (Plate XLII, 17), and by Spes (Plate XLII, 2) with her flower, the hope centred on the heir. Nobilitas (Plate XLII, 10) suggests the high rank of the prince, who came to be known distinctively as 'nobilissimus Caesar'. With the epithets 'P.R.' or 'Publica', Spes has a different shade of meaning and looks rather to the rising generation as the hope of Rome.

A group of virtues, usually associated closely with the Emperor, represent various sides of the activity of a good ruler. Libertas (Plate XLII, 9), with her pileus and wand (*vindicta*), stands for the constitution or the constitutional temper of the ruler. Then follow Clementia, Indulgentia, Justitia, and Tranquillitas (Plates XLI, 13; XLII, 5, 6, 21), expressing the idea of mercy, readiness to grant favours, just dealing and calm judgement. These powers are not very clearly defined; Clementia and Justitia hold patera and sceptre, Indulgentia extends her right hand in a gesture of friendliness, Tranquillitas holds in her arms a capricorn.[1] Patientia (Plate XLII, 11) represents the patient endurance of Hadrian on his long and weary travels. Closely associated with the Empress are Fecunditas (Plate XLI, 16), with a reference to the blessing of children, and Pudicitia (Plate XLII, 18) with her veil – a reference to the personal sanctity of the Empress, who, as consort of the Pontifex Maximus, shares in the honours of the Vestal Virgins. The uncommon type of 'Iuventus' has special reference to the youthful promise of the heir. A few remain to be noted – Bonus Eventus (Plate XLI, 18), with his patera and corn-ears, the giver of success in all undertakings, the various 'Genii' – of the Emperor, the Roman people, the Senate, the army – most commonly represented with the patera, but sometimes with the sceptre or the standard, the 'Fata Victricia' of Diocletian, the 'Bona Mens' of Pertinax, the 'Ops Divina' of Antoninus Pius and Pertinax, the 'Tellus Stabilita' of Hadrian. The 'Saeculum Frugiferum' of Septimius Severus and Albinus seems to be a Roman expression for a native African god of Hadrumetum, presiding over agriculture.

A few general rules governing the use of these personifications on coins need to be remembered. They are usually represented by female figures, standing or seated, seldom by busts on the reverse; when busts occur, the attribute usually carried in the hand is sometimes placed by the neck. They have often several forms of activity, which are defined

---

[1] Is there a reference to Augustus, whose natal sign it was?

by descriptive epithets – 'Augusti' or 'Augustus(a)' – adjective, 'P.R.' or 'Publica', 'Militum' or 'Exercitus'. They have for the most part definite distinguishing attributes, which can however be transferred for special reasons to other powers. Thus we find under Hadrian Pax with a miniature Victory as 'Pax Victrix' and Nemesis – Victory with the olive-branch – as 'Victoria Pacifera'. Providentia under Severus Alexander has the corn-ears and modius of Abundantia, and evidently looks to the provision for the corn-supply. Pax often borrows the caduceus of a closely related power, Felicitas. Examples of such transferred attributes always deserve careful study, for it may be safely assumed that there is some particular meaning to be expressed by it. The patera, the commonest of all symbols of sacrifice, is naturally borne by Pietas, in the sense of piety towards the gods – it is less obvious why it should be attributed to such powers as Securitas, Clementia, Justitia and, occasionally, Victory. In some cases the idea of sacrifice is probably present; in others, it is the virtue herself that is worshipped – the patera, the implement of worship, is, by a curious transference, assigned to her instead of to her priest.

Mythology, as distinct from religion, no longer plays the part that it played on the later Republican coins. On the bronze medallions of the second century, which were not destined for currency, it holds a large place – a sign that they were something apart from the ordinary coins. Antoninus Pius has an interesting series relating to the early history of Rome – the landing of Aeneas, the story of Hercules and Cacus.[1] On the coins themselves, we have the she-wolf and twins on aurei of Hadrian, Aeneas and Anchises on the sestertius of Antoninus Pius, Romulus and Mars and Rhea on aurei of the same reign. A few references on the coins of the moneyers of Augustus – to Tarpeia (Plate XL, 3), to the treaty with Gabii – must be considered to belong rather to the Republican tradition. Professor Grant has recently invited us to see on Roman Imperial coins a very large number of 'anniversary' issues – anniversaries of accessions, foundations of temples, etc. His insistence on the interest of Rome in the past is timely and justified; many of his special suggestions fail to carry conviction.

(f) Historical Types

Historical types are common at all periods of the Empire and, as we have seen, give the coinage something of the character of a medallic

[1] These were issued in preparation for the games celebrating the 900th year of Rome.

series. The history of the Republic is not unnaturally neglected; interests ran in new channels and there was always the danger of reviving old bitternesses. Trajan, the most Republican in sentiment of all Roman Emperors, on the occasion of the calling in of the old Republican silver, reissued a chosen series of types with his own legend of restoration; he deliberately represented the Empire as the natural outcome of the Republic and included among his restorations types of Sulla, Pompey and Brutus – the foremost enemies of the founders of the Empire. The issue represents a notable attempt to see Roman history as a whole, emphasizing its continuity and harmonizing its discords, but it exercised no permanent influence on the choice of Imperial coin-types. History for the mint-masters of the Empire meant primarily the history of the present – the performances of Imperial government, which must be presented – and presented in the proper light – to its subjects. Some reference to earlier Emperors is occasionally found, whether in commemorative issues, in echoing of types or in definite restorations of earlier coins; interest in the past even here is dwarfed by the present. A brief chronological survey, under the general headings of Rome and Italy – the provinces – foreign powers – will give a good idea of this aspect of the coinage.

Rome and Italy. Augustus celebrates his surrender of his exceptional powers and the honours voted to him by the Senate in return, his restoration of the roads of Italy, his election as 'pontifex maximus'. Tiberius, with his type of wreath and curule chair, might refer to the transference of the election of magistrates from the 'comitia' to the Senate, but quite different explanations of the type are now being offered.[1] The 'R.C.C.' of the quadrans of Caligula (Plate XLV, 3) stands for the 'remission of the two-hundredth', the tax of $\frac{1}{2}$ per cent. on sales.[2] The P.N.R. of the quadrans of Claudius attests the restoration of the true weights, 'Ponderum norma restituta'; it has probably nothing to do with the weight of the coins; we no longer think that Caligula had tampered with them.[3] We have already spoken of the types that refer to the share of the praetorian guard in making Claudius Emperor. Nero's 'Roma' and 'Vesta' types allude to the great fire of Rome, his 'Port of Ostia' to the great harbour begun under his predecessor, his

---

[1] C. H. V. Sutherland, *Coinage in Roman Imperial Policy, 31 B.C.–A.D. 18*, pp. 87 ff.
[2] The reference is perhaps more probably to the reduction of the 'centesima' to its half, a 'ducentesima'.
[3] The 'As Gaianus', once thought to be an As of Caligula of reduced weight, is now seen to have a much earlier reference – to Gaius Gracchus, in fact (see p. 19). The Asses of Caligula are normal in weight.

closed temple of Janus to the peace following the successful termination of the Parthian War. Nerva chronicles a series of popular measures, the abolition of the vexatious exaction of the tax on the Jews, the remission of the charges of the Imperial post on Italy (Plate XLV, 8), and the distribution of corn to the people of Rome. Trajan records the building of his new harbour at Centumcellae, the laying out of the 'Via Trajana' from Teanum to Brundisium, and, above all, the alimentary institutions (Plate XLV, 9), which served at once to provide for the education of Italian orphans and to encourage Italian agriculture. These institutions grew and prospered under his successors; a rare and beautiful aureus of the deified Faustina I records the granting of a charter by her husband to the 'Puellae Faustinianae', orphan girls for whom he provided in her honour (Plate XLV, 14). Hadrian records the burning of the bonds of arrears of debt in the forum of Trajan (Plate XLV, 13). His 'Libertas Restituta', with the type of a woman presenting two children to the Emperor (Plate XLV, 10), may refer to his approval of the principle that the children of mixed marriages should be free, even when it was the mother who was a slave; an alternative explanation would see in the type a reference to the restoration of the freedom of testation, by the refusal of the Emperor to accept legacies from fathers, who left children behind them. But, as the type is just that of the 'alimenta' coins of Trajan, the reference may again be to that charity – as an encouragement to the nurture of children. In A.D. 121 Hadrian celebrated the *Parilia* under the new name of *Natalia Urbis* and opened thus a new age of gold (Plate XLV, 11, 12). The various games established from time to time at Rome find occasional mention on the coinage, notably the 'Neronia' of Nero, represented by the type, table of the games, urn and palm. The Secular Games, celebrated by Augustus in 17 B.C., by Domitian in A.D. 88 and by Septimius Severus in A.D. 202, were marked by a succession of moving scenes of sacrifice and prayer, calculated to make a deep impression on the minds of the onlookers. Augustus, whose Secular Games served as a kind of ritual of inauguration of the Empire, strikes several commemorative types (Plate XLV, 1, 2), including one of the preliminary distribution of purifying substances ('suffimenta'). Domitian celebrates his performance with types on gold and silver, showing the herald who announced the games, and a magnificent series of types on sestertius and As, showing the distribution of 'suffimenta' by the Emperor and his colleagues, the reception by them of 'fruges' from the people, the sacrifices to Jupiter, Juno, the Moerae, Terra Mater, and the Eilithyiae, and the choral procession of boys and girls in honour of Apollo and Diana (Plate XLV, 4–7). Septimius Severus strikes a coin with type of Hercules and Bacchus and legend announcing his celebration of the games (Plate XLV, 15); he must, it would seem, have introduced into the ritual some special honours to his two protecting deities. The 'Secular Games' of Claudius in A.D. 48 were distinct in character from these – they celebrated the eight-hundredth anniversary of Rome; it is curious that they have left no numismatic record. The nine-hundredth anniversary in A.D. 148 was celebrated by Antoninus Pius with various mythical types – struck some years before in anticipation.[1] The great event of A.D. 248, the end of the thousand years of Rome, was celebrated by Philip with magnificent games – represented on the coins by types of the beasts exhibited – lions, hippopotami and various kinds of deer; the she-wolf and twins of the foundation legend are rather curiously inserted among them.

It may perhaps seem that the record of events of the capital on coins is a meagre one. The explanation lies partly in the fact that the life of Rome, under the Empire, moved as a rule on quiet lines, the violent interruptions in the shape of new Emperors being represented by the new coinage – often with no special reference to the violent transition – partly by the other fact, that many events were of the kind that is liable to occur at regular intervals and were therefore represented by more or less stereotyped reverses.

The foreign policy of the Empire, its diplomacy and its wars, finds a full and usually explicit record. Augustus commemorates his recovery of the East by the types of Asia Recepta and the crocodile of Egypt (Plate XLIII, 3). His great diplomatic triumph over Parthia and Armenia is represented by the kneeling Parthian offering a standard and by the suppliant Armenia (Plate XLIII, 4, cp. 2). His wars in Rhaetia and Noricum and on the German frontier are depicted in the type of the soldiers acclaiming him as 'imperator' (Plate XLIII, 1), in the type of the barbarian offering a hostage and the German kneeling to surrender a standard (Plate XLIII, 5). The quelling of the Pannonian revolt is only celebrated by the triumph type of Tiberius, Caligula records the great exploit of his father Germanicus in the East – the crowning of Artaxias as king of Armenia (Plate XLIII, 6). Claudius places on his coins a triumphal arch erected for the victory 'De Britannis' (Plate XLIII, 7). The subjection of Britain after the revolt

---

[1] Cp. Professor Toynbee in *Cl. R.*, 1925, pp. 170 ff.

of Boadicea under Nero finds no mention beyond that implied in the
general type of Victory; the government was perhaps unwilling to call
public attention to a success so hardly won. The successful war against
Parthia, on the other hand,[1] finds its record in the triumphal arch, the
closing of the temple of Janus, and the adoption of the praenomen of
'imperator' by the Emperor. The Civil Wars of A.D. 68–69 are fully
represented by the local coinage of Spain and Gaul (Plate XLIII, 10),
with their glorification of the Senate and people of Rome and of the
militant provinces;[2] by the coins of L. Clodius Macer, with reference
to Africa, Carthage and Sicily and to the legions that supported him;
by the coinage of the rebellious legions of Germany, with their insistence on the devotion of the armies and their appeal to the praetorian
guard to assist them in making a new Emperor; by the issues of Vespasian in north Italy, the East, Gaul, and Spain, and by the coinage
of the rebels of the Gallic Empire, who celebrate the capture of the
legion at Vetera, the new loyalty to Gaul, and the restoration of national
liberty. An Eastern aureus, showing Vespasian as restorer, is shown on
Plate XLIII, 9. The conquest of Judaea, the great exploit of Vespasian
and Titus, is recorded by types of the captured province mourning;
the 'Victoria Navalis' on which Vespasian lays such emphasis probably
refers to the pressure of sea-power brought to bear on Rome to end
the Civil War. The victories of Agricola in Britain find their record in
types of a formal character under Vespasian and Titus, Domitian chose
rather to direct attention to the more personal triumph won over the
Chatti on the middle Rhine. We find Germania mourning with her
broken spear beneath her (Plate XLIII, 11), a barbarian kneeling to
ask for mercy, the Rhine prostrate at Domitian's feet. The wars
against the Dacians, the Suevi, and the Sarmatae, with their doubtful
issues, are hardly touched upon. Trajan, the greatest of all the aggressive
Emperors, celebrates his Dacian triumph with types showing a Dacian
mourning defeat, presented by Trajan to the Senate (Plate XLIII,
12), or crushed beneath the heel of Peace. His Eastern wars are presented in all their main phases – the appearance of Parthamaspates
before Trajan at Elegeia ('Rex Parthus'), the addition of new provinces ('Armenia et Mesopotamia in potestatem P.R. reductae'). The
type of Arabia with her camel records the addition of that province to the Empire in A.D. 106. Hadrian, as a lover of peace, prefers

[1] For Armenian Victories, cp. Pl. XLIII, 8.
[2] There is no true Republicanism here; all that is thought of is a true 'res publica',
such as had been realized by Augustus.

to lay emphasis on his work in building up and developing the Empire; the Jewish revolt, the one serious blot on the pacific record of the reign, is recorded only by a type of the Emperor with standards and by a Victory-Nemesis, with the branch of Peace. The building of the wall in Britain is perhaps suggested by the stone – showing distinct traces of courses – on which Britain rests. Antoninus Pius records the suppression of a revolt in Britain and the peaceful diplomacy, which enabled him to assign rulers to Armenia and the Quadi ('Rex Armeniis Datus' – Plate XLIII, 14, 'Rex Quadis Datus'). The Parthian War of M. Aurelius and L. Verus finds record in a 'Profectio' type for L. Verus, in types of Mars and Victory (Plate XLIV, 1), and finally in the giving of a king to conquered Armenia ('Rex Armeniis Datus'). The bitter wars on the Danube frontier, which caused Marcus Aurelius, the philosopher Emperor, to exchange his study for the camp, gave rise to types of arms and trophy, recording the victories 'De Sarmatis' (Plate XLIV, 2) and 'De Germanis'. A 'Victoria Britannica' records the suppression of a revolt in Britain under Commodus. The civil war of Pescennius Niger and Septimius Severus is reflected in the Eastern coinages of the two rivals, while the victorious Septimius has further victories to record over Arabia, Adiabene, and, later, over Parthia herself (Plate XLIV, 3). A Lugdunum coinage of Albinus bears witness to his short independent rule in Gaul. Finally the British campaign, in which Septimius ended his days, produces types of 'Victoria Britannica' (Plate XLIV, 4), of the crossing of a river, of the acclamation of the victorious Emperors by their troops.

The troublous history of the third century, with its succession of short-lived Emperors, of usurpations in the provinces, of wars with the new Persian Empire that rose on the ruins of the Parthian, with the wars on the Rhine and wars on the Danube, that culminated in the great Gothic invasions, is written full in the military types of the Emperors and in the coinage of the usurpers abroad (cp. Plate XLIV, 5, 8, 9, 12, 13). The more picturesque style of reference in the form of special scenes of the campaign or special acts, such as the bestowal of the crown on a subject king, is hardly to be found; we find mainly formal types of Mars, of Fides Militum, of Pax and Victory – occasionally made more explicit by explanatory legends, such as the 'Pax Fundata cum Persis' of Philip I (Plate XLIV, 7), the 'Victoria Carpica' of the same Emperor (Plate XLIV, 6), or the 'Victoria Gothica' of Claudius II (Plate XLIV, 11). Among the more remarkable coinages of usurpers we may signalize the issues of Uranius Antoninus at

Emesa,[1] the uncouth overstruck coins of Regalian in Dacia, the ample coinage of the Gallic Emperors, and the coinage of Carausius and Allectus. Carausius celebrates his welcome in Britain ('Expectate Veni' – Plate XLIV, 14), his establishment of peace ('Pax Aug.'), the peace and recognition that he extorted from his 'brothers' Diocletian and Maximian. Allectus emphasizes the store set by him on his navy, with types of a galley and legends, no doubt giving the names of the two flagships, the *Delight* and the *Valour*.

Rome in these anxious years had come very near the brink of disaster; the 'Ubique pax' type of Gallienus (Plate XLIV, 10) comes strangely from a government which had rather attained a state of universal war. The 'Restitutor' types of Aurelian mark the beginning of a happier era and, by the time of Diocletian and Maximian, we are in the full revival of Roman military prowess, which was to start the new form of the Empire under auspices that must have seemed entirely favourable.

(g) Animate and Inanimate Objects

Animate types, other than those of living persons, gods and personifications, play a large part in the Imperial coinage but can only be briefly reviewed here. The priest ploughing, a type of the founder of the city, is used by Augustus, Trajan and Commodus: the first two seem to refer by it to their extension of the 'pomoerium', Commodus to his foundation of Rome as the 'Colonia Herculea Commodiana'. The herald of the secular games appears on coins of Augustus and Domitian. Soldiers clasping hands stand for military harmony under Vespasian. As a subordinate part of the type, we find citizens attending to receive the Imperial largesses, soldiers listening to the Emperor's harangues, acclaiming him as 'Imperator' or aiding in the celebration of his triumphs. The clasped hands are a natural symbol of concord (Plate XLVI, 18), whether in a civil or military sense – and the further meaning of prosperity can readily be added by a winged caduceus and corn-ears held in them. The sphinx on the coins of Augustus is his signet-ring, the capricorn his natal sign (Plate XLVI, 1). The Pegasus and Siren of Augustus's moneyer, Turpilianus, referring directly to an ancestor, Turpilius, may convey an indirect reference to the great poet Virgil, who had just died in 19 B.C. The phoenix on consecration coins of Trajan is a symbol of immortality (Plate XLVI, 6). The she-

---

[1] These gold pieces have been held by some to be false, but they are undoubtedly genuine.

wolf and twins stand for the foundation legend of eternal Rome (Plate XLVI, 7). The eagle, the bird that is conceived of as carrying the soul of the dead Emperor heavenwards, will represent consecration. The crocodile of Augustus represents the province of Egypt. The butting bull of Augustus has a double reference – a local one to south Gaul and a personal reference to Augustus, who was nicknamed 'Thurinus' – we remember that a bull was the typical reverse of Thurii (Plate XLVI, 3). Often a bird or animal represents the deity with whom it is associated – the eagle Jupiter, the gryphon Apollo (Plate XLVI, 8), the peacock Juno (Plate XLVI, 5), the owl Minerva, the dove Venus (Plate XLVI, 9). The games of the arena are also fully symbolized by the animals there displayed to public view – the lion (Plate XLVI, 11),[1] the rhinoceros (Plate XLVI, 4), the hippopotamus (Plate XLVI, 10), the elephant, the elk, and the stag. A remarkable type of Septimius Severus, with legend 'Laetitia temporum', shows us a vessel disgorging its freight of animals for the public show.

Inanimate objects are used both as literal expressions of current events and as symbols. We may begin with the little columns, set up and inscribed to commemorate acts of the Emperor or decrees of the Senate (cp. Plate XLVI, 25), the triumphal chariots and arches which celebrate the Imperial triumphs, the chariots drawn in the 'pompa circensis', or the 'carpentum', voted in honour of the dead or living Empress. In the same class we may put the laurel-branches planted on either side of Augustus's doorposts, the oak-wreath, 'Ob Civis Servatos', so often decreed by the Senate to the 'Father of the Country'. An altar may be a general symbol of religious worship or may commemorate a particular dedication, such as that of the altar of 'Fortuna Redux' to Augustus in 19 B.C. The chief priestly offices of the State may be represented by emblems of the priests – the simpulum, jug and sprinkler for the pontifex, the lituus for the augur, the tripod and raven for the 'quindecimviri sacris faciundis', the patera for the 'septimviri epulones' (Plate XLVI, 19, 23, 24). Standards naturally symbolize the army (cp. Plate XLVI, 16), piles of arms or a trophy the victory over a foreign foe (Plate XLVI, 15). A galley may stand for the travels of the Emperor by sea, for sea-power or for the service of corn-ships from overseas to Rome. The eruption of Vesuvius in A.D. 79 was expiated by solemn supplications and banquets at the table of the chief gods ('supplicatio', 'lectisternium'). The couches or 'pulvinaria' of the gods appear on the coins of Titus and Domitian.

---

[1] The lion of Postumus is probably a symbol of strength (Pl. XLVI, 12).

We know from our literary sources that the gods were usually represented on these occasions, not by statues,[1] but by 'exuviae' – i.e. the various trappings, which we usually describe as attributes. The great gods figured in pairs at these 'lectisternia' and we may take the procedure after Trasymene as a possible model for this occasion. There is one couch for Jupiter and Juno – represented by thunderbolt on throne; one for Neptune and Minerva, represented by dolphin and anchor and by helmet on throne; one for Ceres and Mercury, represented by corn-ears on throne; one for Apollo and Diana, represented by dolphin, raven and tripod, and by crescents and stars on throne. Vesta and Vulcan will be represented by the altar type, Mars and Venus by the wreath on throne, composed of two curule chairs; wreaths ('struppi') were sometimes used to symbolize the heads of the gods. On other occasions, too, the divine attributes may stand for the god – the thunderbolt for Jupiter, the helmet, aegis and olive-branch for Minerva. The caduceus of Mercury is a regular symbol for prosperity and the cornucopiae, the common attribute of so many 'Virtues', for abundance (Plate XLVI, 20).[2]

(h) Buildings

The Romans, both individually and as a State, always displayed a passion for building, which finds its full expression in the Imperial coinage. The delineation is often, of course, very imperfect and conventional, but, in the absence of other memorials, the coin record of Imperial buildings is of the highest value. Temples are naturally well represented – the temples of Mars Ultor (Plate XLVII, 1), of Jupiter Tonans, of Diana Sicilia, of Divus Julius under Augustus, the temple of Concordia under Tiberius, the temple of the deified Augustus under Caligula, the closed temple of Janus under Nero (Plate XLVII, 10), the restored Capitol under Vespasian and Domitian (Plate XLVII, 11, 12),[3] the round temple of Vesta under Nero and Vespasian (Plate XLVII, 3), the temple of Jupiter under Trajan (Plate XLVII, 15), the temple of Roma and Venus under Hadrian, the temple of Faustina the elder and the restored temple of Divus Augustus under Antoninus Pius. After the second century, this class of reverse falls off in fre-

---

[1] But cp. A. B. Cook, *Zeus*, II, pp. 1170 ff.
[2] Further illustration of this subject will be seen on Pl. XLVI, 13: tiara, bow-case, and quiver as a symbol of Armenia; 14: rudder on globe, representing the government of the world; 17: the table of the games for Nero's festival; 21: a statue on a rostral column; 22: the twin sons of Marcus Aurelius in horns of plenty.
[3] For other temples, built or restored by Domitian, cf. Pl. XLVII, 4–6.

quency; the most interesting types are the temples of Apollo and Roma under Philip I and the round temple of Juno Martialis under Trebonianus Gallus. The Altar of Roma and Lugdunum under Augustus and Tiberius is worthy to be ranked among the buildings, for the coins show not so much the altar itself as its surroundings – an elaborately ornamented plinth, flanked right and left by Victories on pillars. An 'Ara Pacis' of Nero is shown on Plate XLVII, 9. The triumphal arches, which have already claimed a place among military types, are sometimes very slightly rendered: or again they are given on the large scale, with a full rendering of the details of statuary. Chief among these are the Arches of Nero Drusus, Nero, Trajan and Severus. Columns are found under Augustus and Nero – the great column of Trajan does not fail to appear. A memorial column to Antoninus Pius appears on his 'consecration' coins. We have further the 'Macellum' or meat-market of Nero, the praetorian camp of Claudius (Plate XLVII, 2), the harbours of Ostia under Nero (Plate XLVII, 8) and of Centumcellae under Trajan, the Basilica Ulpia and Forum Traianum (Plate XLVII, 7), the Circus Maximus of Trajan (Plate XLVII, 14), Caracalla and Gordian III, the baths of Alexander Severus. Augustus's legate, P. Carisius, gives a bird's-eye view of the Spanish colony of Emerita.

4. RELATION OF EARLY IMPERIAL COINAGE TO ART [1]

The relation of the Imperial coinage to art on the grander scale is a question of high interest and importance. The debt of the coins to sculpture is obviously very great: the portraits of the Emperors must have been modelled at times on well-known busts, and the same will hold good of many divine types of the reverses. Republican Rome had already ransacked the provinces to enrich herself with statuary and the Emperors showed something of the same taste for art, if less of the rapacious brutality allied to it. Augustus placed a wealth of statuary in the temples of Mars Ultor and Concord and Vespasian's temple of Pax was something not unlike an Art Museum. Pliny the Elder gives us a very vivid idea of the treasures assembled in Rome to delight the heart of the art-collector: in his own appreciation there is present what we may perhaps without offence term a Transatlantic element – he is impressed by costs and curiosities, as well as by sheer artistic merit. The most famous statue that has been identified on Imperial coins is

[1] J. M. C. Toynbee, *The Hadrianic School, a Chapter in the History of Greek Art.*

perhaps the Cow of Myron (Augustus – Plate XLVI, 2 – and Vespasian), brought by Augustus to Rome and placed in the portico of
Apollo and, it seems, transferred by Vespasian to the temple of Peace.
The province types of the coins must owe much in the way of general
conception, if not of exact execution, to the statues of the nations
placed by Augustus in the 'porticus ad nationes', and afterwards by
Hadrian in the 'Basilica Neptuni'. The elaborate reverse of Geta,
Bacchus with his crew finding Ariadne, is clearly derived from a group
of statuary.

The historical bas-relief – developed from Pergamene and Alexandrian models but, as far as choice of subject goes, a creation of the
Empire – has certainly had a profound influence on some of the more
elaborate compositions on coins – on such types as the distribution
scenes, the 'adlocutiones', the burning of bonds by the lictor under
Hadrian, the procession of soldiers in his 'Disciplina' type. The
acclamation type of Trajan may be closely paralleled in the sculptures
of his column.

Materials for comparison with paintings and mosaics are not very
plentiful and do not, so far as we know, suggest any close relation.
Very different is the case with metalwork in silver and gold and above
all with the art of gem-cutting. There are striking parallels to coin-types
in such rare survivals of ancient plate as the Bosco Reale cups and the
patera of Rennes. The art of the engraver of gems is hardly to be distinguished in kind from that of the die-sinker – the principles are the
same, only the material differs. Extant gems show the closest of
parallels both to the portraits of the Emperors and to the reverse figures
on coins; it stands to reason, of course, that the standard of gem
engraving is technically on a higher level than that of the ordinary
coin.

Here we may leave our discussion of this fertile and fascinating
subject. We have hardly done more than touch its fringes – to master
its wealth of detail requires a lifetime of study. It is not too much to
say that there is hardly a branch of study connected with the Empire
which cannot be deepened and enriched by a study of the coins.

Coinage in the General Life
of the Early Empire

I. THE OUTSIDE WORLD AND THE PROVINCES

For this third chapter we have reserved the full discussion of the
influence of the Imperial coinage on the general history of the Empire.
The range of our inquiry will be wider than in the corresponding
chapter on the Republic. The Imperial currency travels far beyond the
bounds of the Empire and influences foreign powers. The provinces
now form an integral part of the sytem and must be included in our
survey. And on the life of the State itself – on trade, on the army, on
the people of Rome – the reactions of the coinage are, if not more
important, at any rate easier to follow than in the preceding period.

The foreign politics of the Empire were usually very simple in
character. The only civilized power with which Rome had regular
diplomatic relations was Parthia. For the rest, her territory marched
with barbarian nations, which, if not in a state of war against Rome,
were usually subject to her tutelage. Roman gold soon became a world
currency and found acceptance beyond Roman territories in the
Parthian Empire and as far as India. The Parthian kings struck silver
and copper independently, but never gold: to this extent, they recognized the claim of the Roman Emperor to be 'King of Kings'. The only
gold coinage, other than that of Rome, was struck in the vassal kingdom of the Bosphorus, which was accustomed to a coinage in gold and
copper and did not use silver. It was felt as a sign of the new independence
of the Sassanian monarchs that they struck in their own name in gold.
The Roman silver circulated beyond the Empire. Britain, which first
learned the art of coinage from Gaul, betrays Roman influence from
the invasion of Julius Caesar to the conquest under Claudius. The
German tribes never developed an indigenous coinage; in the time of
Tacitus they were still addicted to the use of Republican silver,
particularly of the older issues, the 'bigati' and the later 'serrati'. The

evidence of finds shows that Imperial denarii in time succeeded the Republican in this field. In Africa the vassal kingdom of Mauretania had its own silver currency: when this ceased, the Roman coinage reigned supreme. On the Danube, as on the Rhine, we find no native coinage; even the Dacia of Decebalus stopped short before this point. In the East, we find Roman silver, as well as Roman gold, penetrating as far as south India. Rome, then, supplied the needs of coinage, so far as they were at all felt, over a very wide area. She became a great importing nation, drawing raw materials such as hides from the North and, far more important, the costly spices and perfumes from the East. To pay for them she had no great mass of manufactured goods to offer – payment had to be made, for the most part, in bullion. The result was a steady drain on the Roman treasury, a steady depletion of the stocks of precious metal, which played its part in the production of the crisis of the third century. The decrease in the purchasing power of gold and silver, which was a main feature of the Republic, reached and passed its height. The Government endeavours by reduction of the weight of gold and silver and by debasement of the silver to protect its stocks of metal. It does nothing to correct the adverse balance of trade and finds itself involved, through the expedients it devises, in worse ills than those originally feared.

How far considerations of foreign trade influenced the Imperial Government in its issues of coin is very hard to determine. We must not assume a negative result, just because our evidence is scanty. It has been suggested that plated denarii of the early Empire, particularly of the famous 'C.L. Caesares' type of Augustus, were expressly issued for the trade with the Far East. This is simply untrue; the coins found in south India are invariably of good metal. The type in question is common in south Indian hoards, it is also often found plated – but these two facts, quite unrelated, have been forced into an unnatural alliance. The practice of subsidizing native princes, in return for their acceptance of Roman suzerainty, was adopted as early as the reign of Domitian for Dacia and is a familiar device of State-craft later. As the debasement of the silver progressed, such subsidies would more and more need to be paid in gold, and we may conjecture that this fact partly accounts for the marked scarcity of gold in the third century. The extreme rarity of aurei of Maximin I is perhaps to be accounted for on another assumption.[1]

[1] The Emperor more and more chose to keep the precious metal in his own hands for the pay of the troops.

Turning to the provinces of the Empire, we find ourselves on surer ground. The details of the arrangements for provincial coinage must be reserved for a separate chapter; all that we are concerned with for the moment is the general principles at stake. Roman gold circulated over the whole Empire without a rival, except in the Bosphorus. Roman silver dominated the market in the West, but in the East had to compete with the old coinage still in circulation, provincial issues in Asia Minor, Syria and Egypt and occasional issues of towns. Roman 'Aes' was at first issued for Rome and Italy; its use soon extended to Sicily, Africa, Spain and Gaul, but not till the reign of Nero was the transition from local coinage here complete. In the East it played a very subordinate part. Small change was issued regularly from a limited number of provincial mints – usually bearing the head of the Emperor or Senate, as token of allegiance, but, in form, the independent coinage of the people or city. At many towns there exists, often beside an 'Imperial' coinage, one purely autonomous in form, only betraying its Imperial date by its general style and fabric. Rome was evidently only too thankful to decentralize this difficult question of supply and to profit by the long experience in coinage of her Eastern subjects. The vassal states of the Empire struck gold (in Bosphorus only), silver (in Macedonia, Thrace, Pontus Polemoniacus), and copper (Thrace, Pontus, etc.). These vassal coinages are mainly a feature of the first century of the Empire; only in Bosphorus does gold and copper continue to be struck down into the third century.

The decay of the Roman silver currency brought down this system in ruins. Bankers became reluctant to give small change for the wretched billon of Gallienus. Local and provincial coinage declined and came to an end under Tacitus. The tendency that already existed to establish provincial mints received an immense impetus – the only solution was to carry the debased Imperial silver over the whole Empire. Mommsen has assumed on inconclusive evidence[1] that the silver coinages of the East were given general currency in the third century to eke out the failing Imperial stocks. It is perhaps enough to suppose that the Government was unwilling to reserve special funds for provincial use. Egypt, which was the last province to maintain its independent issues, coined its base billon till the reign of Diocletian; its tetradrachm, already a base coinage in the reign of Tiberius, ends as a small dump of metal indistinguishable from copper.

---

[1] Tetradrachms of Philip I in Antioch style are sometimes marked MON. VRB.; this is good evidence as far as it goes; but it only proves one special instance.

The Roman Government seems to have shown wisdom in making one form of debased silver standard for the whole Empire, instead of attempting to maintain it in various provincial forms in relation with the Imperial.

The Roman Emperors, then, made some serious attempt to consider the coinage problems of the Empire as a whole. They based all reckonings, even in the East, on the Roman standards. They supplied an Imperial coinage in gold and silver, eked out by Eastern issues of silver. They solved the problem of small change by calling in the aid of the city-state. So far as this policy gave a chance for local cults and interests to survive, we may be thankful that they were not more thorough; and, however attractive the idea of a uniform system of coinage for East and West may appear, we much remember that its introduction in the East would have involved a difficult breach with a multitude of old traditions and connexions. A more serious complaint may be urged against them for neglecting at times to provide an adequate supply of coinage. The existence of local imitations of Imperial coinage, particularly in the West under the early Empire, seems to point directly to a failure in supply. And the provincial silver of the East, supposing it to have served a really useful end, should have been coined with far greater regularity than we find to be the case.

2. OCCASIONS OF COINAGE. LEGAL TENDER

With the settled peace, established by Augustus and preserved with little break for many years after him, trade began to develop on a scale unknown before. Not only were raw commodities freely transported from place to place, but a trade grew up in such manufactured articles as tiles and pots. It was only suitable, then, that the Emperors should regularize the supply of coinage and keep the mints permanently at work. In the early years, it is true, we still find occasional intermissions of coinage; by the end of the first century, regular issues in all metals had become the rule, fuller at some times than at others, but at no time entirely in abeyance. The money was put on the market either in the form of payments to the army, civil service, and State creditors or through the banks ('mensae'); the existence of 'nummularii' among the mint officials suggests that some of these banks were official. Tiberius, at the great financial crisis of A.D. 33, placed 100,000,000 HS in the banks, to be lent free of interest to those in need of money, on the giving of sufficient security.[1] The supply of bullion was maintained partly from the mines, partly from the existing stocks of coined metals, as the coins became obliterated and were called in: it is probable that individuals could bring bullion to the mint to be coined for them for a small royalty.

In this connexion we have to face the problem of legal tender. Over what areas and for how long a period were coins under the Empire current? Our evidence must be drawn mainly from finds, countermarks, 'restored' issues, and some general considerations; without dogmatizing as to theory we shall be able to form an approximate idea of the practice.

Finds show us that Republican denarii circulated beside the Imperial down to the time of Nero, and, less commonly, beyond it; the last to continue in use are the base pieces of Mark Antony, which still occur in hoards of the middle of the third century. After the reduction of the weight of the denarius by Nero, pre-Neronian coins are usually absent – they must have gone in masses to the melting-pot. Even in the third-century hoards stray coins from Nero onwards occur – they evidently ranked as equal to the later denarii. 'Antoniniani' and denarii are quite commonly found in the same hoards. The increasing debasement of the silver has no influence at first; only at the complete breakdown under Gallienus do we find a clear line drawn – the utterly debased billon of Gallienus, Claudius II and the Gallic Emperors is found in vast quantities in hoards, but seldom in conjunction either with earlier or later pieces. The Gallic money found admission to a limited extent to the Roman market and the Roman to the Gallic; the standard of the coins was approximately the same in both. The reformed coinage of Aurelian and his successors is normally kept distinct in hoards from the base money preceding it. Hoards then indicate three critical dates for the silver, A.D 65, A.D. 258, and A.D. 272–3.[2] Gold is not very commonly

---

[1] The action taken by Tiberius in A.D. 33 demands a closer investigation. A financial crisis had been brought about by an enforcement of the laws governing usury, which were being widely infringed. To put their affairs in order, creditors called in their debts. The money lent had been largely invested in Italian land; the forced sales that followed led to a collapse in prices and a great scarcity of ready money. Tiberius came to the rescue by lending 100 million sesterces, free of interest, on security. This is an isolated case, in our present state of knowledge; in reality, it is probably only one of many similar cases. The Emperors seem to have been ready to make a wise use of their control of coinage to meet the financial needs of their times.

[2] Nero, in A.D. 65, may have called in the old coinage, and Aurelian in A.D. 272–3 certainly did so. Whether Gallienus did the same in A.D. 258 is very doubtful; it seems more probable that he did not intend to make a break with the past, but only to profit by the issue of base metal; it was the refusal of the commercial world to accept his coinage at the old rates that led to the cleavage.

found in hoards. Mommsen has concluded from the evidence of a few hoards that gold was very soon withdrawn from circulation. The evidence of other finds such as that of Corbridge (Nero-Antoninus Pius) suggests that the period of circulation was fairly long. The reform of Nero of A.D. 65 marks a critical division for gold as for silver; the pre-Neronian gold was largely melted down. The brass coinage was not often hoarded until the third century, when, with the debasement of the silver, it began to have a real value. Eastern coinages, so far as their denominations fitted in with the Imperial, are occasionally included in Imperial hoards; the Lycian drachm of Trajan not infrequently appears with denarii.

Countermarks[1] on Roman coins are, practically speaking, confined to the years from Augustus to Nero – there are a few outlying examples. They are common on the As, less common on the sestertius and dupondius, unknown on the quadrans. A countermark of its very nature does something to modify the use of the coin on which it is placed. It may enable a worn coin to continue to circulate at a reduced value – sestertius as dupondius, or dupondius as As. It may appropriate a Roman coin for use by a city; Eryx and Lilybaeum are examples. But most countermarks serve other uses and, today, we are in grave doubt as to what those uses were. It was once generally thought that these countermarks affected the circulation of the coins – gave them currency, perhaps, in Gaul and Germany; this was particularly thought to be true of a group of countermarks found mostly on late coins of the reign of Augustus. Two very serious – nay, fatal – objections have risen against this view: (1) The same countermarks have been found sporadically on coins of middle to late Tiberius; (2) At sites like Vindonissa s.c. coins have been found in mass without countermarks beside much fewer countermarked. The old theory, then, must be abandoned. What can we put in its place? Some think that the countermark, normally the name of a commander, makes the coin on which it is placed a kind of war medal awarded by the man in question. Professor Grant thinks that some countermarks may have paid posthumous honour to illustrious generals. Perhaps, we may not be far wrong in saying that these countermarks call attention to changes in the command.

What is one to make of the fact that some countermarks belong mainly to coins of a late Augustan date, but occur very rarely on

---

[1] M. Grant, *The Six Main Aes Coinage of Augustus*, 1953, pp. 14 ff.; *Roman Imperial Money*, 1934, pp. 122 ff.

later coins? Is it reasonable to date them all by the exceptional late occurrences? Before we do that, we must determine beyond a doubt that the late countermarks are really exactly the same as the earlier. Here is one apparent absurdity, well authenticated. The mark IMP. AVG. is quite frequently found over TIB. IMP. or TIB. AVG. – an obvious absurdity if the former stands for Augustus, the latter for Tiberius. The ingenious theory, that in 6 B.C. an army group actually proposed to raise Tiberius to the rank of Augustus, breaks down on general improbability and questions of date. The only explanation that occurs to me is that the countermarks belong to the mutinies at the beginning of the reign of Tiberius; the men, repenting of their allegiance to Tiberius, went back to the name of his predecessor. Others escape the difficulty by saying that IMP. AVG. need not mean Augustus. If you can believe that, it is a possible way out. Countermarks of Claudius, which, despite the similarity of names, can be distinguished without much uncertainty from those of Tiberius, may have stamped coins for circulation in Britain. Professor Grant has not rendered any good service to our studies by reintroducing confusion, where order was largely being established.[1] Countermarks of Nero mark something like a revision of what was worthy to survive of the old coinage. BON. and PROB. speak for themselves. NCAPR, the commonest of the group, has been read 'Nero Caesar Augustus probavit'; but, though the reference to Nero is certain, other readings are possible – for example, that of Kraay, 'Nero Caesar Augustus populo Romano', coins countermarked for a largesse. After Nero, countermarks of SPQR and PR mark coins of the rebels in Gaul or Spain. Rare countermarks of Vitellius and Vespasian follow. An uncommon countermark of Trajan may mark coins for circulation in Dacia.

We can no longer claim, as we used to do, that countermarks tell us a lot about the circulation of the *Aes* coinage. But they *do* carry their information, which it is now our task to find out again. Something can be learned about the length of circulation of *Aes* coins. It was not apparently very long. By the reign of Nerva the coinage of Nero seems to have almost completely disappeared. But were coins withdrawn after a stated term of years? Or were they allowed to circulate as long as they were not too worn?

The 'restored' coins require a word of explanation. Vespasian and his sons deliberately revived a number of types of Augustus in all metals. Titus and Domitian struck a series of *Aes*, with a formula

[1] M. Grant, op. cit., pp. 28 ff.

announcing that they had restored them, from Augustus to Galba; the coins, apart from this formula, are closely copied from the originals. Nerva restored the 'capricorn' type of the denarius of Augustus and various types of his in *Aes*, but with a freedom not met with under Titus and Domitian. Trajan, in A.D. 107, in connexion with the melting down of the old 'worn-out' silver, issued a 'restored' series of Republican denarii and Imperial aurei – the former close to their originals, the latter in most cases essentially new coins, except for the portrait. This great issue certainly marks an extensive calling-in of the old coinage; but it has another purpose, in the presentation of Roman history as a whole – the Empire succeeding in natural order to the Republic; obviously the coins of Nerva, if not those of Vespasian and Titus, cannot have yet been out of date. Hadrian restruck great numbers of 'cistophori' of Mark Antony, Augustus and Claudius with his own types. Finally, Marcus Aurelius and L. Verus restored the type of one legion of Mark Antony.[1]

Finally, there are a few general considerations that seem to bear on the case. The withdrawal of worn-out coin is a natural and almost inevitable measure at any time. Again, after a change in the money-system, old and new coins can hardly circulate together, unless they are definitely tariffed to one another in terms acceptable to the general public. And the existence or non-existence of provincial coinages in silver and brass enables us to form conclusions as to the range of circulation of the Imperial money.

Let us try to extract from the above evidence the rules of circulation under the Empire. First, as regards range of circulation in place. Imperial gold is current everywhere; so too is Imperial silver, but only in competition with provincial coinages in the East. The s.c. coinage certainly served Rome and Italy primarily. It was not barred from the West and, perhaps, wandered out occasionally to the East. But the East has its own abundant supplies. That the West was not adequately supplied from Rome appears from the fact that Lugdunum was used at various times to supplement the Roman issues. The Lugdunum coins predominate over the Roman in Western hoards of their periods. In Syria the place of the s.c. coinage seems to have been taken by an analogous coinage of Antioch, bearing the same mark s.c. Money was withdrawn as it became obliterated by wear or as it was ousted by new denominations. Trajan certainly withdrew the mass of Republican

---

[1] Cp. here Grant's *Anniversary Issues*, a book of very great interest, but needing to be used with some caution.

denarii from circulation; it is possible that he definitely demonetized them. In the third century, the coinages of A.D. 258 and 272 were definitely separated off both from the earlier and later coinage. Aurelian certainly demonetized the coins of Gallienus in the sense that he did not give them parity with his new money; if he allowed them any legal status, it must have been on a scale unsatisfactory to the owners – only so can we account for the immense quantities of them that were buried away.

3. FINANCIAL POLICY.[1] LARGESSES AND DONATIVES

The general policy of the early Empire was, it seems, a sound one. The gold and silver were struck true to weight and of an exceptional fineness. They could command acceptance on their merits, without any pressure on the part of government. The brass and copper only represented part value, but, as they were not ordinarily used in large payments, this did not seriously matter. Serious doubts, however, are raised by the existing masses of plated denarii of the period. If these were official issues, the Government largely stultified its own endeavours, by secretly going back on its avowed policy. A definite decision is hard to reach. We shall probably not be far wrong if we credit Augustus and Tiberius with a faithful maintenance of their policy, while admitting that official debasement, by means of the expedient of plating, may have to be debited to the account of Caligula and Claudius. For the most part the plated coins are the work of false moneyers whether or not in official connexion with the mint. After the debasement of the silver under Nero had begun, the plated coin as an official issue lacks a *raison d'être*.

How was it that the Imperial Government left the sound lines which it had at first followed and took the devious path that led to the financial collapse? We have already seen one cause of this in the loss of precious metal in foreign trade and in articles of luxury: the stocks of metal were no longer adequate for the needs of coinage, and the Government under Nero began to protect itself by reduction of weight and debasement of the silver. But some further cause must be sought and this we shall find in two directions – in the ever-increasing demands of the poorer citizens of Rome and of the armies. The practice of giving gifts in kind to the poor of Rome goes well back into the Republic. Caesar introduced the practice of distributing money

[1] Cp. Sture Bolin, 'State and Currency in the Roman Empire to 300 A.D.'

and his successors followed in his footsteps. It was not, however, till the reign of Trajan that these 'liberalitates' assumed such proportions as to constitute a serious drain on the exchequer. Trajan distributed no fewer than 650 denarii per head, Hadrian 1,000, Antoninus Pius 800. From this time on the 'liberalitates' were a heavy item in the debit account of the Imperial budget. The motives that underlay them were mixed and, to some extent, pardonable or even laudable. The Emperors, who did most to increase the burden of the 'liberalitates', were among the best and wisest that Rome ever had. They still respected the position of Rome as head and centre of the Imperial system and they found in her masses of citizens hardly able to bring up their families to a decent standard of livelihood. What more fitting than that the Imperial funds should contribute to the material well-being of the Roman people, on which the supply of a healthy and vigorous population depended? The mischief, of course, lay in the fact that these doles only palliated, without relieving the cause of the trouble. The people of Rome were not taught to be self-supporting, but only to depend more and more on the Imperial bounty. The consequence most to be desired – the rearing of a large and vigorous population of native Romans – was only imperfectly realized, though the 'Spes P.R.' types representing all the hopes reposed on the rising generation, bear eloquent witness to the good intention. We in our day, who have seen the necessity of doles as an alternative to worse evils, are not likely to condemn the Romans too hastily. All we can say is that the empire of the Antonine and succeeding period found itself burdened with a permanent expenditure on the poor of Rome which brought in no adequate return.

To this must be added the needs of the army. Augustus had put the soldier in his right place; he had shut him out of interference in politics and, whilst providing for him generously on his discharge, had compelled him to serve for a long term at a very modest rate of pay (225 denarii – 9 aurei per year – for the legionary). Domitian, who depended so much on the support of the army, raised the pay by a quarter – to twelve aurei. Then, after an interval of a century, Commodus and Septimius Severus again raised the pay and Caracalla followed him with a further increase. To all these regular payments fell to be added the donatives which corresponded to the doles for the civil population, which, like them, were always increasing and came more and more to be looked on by the soldiers as their right. The story of the putting up of the Empire to auction by the praetorians after the death of Pertinax is certainly in its essence true. The accession of Severus brought no real improvement. His dying advice to his sons 'to enrich the army and care nothing for anybody else' sufficiently well indicates the trend of his policy. In one way and another, direct and indirect, the army was becoming an ever heavier burden on the budget, and the third century, with its lack of long settled dynasties and its quick transferences of power, only made matters worse. With the increased pay of the troops, with the donatives and doles, the expenses of the Government were brought to a dangerous height. What could be done to balance the budget? Our knowledge of provincial taxation is too imperfect to allow of a very positive answer, but we can feel fairly safe in saying that no great increase in taxation was possible. The provinces were already paying as much as could reasonably be required of them and, at times, a remission of old bad debts was considered necessary. The Government, then, perhaps hardly realizing the full scope of its action, plunged deeper and deeper down the dangerous path of debasement and reduction of weight. It had the command of the coinage and could apparently increase its resources by these expedients; it did not sufficiently realize that it was only attempting to raise by an inequitable form of indirect taxation what it could not trust itself to raise by direct.

4. THE CRISIS OF THE THIRD CENTURY. ATTEMPTS AT RECOVERY

The debasement of the denarius, we have seen, proceeded by a series of regular drops from Nero to Caracalla. The weight of the aureus, reduced by Nero, was restored by Domitian – probably out of regard for people and army – but was again reduced by Trajan. Caracalla reduced the weight again to one-fiftieth of a pound and, to increase the profits of the silver coinage, introduced his new Antoninianus', or double denarius, at less than the weight of two denarii. The victory of this new coin over the denarius after Balbinis and Pupienus marks a critical stage; it was a victory for immediate necessities over a further-sighted policy. Even so, however, a stand was not called; debasement of the silver proceeded and, at last Gallienus, at the crisis of his reign, broke clean away from sound tradition and attempted to impose the basest of bad billon in place of a silver currency. Up to now, the Imperial silver seems to have been accepted at its normal face value; the evil day was postponed and the owner of debased silver could still flatter himself with the hope that his coin was exchangeable for its equivalent in good metal. Now at last the harvest had to be reaped. The Imperial silver was no longer accepted as what it pretended to be – its course must have fluctuated up and down, till it reached bed-rock. Money-changers in the East refused to give small change for it and had to be commanded to do so – with how much permanent success we can readily imagine – by Imperial edict. The gold coinage lost all stability and regularity; it could not bear the impossible burden thrown on it by the collapse of the silver. The Empire had, in all but words, declared itself bankrupt and thrown the burden of its insolvency on its citizens. It had begun, in the third century, to attempt to collect provincial taxes in bullion, so as to escape itself the consequences of its own debasement. Obviously there were limits to the unjust gains that could be procured thus; in the long run the Government must have been compelled to accept payment to some extent in its own coin and so find itself no better off than before. The results of the crash must have been disastrous. Trade must have been shaken to its foundation, prices must have risen to fabulous heights and individual fortunes must have been swallowed up in the cataclysm. No doubt, then as in our own time, the violent disturbance of credit gave occasion to the daring speculator to build up gigantic fortunes. The net result for the hard-working citizen must have been, almost without mitigation, evil.

By the time that Aurelian was ready to reform the coinage, the worst of the mischief must already have taken place. Any hopes that the holders of the old billon may have had of recouping their losses were certainly buried, when he refused to admit the old coin on a parity with his new. Many owners, sooner than part with their money at unfavourable rates, hoarded it in the ground – to make up those huge finds, which are constantly coming to light. Demonetization of this kind, however, was a necessary step towards any reform. All that Aurelian could hope to do was to leave the past with its losses and build for a happier future. The local and provincial silver and copper of the East had begun to collapse with the breakdown of the Imperial silver under Gallienus. Aurelian made no attempt to restore them – they cease entirely under Tacitus – but prepared to supply the whole Empire with Imperial coin. For the senatorial copper of Rome he substituted new Imperial issues, while leaving the East as a whole without any fresh supplies of small change. Only in Egypt did the old provincial coinage continue, reduced in weight and debased to match the Imperial. Aurelian's reform cannot be accounted an entire failure

– it provided a makeshift coinage and paved the way for the more far-reaching reform of Diocletian. But he gave the world no regular and dependable coinage either in gold or in silver; the main supply was still to consist of a billon coin, with a delusive coating of silver, not much more valuable intrinsically than the worst productions of the mint of Gallienus. Prices must have remained at an abnormally high level and, worse than this, there must have been all the uncertainty and instability that attends a coinage which does not rest on an adequate reserve. The one genuine remedy – the restoration of a regular coinage of gold and silver – was not yet resorted to. The supplies must have been inadequate and, in the case of the silver, the good metal had been frittered away over the supply of vast masses of inferior billon. How Diocletian found sufficient gold and silver to inaugurate his reform must remain to some extent a mystery; probably his Eastern conquests actually placed fresh supplies of bullion at his disposal. With his new attempt to reform the coinage and with the doubtful success that attended it we shall have to deal in the first chapter of our third book.

Looking back then we see that the financial miseries of the third century amounted to a formal State-bankruptcy, brought about by a long failure to adjust expenses to income. The best of all remedies would have lain in a cutting down of expenditure, but the political conditions of the time forbade any saving on the least justifiable of the charges – those for the poor of Rome and for the army. A second alternative would have been the recognition of the deficit and the funding of a national debt. This was something as much beyond the ken of the Imperial as of the Republican statesman. The real insolvency of the State was dissimulated up to the last possible moment and then the whole burden was thrown on the private citizen. The State emerged, as modern Germany has emerged from a similar crisis, but only at a cost of individual happiness and well-being that is well-nigh incalculable.

Again, I must apologize for leaving many questions barely formulated and very imperfectly argued, and again stress the need for further research on them.

CHAPTER IV

The Provincial and Local Coinage
of the Early Empire

I. GENERAL PRINCIPLES

The place of the local and provincial issues in the coinage of the Empire has already been defined in general terms in the preceding chapter. Our present task is to pursue this inquiry into further detail and to give some idea of the conditions under which these coins were struck, the denominations which they represented and the subjects which were chosen for their types. In no part of this handbook is the author more aware of the imperfection of his equipment for his task and of the inadequacy of the space at his disposal. Some indulgence may perhaps reasonably be claimed for an attempt, however imperfect, to draw a faithful sketch of a subject which really requires a book to itself.

The task of providing coinage in all metals for the whole Empire was not even attempted by the early Imperial Government. Coinage in gold was almost entirely Imperial. Coinage in silver was Imperial over almost the whole of the West; but in the East local and provincial issues helped out the demand. Coinage in base metal was issued by the Senate, first for Rome and Italy, after Nero for the whole of the West; in the East, local and provincial issues took its place and continued in use till late in the third century. We will try to give some idea of the arrangements made, province by province, first for the Western, then for the Eastern provinces.

Spain had a large number of city mints striking bronze under Augustus (cp. Plate XLVIII, 1, Emerita), many of which were still active in the reign of his successor; under Caligula (cp. Plate XLVIII, 2, Caesaraugusta) only a handful are still at work and after him the mints are closed. It is probable, however, that here and in Gaul the supply of senatorial 'Aes' was inadequate and was eked out by local imitations till the reign of Nero, who provided a more satisfactory supply for local needs. Gaul, in the latest period of the Republic, had

188

had a silver coinage at Lugdunum, Nemausus and Cabellio and a coinage in bronze at Lugdunum and Vienna. Under Augustus the coins of Nemausus formed something like a provincial currency for Gallia Narbonensis (Plate XLVIII, 3). In Gaul, however, the city played a much smaller part than in Spain; and in 11 B.C. Augustus instituted the provincial issues of the 'Commune Galliarum' at Lugdunum, with the famous reverse type of the 'Altar of Rome and Augustus'. This coinage was suspended by Tiberius, perhaps out of fear of nationalist movements, and only resumed for a moment by Claudius; but the branch of the Roman mint, opened by Nero at Lugdunum for the supply of the West, may be regarded as in some sense the successor of the provincial mint. Britain had no provincial coinage of its own; in the days preceding the Roman conquest, however, the influence of Roman types is clearly to be seen on the silver and bronze issues of the native princes. Africa had a local city coinage in bronze under Augustus and Tiberius, Mauretania had a silver coinage under its kings, Juba II (Plate XLVIII, 7) and Ptolemaeus, and very rare coins in gold. The colonial coins hitherto supposed to belong to Babba (Plate XLVIII, 6) and Banasa are now thought to belong to Buthrotum.[1] Sicily has a few issues of bronze down to Tiberius (cp. Plate XLVIII, 5, Panormus), and to these we may add a group of coins of the moneyers of Augustus, countermarked for local use. The Sardinian coins of C. Atius have sometimes been attributed to the reign of Augustus; the small coinage of the Balearic Isles extends down to the reign of Claudius. Italy itself depended on the mint of Rome; only in the South did the mint of Paestum issue small bronze coins down to the reign of Tiberius (Plate XLVIII, 4).

The general lines of the development are clear enough. Coinage in the West was not highly developed and there was never any question of establishing regular mints for the supply of gold and silver. For the base metal Augustus made an experiment in local issues. But the nationalist movements in Gaul and Africa led Tiberius to revise this policy and in the end we find it completely abandoned. The Imperial coinage itself was largely issued by Augustus from Spanish and Gallic mints. Here too a change of policy set in; after the reign of Caligula provincial issues of Imperial coin are a symptom only of the Civil Wars, not a permanent part of the system. Authority to coin was given either by the Emperor himself for a town or even for a whole province or by the provincial governor.

---

[1] J. Mazard, 'Les Monnies Coloniales supposées de Babba et de Banasa', *Revue Africaine*, 1955, pp. 53 ff.

The East presents us with a mass of coinage of diverse kinds, which by its detail baffles any attempt at a full description here. The vassal kings, held in a relation of dependence on the Emperor, issued semi-independent coinage, on which the heads of the local ruler and Emperor often appear on opposite sides of the coin. The kingdom of the Bosphorus is remarkable in having a coinage of gold (Plate XLIX, 1) and bronze, but no silver. Silver coinage is found in Thrace, Galatia, Cappadocia, Nabathaea – bronze in the same kingdoms and also in the small principalities round Palestine and in Commagene. These coinages, for the most part, came to an early end and represent a passing and unimportant phase.

2. PROVINCIAL ISSUES

Of far greater interest are the provincial issues. Under the Republic the East had never fallen under the sway of the denarius; it still maintained local standards and possessed masses of struck coin. The Roman Empire accepted the *status quo* and issued coins, Imperial as far as the authority was concerned, but provincial in their standard and in their general style and appearance. For the province of Asia Augustus, Claudius (Plate XLVIII, 8, 9), Vespasian, Domitian, Nerva and Trajan struck tetradrachms of the cistophoric standard, equated in value to three denarii. Hadrian struck similar coins for Asia and also for Bithynia and recoined masses of earlier pieces (Plate XLVIII, 10); after him, except perhaps for a moment under Septimius Severus, the series ends. Crete has a silver coinage from Caligula to Trajan (cp. Plate XLIX, 3), Cyprus *Aes* under Vespasian (Plate XLIX, 7) and his sons. Caesarea in Cappodocia strikes silver, mainly drachms, from Tiberius to Gordian III (cp. Plate XLIX, 9–11).[1] These drachms seem to belong to the same system as the tetradrachms of Syria. These Syrian tetradrachms were struck mainly at Antioch, later at a number of other mints (cp. Plates XLIX, 12, 13; L, 1, 2). Mesopotamia had a small silver coinage under Marcus Aurelius and L. Verus. Finally, the great mint of Alexandria in Egypt from the reign of Tiberius issued its base billon tetradrachms (Plate L, 3), to which no higher value than that of one denarius was assigned.[2] The Lycian League had an autonomous silver coinage down to Claudius and a provincial coinage after him under Domitian, Nerva and Trajan (Plate XLIX, 5). As an appendix

---

[1] The coin shown on Pl. XLIX, 8, was possibly struck at Caesarea, but for circulation in Cyrene.

[2] Perhaps the passage in the *Gnomon of the Idios Logos*, s. 106, implies an attempt to keep the tetradrachm down to par.

to these provincial issues we may place a few sporadic issues of cities –
Byzantium under Claudius (? Plate XLIX, 2), Chios under Augustus,
Stratonicea under the same Emperor, Amisus in Pontus under Hadrian
(Plate XLVIII, 12), Aegeae in Cilicia under Hadrian, Mopsus under
Hadrian and Antoninus Pius, Nicopolis under Antoninus Pius (Plate
XLVIII, 11), Thessalonica under Commodus, Cydonia, Hierapytna
(Plate XLIX, 4) and other Cretan cities under Tiberius, Tarsus under
Domitian and succeeding Emperors down to Caracalla (cp. Plate
XLIX, 6). In the Syrian district we find autonomous silver of Seleucia,
Laodicea and Tyre during the first century A.D. and coins with the
heads of Emperors later at Tyre, Berytus, Damascus, Emesa, Heliopolis,
Tripolis, etc. Some of these town issues are really to be regarded as
provincial issues, struck at a number of centres. In general we may say
that silver was restricted to a few great provincial issues and formed no
part of the general local coinage.

With bronze the case is entirely different. We find associated with
the provincial 'concilia' a number of issues for such provinces as
Bithynia (Plate L, 7), Asia, Crete, Cyprus, Galatia, Macedon (Plate L,
6) and Pontus. Alexandria (Plate L, 5) has a great coinage of bronze,
running parallel to its billon coinage, and Antioch strikes bronze with
the Latin legend S.C. on the reverse (Plate L, 4). This S.C. can only
refer to the Senate of Rome, and, strange as the fact may appear, we
must recognize in this coinage a sort of Eastern counterpart of the
senatorial 'Aes' of the West. Dacia (Plate L, 9) from Philip I to
Valerian has its own provincial coinage and the coinage of Viminacium
(Gordian III to Valerian – Plate L, 8) should perhaps be regarded as a
provincial coinage for Moesia Superior. There are other instances (e.g.
Corinth and Patrae) in which the coinage of some important city seems
to take the place of a provincial.

3. LOCAL ISSUES

These provincial issues of bronze, however, fade into insignificance
before the vast masses of coin struck by a number of city mints over
the whole of the East. Of special grants of the right to coin we hear
little[1] – we may quote the 'indulgentia Augusti moneta impetrata' of
Patrae and the 'perm. Imp.' of Corinth under Domitian. As a rule we
must suppose that the right to coin in bronze was conceded almost as a
matter of course to every organized civic body, capable of meeting its

---

[1] The governor certainly enjoyed general powers of supervision; cp. *Digest*, XLVI,
31–2, bad silver demonetized by governor.

own needs of small change. Such coinage, while bearing the 'ethnic' or city name as a mark of authority, indicates its dependence on the Empire by complimentary reference to the Emperor, the Senate, or, less commonly, to the people of Rome. Many cities, however, strike a coinage, either alone or parallel with that just described, which is purely autonomous in character. Such a display of independence has nothing to surprise us at a city like Athens that still enjoyed nominal independence. But the autonomous coinage is far too widespread to be fully explained on this one hypothesis. The explanation perhaps is that local coinage was always in theory autonomous and that the omission of any reference to Rome had no constitutional significance. A special place is taken by the coinage of the Roman colonies and by the 'municipia', which, though not actually colonies, were organized on the Roman model. The theory of the Republic had made the colony dependent on the capital for its coins. Under the Empire all this was changed. The colony strikes like any other city, but is distinguished by its use of Latin instead of Greek and by selection of types of a more Roman character, particularly such types as the priest ploughing which bears directly on colonization.[1]

To study the distribution of mints over the Eastern provinces is more than we can attempt here. The foundations of the coinage were almost everywhere laid by Augustus, but scarcely a reign passed without some addition to the number of mints. At certain periods in particular provinces the increase is peculiarly marked – e.g. under the Flavians in Bithynia, under Trajan in Lydia, under Septimius Severus in Achaea, under Gordian III in Lycia. If ever the great task of presenting the local coinage of the Empire chronologically is successfully achieved, it is certain to add considerably to our knowledge of the Imperial Government in its relation to the provinces. In some provinces, such as Asia, the mints are extremely numerous, in others the burden falls mainly on a few cities, which must have ministered to the needs of large countrysides.

This is perhaps the best place in which to refer to the important and difficult question of countermarks. In coinage, as elsewhere, things are not always what they seem and the countermarked coin is an excellent example of this truth. In every case the countermark effects some alteration in the piece on which it appears; it may bring an obsolete coin up to date, it may alter the nominal value of a coin, it may claim the

---

[1] The type of Marsyas, taken from the statue in the Roman forum, was used as a symbol of the 'ius Latii'.

coin of one city for the use of another.[1] The last mentioned is probably the most common function of the countermark. For example EPYX and LILYB on moneyers' coins of Augustus appropriate the pieces to the local uses of Eryx and Lilybaeum. Spanish countermarks of a number of towns (C.A. – Acci, CAS – Cascantum, CLV or boar – Clunia – Turiaso, etc.) were probably affixed after the cessation of the Spanish city coinage; there was a dearth of money and cities, forbidden to strike new money, had to content themselves with seizing as many as possible of the worn pieces already in circulation. In Bithynia coins of Nicaea of the early third century A.D. seem to have been countermarked for use in other towns during the distressful years of the reign of Gallienus. Other countermarks, such as those of a governor (e.g. VAR at Laodicea in Syria, KOP – Corbulo (?) on Commagene coins of Tiberius) or of a legion seem to be used to extend the circulation of local issues for particular purposes.

4. MINT AUTHORITIES

We pass on to the question of the authorities controlling these coinages. The provincial issues of silver, which bear no 'ethnic', may safely be assigned to the provincial government; they are essentially Imperial in nature, only the standard being provincial. The coinages of the provincial councils were presumably issued by those bodies under the supervision of the governor. The issue of local coinage was a part of the local administration and fell to the local senates and to local magistrates. Reference to the governor is common enough, but it is normally in the form of ἐπί with the genitive case – a date, not a mark of authority. Portraits of governors only appear for a very short period in the reign of Augustus and are restricted to Asia and Africa; they seem to mark a temporary grant of privilege by the Emperor. The local arrangements were very various. Most often one of the permanent boards of magistrates was entrusted with the issue. Thus we find στρατηγόι, ἄρχοντες, γραμματεῖς in Asia, ephors at Sparta, suffetes at Carthage, duumviri in Spain, and elsewhere. The name of the authority is either in the nominative case or in the genitive with the preposition ἐπί or διά, less commonly παρά. The issuer of coin sometimes adds other titles of honour, not relevant to his function as moneyer, either the name of some other office held by him, or simply some general

[1] Cp. *Num. Chron.*, 1913, pp. 389 ff.; 1914, pp. 5 ff.; *N.Z.*, 1915, p. 86; 1921, p. 144; *R.N.*, 1911, p. 423 f.; *M.N.*, 1875, pp. 101 ff.; *Bull. Soc. Num. Rom.*, 1924, pp. 53 ff.

title of honour, such as πρῶτος πόλεως, ᾿Ολυμπιονίκης, or φιλόκαισαρ. The expense of an issue was sometimes borne by a private citizen and is then distinguished by the description ἀνάθημα or by the verb ἀνέθηκε. A dative may denote the person to whom an issue is dedicated or an accusative the person who is complimented thereby. Such formulae as αἰτησαμένον or ἐισαγγείλαντος seem to mean that a coinage was decided upon on the request or proposal of some individual. For many provinces the evidence on these points is almost nil; for the province of Asia there is a mass of evidence, which gives us a considerable insight into the way in which the cities of the Empire managed their finances.

5. SYSTEMS OF RECKONING

Our knowledge of the systems of reckoning in use is very slight indeed. It is, however, tolerably certain that Roman reckoning was in use over the whole Empire, at any rate for all larger transactions, either alone or beside the local systems. All the coinages of gold and silver were undoubtedly tariffed in terms of aureus and denarius. The gold piece of the kingdom of the Bosphorus was equated with the aureus. In the late second and the third centuries it came to be very heavily alloyed with bronze and ends as little more than a piece of base metal; it may perhaps have retained its nominal value in terms of sestertii, while the Roman aurei of good metal were at a very great premium. The 'cistophoric' tetradrachm was equated to three denarii, its fourth part, the 'Rhodian' drachm, to twelve Asses, three-quarters of a denarius; a lower value of ten Asses is also attested, but is certainly exceptional.[1] The drachm and didrachm of Caesarea in Cappadocia were probably equated to one and two denarii, whilst the Syrian tetradrachm, heavier than the 'cistophoric' but less pure, was, like it, valued at three denarii. The Alexandrian tetradrachm, struck in very poor billon, was valued at one denarius only but was often at a premium. The fact, indeed, that there was an official prohibition against giving more small change for a coin than it was worth seems to indicate that it tended so to stand. The drachm of Crete was, by weight, only equal to about two-thirds of the denarius; Mommsen inclines to the belief that it was valued at three-fourths of that coin, but the facts of the coinage seem to be against him. Turning to the bronze, we find the Italian As in common use as a unit of reckoning; whether there were other Asses in use beside it, e.g. an

[1] Cp. here and below, Mommsen in *Z.f.N.*, 1887, pp. 40 ff.

As that is one-sixteenth of the Rhodian drachm, is extremely doubtful. In the case of great provincial issues like that of Antioch it is possible that denominations were actually known by the Latin names of Dupondius, As, etc. In the case of the small change of the cities we do not know to what extent Latin names replaced local ones – all we can say with certainty is that all such coins were tariffed in terms of the denarius. Chios has a system in which Roman As and Greek chalcus appear side by side; the As seems to be the sixteenth part of the denarius, the chalcus the forty-eighth part of the 'Rhodian' drachm or one sixty-fourth of the denarius. Marks of value are never common on the local coins.[1] We find δίδραχμον on copper of Rhodes, ὄβολος on a coin of dupondius size of Seleucia in Pieria. In the early third century Sparta has pieces of 2, 4, 6 and 8 Asses, Argos of 6, 7 and 10 Asses, Syros of $1\frac{1}{2}$ Asses, Thessaly of 3 and 4 Asses, Thessalonica of 2 and 4 Asses. On the western coast of the Euxine from Septimius Severus to Philip I we find pieces of 1, 2, 3, 4, $4\frac{1}{2}$ and 5 Asses. In the south of Asia Minor from the reign of Valerian and Gallienus we find a reckoning, apparently in Asses, with pieces of 2, 3, 4, 6, 8, and 12, later with pieces of 5 and 10 Asses. Here there seems to be a transition from a duodecimal to a decimal reckoning. A private letter, in an unpublished papyrus, probably of the reign of Diocletian, shows that Italian money was reduced to one-half of a νοῦμμος;[2] the reduction was probably absolute, not merely relative to Egyptian coins. At the end of this period local coinage decays and Roman coin, as well as Roman reckoning, holds the field unchallenged.

6. OCCASIONS OF ISSUE

The occasions of issue were no doubt determined mainly by the needs of everyday life and trade. Religious ceremonies seem, however, to have played no inconsiderable part – in particular, the great festivals and games which formed so remarkable a feature of the life of the Empire. Such occasions as an Imperial visit would call forth special issues; and the so-called alliances of cities in the same or in different provinces, which represent acts of courtesy rather than real diplomatic engagements, are frequently commemorated by large bronze coins, or 'medallions'. In general, we can distinguish with some certainty the

---

[1] Cp. Imhoof-Blumer, *Griechische Münzen*, pp. 680 ff.; L. Cesano in *Analecta Numismatica*, pp. 3 ff.; *Num. Chron.*, 1876, pp. 307 ff.; 1923, p. 225.
[2] *N.Z.*, 1920, p. 158.

smaller unpretentious pieces of everyday use from the larger show-pieces, struck to celebrate special occasions. In the case of the provincial silver military considerations seem to have played a very large part in determining the extent of the output.[1]

When we come to the types of the local and provincial coinage we feel like a man who should take a bucket to draw up the sea. The utmost that we can hope to achieve is to draw the main lines of the picture and to supply a little illustrative detail from widely separate sources.

7. OBVERSE TYPES AND LEGENDS

The general rule of the obverse is that it is given up to the portrait of the Roman Emperor, with his appropriate style, expressed in Greek, but modelled on the Latin. It is certainly not as mint-authority that the Emperor appears; the right of coinage was vested in the local senate. The Imperial portrait is rather a sign of loyalty to the Empire as expressed in the person of its ruler; and, as the worship of the living Emperor was accepted over a large part of the Empire as a perfectly natural form, we may see in it something very much like religious veneration. In the names and styles of the Emperors irregularities and curiosities occur – the local authorities were not always very well informed about such matters. Thus we find names like *Βηρίσσιμος* for Marcus Aurelius, *Βασσιάνος* for Caracalla, *Χρυσογόνη* for Salonina. Occasionally a picturesque phrase, like the *Κομμόδου Βασιλεύοντος κόσμος ἐυτυχεῖ* of Nicaea relieves the monotony of formal etiquette.[2] Beside the Emperor a place is found for Empresses and princes and princesses of the Imperial house. In the early Empire we find Agrippa, C. and L. Caesares, Livia, Drusus and Germanicus, Nero and Drusus Caesares in Spain and elsewhere. Apart from these cases portraits of Romans are very rare; there are a few portraits of governors of Asia and Africa during a short period in the reign of Augustus, a portrait of Cicero (Plate LI, 4), struck when his son was governor of Asia, a portrait of Corbulo at Dioshieron. Quite by itself stands the series of coins commemorating Antinous, the favourite of Hadrian.

In the senatorial provinces the bust of the Senate (cp. Plate LI, 1) or of Rome may replace that of the Emperor, and, in these cases, the

---

[1] Cp., for example, the extensive issues of Caesarea in Cappadocia for Nero's Parthian War.

[2] Cp. Muensterberg in *N.Z.*, 1925, pp. 37 ff.

titles Θεὰ Σύγκλητος, Θεὰ ʿΡώμη are often found. The personification of the Roman people is rather less common. The formulae s.c., s.p.q.r. seem to refer to the senate or to the Senate and people of Rome; whether they imply in every case that the issue was something more than an ordinary city one is not quite certain.

The 'autonomous' coinage, which is found in many cities, either alone or parallel to the issues with head of Emperor, has generally on the obverse the head of some divinity. An interesting variation consists in the substitution of the portrait of some local celebrity – real or mythological. Thus we meet with representations of Homer at Chios (Plate LI, 2), of Anacreon at Teos, of Herodotus at Halicarnassus, of Sappho at Mytilene (Plate LI, 3), of Theophanes at the same mint, of Chrysippus and Aratus at Soli. Sometimes later personages are introduced, as for example Pancratidas and Dada at Mytilene (Plate LI, 5). Very common in some parts of the East is the bust of the city 'Tyche' or 'Fortune' – the symbol of the city life, characteristically represented with her crown of towers.

8. REVERSE TYPES AND LEGENDS

If the rules governing the choice of obverse type are relatively simple, the same cannot be said of the reverse. These reverse types are a treasure-house of information about the religious and social life of the Empire; and the scholar who really commanded this subject would be in a very favourable position to understand what local life in the first three centuries of our era was really like.

(a) Religious

The predominating interest is undoubtedly religious. Most of the great Olympian deities – Zeus, Hera, Apollo, Artemis and the rest – are frequently represented. Asclepius enjoys a very wide worship, and so too, in particular districts, do Demeter, Kore and Dionysus. Ares, the war-god, is rather neglected under the peace that was the prevailing atmosphere of the Empire. As a rule the gods are Greek; specifically Roman forms are occasionally found – we may quote the Capitoline Triad, Jupiter, Juno and Minerva at Cadi in Phrygia. Very often it is neither the Greek nor the Roman deity that is honoured, but some local divinity, loosely identified with one of the Olympians, but really enshrining the memory of some older power. Asia Minor, in particular, is the home of a vast system of cults, in which qualifying epithets, attached to the name of the Olympian deity, still preserve something of the original character of the local god. Zeus Labrandeus, the god of the double axe, has a special worship in Caria, for example at Euromus and Mylasa (Plate LI, 6). Zeus Osogoa, a blend of Zeus and Poseidon, has a special cult at Mylasa. Laodicea and Helipolis worship each a special Zeus of its own. And further we find special by-names of the god at many towns – Panameros at Stratonicea in Caria, Larasios at Tralles, Ammon at Beroea, Lydios at Sardis, Hyetios at Ephesus, Hagios and Tripolis in Phoenicia, Syrgastes at Tium. Apollo too has many secondary names – Smintheus at Alexandria Troas, Clarios at Colophon, Didymeus at Miletus, Amyclaeus at Sparta, Tyrimnaeus at Thyateira, Propylaeus at Cremna. Leto and the Python appear on coins of Mastaura in Lydia. Artemis, the many-breasted, is the great 'Diana of the Ephesians' and of other Asiatic cities. Artemis of Perga is only another form of the same great nature-goddess. We find Artemis Leucophrene at Magnesia in Ionia, Artemis Anaitis at Hypaepa in Lydia. Cybele enjoys high honour in many towns of Asia, as do also Demeter and Kore. The worship of the moon-god, Men, is particularly widespread in Phrygia (Plate LI, 8). The worship of the triple Hecate (Plate LI, 7) and of Hades has a similarly wide extension. The cult of the Dioscuri has special local importance at Tripolis in Phoenicia. Others of the Olympians figure less prominently in the local cults. We find Hera at Samos, Athena at Athens, Athena and Hephaestos at Thyateira, Aphrodite at Aprodisias in Caria and at Paphos in Cyprus; Bacchus and Hercules are worshipped together at Leptis Magna in Africa. The rude cultus-statues, which are often used to represent these local deities, force us to realize what very primitive idols were worshipped under the dignity of great Olympian names. In many cases the local deity seems to have little beyond the name in common with the Olympian and we find it hard now to understand how the identification was originally arrived at.

(b) Mythological

Close to religion in importance and in breadth of diffusion comes mythology. The local coins provide a remarkable set of illustrations of a great number of legends – some purely local, others drawn from the great Greek stock. The Trojan war is represented by a group of Hector, Priam and Patroclus at Ilium (Plate LII, 1), by Ajax at Prusa in Bithynia, by Aeneas and Anchises at Apamea, at Dardanus and at Otrus in Phrygia. Diomedes with the palladium appears at Argos. We find reference to the myths of Io at Gaza, of Marsyas at Apamea, of Cadmus at Tyre, of Amphion, Zethus and Dirce at Acrasus in Caria, of Ganymede and the eagle at Ilium, of the rape of Proserpine at Elaea. Corinth honours her mythical hero, Bellerophon, and Athens her Theseus. Atalanta and the Calydonian boar figure appropriately on the coins of Tegea. Other examples of local mythology are to be seen in Dido at Tyre (Plate LI, 12), Hero and Leander at Sestos (Plate LI, 11), and the dutiful brothers, who saved their aged parents from an eruption of Etna, at Catana in Sicily. Halfway between the religious and the mythological may be placed the types referring to the labours of Heracles at Aspendus in Pamphylia and at Heraclea Pontica, to Apollo and Daphne at Apollonia ad Rhyndacum, to Apollo and Marsyas at Germe, to Dionysos and Ariadne at Perinthus, to Theseus at Troezen, to Athena and the giants at Seleucia ad Calycadnum. Somewhere between myth and history falls the vision of Alexander represented on coins of Smyrna (Plate LII, 2). This is but a small selection from an immense repertory, but it will give some idea of the extent to which Greek mythology had permeated the East and had associated itself with the life of the cities. A most remarkable type is that of the Ark with a Noe, actually identified by name, at Apamea in Phrygia. Why this one selection from an alien mythology should have been made is not exactly known; presumably there was a local legend of a flood, which could be aptly fitted on to the Bible story, and we naturally suspect that Apamea had a strong Jewish colony. Various local myths are represented by the bull at Nysa, the radiate horseman at Mostene, the winged horse at Lampsacus, the sacred serpent at Aboniteichus (Plate LII, 3), Cabirus at Thessalonica and Tylos and Masnes at Sardes.

(c) Emperor-Worship

Before passing on from the sphere of religion we must ask ourselves what part in the religious life of the Empire was played by the cult of the deified Emperors. Curiously enough 'consecration' issues do not enjoy the importance that we might have expected. $Θεὸς \ Σεβαστός$ is widely honoured, Divus Claudius appears on a series of silver coins struck at Caesarea in Cappadocia, and other Emperors are, here and there, honoured after death. But, whereas in Rome the Imperial worship only began at death, in the provinces it would naturally begin at accession. The posthumous issues have therefore relatively a much smaller importance, as worship is naturally offered first to the living occupant of the Imperial throne. One remarkable case of consecration,

unknown to the Roman series, is that of Θεὸς Μάρεινος, the father of
Philip I, at Philippopolis in Arabia (Plate LI, 10). A striking series of
types of deified Emperors, with Latin legends, has been assigned to
Patrae,[1] but should perhaps be given to Philippopolis in Thrace
(Plate LI, 9). It seems to belong to the reign of Trajan Decius and, if
so, finds its parallel in his Roman series of the 'Divi'. It seems not
improbable that the ardent belief in immortality, which we know to
have been a characteristic of the Dacians, lived on in the Balkans and
ensured a special respect for the cult of the deified Emperors.

(d) Personifications

The personifications, which are so prominent on the Imperial coins,
play a very subordinate role on the local. At one or two mints – e.g.
Alexandria in Egypt and Caesarea in Cappadocia – something like the
Roman custom prevails; but these two mints strike provincial coinage
in the Imperial tradition and cannot be held characteristic of the East
at large. The commonest of personifications found elsewhere are Salus
(Ὑγίεια), the attendant spirit of Asclepius, who was extensively worshipped, and Fortuna (Τύχη), whose cult was world-wide. Victory
(Νίκη) and Virtus (Ἀρετή) occur not infrequently, as for example
at Antioch in Pisidia. Aequitas (Δικαιοσύνη) appears at Prymnessus,
and her distinctive attribute, the pair of scales, is often used as an
independent coin-type. Quite unusual for the East is the Ὁμόνοια
Αὐτοκρατόρων of Marcus Aurelius and L. Verus at Pantalia in Thrace.
A rare instance of allusion to the genius of the Emperor is seen under
Commodus at Apamea. The worship of Nemesis or of the two Nemeses
is common in Asia, particularly at Smyrna; but here we should speak
rather of goddesses than of personifications. So far as this evidence goes,
it seems to bear out the conclusions at which we arrived in Chapter II of
this book, that there was something peculiarly Roman in the worship of
these secondary powers, associated with particular areas of human life
– that we have, in fact, the later development of beliefs in the spiritual
counterpart of the material world which were never very familiar in the
Greek East. If so, this is perhaps the most important contribution that
Rome made to the religious and philosophical thought of the world.

(e) General History

Direct references to the general history of the Empire are not very
numerous, though indirect references are probably common enough, if

---

[1] Meunsterberg in *Bl. f. Mzfr.*, 1923, pp. 361 ff.

only we were able to detect them. Philippi has a type of Augustus and Divus Julius (Plate LII, 4), Mytilene a figure of Augustus in a car drawn by elephants, Philippi a type of the children of Claudius. A 'Parthia Capta' type of Ephesus celebrates the chief Eastern success of Trajan (Plate LII, 5), while Tripolis in Phoenicia shows the same Emperor as conqueror of Dacia, with a Dacian captive. The Emperor crowned by Victory appears at Maeonia, a triumph type of Macrinus at Nicopolis ad Istrum. Commodus in a triumphal procession and later the Imperial brothers, Caracalla and Geta, appear on coins of Mytilene, and Septimius Severus is represented striking down a foeman on a coin of Bageis in Lydia. Phocaea has a type of Maximin I and his son Maximus seated on curule chairs. A series of large bronze at Edessa shows Gordian III granting the crown of Osrhoene to Abgar X (Plate LII, 6). Imperial journeys and arrivals are not infrequently celebrated by types of ships, etc., sometimes with explanatory legend. The provincial issues, not unnaturally, reflect contemporary history far more closely. The 'Cistophori' of Augustus refer to his Parthian successes, those of Domitian to his restoration of the Capitol. Alexandria, in particular, offers a commentary on Roman affairs, which is sometimes comparable to that of the Imperial series.[1] But the general rule of the local coinage is absorption in local interests, with very scant heed paid to the larger movements in the Empire.

(f) Local Interests

What then are the local interests which to such an extent monopolize attention? They are in the main religious – celebrations of sacrifices in honour of special deities, the adoption of the official worship of 'Roma and Augustus' or of the deified Emperors, offices which earn for the city the title of Νεωκόρος Δὶς Νεωκόρος and the like, alliances which have barely any political significance, but which indicate relations of special goodwill between States. Asia, the home of the most intense development of city life, is the best source from which to illustrate this phase of the coinage. Finally, there were the athletic games and contests of various kinds which spread from Greece Proper over the East and made up perhaps the chief interest of the inhabitants of the Empire. They were calculated to occupy men's minds and to inspire healthy rivalries and, as such, they were definitely encouraged by the Emperors, who often contributed to the prize-money and, in the case of the important games, the Εἰσελαστικοί, victory in which earned the winner

---

[1] Cp. here Vogt, *Die Alexandrinischen Münzen*, Stuttgart, 1924.

an entry in triumph through a breach in the city walls, actually settled pensions on the victors. The connexion of these games with religion was, as in the case of the Greek prototypes, a very close one. The most common types that celebrate these were the vases, wreaths or urns, which we find, for example, at Anazarbus and Perinthus; the purses that were given as prizes may be seen on coins of Magnesia in Caria, of Perge and of Corycus. The parsley-wreath, the prize of victory at the Isthmian games, appears on coins of Corinth. A table set for the games, with urn, vase and palm (?), is seen on coins of Nicaea. Not infrequently more graphic views of the games are given – a group of three athletes at Aphrodisias, an athlete with urn at Cyme, a group of athletes at Nicaea (Plate LII, 8). Cyzicus shows both a show at a festival and a race, Nicomedia a body of spectators looking on. Games in the arena are shown at Synnada (Plate LIII, 1).

To the Roman, games of the Greek type seemed foreign and unmanly; and, although the Emperors found it politic to encourage them in the East, they never introduced them to any great extent in Rome itself. To modern tastes these bloodless shows, which at worst encouraged interest in insignificant themes and a certain vanity and at best developed healthy qualities of body and ministered to general culture, appear vastly preferable to the bloody gladiatorial shows which most Romans justified as ministering to the military spirit. The games of the circus, the other madness of the capital, were of course familiar in all great cities of the East, notably at Antioch and Alexandria where they formed the centre of men's interests.

It would not appear from the coins that interest in local politics was very lively; but perhaps we must not press this negative evidence too far. Reference to the local senate is found at Tiberiopolis and Sagalassus, at Miletus and Alexandria Troas, to the Demos at Sagalassus. Indirectly, the connexion with local politics is no doubt close; particular issues would be determined by the accession of particular men to office. The legends here teach us more than the types.

(g) *Military Types*

Direct military references are rare except in a few series like that of Alexandria. The worship of the legionary eagle is shown on a coin of Tomi (Plate LII, 7), an eagle in a temple on a coin of Perga, an eagle between standards at Amorium. But the Empire was after all predominantly an age of peace and it was precisely the most settled provinces that developed the art of coinage to the fullest extent. On the

Balkan frontiers there is more suggestion of military activity in the favourite type of city gates, to which we shall come back in a moment.

(h) Buildings, Statues, etc.

The representations of buildings are extraordinarily numerous and interesting and might well form the subject of an independent study. The temples claim the first place of importance – we may instance the temple of Aphrodite Paphia in Cyprus, the temple of Astarte at Berytus, the temple of Artemis Ephesia at Ephesus, the temple of 'Roma et Augustus' of the Κοινόν Βιθυνιών at Pergamum, the temple of the 'gens Iulia' at Corinth. Nicomedia with its three temples claims the proud title of Τρὶς Νεωκόρος. Neapolis in Samaria has an interesting type showing the sacred buildings connected with Mount Gerizim (Plate LIII, 3). The common council-hall (Κοινοβούλιον) appears on a coin of Tarsus. Buildings of local interest are common enough – the city gates at Nysa, bridges at Mallus, Zeugma, Antiochia ad Maeandrum, the harbour at Caesarea Germanicia, the circuit of walls at Nicaea, a view of the city at Amasia, the acropolis at Corinth (cp. Plate LIII, 6), Argos and Troezen. Corinth also shows its harbour and the celebrated tomb of the courtesan, Lais. The Theatre of Dionysus is shown on a coin of Athens (Plate LIII, 5). The city gate, as a symbol of the defence of the city against barbarian attack, is particularly popular in Thrace and Moesia (at Anchialus, Nicopolis ad Istrum – Plate LIII, 4 – and elsewhere) – the problem had there an immediate practical bearing. Of special antiquarian interest is the Labyrinth at Cnossus in Crete (Plate LIII, 2).

For examples of illustrations of ancient statues on coins we may refer to the *Numismatic Commentary on Pausanias* of Imhoof-Blumer and Gardner. Athens is perhaps the richest mine of such information, but instances occur sporadically at many places and often yield valuable information about works of art, not otherwise known in picture.

(i) Various Types

Miscellaneous types of local reference are far too numerous to summarize here. The lion of Miletus is the badge of the city, the camel of Bostra suggests the caravan trade. Mons Argaeus, the sacred mountain of Caesarea in Cappadocia, is the most characteristic type of that town. Crescent and star or stars, as symbols of sun and moon or of the sky, are common at many cities, such as Smyrna. Signs of the Zodiac are seen on coins of Amastris, Perinthus, Rhesaena, Singara and Sidon.

9. TYPES OF COLONIES AND 'MUNICIPIA'

The coinage of the colonies and 'municipia' demands a word to itself. Here the language was normally Latin; the communities considered themselves definitely Roman. This fact was expressly commemorated by particular types, such as the she-wolf and twins, Aeneas and Anchises, the priest ploughing to mark out the boundaries of the new colony. Reference to matters of Roman interest is in general more common here than in the rest of the local coinage. The coinage of the Western provinces, short-lived as it was, was mainly of the colonial or municipal pattern (cp. typical coin of Bilbilis, Plate LIII, 8). The worship of Roma and the Emperor was the main theme of the coinage of Lugdunum, the temple of Divus Augustus is shown at Tarraco (Plate LIII, 10). In Spain there is lively interest in the Emperor and his family – Livia (cp. Plate LIII, 9), Agrippa, C. and L. Caesares, Drusus and Germanicus, Nero and Drusus Caesares. Types drawn from the ordinary Roman symbolism are common; globe, globe and cornucopiae, capricorn, shield in laurel-wreath, she-wolf and twins, Roma, the Genius of the Roman people (Plate LIII, 7). The early extinction of this coinage deprives us of a most valuable side-commentary on Roman affairs.

Of the use of the two Imperial languages, Latin and Greek, something has already been said. Latin was in universal use in the West, except in Africa where Phoenician legends still occur. In the East, Latin was the language of the colonies and 'municipia', but only occurs quite exceptionally elsewhere. In the third century there are definite traces of a decline of Latin; Greek begins to intrude on the coinages of colonies – as for example at Thessalonica, Philippopolis in Arabia and the colonies of Mesopotamia. The Byzantine coinage, as is well known, developed a strange mixed alphabet, in which Latin and Greek forms are blended together in strange confusion.

10. LOCAL ART

The art of the provincial and local issues is of interest for the study of local styles, but falls a long way behind the best Imperial standards. Evidently the best skill of the Empire, whatever the nationality of the artists, was steadily drawn in to the capital. The West supplies little of artistic value; in Spain we can trace what may be termed a distinct provincial style, but it has small artistic merit. It is more surprising to find a low standard prevailing in the local coinage of the East. Fine work is occasionally found on the 'Cistophori' and on the silver and billon of Alexandria; the large bronze 'medallions' of Asia sometimes present portraits that may rank with the better work of the Imperial mint. As a rule the claims of art are not much considered; the coinage of the Roman period in the East falls as far behind that of earlier ages in beauty as it rises above it in the wealth of its subject-matter.

11. LOCAL COINAGE IN THE THIRD CENTURY A.D.

The local coinage of the West, we have seen, did not survive the first century of the Empire. In the East it struck firm root in the early Empire and actually extended its range steadily throughout the second and early third centuries. In spite of the official policy of developing Imperial coinage at local mints, there seems to have been no discouragement of local coinage. As late as the reign of Gordian III we find a number of new mints bursting into activity in Lycia. It was the financial crash under Gallienus that ruined the local currency of the East. The debased Antoninianus was still supposed to circulate at its former value, and, naturally enough, bankers began to refuse to give change for it. We have an Egyptian papyrus, giving us the terms of an Imperial edict, requiring bankers to accept this money, unless it was 'altogether bad and rotten'. Had the Government taken timely steps to withdraw the bad money or to assign to it a suitable market-value, all might still have been well. As a matter of fact, it did neither, with the result that vast masses of bronze coin were hoarded and issues stopped abruptly over a large part of the East under Gallienus. Eastern bronze is said to appear occasionally in hoards along the Western frontiers, and it is thought that it was at this time that it came West. Now, too, may have originated the practice of collecting great sums of bronze coin in purses or 'folles' to effect large payments. In Egypt the provincial money continued to be issued; but the trouble was to some extent met by debasement and reduction of size in the tetradrachm; the later tetradrachm of Alexandria was a fair match for the basest of Roman billon. After Gallienus local coinage lingered on only at a limited range of mints in the south of Asia Minor – particularly in Pamphylia, Pisidia and Cilicia, provinces which were not near the supplies of any one of the new Imperial mints, such as Cyzicus. This coinage extends as late as the reign of Tacitus and bears a number of marks of value – Greek letters denoting 2, 3, 4, 5, 6, 8, 10 and 12. The mark IA, which seems to be interchangeable with I, cannot therefore denote eleven, and must mean ten Assaria. The reckoning, then, is in Asses, and a decimal reckoning supplants the duodecimal of the earlier period. The letter ε (five) occurs commonly as a countermark on coins on which we should expect the mark I (ten). This seems to involve a reduction of face values by a half, and can be paralleled both by the Egyptian papyrus, which records a reduction in value of Italian money (cp. above, p. 195), and by the marks I, x, which occur occasionally on coins of Tacitus and Carus, in place of the normal κ, xx. The debasement of the denarius and of its multiple, the Antoninianus, seems to have led to the abandonment of reference to these coins in the local currency. The attempt was made to base a new system on the As; and after the reform of Aurelian this As was, it appears, identified with his new unit of account, the 'libella' of the sestertius. It may well be that the system of Aurelian was really one that had gradually been growing up in the East, during the financial miseries under Gallienus.

It has been maintained by Mommsen that the Emperors, during the financial crisis, drew on the silver issues of the East to help out the Imperial coinage as it became more and more debased. The question centres round the billon tetradrachms of Antioch. Now, it is true that in the reign of Philip I we find some tetradrachms signed in the exergue 'Mon. Urb.', while others are marked 'Antiochia'; the style of the former series is vastly superior to that of the second and recalls that of the Roman mint. It certainly appears probable that 'Mon. Urb.', 'Moneta Urbica', denotes mint or coinage of the capital, and marks a part of the coinage as coinage of the Empire. So far Mommsen's theory seems to be correct, though we may question the reason that he has assigned to it. Perhaps all that was intended was to introduce a larger denomination than the denarius – a step that might well appear desirable, when prices were rising so high.

The decay of local coinage was, we have seen, rather the unforeseen result of a vicious financial policy, than the outcome of a direct official endeavour. The process once accomplished, however, the Emperors made no attempt to restore the old conditions. Bronze was not suited to be an independent coinage, and the good silver, in terms of which it had been tariffed, was steadily being lost. It seemed a simpler matter to substitute everywhere for silver and bronze the intermediate coinage of base billon, which Aurelian tariffed on what we might call a 'nickel' basis. In point of policy, too, there was no difficulty. The Government was tending in the direction of a dead uniformity, and, finding so much effected, as it were by accident, in the coinage of the East, it readily fitted this in with its general aims. The fact that Diocletian closed the one remaining mint of the old style, Alexandria, shows in what direction his wishes lay. While recognizing the naturalness and the expediency of such a policy in the long run, we need feel no regret that the Emperors were so slow in coming to it. Had uniformity been established earlier, we should be without one of our most important sources of information for the local life of the cities of the East.

It is obviously impossible to deal with so large a subject adequately in one short chapter. The sketch that I have given must be regarded as no more than an introduction to the subject. Readers who wish to know more are invited to study the collections and articles, collected in the Bibliography.

BOOK III

The Empire – Diocletian to Romulus Augustulus

CHAPTER I

The External History of the Later Imperial Coinage : Mints, Money-Systems, etc.

I. REFORM OF DIOCLETIAN AND ITS DEVELOPMENTS: MINTS

In A.D. 295 Diocletian carried through a reform of the coinage, which may have been in preparation for two or three years before. He closed the one remaining provincial mint of the old style, Alexandria, and arranged for the supply of the whole Empire from a number of Imperial mints in the provinces, all issuing coins of the same general types and the same denominations, but distinguishing their issues by letters or signs denoting mint, officina and series. At the same time he made sweeping changes in the money-system, striking in place of the old aureus a new one of one-sixtieth of a pound and a pure silver coin, corresponding to the denarius of Nero. The details both of this reform and of its subsequent developments are very obscure and will be discussed fully a little later on; for the moment we can only note the salient features of each change as it occurs. The mint-system of Diocletian was the logical completion of the developments of the third century and faithfully represented the changes that had come over Imperial institutions. The centre of the Empire now lay, not so much in any one site, as in the 'sacra domus', the entourage of the two Augusti and the two Caesars of Diocletian's tetrarchy. The exact local *habitat* of the 'domus' mattered little – in the nature of the case there were bound to be several capitals. Rome (Plate LVIII, 3) was still one of these, the headquarters of the Augustus of the West; but beside it stood Treveri, as the capital of the Western Caesar, while Diocletian made Nicomedia his capital in the East, leaving Antioch to his Caesar, Galerius. The Imperial coinage was now uniform and without a rival; the local and provincial issues disappeared. So far as institutions could affect the case this meant the loss of local traditions and peculiarities and the spreading of a monotonous culture over the whole of the Empire.

The practical advantages gained by the unification of administration and control were obviously great; supplies of coin were now everywhere available without any great expense or difficulty of transport. As we study the allocation of local mints, we shall find that it does not correspond exactly to the system of provinces and dioceses. Britain had its one mint of Londinium (Plate LVII, 9) – the 'C' mint of Carausius and Allectus was closed. Gaul had two mints – Treveri (Plate LVII, 10) and Lugdunum – Spain none; in Africa the mint of Carthage (Plate LVIII, 11) was closed after the revolt of Alexander (A.D. 308–11). Italy had Rome, Ticinum and the new mint of Aquileia (Plate LVIII, 5) – important for the service of the armies on the north-eastern frontier. In the Balkans we find Siscia and Serdica (Plate LVIII, 7), in Macedonia Thessalonica (Plate LVIII, 8), in Thrace Heracleia, that is to say, the old Perinthus, Nicomedia (Plate LVIII, 10) and Cyzicus, in Syria Antioch (Plate LVIII, 13), in Egypt Alexandria (Plate LVIII, 12). Evidently the general plan of supplying the needs for coinage locally was modified by considerations of movements of troops and trade. The most striking feature is the absence of a regular mint for Spain and after A.D. 308 for Africa. Both these provinces stood outside the main movements of the age and were dependent for their supplies on Gaul and Italy respectively.

The coinage system of Diocletian was the model for all that succeeded it, but in itself it only achieved a partial success. The introduction of reliable denominations of gold and silver was a permanent gain. But the silver-washed bronze, which was certainly tariffed too high for its intrinsic value and was apparently used as legal tender for large amounts, was less satisfactory. Prices again rose to absurd heights, and Diocletian felt himself called upon to interfere with direct legislation in the shape of his famous edict, 'De maximis pretiis', fixing prices above which articles must not be sold and proposing savage penalties for infringements of his law. We need hardly say that force was impotent to effect permanent improvement here. And matters became worse when Diocletian's successors, A.D. 305–12, began to diminish the weight of the follis or two denarius piece. The 'denarius communis', the new unit of reckoning, fixed by Diocletian at one fifty-thousandth of the gold pound, rapidly fell to much lower values. When Constantine I and Licinius divided the Empire in A.D. 312, there was a partial break between East and West; while Licinius in the East still struck the gold and silver of Diocletian, with a follis of reduced size and value, Constantine instituted a new system based on the solidus. The victory of Constantine in 324 led to the spread of his system over the whole Empire. Under his sons and their successors the *Aes* coinage undergoes a series of puzzling changes; coins that may be roughly defined as Æ 1, 2, 3, and 4 come and go. After this the only base-metal coin is a small piece of about twenty grains (1·3 gm.) which gradually dies out in the Western mints and in Illyricum, and is only found in Rome and Italy, at Thessalonica and the other Eastern mints. For the details of the silver coinage we must refer to section 3. For some reason not yet clearly understood, the silver of the late fourth century is rare except at the Western mints and hardly appears in any but British finds. The decay of the coinage of silvered bronze in the West and in Illyricum faithfully represents the weakening of Roman grip on these parts of the Empire. In the general plan of mints laid down by Diocletian no radical change was made. Ostia (Plate LVIII, 1) was opened as a mint by Maxentius; after his defeat in 312 the mint was transferred bodily to Arelate (Constantina) in southern Gaul (Plate LVII, 12). Ticinum and Londinium ceased striking a little after 326 – the latter not to reopen except for a brief space under its new name of Augusta under Magnus Maximus. The staffs of these two mints were possibly drawn upon for the new mint of Constantinople – opened by Constantine in 326 (Plate LVIII, 9). In the Balkans Siscia remained the chief mint; Serdica closed in about 308, while Sirmium was opened as a mint by Constantine and struck at intervals down to the reign of Theodosius I (Plate LVIII, 6). Ambianum (Amiens) struck for a short time for Magnentius and Constantius II (Plate LVII, 11). After about 386 the Balkan mints one and all began to suspend operations; the Romans never fully recovered from the Gothic disaster of Valens at Adrianople in 378. Thessalonica, Heracleia, Nicomedia and Cyzicus continue to strike busily into Byzantine times. To these must be added the mint of the Eastern capital, Constantinople. Antioch continued to supply the needs of Syria, as did Alexandria those of Egypt; but the latter scarcely issued any but base-metal coins after 324 – an arrangement which led to curious local developments of currency. The mint of Mediolanum (Plate LVIII, 4) in north Italy was opened by Constantius II about 353 – that of Ravenna (Plate LVIII, 2) by Honorius, in about 400. Both of these two mints play a prominent part in the coinage of the last century of the Western Empire.

A marked feature of the coinage after Diocletian is the rigid control now exercised. Every coin now bears not only a mint-mark, usually the first letter or letters of the city (e.g. L for Londinium, TR for Treveri,

L or LD for Lugdunum, AR or CONST for Arelate, R for Rome, T for Ticinum, AQ for Aquileia, K for Carthage, SISC for Siscia, SD or SERD for Serdica, SIRM for Sirmium, TS for Thessalonica, CONS for Constantimope, HT for Heracleia Thracica, K for Cyzicus, N for Nicomedia, A or ANT for Antioch, ALE for Alexandria), but also a mark (Latin or Greek letters or Latin numerals) for the officina and further marks to distinguish the particular issue. The letters S.M. ('sacra moneta') often accompany the mint signature. The marks that define the issue are as yet only imperfectly understood. They consist sometimes of symbols, sometimes of combinations of letters, often apparently arbitrary. References to Jupiter and Hercules, as patrons of Diocletian and Maximian, have been traced and other similar references probably await discovery.[1] Despite these doubts as to the exact meaning of these formulae, their general meaning is clear; they serve to facilitate control, by marking the exact period of a mint's activity to which the individual coin belongs. Jules Maurice has claimed to have found traces of the employment of groups of workmen, outside the regular personnel of the mint. His arguments – based on the recurrence of characteristic misspellings in particular issues (e.g. at Londinium) – are perhaps not quite conclusive.[2] His general theory is, however, attractive; but we must also remember that forgery was rife – as is proved by the moulds that are so frequently found and by a string of edicts in the Codex of Theodosius. Curiously enough, the system of mint-marks is far more fully developed on the silvered bronze than on the gold or silver. It would appear as if in each mint the striking of the precious metals was reserved for particular groups of workmen, to whom any fraud could at once be brought home; the possibility of the use of secret marks too must not be forgotten. Towards the close of the fourth century the marks OB and PS begin to appear on gold and silver respectively. They certainly denote pure gold (obryziacum)[3] and pure silver (pusulatum) respectively, and were affixed by special officers responsible for the quality of the metal. In the East the letters OB are attached to the mint name; in the West the formula COMOB becomes universal after about 395 – a single official of high rank, the 'comes auri' or 'comes obryziacus' vouched for the quality of the gold, wherever struck. Bars of gold and silver, stamped with the names of the control-officers, are occasionally found.

[1] Note $EP\Omega\Sigma$ (= AMOR, anagram of ROMA) on Roman issue of about A.D. 320. Such letters as S F, T F, may stand for 'Saeculi', 'Temporum Felicitas'.

[2] *Numismatique Constantinienne*, Vol. II, pp. c ff.

[3] Probably also denotes 72 – the number of solidi in a pound.

2. ADMINISTRATION

Administration, we have said, was highly centralized. Under the tetrarchy of Diocletian the division of the Empire into four great districts was decisive. The mints in each received their orders to strike from the Chancellery of their own Augustus or Caesar. When no reliable portrait of a distant colleague was available the portrait of the lord of the mint was often made to serve for him. From 313 to 324 there was the division into East under Licinius and West under Constantine. After the death of Constantine the one great division of East and West becomes normal and, with only short exceptions, permanent. On the death of Theodosius I the schism proceeds to become final. The West drifts slowly along to its inevitable decay, occasionally brought into line with the East by political considerations, but for the most part running an independent course. The East begins to develop the new tradition, which ends in the fully developed Byzantine coinage of Anastasius and his successors. The close dependence of the provincial mints on instructions from headquarters rules out the possibility of real autonomy. Individual styles are still well marked and enable the trained eye to distinguish mintage, even without the aid of mint-marks. Fabric, however, tends to become more and more uniform, and special local references and allusions on the reverse, though still occasionally prominent, as for example in the mint of Carthage from 296 to 308, are in general on the decline. The main feature of the age is a stale uniformity, which proves at least that the central control, however destructive of local vigour, was functioning well.

3. MONEY-SYSTEMS [1]

It has been found necessary to rewrite the whole of this section – not, alas, because new certainties have been attained, but because we have come to realize how incomplete our knowledge is. The coins are there for us to study; they even bear some marks of value – but these are often obscure in meaning. References to coins in literature and in the legal Codices supply some valuable information, but many uncertainties arise about interpretation. Metrological notes, being almost always undated, can only be used with the greatest caution. How far astray

[1] Cp. H. Mattingly, 'The Monetary Systems of the Roman Empire from Diocletian to Theodosius I', *Num. Chron.*, 1946, p. 113: J. W. E. Pearce, *Roman Imperial Coinage*, Vol. IX, pp. xxvi ff.: G. F. Hill, 'Roman Legislation Concerning Coinage: Excerpts from the *Codex Theodosianus*' (typescript in B.M.). There are also medallions of gold, silver and bronze. Contorniates – pieces of base metal of about sestertius size, with turned-up edges, are not coins – perhaps pieces played for in some game connected with the circus.

may one not go, if one applies a gloss of the seventh century, say, to the fourth? Our modest plan will be to offer a few general considerations which will find their special applications as we advance and, then, to present the coinage, period by period, noting what is certain, making an occasional guess, but always marking the borders where uncertainty begins.

The gold was struck true to weight and very pure; plated forgeries *do*, however, occur. The gold coin held a peculiar position in the system, being treated not as a coin proper, but as a privileged piece of bullion. You took your solidus to the market and sold it for as much small change as it would fetch on that particular day. There were official bureaux at which solidi were bought and sold at fixed rates. There may have been a 'par' value of the solidus in small change ('pecunia'); but it was not pegged at it – it could rise and fall. The gold became a general measure of value; with its rise or fall prices rose or fell. When taxes were being paid, the Government, to avoid any risk of getting base solidi, insisted on having all that were brought in melted down and assayed. This meant, of course, a never-ending process of restriking.

Silver was struck very pure, as a rule, but often well below its theoretical weight. The value of silver in terms of gold varied quite a lot. A pound of silver was sold, at different times, for four or five solidi; this gives a rate of 1 to 18 or 1 to $14\frac{2}{5}$. We are inclined to suppose that in theory the silver stood in definite fixed relationships to the gold; in fact, it may have varied, as did the 'pecunia'. We shall call attention later to some curious behaviours of this metal.

The subsidiary coinage ('pecunia') – bronze often with a small admixture of silver – presents a curious problem. Was it tariffed at its metal value, determined by the quantity of silver contained in it? Or was the coinage always of a token character, tariffed well above metal value? And was the amount of silver contained matter of mint practice, not of exact valuation? The coins occasionally present a silver surface; a few contain no silver at all, most of them silver in small, varying proportions. The view that we shall adopt is that the whole of this coinage was considered as bronze, enhanced in value by a little silver and that it was valued above its metal content – on what we might call a nickel basis. The amount of silver was no doubt fixed for each denomination by the mint. But forgery was rife and frequently took the form of separating out the silver from the bronze. It is the worst specimens that tend to survive. Compare with the bronze of the fourth century the *Aes* of Augustus earlier and of Anastasius I later. They too may have been tariffed above their metal value – but a reasonable quantity of brass or copper was offered. The fourth-century bronze seems to need silver to give it any considerable value at all. This, if true, is very interesting; but it means that we shall always be guessing at what the coins were worth.

The question of the unit of account will be troubling us from time to time. In the 'Edict of maximum prices' of A.D. 301 the reckoning is in 'denarii communes', 50,000 to the pound of gold. This reckoning continued down into the fifth century. But from time to time we meet with 'nummi' which seem to be small units of reckoning, but which we cannot relate with certainty to the denarius. The old sestertius reckoning was, perhaps, not completely forgotten. We have guessed that the two-denarius piece of Aurelian may have been a sestertius and so too may have been the piece of Diocletian. But did the reckoning last on later? The 'nummi terentiani' of Anastasius I have been taken to be 'terunciani', referring to the old valuation of the sestertius at forty teruncii; the M, forty-nummia piece would be in question. This is best left as a fascinating possibility.

In a little Appendix at the end we will assemble a few items of possible use – marks on the coins, passages from literature, the codices and metrological writers, etc. We can now advance to the study of the coins.

At his reform of A.D. 295 Diocletian struck the following coins:

(1) In gold, a piece of sixty to the pound, sometimes marked with the Greek numeral *Ξ*.

(2) In silver, a piece of ninety-six to the pound, marked as such in Latin numerals (XCVI), usually struck well under weight.

(3) In silvered bronze three denominations:

(a) A large piece, the follis, as we usually call it, of c. 150 gr. often with reverse legend, GENIO POPVLI ROMANI. Emperor laureate.
(b) A piece of c. 60 gr. Emperor radiate.
(c) A smaller piece of c. 20 gr. Emperor laureate.

This system looks very much like a return to that of Nero – a gold piece equal to twenty-five silver pieces equal to a hundred sestertii of brass. We could interpret it on these lines:

1 gold lb. = 60 aurei = 1,500 silver pieces = 6,000 first bronze = 12,000 second bronze (denarii).

But there are two difficulties. One concerns the relation of gold to silver. It works out as 1 to 15⅝ – 1/60th pound gold equals 25/96th pound silver. But, as early as 323, we find 'siliqua' as the name of a silver coin – and the only such coin that we know is this ninety-sixth of Diocletian. Now, a siliqua is the 1/1728th of a pound – as name of a silver coin representing that part of the pound of gold. That would give a rate of gold to silver as 1 to 18, a value of the aureus as 28-odd silver pieces. Perhaps the solution of this apparently hopeless difficulty is that the value of silver dropped between 295 and 323 and that, with the drop, the name 'siliqua' became appropriate to the silver piece, which originally had been worth more.

The other difficulty concerns the bronze coins. The largest piece is the two-denarius piece of Aurelian, now expressed by a larger coin; it occasionally bears the mark of value XXI. The second piece is the coin of Aurelian, reduced to one denarius, half its original value. The third piece should be a third of the second. But the price of the gold pound in the Edict is 50,000 denarii, not 12,000 as we have made it. We must therefore revise our system to read:

1 lb. gold = 60 aurei = 1,500 silver pieces = 24,000 first bronze = 48,000 denarii,

perhaps a sufficiently close approximation to the price of the Edict.[1]

One interesting possibility must be kept in mind. The 'enormitas pretiorum', the calamitous rise in prices that set in between 295 and 301, may not have been completely cured by the Edict. The gold price of 50,000 to the A͡ pound may have been much higher than that of 295. The system of 295 might have been so far distorted that the two-denarius piece had lost three-fourths of its value. Beginning as a sestertius of the system of Nero it might have sunk to be no more than an As. Lactantius tells us that Diocletian by various ill-considered measures contributed to that rise in prices which he had to fight. The reduction of the second bronze to half its value might be one of these measures. It was well intended – for deflation rather than inflation – but the public took alarm and feared further reductions. It rushed to turn coin into goods and drove prices sky-high.

The first bronze began after A.D. 305 to lose weight and fell by a series of declines to c. 120 gr., c. 100, c. 70 and finally c. 50. As the same

---

[1] The figure of the Edict is certain; it has recently been confirmed by a new fragment. Gold in other forms than coin is tariffed much lower – perhaps because it was not pure.

types are carried on from reduction to reduction it seems probable that the same denomination was represented throughout, by declining weights of metal. If so, the value of gold in terms of these reduced coins must have risen and the denarius must have fallen far beyond the 50,000 to the pound of the Edict. Egyptian documents show over 100,000 denarii to the pound of gold in 308, over 313,000 in 323; but the drop may have been more extreme in Egypt than in the Empire at large.

In or a little before 312 Constantine I introduced his famous gold piece, the solidus, at 72 to the pound; Licinius in the East retained the 60th down to his fall in 324. It was still struck occasionally after him and the chief subdivision of the gold piece, down to Theodosius I, was a third ('triens') of the 60th. The issue of silver seems to have been suspended – perhaps some years before 312. The one common piece of silvered bronze was the piece of c. 50 gr., still tending to lose weight. As it only weighed under a third of the large piece of Diocletian, the 60th aureus should equal 1,200 instead of 400 of these pieces. The solidus, 5/6th of the aureus, would then equal 1,000. As there is clear suggestion in the Codices that there was a 'nummus' of just that value we are inclined to take this guess as a happy one. We get the system:

1 solidus (1/72nd pound) = 24 siliquae (perhaps not struck) = 1,000 silvered bronze = 2,000 denarii – 144,000 denarii to the gold pound.

The system of Licinius in the East would be a little different:

1 aureus (1/60th pound) = 25 (?) siliquae = 1,200 silvered bronze = 2,400 denarii – again, 144,000 to the gold pound. The mark of value XIIΓ on the bronze had not been explained.[1]

Let us check our guess by one of the few pieces of evidence of the period – the inscription of Feltre of 323. It regulates the administration of an estate. An annual income of 60,000 denarii has to supply payments of 10 aurei and one siliqua, and 'n. CCCLXIII'.[2] One reading of this is 241 plus 363 siliquae, 604 in all, or 25 solidi 4 siliquae. If that was the full value of 60,000 denarii, the denarius would go at 172,800 to the

[1] Could it possibly mean 'twelve hundred'? – the number to the aureus?
[2] The 'n' is uncertain – 'nummi' (?) or 'numero' (?). But the 10 aurei 1 siliqua make 241 siliqae and the other number, 363, is exactly one and a half times it; that inclines one to take the 363 also as siliquae – whatever 'n' may mean.

gold pound; if the denarii were not fully expended, the rate would be lower. This seems to agree very well with our guess. The higher figure found in Egypt may be peculiar to that province.

For the rest of the reign of Constantine and for that of his sons down to A.D. 348 there is little change to record. The solidus now rules the gold currency. Silver was again struck in some profusion. The silvered bronze had fallen by 330 to c. 40 gr., and in 335 was further reduced to c. 30. As the common type of GLORIA EXERCITVS is carried over into this last reduction, we again assume that the denomination remained the same. A further drop of the denarius to c. 240,000 to the gold pound is to be assumed.

The year 348, the eleven hundredth year of Rome, witnessed a striking reform of the bronze coinage. Constantius II and Constans struck a piece of c. 80 gr. and its half, of c. 40 gr. The larger piece (Æ 2) rose in 350 to c. 100 gr. only to fall again by degrees to 40 gr. or less in 355. The rebel Magnentius struck pieces of c. 80 and 40 gr., then, towards the close of his reign a larger piece of c. 120 (Æ 1); it looks like an attempt to revive the follis of Diocletian. Julian in 361 made a similar attempt with a slightly lighter coin. The solidus, of course, continued to be struck. The silver piece was reduced in 356-7 to c. 35 gr., while heavier pieces of c. 65 and 80 gr. were commonly struck. We usually call this piece of c. 35 gr. the siliqua, but, as we have seen, the name belonged originally to a larger coin. Mickwitz thought that the new coin was a half siliqua. It seems more probable that the coin was really still the siliqua; the price of silver had risen – and, even so, the coin was struck light. Of the two heavier pieces, that of c. 65 gr. was perhaps the double siliqua; we usually call it the 'miliarense'; while the piece of c. 80 gr. was a special coin, given in largesses.

The two coins, 'miliarense' and 'centenionalis', are only mentioned at dates after 348. By correct linguistic use they should mean 'pieces of one thousand and one hundred units, respectively'. The 'miliarense' would presumably be a silver coin, equal to ten 'centenionales' of silvered bronze. The use of the names would have been suggested by the one thousand one hundredth year of the city. We can now construct a system:

1 solidus = 12 miliarensia = 24 siliquae = 1,200 centenionales = 2,400 half-centenionales = 12,000 'nummi' – the little units in which 'miliarense' and 'centenionalis' were reckoned.

Where does the denarius come in this system? Was it the half centenionalis? Was the 'centenionalis' now the double denarius? Then 172,800 would go to the gold pound – a reduction from what we guessed for the previous period.[1] Or was it half that? The rate would then rise to 345,600. The lower rate seems preferable. The 'nummus' would be two-fifths of the denarius.[2]

The 'centenionalis', alternatively called by its popular name of 'pecunia maiorina', was demonetized by an edict of 395. By the end of the century the name seems to have been applied to a much smaller coin – an Æ 4 instead of an Æ 2; for the 'centenionalis' is allowed to continue in circulation while a larger coin is withdrawn, and the Æ 4 was the only denomination that continued in common use down into the fifth century.

For the rest of the century we may sum up what is known very briefly. In gold and silver, solidus,[3] siliqua and miliarense are struck as before. In silvered bronze we find (1) an Æ 2 (the Æ 1 stops just after Jovian) of c. 80 gr. (2) An Æ 3 of c. 40 gr. – dominant under Valentinian I and his family. (3) An Æ 4 of c. 20 gr. – dominant at the end of the reign of Theodosius I. At the value of the denarius in this period we can only guess. If the centenionalis of c. 80 gr. went at 1,200 to the solidus, the reduced centenionalis of c. 20 might go at 4,800. Can we now consider the centenionalis as equal to one denarius, not to two? We should then get 345,600 denarii to the gold pound – a figure which seems to be more or less correct according to the progress of decline.

A coin, called the 'decargyrus nummus' or 'pecunia maior' was withdrawn from circulation by the Edict of 395. Was it our Æ 2 or our Æ 3? And was it called 'decargyrus' because it contained a tenth part of silver or because ten of it went to the 'miliarense'? We are reduced to guessing here. The real difficulty is that the Edict seems to know of only two coins, whilst our trays show us three.

This statement of the facts of fourth-century coinage may seem naked and incomplete. But, at least, it avoids too many unverifiable hypotheses and may help future investigators to advance to completer knowledge. We must not expect to hit distant targets, which are hardly yet in sight.

[1] This view would mean a drop in the price of gold, such as we seem to deduce also from the behaviour of the silver coinage.

[2] I have not attempted to reconstruct the system of Magnentius and Julian. Their Æ 1 might be expected to rank as about the 400th part of the solidus. On Julian, see Elmer, 'Die Kupfergold Reform under Julianus Philosophus', *N.Z.*, 1937, pp. 25 ff.

[3] For the value of the solidus in the fifth and sixth centuries, see Philip Grierson, *JRS.*, 1959, pp. 73 ff.

APPENDIX

Marks of Value

We have already spoken of the 60 and 96 on gold and silver of Diocletian and the XX on the follis. The solidus is marked by OB, 72; the letters also seem to denote 'obryzum' – 'pure gold'. PS on the silver stands for 'pusulatum', the name for the pure metal. LXXII occurs on bronze of c. 354, apparently stating the number that went to the pound. Other marks of value are CMH on bronze, c. 100 gr., of Nicomedia and Cyzicus (c. 308), XIIΓ on bronze, c. 50 gr. in Eastern mints of Licinius I, after c. 317, NKYX C on gold of Nicomedia (c. 309).

Other marks are quite uncertain and not worth quoting here.

Value of the Metals

An Edict of 388 values the solidus at 25 lb. of bronze; gold is to bronze as 1 to 1,800. Prices of the silver are given as four or five solidi – gold to silver 1 to 18 or 1 to 14⅔; the lower rate is the earlier. A passage in the *Codex Theodosianus* (XI, XXI, 3) seems to make gold equal to 100 times a particular kind of bronze – perhaps silvered bronze, valued high above its metal. We can put this to a test with the solidus and centenionalis of 348. 1 solidus, 1/72nd pound, would equal 1,800 pure bronze pieces of the same weight, or c. 1,570 pieces of centenionalis weight. But the relation of the solidus to the centenionalis is 120 to 1, about thirteen times its value as pure bronze.

This is perhaps evidence enough that the silvered bronze was valued high above its value as pure bronze.

Prices of Pork

In the Edict of 301, 1 lb. pork costs 12 denarii.

In 363 1 lb. of pork costs 6 folles.

In 389 80 lb. of pork cost 1 solidus.

In 419 20 lb. of pork cost 1,200 denarii (1 lb. = 60 denarii).

It is a little difficult to make a proper use of these figures, as the denarius is changing in value all the time.

In 301 1 lb. pork = 12 d, 80 lb. pork = 960 d = $\frac{50,000}{960}$ lb. A∕

In 389 80 lb. pork = $\frac{1}{72}$ lb. A∕ (1 solidus).

The price, then, has dropped by nearly a third. If we apply this correction to all our figures:

The 1 lb. pork of 363 (6 folles) would equal 9 folles, unlowered.
The 1 lb. pork of 419 would equal 90 denarii, unlowered.

If, as we guess, the solidus (60 d) of 389 equalled 4,800 d, the lb. A/ would equal 345,600 d – a drop by nearly 7 times since 301.

The 6 folles of A.D. 363 would equal 9 folles, unlowered.
9 folles then = 12 denarii of A.D. 301 = perhaps some 84 denarii of reduced standard.

We must look, then, for a coin of the value of c. 9 denarii: this seems a high valuation even for the Æ 1 of Julian I.

Folles. A passage in the *Codex Theodosianus* (VI, 4, 5) states allowances for the different praetorships:

25,000 folles and 50 lb. of silver.
20,000 folles and 40 lb. of silver.
15,000 folles and 30 lb. of silver.

It will be noted that there is a balance between 500 folles and a pound of silver. 'Follis' here seems to be coin rather than bag of coins.

St Augustine (*Sermons* 389, 3) tells of a man who, whenever he sold a solidus, gave two folles, a trival proportion of the whole, to the poor. This little follis is presumably the Æ 4 of the late fourth to fifth centuries.

Metrological Writers

A λεπτόν equals 1/6,000th solidus. 1 κοδράντης equals 2 λεπτά. 1 follis equals 4 κοδράνται or 8 λεπτά. 1 lb. gold is a follis, containing 72 solidi, 864 miliarensia, 1,728 siliquae. 1 lb. silver is a follis containing 100 denarii, 6,000 λεπτά. There is a silver follis equalling 125 miliarensia. 1 follis contains 250 denarii of $\frac{1}{4}$ lb. each, $312\frac{1}{2}$ lb. in all.

There are references in the *Codex Theodosianus* to a strange term 'denarismus'; 'denarismo vel unciis' or 'φόλλις δύο λεπτὰ κατὰ τὸν δηνάρισμον ἀλλ᾽ οὐ κατὰ τὸν ἀργυρισμὸν'. The meaning remains obscure.

The 'follis', bag of coins representing quite a large value, was a regular feature of the fourth century.[1]

4. SUCCESS AND FAILURE

The great gain of the fourth century was the improved supply of the

[1] See A. H. M. Jones, 'The Origin and Early History of the Follis', *J.R.S.*, 1959, pp. 34 ff.

precious metals – due in part to the Eastern conquests of Diocletian, in part to the ruthless calling in of private stocks for the Imperial account, in part again to the release of temple treasures at the decline of paganism. The rise in value of gold as compared to silver in the late fourth century is very remarkable,[1] for it occurs at a time when the silver coinage was beginning to decline and when the silver coins, miliarense and siliqua, were both being struck below standard weight. And then, too, there is the curious fact that silver of the period is very rarely found except in Britain. The calling in of the 'pecunia maior', too, in 395 suggests that the Government wished to recover the silver content of that coin. Everything, in fact, except the ratio of gold to silver, points rather to a scarcity than to a superabundance of silver. A possible explanation might be that silver was replacing gold on a large scale for articles of luxury in trade, and that, for this reason, silver, though not actually scarce, was not readily available for the coinage. The Byzantine Empire, we must remember, was run mainly on a coinage of gold and bronze.

One evil inheritance from the third century was the use of bronze, with a coating and slight admixture of silver, to represent values above those of the ordinary bronze. All the systems of the fourth century suffered to some extent from this evil, and to it we may attribute the instability of values and the tendency of the unit of account to keep on falling. Constantine I in 324 seems to have arrested the fall of the denarius at the figure of 172,800 to the gold pound. But, in one province, Egypt, he did not back the silvered bronze with money of gold and silver. The result was that, in Egypt, and, so far as we can tell, nowhere else, the unit of account fell further and further away, till many millions were reckoned to the gold pound.[2] Evidently the bronze coinage was quite unfitted to bear the whole burden of the currency. It was treated more and more as a pure token or 'paper' currency, which hardly represented real value at all and to which ever-increasing nominal values were attached, without increasing its actual purchasing power. We shall see below in Chapter III how the general policy of the Empire made it possible for one province to run a course so far distinct from the general course of the Empire. The decay of the bronze coinage n Illyricum and the West in the closing years of the fourth century is simply a symptom of the decline of Roman authority in

---

[1] Cp. above, p. 186.
[2] Cp. Wessey, *Ein Altersindizium in Philogelos, Abh. d. Kais. Ak. d. Wiss.*, Vienna, Phil.-hist. Klasse, CXLIX, pp. 1 ff.

those parts. The Government had not yet abandoned its claim to possession, but showed itself more and more incapable of ministering to the requirements of local trade, of which the bronze coinage was an essential part.

The financial administration was simplified by the elimination of the Senate from all Imperial affairs; it was now no more than the city council of Rome and Constantinople. The only divisions of authority were those that resulted from the division of the Imperial power – at first between the two Augusti and the two Caesars of the tetrarchy of Diocletian, afterwards between the Augustus of the East and the Augustus of the West. Even so, a large measure of uniformity was secured by conference between the heads of departments. It is only after the final division of the Empire under Arcadius and Honorius that the coinages of East and West really parted company. The chief financial officer was the 'comes sacrarum largitionum', assisted by some subsidiary 'comites', such as the 'comes auri'. The individual mints were still controlled by the 'procuratores '. For the personnel of the mint we find the term 'monetales' employed. Service in the mint came to be an hereditary profession, from which no one could escape except by providing a substitute. The system of control was now most elaborate and aimed at nothing less than the fixing of responsibility for every issue. But the question here was that of Juvenal, 'quis custodiet ipsos custodes?' In spite of all the machinery of control, fraud of various kinds was rampant.[1]

Looking on the system as a whole, we must grant it a certain limited success. No financial crisis on the scale of that of the third century recurred. The financial resources of the Empire were carefully husbanded and the gold coinage in particular enjoyed a well-deserved respect even beyond the bounds of the Empire. The main weakness was the prevailing corruption in and about the mint and the unsatisfactory character of the coinage of silvered bronze, which could not be maintained in stable relations with the gold and silver.

5. ORGANIZATION OF THE MINTS

Of the details of mint organization we know little. There was a careful subdivision of the work of the mints over a number of officinae and perhaps a distribution of the work inside the officinae to smaller groups of workmen. Fabric becomes more and more uniform everywhere.

[1] See below, Chapter III.

The style is on the decline. Portraiture, the *chef d'œuvre* of the early Empire, is still on a high technical level. But the growth of the 'hieratic' principle – the principle, that is to say, of representing the Emperor rather in his formal aspect than as a living individual – is in the long run fatal to real life. Stress is laid more and more on the attributes of power, the diadem, the mantle, the sceptre, the orb; these attributes, which assume ever more stereotyped forms, crowd out the living interest, and Emperor after Emperor is represented with little to distinguish him from his fellows. In the reverse types we have to report a growing barbarism both of theme and of rendering. In the East a new life gradually pushed through and blossomed in the development of Byzantine art, which has a conscious theory of its own, unlike the Greek, but not unworthy of respect. In the West the life impulse slowly died and left at the last little beyond an elaborate formalism. When the early medieval art appears in the West it is found to be aiming at a beauty of ornament and pattern rather than of life.

6. MINTS AND CHRONOLOGY

Questions of mint hardly trouble us in this period, when the mint-mark is a regular part of the coin. Each mint, however, has an individual style of its own, marked enough to allow of the attribution of unsigned issues. Dating, of course, still depends mainly on the Imperial portrait, though the omission of Imperial titles with numbers makes it often difficult to attribute coins with certainty to their exact place in a reign. A few cases of attribution where knowledge is required, may be noted. The coins of 'Divus Claudius', 'Divus Maximianus' and 'Divus Galerius' were issued partly by Constantine I, partly by Maxentius, at war with their rivals. The coins of Theodora were struck after her death by Constantine I (c. 336–7). The coins of Helena and Fausta with obverse title 'N(obilissima) F(emina)' and reverse type, star, have been the theme of a long controversy.[1] There can be little doubt, however, that they were struck for Helena, the mother, and Fausta, the wife of Constantine I. It has been supposed that they were issued some time after their deaths. But why should not 'nobilissima femina' correspond to 'nobilissimus Caesar', as a title preceding 'Augusta'? The weights and mint-marks also suggest early dates. A remarkable series of anonymous types, with reference to Egyptian religion – Serapis, Isis Pharia and

[1] Cp. Maurice, *Numismatique Constantinienne*, Vol. II, pp. 451 ff.

Anubis – is attributed with strong probability to the late fourth century.[1] A similar, but smaller, series of Antioch has also been attributed to an earlier date.

Our knowledge of the finds of this period is far from satisfactory as yet. The chief facts that emerge are (1) the separation of the coins of Diocletian from the coins of Aurelian and his successors down to the reform of 296; examples of sestertii, however, in finds of the age of Diocletian have been recorded; (2) the joint appearance in hoards of the small bronze issues of Constantine I and Licinius I in the period from 312 to 324. A curious problem, as yet unsolved, is presented by the imitations of the bronze coinage. When the module of the imitation is approximately the same as that of the original we may attribute the imitation to contemporary forgery. More puzzling are the 'minimi', pieces of very small module and, often, of great barbarism of style, copying not only the diademed heads of the fourth century, but also the radiate heads of the third. Certain Egyptian 'minimi', known chiefly from Egyptian hoards, copy closely the small bronze coins of Eastern mints of the late fourth century, and were possibly issued irregularly in Egypt – perhaps by the great landowners, who asserted a half-independence of the Imperial Government.[2] More familiar to us are the 'minimi', diademed or radiate, of the West, which are peculiarly plentiful in some British finds. Failing any definite evidence of date, we are inclined to see in them an emergency local coinage in Gaul and Britain during the latter years of the fourth century and perhaps even more in the early years of the fifth, in the decay of the Roman power. If anyone objects to this view that the types imitated are often of much earlier date, we may remind him that the earliest Anglo-Saxon sceattas, which occasionally show some points of resemblance to the 'minimi', often hark back to much earlier types – to the radiate heads of the Gallic Emperors or to the type of the she-wolf and twins of the years 330 to 337.[3]

[1] Cp. A. Alfoeldi, *A Festival of Isis in Rome*, etc., 1937.

[2] Cp. J. G. Milne in *Num. Chron.*, 1926, pp. 43 ff., especially p. 61.

[3] This question of barbarous imitations is still a most vexed one. Some scholars regard all imitations as more or less contemporary with their originals. Others place many of them very much later. I would make one or two points plain here:

(a) The temptation to date all imitations downwards must be resisted: many were certainly contemporary.

(b) The case for the early date of radiate imitations is often taken as proved, particularly on the evidence of the hoard in the theatre of St Albans. But one hoard at least – that of Richborough – must be later: for it contains a number of apparent imitations of fourth-century types, it has some strange types of its own – apparently attempts at expressing new ideas: it shows definite kinship to some early Anglo-Saxon sceattas.

(c) The 'minimi, or 'minimissimi', pieces of tiny module, seem likely to belong to a time when even bronze was very scarce.

(d) The sceattas copy radiate, as well as diademed types. Radiates, then, were, as we must have expected, still known. If a number of radiates were found and imitated later, we have to consider two dates as possible – the date of the originals and the date, quite possibly much later, of the copies.

Evidence on this subject is still accumulating and being keenly studied. More certainty on the dubious points may be hoped for before long.

CHAPTER II

The Content of the Later Imperial Coinage. Types and Legends

I. GENERAL TENDENCIES

Gradual as was the actual transition from the Empire of the third century to the new Empire of Diocletian, the change once made was soon found to be a decisive one. It was not so much that new features were introduced, as that the whole emphasis was shifted to a new class of subjects. The forms of the Empire down to Diocletian had been, with few exceptions, those of the free State under its 'Princeps'; those of the new Empire were those of an Eastern monarchy under its king. The types of the new age faithfully mirror its new tendencies. Apart from changes in detail, we find a new conception of the Imperial office, a new relation towards religion, a new attitude towards the celebration of contemporary history; and, perhaps as striking as any other change, a new spirit, tainted with savagery and boastfulness, informs the whole coinage. Before we come to the more detailed discussion of different classes of types, a few words on these main changes will help to clear the way.

The principate of Augustus was dead. The Emperor of the fourth and fifth centuries is the traditional 'Great King', the master of his subjects, worshipped almost as a god. The triumph of Christianity, it is true, forced into the background the divinity of the Emperor or rather shaded it off into something like the doctrine of the 'divine right of kings'. But the word 'sacer' is now used as an almost exact equivalent of 'Imperial', and the personality of the Emperor dominates the entire coinage. The exact form of division of the Imperial power designed by Diocletian was not permanent. But the fundamental distinction between East and West, which had never been entirely overcome, was definitely recognized by the foundation of the Eastern capital of Constantinople in A.D. 326. The restorations of the Imperial unity under Constantine I, Constantius II and Theodosius I were only provisional, and the East, in the end, disengaged itself from the sinking Empire of the West and carried over its own age-long history, touched with something of the Roman tradition, into the Middle Ages. The West gradually relapsed into the barbarism from which Rome had raised it, while Rome herself and Italy stood in an equivocal middle position, partly saved from barbarism by the influence of the East. The Senate, of course, had now lost its last remnants of political power. It has no influence on the coinage and is entirely confined to its local dignity in the two capitals.

The age was one in which religion occupied a great place in men's thoughts and emotions. It begins with the decisive battle between paganism and Christianity; it continues with the intestine struggles of the Christian Church and the abortive pagan revival of Julian: it ends with the stamping of a definite Christian mark on the coinage. Diocletian attempted to associate his dynasty in the closest possible way with the old paganism in the persons of Jupiter and Hercules.[1] Then follows a short period in which the 'invincible Sun-god', now, it may be, closely associated with the worship of Mithras, comes to the front. Then follows an interval of neutrality, in which, as if by common consent, direct religious references were banned and the field was left to vague allegorical conceptions of neutral character. Finally Christianity, which had already begun to find expression in the form of symbols on the coins, gained the day and definite Christian types appear. The labarum, or standard, emblazoned with the monogram of Christ (☧) became the sign of the Christian Emperor. Julian's apostasy is represented by his 'Apis bull' type. After his death the invasion of the coinage by Christian forms proceeds to its completion. The cross and labarum constantly appear and the Emperor is celebrated as the Defender of the Faith. The full exploitation of the symbolism of the new faith was, however, reserved for the Byzantine Empire.

The worship of the Sun-god, to which Mithraism was closely allied, might seem to have much in common with Christianity. Its morality was often high; in Mithraism, some features seemed to the Fathers to have been stolen from Christianity. Julian was the last to maintain the Sun-god in supreme honour in his religious scheme. The bitter factions of the Christian Church, distracted between Arians and Athanasians, have hardly left a mark on the coinage – unless there still

---

[1] This system of god the father and god the son may be regarded as an attempt to restate the old paganism in a form that might be acceptable to minorities like the Christian. Diocletian may have known just enough of the Faith from his wife and sister, who were Christians, to imagine that his system was not so far from the Christian. He certainly did not contemplate persecution at first.

remain allusions to be discovered that have as yet escaped us.[1] In fact, Christianity, in the early day of its triumph, seems to have been singularly moderate in its self-assertion; we may safely conclude that there were powerful pagan elements still surviving in the official classes.

The worship of the personifications or 'Virtues' is, on the whole, on the decline. It had always been closely associated with the person of the Emperor and it may be that Christian belief interposed difficulties here. One personification, that of the Genius of Emperor or State, plays a very large part and we know from literature that it held a central position in the thought of the time. We shall see later how Christianity took over under its own forms the great conception of the 'Victory', who accompanies the march of Rome from age to age.

The coinage of the fourth century did not cease to offer some kind of medallic history of the Empire, but something definite was lost for ever. The propagandist element is still strong – the Government is concerned to present its policies in an attractive light to its subjects. But there is on the whole a decline in active political interest and in the commemoration of particular events: vague general conceptions associated with formal types tend to supplant the definite portrayal of current happenings. The army, now strongly felt to be the only pro-tection of civilization against insurgent barbarism, is constantly in the picture and, in the incessant references to the 'Safety', the 'Security', the 'Glory' of the State we see the genuine concern of the Government to steer the ship safely through to its haven. As we advance, we find the forms of the coinage gradually stiffening into a lifeless conventionality. Each denomination tends to gain a type of its own which remains unchanged for years at a time. It is perhaps a feature of the exhaustion of the time that interest could not be shifted from year to year over the moving course of events, but had to be concentrated on the contempla-tion of a few quasi-permanent features of the life of the State.

The general change in the moral tone of the coinage is easier felt than described. Rome of the great days had indeed celebrated her victories, but usually with a strict sense of proportion and reality and without any vainglorious mouthings. Now we are constantly hearing of the 'Glory of the Romans', the 'Glory of the State' – the word 'Gloria' itself is new to the language of the coins. This is, however, at

---

[1] But the type of Magnentius, SALV̩S DD NN AVG ET CAES, with the Chi-Rho and Alpha and Omega, shows us that pagan Emperor making a bid at the last for Christian support; his type, throwing the emphasis on the person of Jesus Christ, reflects the fact that the West was strongly inclined to the Athanasian position.

worst a minor fault of taste. More serious is the element of savagery, which the conflict with a barbarian world introduced. The Emperor is portrayed, with a special complacency, as the 'Conqueror of the whole world', the 'Conqueror of the barbarian nations', and is shown setting his foot in triumph on a crouching captive. The famous 'Fel. Temp. Reparatio' of Constantius II shows a Roman legionary in act to transfix with his spear a fallen Persian: in the 'Gloria Romanorum' of Valentinian I the Emperor drags a captive by the hair. We are familiar with the thought that the Empire fell, not by the barbarians without, but by the barbarians within: such types as these are an eloquent comment on the justness of that reflexion.

The obverse of the coin is, of course, reserved for the Emperor, though, in the new order of things, several Emperors often strike concurrently at the same mint. The right of portraiture is still extended to the Caesars, the Emperors to be, and occasionally, but not so commonly, to the ladies of the Imperial house. Remarkable is the small coinage of Hannibalianus, the nephew whom Constantine I appointed King of the Bosphorus but who was murdered, after Constantine's death, by the troops. The foundation of Constantinople was commemorated by special issues with the heads of Roma, Constantinopolis, and the people of Rome on the obverses. Such substitutions of the obverses for the Imperial are decidedly rare. Almost the only other exceptions are in the little series of coins, with religious types of the mints of Alexandria and Antioch, struck, in part at any rate, under Julian.[1]

The Imperial title is much less open to variety than before. The title 'Imperator' gives place to that of 'D(ominus) N(oster)' under the sons of Constantine I and the description 'P(ius) F(elix)' becomes an invariable part of the style. The praenomen is seldom given, the gentile name (cp. 'Iulius', 'Valerius') more commonly. The consulship is occasionally mentioned on the reverse and so too the proconsular power, which in the early Empire had hardly ever found expression. The tribunician power, the chief pontificate, the title of 'pater patriae' are almost obsolete. There is one exceptional use of the cognomen 'imperator' with a number to represent the regnal years of Theodosius II. The Caesar is regularly designated by that name with the distinguishing epithet 'Nobilissimus'. With Gratian the custom was introduced of giving the full Imperial title 'Augustus' to the junior colleague: the title 'Augg. Aug.' which Gratian bears on his earliest coins seems to describe

[1] But see p. 226 f. above.

him as the 'Augustus dependent on the two (senior) Augusti'. The Empress is still the 'Augusta'. The title 'N(obilissima) F(emina)', which is given on rare issues to a Helena and Fausta, has been discussed above.[1]

The laureate wreath is still at first the normal wear for the Emperor. Later the diadem of Eastern monarchy, interwoven with flowers or pearls, takes its place. The radiate crown of the Sun-god is still found under Constantine I, while military portraits, with helmet, spear and shield, become increasingly common. Common too is the portrait with Imperial mantle and eagle-tipped sceptre, later with the sceptre and orb, which became the choice symbols of Imperial power. With Constantius II comes in the facing military portrait, which was to play so large a part in the Byzantine coinage. In general, we notice a great elaboration of ornament and ritual – the Emperor is represented less as an individual than as the holder of a great symbolic office.

2. TYPES CLASSIFIED

The reverses can only be studied satisfactorily under different subject groups. We may adopt the following provisional classification:

(*a*) Types in which the person of the Emperor is the main interest.

(*b*) Types showing the care of the Emperor for the State.

(*c*) Types relating to provincial and foreign affairs.

(*d*) Military types.

(*e*) Religious types, with personifications and the 'consecration' issues, so far as they continued to exist.

(*f*) Various animate and inanimate types.

(*g*) Buildings.

The reverse legends naturally, as a rule, describe the types; but the practice becomes more and more common of associating with a composite type a legend vaguely characterizing, rather than describing it: to take one or two examples – Constantine and his sons are described as the 'Safety and Hope of the State', a warrior spearing a fallen foe symbolizes the 'Restoration of Happy Times', a Victory stands for the 'Security of the State', the Emperor setting his foot on the 'ancient serpent' is an emblem of the 'Imperial Victory'. The tendency deserves close attention, for it is markedly characteristic of the age.

[1] See above, p. 226.

(a) *Types of the Emperor*

The Emperor, in his formal aspect of head of the State, is mainly represented by the portraits of the obverse. On the reverse he is occasionally represented in his robes as consul or in his chariot, scattering largesse to the people. In an age where there were usually several colleagues in the Imperial power, there was a strong preference for types emphasizing the good relations of the colleagues: such are the 'Perpetua Concordia Augg.' of the aureus that shows Diocletian crowned by Jupiter and Maximian crowned by Hercules, the 'Gloria Romanorum' of the aureus that shows Valentinian I and Valens throned together, holding their orbs, or the 'Victoria Augg.' of the later solidi, showing the two Emperors seated side by side, while over them broods the Imperial Victory. Maxentius took pains to commend himself to his subjects, by picturing on his coins the divine powers that help him to preserve his cities (Plate LIX, 2) or his ceremonial appearance at his consulship (Plate LIX, 3). A series of 'Pietas' types shows the Empress Fausta with her children and Constantine and his sons often appear together in military dress, with such legends as 'Felicitas Romanorum' or 'Salus et Spes Reipublicae'. Anthemius and Leo I are represented together, holding spears and crosses, with the legend 'Salus Reipublicae'. The Empress Aelia Flaccilla, wife of Theodosius I, appears standing, with her hands clasped on her breast in prayer, as 'Salus Reipublicae', and the marriage of Marcian and Pulcheria is represented by figures of the two rulers, united in holy wedlock by Christ, with the remarkable legend 'Feliciter Nubtiis'. The princes still bear the title 'Princeps Iuventutis' (Plate LIX, 1, 10) and appear with such military attributes as spear, shield and standards; sometimes the legend reads 'Principia Iuventutis', the first stage of military training for the career of Emperor. The 'Spes' type still bears witness to the hopes centred in the heir (Plate LX, 2),[1] and Arcadius is acclaimed on a solidus as the 'Nova Spes Reipublicae'. Gratian, with labarum and spear, is hailed as the 'Gloria Novi Saeculi'[2] on his accession to the throne; another type shows him as the 'Spes P.R.' standing between his seated senior colleagues (Plate LX, 9). A new turn is given to the same thought by the legend 'Bono Reipublicae' or 'Bono Reipublicae Natus' (cp. Plate LIX, 4), which was used by Constantine I and Magnus Maximus and continues in use in the fifth century.

---

[1] Cp. Pl. LIX, 9, Fausta and children.
[2] There is a clear reference to the 'decus hoc aevi', the child of promise in Virgil's fourth Eclogue; we know that Ausonius applied the imagery of the Eclogue to Gratian.

The Imperial largesses are no longer represented by scenes of distribution with the Emperor on a platform: the new equivalent is the scattering of coins by the Emperor from his chariot (Plate LIX, 14). The occasion of the arrival of the Emperor in one of the chief towns of the Empire is still represented by the Emperor riding on horseback and such legends as 'Felix Adventus Aug.'.

The Imperial vows were celebrated as ever with especial emphasis at the expiry of each five years of the reign, with such formulae as 'Vot. V. Mult(iplicatis) X' or 'Sic X Sic XX'. The most common type is the plain legend in a wreath (cp. Plate LXI, 1, 2), but the allusion to the vows is often introduced as a detail of a larger type – on the base of a statue, on the shield held by two Victories – or associated with a type of Victory (Plates LX, 18; LXI, 4). The 'Vota' legend is sometimes illustrated by more elaborate types – by the two Emperors enthroned together (Valens), by the figures of Roma and Constantinopolis (Honorius – Plate LXI, 3), by the Emperor and a kneeling figure of Rome (Valentinian III – Plate LXI, 5). An unusually full expression of the vows appears on the big silver coin of Constantine I, with the legend 'Vota orbis et urbis sen(atus) et p(opuli) R(omani)'. Of the remarkable series, celebrating Egyptian deities, we have already spoken; it is to some extent an expression of the struggles of the later paganism. These 'Vota' types are of great importance as a help to chronology; we have to remember, however, that the vows were sometimes celebrated in advance of the right time and that vows, appropriate to a senior Emperor, may sometimes appear on the coins of a junior colleague.[1]

Of the consecration issues we shall have to speak under religious types. The special occasion of the abdication of Diocletian and Maximian is appropriately marked by coins, celebrating the 'Quiet Retirement of the Emperors', and the 'Providence' that had arranged for the succession. The anti-climax of the return of Maximian to active political life is represented by coins, giving him the title of 'senior' Augustus.

(b) Types of the Emperor and State

The care for the State, which seems to have been ever present in the mind of the rulers, is reflected in the number of legends acclaiming the

---

[1] Cp. Mattingly in *Proceedings of the British Academy*, 1950, 1957. The vows were usually celebrated according to a set plan. 'Vota V Mult. X' began after the completion of the fourth year and so on. But the formula could sometimes mean that five years' vows were paid, vows for ten years undertaken with increase. Usage varies and has to be studied from period to period.

'Peace' (Plate LX, 1), the 'Happiness' (Plate LIX, 8, 15), the 'Glory' (Plate LX, 7, 11, 12, 14, 15, 16), the 'Safety' (Plate LX, 8), the 'Security' (Plate LX, 4), of the State. Constantine I (Plate LIX, 6, 8) and Magnentius claim the credit of having restored the liberty of Rome, Vetranio appears as 'Saviour' ('Salvator' – Plate LX, 3), Valentinian I and Valens as 'Restorers' ('Restitutores') of the State (Plate LX, 5, 6). Under Theodosius I the conception of the 'Reparatio Reipublicae' is conveyed by a type, showing the Emperor stretching out a hand to raise a kneeling woman. The well-known series of types of Constantius II and Constans with the legend 'Fel(icium) Temp(orum) Reparatio' presents the general idea of 'reconstruction' under a variety of aspects – by the Roman legionary spearing a fallen Persian, by the Emperor dragging a barbarian from his forest hut – presumably to settle within the Empire – by Victory steering the Emperor's bark, by the phoenix as the type of eternal Rome (Plate LIX, 11–13).[1] Magnentius repeats the same conception, with fresh emphasis, when he represents himself, a victorious general, as 'Gloria et reparatio temporum'. Very commonly the idea of the 'Glory of the State' is conveyed by the old and new capitals, Rome and Constantinople, seated enthroned side by side. Later the idea of the 'Victory of the Augusti' is expressed by a figure of the Emperor, trampling down a foeman or a human-headed serpent (Plate LX, 10, 13). Many similar types have a definite military setting and will be considered below under the military heading. We may almost say that the thought of the State was an obsession with the Government, which devoted so much effort to preserve it intact, at whatever cost to individuals. The remarkable types of Constantine I representing the 'Senate' by a man in robes of State and the Roman knights by a figure on horseback (Plate LIX, 5) show the interest of Constantine I in the Roman aristocracy. For the most part the orders are confounded in the one general conception of 'respublica'.

(c) *Types of Provinces and Foreign Powers*

We have already mentioned that definite and particular reference to current events tends to yield place to more general forms of allusion. Exceptions, however, still occur. The great hoard recently discovered at Arras has enriched us with some splendid medallions of gold,

[1] The 'reparatio' falls at the eleventh century of Rome and references to Virgil's fourth Eclogue seem to be present. The soldier may be Achilles, striking down a Trojan; the Victory in ship may suggest the new Argo; the 'barbarian dragged from a hut' is possibly something quite different – the child of promise led by a warrior to take up the valorous tasks of his prime. Cp. H. Mattingly, 'Fel. Temp. Reparatio', *Num. Chron.*, 1933, pp. 2 ff.

commemorating the recovery of Britain by Constantius I: one of the largest and finest of them shows Constantius riding up to the gates of a town at which kneels a suppliant woman, expressly identified as 'Lon(dinium'), while on the river below a boat with armed men is in attendance. The mint of Carthage celebrates the city herself and the province of Africa (Plate LXI, 6, 7). Constantine I celebrates by name his Sarmatian victory and represents 'Francia' and 'Alamannia' (Plate LXI, 8), seated with hands bound behind their backs in the old tradition of the 'capta provincia'. A type of a sea-god for Hannibalianus represents his kingdom of the Bosphorus (Plate LXI, 9). Julian honours the valour of the Gallic army, which fought for him so gallantly to recover the province from its German invaders, and later the valour of the Roman army with which he sought to conquer Persia. Honorius has a type of the solidus, in which the lion under his foot symbolizes his African victory of A.D. 413. The remarkable type of Constans, 'Bononia Oceanensis', that shows his departure for the campaign in Britain, is only found on a contorniate and has, strictly speaking, no place in our present discussion. The great victory of Aetius over the Huns at Chalons comes too late to receive the numismatic commentary that its signal importance deserves.

Events of a more peaceful character find even scantier commemoration. One or two interesting types record the transference of the mint of Ostia to Arelate by Constantine the Great. The foundation of Constantinople was, as we have already seen, commemorated by special issues in honour of the two capitals, the old and the new, and Roma and Constantinopolis constantly appear as types of the 'Glory' or the 'Safety' of the State. The 'Invicta Roma Aeterna' on the coins of Priscus Attalus, the puppet-Emperor of the Visigoths, has a curiously ironical sound. A small silver coin of Julius Nepos shows Ravenna, the last capital of the West, as a towered woman, with her foot set on a prow, holding spear and cornucopiae.

(d) Types of the Army

The all-important role of the army, the bulwark of Rome against the insurgent barbarians, is faithfully represented by the general character of the coinage. The Emperor is depicted, commonly in military garb, often setting his foot on a captive, under the proud title of 'Debellator', 'Triumphator gentium barbararum'. A multitude of 'Victoria' and 'Virtus' types (Plate LXI, 12, 15)[1] celebrates the victorious course of

---

[1] Pl. LXI, 13, seems to show the plan of a camp.

Roman arms and the Roman valour by which it is secured. Favourite types are the Victories supporting a shield, Victory with trophy and captive, the Emperor setting his foot on a captive, a Roman legionary dragging a prostrate foeman, the Emperor standing armed or riding on horseback, the legionary standards (Plate LXI, 16); these types are associated with such legends as 'Pax Aeterna Aug.', 'Pacatores Gentium', 'Ob Victoriam triumfalem', 'Ubique Victores', 'Victor omnium gentium', 'Victor totius orbis', 'Victoriae Laetae Princ(ipum) Perp(etuorum)', 'Virtus Exercitus Romanorum', 'Salus Reipublicae', or 'Securitas Perpetua'. The military attendance of the Emperor is shown by mounted figures on the aureus of Maximian (Plate LXI, 10). A remarkable solidus of Constantine I represents the 'Safety of the State' by a group of the Emperor crowned by Victory and attended by nine soldiers. The famous fort on the Danube, 'Constantiniana Dafne', is celebrated on a coin (Plate LXI, 11). Very prominent is the conception of the 'Glory of the Army', which is represented by two soldiers with spears and shields on the common copper coins of Constantine and his family (A.D. 330–7). There is no mistaking the importance attached to military prowess in this age of the decline of the Roman arms. But one evil of the previous century had to some extent been overcome. The legions had been taught their place and were no longer so ready to seize the first opportunity of putting a pretender on the throne; the establishment of the dynastic principle no doubt contributed its share here. Pretenders indeed there still were; but, considering the opportunities for rebellion provided by the general unsettlement of the times, we are disposed rather to wonder at the loyalty of the troops to the established régime. The period of the ascendancy of the barbarian 'magistri militum' in the fifth century has left little mark on a coinage that was gradually falling mute.

(e) Religious Types

We have first to consider the records of the last rallies of paganism on the Imperial coinage. Diocletian associated himself in a special way with the great father of the Roman gods, Jupiter, and was commonly known as 'Jovius'; his colleague, Maximian, added to the wisdom and foresight of the Imperial Jupiter the strength and valour of his patron Hercules, after whom he was named 'Herculius'. The worship of these two great deities is the keynote of the religious types of the tetrarchy. Jupiter is usually represented simply with his thunderbolt, sceptre and eagle: the myths relating to Hercules gave scope to more varied treatment and a number of his labours figure on the gold of Maximian (Plate LXII, 3, 4). The only other deities to claim a large part are Mars, the god of war, and 'Invictus Sol', the Eastern divinity so closely associated with Mithraism and so deeply enshrined in the affections of the troops. In the period after the defeat of Maxentius, 'Invictus Sol' became for a moment the dominant power in the Roman religious world, but his ascendancy ended with the growing devotion of Constantine to the Christian Church. The Dioscuri appear on coins of Constantine I and Maxentius (Plate LXII, 1, 2). The cult of the Roman goddesses is hardly represented except by the 'Venus Victrix' of Galeria Valeria, wife of Galerius (Plate LXII, 15). Roma, as the patron-goddess of the old capital, enjoyed a special worship under Maxentius and held her place – perhaps as a personification rather than as a true divinity – even later (Plates LXII, 9-12; LXIII, 13). Jupiter is honoured by preference with the title 'Conservator' (Plate LXII, 5), as also is Mars (cp. Plate LXII, 6, 7, 8): Sol is 'Invictus', 'Invictus Comes' (Plate LXII, 13, 14), or 'Aeternus', or may appear as 'Claritas reipublicae'. Jupiter as 'Fulgerator' is the triumphant conqueror of the giants, Hercules takes various titles from his various labours. The decline in the cults of goddesses, no doubt, is partly accidental – due to the comparative unimportance of the ladies of the dynasty of Diocletian. It may, however, be symptomatic of the strongly virile and military character of the later paganism. Mithraism, which was peculiarly a religion of the troops, hardly allowed women any place at all and, to that extent, it has been conjectured, suffered in its final struggle for mastery with Christianity.

Christianity first insinuates itself on the coins in the form of minor symbols – cross or Christian monogram. A type of Constantinople shows the cross set on a serpent as the emblem of the 'Hope of the State' (Plate LXIII, 7). The upward-turned heads of Constantine and his sons on late solidi of his reign were meant very probably to suggest an attitude of prayer and aspiration. The Christian Emperors assumed the 'labarum', the standard emblazoned with the monogram of Christ, as their distinctive emblem, and with Magnentius and Vetranio we reach such definitely religious types as 'Salus DD. NN. Aug. et Caes.' the ☧ between A and Ω, or the 'Hoc signo victor eris'. Later the hand of God, which is sometimes shown extending a crown over the Emperor's head, has a definitely religious flavour, and the fifth-century type, with the Emperor setting his foot on a human-headed serpent, probably represents him as the Defender of the Faith, the guardian of Christian civilization, against the ancient serpent of spiritual evil (Plate LX, 13). The cross (Plate LXIII, 11) or the ☧ (Plate LXIII, 9, 10) become common types. The 'Salus Mundi' solidus of Olybrius, with the cross as main type, has an almost medieval character (Plate LXIII, 12). What strikes one most is the guarded nature of religious reference on the coinage. The pagan revival of Julian is hardly signalized by anything beyond the 'Apis bull' reverse of his copper. The world under the early Christian Emperors remained fundamentally pagan in its conceptions. Christianity first adopted pagan forms and interspersed them with its own symbols: only very slowly and tentatively did it proceed to substitute types that had no foundation in Paganism. The general policy followed was one of compromise and assimilation, rather than of direct change.

The worship of the Emperor, forbidden at Rome under the early Empire, was almost undisguised under Diocletian, and he and his colleagues enjoyed all the honours of the earthly representatives of the great gods. Had paganism held its own, the divinity of the Emperor would unquestionably have become a main tenet of the orthodox. The triumph of Christianity interrupted the development. The Emperor is closely associated with the emblems of the new faith, cross and labarum – he is crowned by the hand of the Lord or by the Angel of Victory – but he remains a man. The conception of the divine in human nature was for ever dissociated from mere place and power. The consecration of the dead Emperor naturally continued so long as paganism held the field, though the merits of the great Diocletian missed this particular form of recognition in the party strife after his death. Constantine paid divine honours to his father (cp. Plate LXIII, 1), and to his ancestor, Claudius Gothicus – Maxentius to his father Maximian (cp. Plate LXIII, 3, 4) and his son Romulus (Plate LXIII, 2), Maximin II to Galerius. Even Constantine himself, though he died a Christian, was celebrated as 'Divus' after his death – a new shade of meaning must have been attached to the term (Plate LXIII, 5, 6). The reverse types show him as a standing figure, with the legend 'Veneranda Memoria' (VN. MR.), or in a chariot beckoned on by the hand of God; some reminiscence of the ascent of Elijah may be mingled in the latter type. These are the last formal issues of consecration. But the conception of immortality in the world of the stars was deeply rooted in the imagination and could easily be provided with Christian parallels.[1]

---

[1] References to the immortality of the good Emperors are common in Claudian. Cp. *On the Third Consulship of Honorius*, IV, 105 ff., 158 ff.

The worship of the minor deities or Virtues has still a place, though only a restricted one, on the coinage. Fortuna still appears with her rudder and globe (Plate LXIII, 18), Spes with her flower, Securitas leaning on her column (Plate LXIV, 6). Moneta with her scales still stands under Diocletian for the activities of the Imperial mint (Plate LXIV, 4).[1] These virtues, however, had usually been associated with the person of the Emperor as a semi-divine being. With the triumph of Christianity this conception declines and the Virtues, so far as they are worshipped, tend rather to be associated with the State or the people of Rome. The use of abstractions to convey general conceptions of the State was actually a main feature of the time; but the abstraction is frequently not personified, but expressed instead by a symbolical type. We have already spoken of the types associated with such ideas as 'Pietas', 'Salus' and 'Virtus'. Specially characteristic of the times is the thought of the 'Glory of Rome' or 'the Army', which is exceptionally personified as a woman holding branch and leaning on a column (Plate LXIII, 17); more often the idea is conveyed by a type of Rome and Constantinople or of the Emperor as a victorious general. The worship of the Genius of the Emperor, or of the people of Rome, was especially popular; the Genius is usually represented as a youth holding cornucopiae and patera for sacrifice. The history of one personification, Victoria (cp. Plate LXIV, 7–14), is peculiarly interesting in the development of religious belief. The Roman people clung closely to this great power that symbolized the triumphant progress of Rome in the world, and over the great statue of Victory in the senate-house at Rome one of the main struggles between Christianity and paganism developed. The Christian party succeeded in A.D. 382 in inducing the Emperor Gratian to order the removal of the statue; but, to our surprise, we find the Victory type still appearing on the coinage and even being associated in the closest possible way, not only with the person of the Emperors, but also with the symbol of the cross. We can easily guess what it was that happened. Christianity was unable to eradicate the worship of Victory entirely; there remained a second course – to retain it with a definitely Christian stamp.[2] The pagan goddess becomes the Christian Angel of Victory, retaining her wings and her emblems, wreath and palm, and now bearing as a new emblem, the Christian cross. It is a striking example of the same subtle policy that

[1] For other examples, cp. Pl. LXIII, 14, Concordia; 15, Fata Victricia; 16, Fides Militum; LXIV, 3, Pietas; 5, Providentia deorum Quies Augg. – the abdication type of Diocletian and Maximian.
[2] Cp. St Augustine, *De Civitate Dei*, Bk. IV Ch. 14.

merged the worship of pagan gods in the veneration for Christian saints.

(f) *Animate and Inanimate Objects*

The use of various animate and inanimate types as symbols of general ideas is decidedly on the decline; fond as the age was of abstractions, it was forgetting the art of clothing them in symbols. The she-wolf and twins still suggests the legend of Rome (Plate LXIV, 15). The lion, as a type of strength, appears on the reverse of Divus Maximian, and again, with an added punning reference, on the coins of Leo the Great. The eagle, associated from of old with consecration, appears on post-humous coins of Constantius I. The phoenix is associated with the two kindred conceptions of renewal ('Fel. Temp. Reparatio' – Plate LXIV, 16) and durability ('Perpetuitas'). The wreath is freely used as a frame for the 'Vota' reverses and occasionally to enclose a star; but the old use of the 'corona civica' can no longer be traced. The military standards still convey the idea of the reliability of the army, and the altar, associated with the legend 'Beata Tranquillitas', suggests offering of thanksgiving for the blessing of peace. The Christian monogram, ☧, is first associated on the coins of Magnentius with the idea of the 'Salvation of the State': the A and Ω that flank it refer to the description of Christ in the Book of Revelations. In the fifth century both ☧ and cross were used freely as main types – the cross becoming the set type of the gold tremissis. The idea associated with it is usually that of the 'Victory of the Augusti' – we have already noticed the remarkable legend 'Salus Mundi' of Olybrius.

(g) *Buildings*

Apart from these Christian types, the most remarkable creation of the new age was the type of camp or city gate, which occurs at intervals throughout the fourth century (Plate LXIV, 17–19). The frontier-defence was no longer a solid bulwark as it had been in the great days: it was at best a serviceable sea-wall, which could bank back the normal tides but was liable to be overflooded when the tide was at the spring. The defensibility of the great cities of the Empire became a prime concern and the care of the Emperors for their defence is symbolized by the type of a city gate with such legends as 'Providentiae Augg.' or 'Virtus Augg.'; it is the wisdom and valour of the Emperor that ensures defence. The types of the silver of the tetrarchy that show a scene of sacrifice outside a gate are probably to be taken rather as types of thanksgiving for victories in the field; they are associated with the legends 'Victoria Sarmatica' and 'Virtus Militum'. Magnus Maximus in Gaul defines the city gate as the 'Hope of the Romans' (Plate LXIV, 17), and contemporary coins of Theodosius and his contemporaries at Thessalonica mark it as 'the Glory of the State' (Plate LXIV, 18). Representations of actual individual buildings are now very rare. The two most famous occur on the double solidus of Constantine I, showing with some attempt at fidelity to detail the bridge and gate of Treveri, and the Arras medallion of Constantius I, showing Londinium kneeling before her gates to welcome the deliverer.[1] The remarkable legend 'Redditor lucis aeternae' has probably no special Mithraic symbolism, but draws on the natural thought of light as an equivalent of good, which was familiar enough to the Romans and was afterwards to supply the inspiration of some of the noblest Christian hymns. The representation of the gate and walls of London is no doubt conventional, but it may at least convince us that the city was not unwalled in A.D. 296.

We have seen that the coinage of the age was rich in its comment on the persons of its rulers, on the valour and renown of the army, on the happiness and safety of the State. We miss the full record of contemporary events and the full series of Virtues of the earlier period. We miss too the interest in mythology, archaeology and in the past history of Rome, which at various times played an important role in the coinage. Some allowance must be made for the influence of the new faith; but we may still conclude with safety that interest was more closely concentrated on the immediate present than in early times. If we read the coinage superficially, we may gather the impression of a certain preoccupation with immediate necessities, coupled with a poverty of new ideas, that leads to bombastic phrases that convey little meaning and to the repeated use of a few well-worn types. We need to look a little deeper into the history as revealed by such historians as Ammianus Marcellinus and such an historical document as the great *Codex Theodosianus* to learn something of the desperate struggle of civilization to maintain itself against an increasing weight of difficulty, the ever-repeated effort to hold the frontiers against the barbarians, the fettering of individual life in the system of hereditary castes, the terrible burden of the machinery of civil and military government, which gave

[1] Cp. A. Alfoeldy, 'Die Donaubrücke Konstantins des Grossen und verwandte. historische Darstellungen auf spätrömischen Munzen', *Z.f.N.*, 1926, pp. 161 ff.; *Num. Chron.*, 1926, pp. 43 ff.

the Empire the chance to live on but almost crushed it in the process. These were the dominant facts of life as they presented themselves to the subjects of the Empire and we, who are living in a time of not dissimilar stress, should find no difficulty in entering into sympathy with their struggles and in judging with leniency a world so hard put to it in the fight for sheer existence. The language of the coins has little to say of the reverse side of the picture; it gives us rather the great watchwords of encouragement that were used to buoy up sinking courage. 'The Happiness of the State', 'The Safety of the State', 'The Restoration of Prosperity', the 'Glory of the Army', the 'Joy of the Romans' – all these no doubt conveyed some positive meaning to the men who handled the coins; but we shall understand them better if we see their bright encouragement in black contrast with the dark abyss of national danger and humiliation, of misfortune and misery, into which the Western Empire finally sank and from which the East was only saved by what sometimes appears to us almost as a miracle.

CHAPTER III

Coinage in the General Life
of the Later Empire

Once again we must try to discover the importance of the facts of coinage which we have been investigating in the general life of the State. The uncertainties with which we have had to contend will still occasion difficulties, but we shall be helped by a number of precise indications in the *Codex Theodosianus* and other documents.

I. FOREIGN POWERS

Let us look first at the relations of the Imperial coinage to the world outside the Empire. The failing reputation of the Roman arms was for a time triumphantly restored by Diocletian; and it is perhaps to this, as well as to the intrinsic merits of the coin, that we may attribute the world-wide reputation of the Roman solidus. Even the Sassanian kingdom of Persia, with its strong nationalist bias, struck gold but seldom; apart from this one exception the whole world gladly accepted the Roman standard. Never, even in the days of Augustus, had the right of the Roman Emperor as King of Kings over gold coinage been so completely recognized. So strongly was this unwritten law established that, even after the fall of the Western Empire, its barbarian successors continued to strike with the head of the Emperor of the East, adding at most their own monogram; and it was felt to be a grave violation of tradition when a Merovingian king took the bold step of stamping his own portrait on the solidus. Many of the large gold pieces, 'medallions', or multiples of the solidus, seem actually to have been struck for presentation to native princes – a fact which is attested both by definite testimonies and by the appearance of such pieces in hoards found outside the Imperial frontiers. A passage in the *Codex Justinianus* (IV, 63, 2), which may well have some meaning for earlier times too, forbids the supply of gold to barbarians and recommends the use of craft to recover it for Imperial use; evidently the export tended to reach dangerous dimensions.

Of Roman silver outside the Empire we have nothing to say. The Roman silvered bronze was freely imitated both in East and West. In the West we are familiar with the so-called 'minimi' – pieces of very small module, bearing types more or less loosely copied from Roman coins of the fourth and even of the third century. These pieces are particularly common in finds in Britain and Gaul and it seems highly probable that these imitations filled the place of a regular currency after the departure of the Romans. The fact that radiate heads of the third century are among the imitations need not seriously alarm us; the series of Anglo-Saxon sceattas, beginning about A.D. 700, is partly dependent for its types on coins quite as early. In the East somewhat similar imitations of Imperial bronze are found in great quantities in Egypt. They have been assigned, somewhat hastily, to the Vandal occupation of Africa. We prefer to follow J. G. Milne in giving them a local Egyptian origin and regarding them as the token-money of the great landed proprietors, striking in practical independence of the Government.[1] The types imitated in Egypt are on the whole decidedly later than those imitated in the West – a fact which may be fully accounted for when we contrast the continuance of the official coinage in the provinces of Egypt and Syria with the closing of all the Roman mints outside Italy in the West soon after the beginning of the fifth century.

The curious imitations of late fourth-century Roman coins which are found occasionally in Ceylon rouse our curiosity about this little chapter of forgotten history. They are all of bronze, and, as the one Roman province (Egypt) in close touch with Taprobane was precisely the one in which gold and silver coinage came to an early end, we need not wonder at this. It seems that Roman merchants still carried on a lively trade with the distant island and that they actually found it convenient to export small change with them which was then multiplied by imitations on native soil.

2. THE PROVINCES

We turn to the provinces. In the early Empire we found a definite centre – Rome and Italy – and round it the provinces, moving but slowly to full political and economic equality. With Diocletian this

---

[1] Cp. *Num. Chron.*, 1926, pp. 43 ff.

movement is complete. The Empire has no longer one centre, but a number of foci – residences of the Augusti and Caesars and of their praetorian prefects. Beside Rome we can now set Nicomedia, Antioch, Treveri, Constantinople and other cities which at one time or another were raised by Imperial favour to special importance. All the subjects of the Empire, as far as geographical position is concerned, have now equal rights – or, perhaps we should rather say, equal responsibilities. This new unity and equality, however, has nothing to do with true local independence. The provinces are made equal to Rome and Italy in servitude and not in freedom; the same omnipotent central government grips all alike and demands a general obedience to its stereotyped instructions.

The advantages of the new system in its relation to coinage are obvious and indisputable. There is no longer a confusion of Imperial, provincial and local issues, involving constant difficulties in tariffing and exchange: the same Imperial coinage is current everywhere. The supply too is well adapted to local needs. Almost every diocese has its own mint or mints and the need for transport of coin from a distance is removed. The Government, however, seems to have impaired the value of this well-planned system by occasional displays of capricious tyranny and by a general lack of sense in its legislation regarding coinage. Let us look at one or two cases of capricious tyranny. While the Roman world at large was carefully supplied with coinage, a few provinces were excluded from the general boon. Spain had no mint of its own and depended on southern Gaul for its supplies. Africa had no mint after the brief activity of Carthage from A.D. 296 to 311 and was dependent on Italy. The military insignificance of these provinces no doubt explains the lack of mints, but the effect on local trade must have been depressing. Britain had its mint of Londinium from A.D. 296 to 324, but no coinage thereafter except for a moment under Magnus Maximus. The military argument hardly applies here, and we are forced to accuse the Government of a lack of consideration for a province from which no important income was derivable. A curious fact of late fourth-century hoards – the finding of miliarensia and siliquae in Britain and very seldom elsewhere – may find its explanation in the arrangements made for coinage. We may conjecture that Britain was but scantily supplied with gold and therefore thrown back on the use of silver for all larger business transactions. This alone would account for the prevalence of silver in British hoards; and, if we may credit the Government with the intention of withdrawing the silver as well as the gold from the island, the hoards may be regarded as evidence of an attempt to preserve treasure not so much from the barbarian invader, as from the even more terrible government official. That the Government was capable of ruthlessness in its policy is proved beyond question in the case of Egypt. After about A.D. 324 Egypt has, practically speaking, no gold or silver of her own. Forced to trade with no better medium than the small silvered bronze the Egyptians found it impossible to maintain the standard of reckoning. Prices rose to fabulous heights and there was no remedy but to assign ever higher values to the almost worthless coins. Such a process of collapse has theoretically no limit, and in Egypt, in fact, depreciation reached an amazing pitch. Now, two things are obvious here at once. Such conditions must cause a vast amount of unnecessary misery; and for such conditions the Government is primarily responsible. Perhaps it was fear of the unruliness of Egypt that made the Romans inflict this policy on the province; the Egyptian taxes were collected mainly in kind and the poverty of the province in metal would not react immediately on its oppressor. The mere omission to strike gold and silver in a province is not in itself enough to bring it to this sorry pass; we should naturally expect supplies to flow in from outside as required, in the ordinary course of trade. We conclude that the Government must have made it a part of its policy to hinder the free movement of money; and this conclusion is in fact confirmed by ancient evidence.[1] Merchants are definitely forbidden to carry with them more than a very modest allowance of money for their personal requirements; the selling of coin is strictly forbidden; coin is to be an instrument of public use, not an article of commerce. Let us reflect for a moment on what is involved in this policy. Each province is condemned to subsist on such supplies of coin as the Government thinks fit to provide. If the supply is anywhere inadequate either in quantity or quality there is no help to be had; any definite attempts to remedy it are punishable in law.[2] We catch an alarming glimpse of that tyrannical control, so characteristic of the age, which entirely subordinated the interests of the individual to those of the State. We suspect that the Government in its issues of money for the provinces was mainly concerned with its

---

[1] *Cod. Theod.*, IX, 23 (speaking primarily of bronze).

[2] The third-century coins of the mint of Alexandria which are commonly found in Britain may have been brought to the island in the fourth century. Merchants would bring in this obsolete coinage to meet provincial requirements. This would be one example of those activities on the part of merchants against which the Government issued its Edict.

own interests, not with those of trade or of private life. Where the requirements of the army particularly demanded it or where the Government itself needed masses of coined money, there the supply was ample; where these conditions did not exist, it refused to go to the trouble and expense of supplying trade with its most vital necessity.

3. OCCASIONS OF COINAGE

What then were the main occasions for which coin was issued? In the first place we must set the supply of pay to the troops and, perhaps even more, to the Civil Service,[1] which after Diocletian was almost a heavier burden on the State than the army. The mint of Aquileia is a good example of a mint serving military needs, supplying, as it did, the pay for troops moving eastwards from Italy into the Balkans. The mint of Sirmium, which is often found striking gold and silver with very little bronze, is another example, the mint of Treviri after Valentinian I is a third. In the second place will come the supply of coinage for the doles to the people, whether made by the Emperor himself or by leading officials in the big cities. Legislation has come down to us, regulating the size of the coins to be used in these largesses; the miliarense was particularly used for such purposes and, according to one etymology, certainly a false one, got its name from being distributed to the 'milites'. The formal bounties of the early Empire cannot be traced beyond Diocletian and Maximian, but the practice of winning popular goodwill by a display of generosity was too valuable to be lightly discarded. We have coins of Valentinian I and II showing the Emperors in their chariots flinging largesse to the mob. Such gifts seem now to be restricted to a series of special occasions, such as the visit of the Emperor to a town; the regular provision for the poor of the capitals by this means was apparently abandoned. Whether more was gained or lost by the change is hard to determine. Probably only in the third place came the requirements of trade and private life. Taxes were now so commonly collected in bullion or in kind that the lack of coined money caused little embarrassment to the treasury; and, as we have seen above, of a far-sighted and disinterested care for private needs there is very little trace. We shall see later how this policy gave rise to false coinage on the largest scale and to the irregular extension

---

[1] But we must remember that the Government made a determined stand for paying salaries in kind and against payment in cash, 'Adaeratio'; in the age of Valentinian I it was beginning to give way on the general principle.

of mint privileges to private individuals – practices which the Government first stimulated by its unwise regulations and then endeavoured to repress with the utmost rigour.

4. SUPPLIES OF PRECIOUS METAL

One notable feature of the period was the restoration of an ample coinage in the precious metals – in itself an excellent thing for trade. Whence these new supplies came is not at first quite obvious, as the State mines were in many cases approaching exhaustion and new metallic resources within the Empire were not easily to be found. It is highly probable that Diocletian's Eastern victories placed large new stocks of gold and silver at his disposal. Even more importance must be attached to the severity of government methods of inquisition and taxation. Little by little the metallic reserves of the Empire must have been drawn into Imperial use; the vast quantities of precious metal, hitherto immobilized in articles of luxury, must to a large extent have found their way to the melting-pot. Another most important source of supply was the temple treasures, which as paganism died, came again into the market. After c. 400 (was the loss of Britain a possible cause?) the supplies of silver began to fail and later we find the Byzantine Empire with a coinage mainly of gold and bronze. The reasons for this relative scarcity of silver are not hard to guess. The gold coinage was the main concern of the Government and the inquisition for gold was correspondingly keen. Further, silver was being continually squandered on the silvering of the bronze. And finally, as articles of luxury cannot have gone entirely out of vogue, the less costly silver probably tended to replace gold in this field. That the decline of silver coinage was not due to an absolute scarcity of the metal is proved by the fact that the relation of gold to silver, far from declining, was actually on the rise.

The supply of small change, ample in the early stages, became meagre towards the end of our period. Here there was no question of larger Imperial needs – it was private convenience that was mainly at stake, and private convenience, as we have already seen, did not lie very near the heart of the Government. It is in its treatment of this branch of the coinage that the administration is most open to criticism; such criticism will lead us naturally on to our next subject – that of the general financial theories prevailing in this age.

5. FINANCIAL THEORY

The Emperors of the third century, unable to balance their budgets, had resorted to the fatal expedient of assigning fictitious values to their coinage. They exploited the false theory that the State can, by an act of will, enforce the circulation of its own money at its own rates. This theory needs no refuting today; such inflation is no more than a dishonest form of taxation, when the Government pays in bad money and exacts payment in good. What was the attitude of Diocletian and his successors to this problem? T̶e bad old practice lasted after them down into medieval times; were they responsible for endorsing it themselves? The answer to this question cannot be quite simple. To a certain extent – particularly in the supply of a pure gold and silver coinage – they seem to have adopted the sound policy of giving the world a currency that could command confidence on its merits. That the silver was constantly struck below its normal weight was, perhaps, no very serious disadvantage, since it was tariffed in terms of a reliable gold coinage. It was the smaller change – the coinage of silvered bronze – that was now as before the weak point of the system. It had originated in the third century as a fraudulent substitute for silver. Diocletian, indeed, distinguished it sharply from the coinage of pure silver and assigned to it values more in accordance with its actual worth. The fact, however, remained that a coinage, essentially of bronze, was offered to the world at rates well above its bronze values. The bitter memories of the third century still survived and expressed themselves in a steady distrust of the new coins. The result was a continuous decline in the value of the new unit of reckoning, the denarius, from 50,000 to the pound under Diocletian to 172,800 under Constantine. With Constantine relative stability was attained, but even now the value of the denarius tended to fall and, in the fifth century, we find as many as 2,880 denarii (7,200 nummi) to the solidus. If we ask why the Government was not content to treat this silvered bronze as a token coinage, dependent on the gold, we may hesitate for an answer; gold, we should have thought, was plentiful enough to carry the weight of the whole coinage. The Government must have insisted on making the bronze a source of profit. As a matter of fact, the silvered bronze seems to have been used, not merely as small change, but as real money to effect large payments; and, when put to this use, its inherent defects became obvious.

The difficulties of maintaining two metals in the same system are sufficiently well known. How much more serious was the problem, when, beside gold and silver, a place had to be found for silvered bronze! The solidus, nominally worth 6,000 nummi, reached a value of 7,200.[1] It became more and more the custom to make the pound of metal – gold, silver or bronze – the unit and to treat the individual coins simply as fractions of those pounds.[2] The pound of metal would rise or fall in market value and the coins would vary with it. The coin is, in fact, relapsing from a measure of value to an article of commerce like any other. The tendency was accentuated by the practice of collecting a large proportion of the taxes in kind. The taxpayer found himself called upon to pay over either certain amounts of necessaries in the form of foodstuffs, clothing or the like or certain values of metal; the payments might be made either in bullion or in coin indifferently. The system, in this respect, represented a decided relapse from that of the earlier Empire; the needs of the Government may have been satisfied by it, but the ordinary requirements of trade must have suffered serious loss.

6. FALSE COINAGE

On a number of points relating to the coinage, the *Codex Theodosianus* preserves for us valuable information. False coinage was remarkably prevalent and was met with correspondingly severe penalties. It took various forms and was perpetrated, partly by the mint officials themselves, partly by irresponsible persons outside.[3] One form of abuse consisted in the clipping of the edge of the solidus and called forth a special edict of repression. The clipping of the silver, which, as our coins show us, was extensively practised, was less serious, as the silver may have been in any case partly token money. Another form of abuse consisted in the melting down of the bronze, to extract the silver and, no doubt, reissue a baser bronze in its place. In general, it was the

[1] The *Cod. Justin.*, XI, 11, 2, shows an attempt to make the solidus a standard for all prices; 'pro imminutione, quae in aestimatione solidi forte tractatur, omnium quoque specierum pretia decrescere oportet'.

[2] The proof of this is to be found in the constant reckoning in pounds in the *Codex Theodosianus*. The *Historia Augusta*, which reckons similarly, probably often reflects the practice, rather than the fourth than of the third century.

[3] Cp. *Cod. Theod.*, IX, 22 ff., penalties for forgers, 21, 6; penalties for 'flaturarii', who separate the silver from the bronze in the 'pecunia majorina', 21, 9; forgery is 'maiestas', high treason, 22; penalties for clippers of the solidus, XII, 7, 2; 'zygostatai' appointed in each city to test solidi that have been cut or rubbed down. The most exact description of the commonest form of forgery is 'nummum falsa fusione formare' – the casting of silvered bronze, no doubt of inferior quality. The anonymous writer who recommends various reforms to two Emperors (Valentinian I and Valens?) has one remedy for abuses at the mint; remove all moneyers to one island, where at least they cannot spread their corruption!

bronze that was most open to attack; the general public can have had no ready method of distinguishing between coins containing the full official allowance of silver and forgeries with an inferior proportion. The penalties for the forger were severe. Offenders were held to be guilty of high treason and were liable to the death penalty or to long terms of penal servitude. They were expressly excluded from the amnesty granted to ordinary malefactors on Easter Day. Not only the forger himself, but the owner of the property on which forgery took place, was liable to give account, though here some merciful allowance was made in the case of minors. The *Codex* leaves us with the impression of a very widespread evil, which defied the efforts of the law to repress it.

We have seen above that the State supply of money for trade purposes was probably often inadequate. It is not surprising to find, then, that private persons contrived to secure licences to have money coined for them at the mint.[1] An edict of Valentinian I revokes all such licences in existence at the time and another edict confiscates all private bullion brought to be struck at the mint; as this second edict defeated its purpose by its severity, a further edict decreed that two ounces only in the pound should be appropriated by the State.[2]

The Government certainly seems to have claimed the right to determine exactly how and where money should circulate. The transport of coin from province to province for purposes of sale was expressly forbidden by an edict of A.D. 354. In A.D. 395 one of the two larger bronze coins then in circulation, the so-called 'pecunia maior', was withdrawn from currency, only the 'centenionalis' being retained. The prohibition of the transport of coin was a serious matter; it meant that the Government insisted on the validity of its arrangements even when experience clearly demonstrated their inadequacy.

7. CONTROL OF PRICES

The standard example of the attempt to control prices by legislation is the famous edict 'de maximis pretiis' of Diocletian (A.D. 301). It was probably by no means the only attempt of the kind; but it is the only one any details of which have come down to us, and it may stand here for its class. Diocletian had in A.D. 296 provided what he regarded, with some justification, as a satisfactory coinage. The business world could not reject it, but it refused to accept the values assigned to the

---

[1] *Cod. Theod.*, IX, 21, 10.
[2] ibid., IX, 21, 7 (A.D. 369), amended IX, 21, 8 (A.D. 374).

coins by Diocletian; prices in fact rose to enormous heights. To Diocletian this seemed nothing more or less than downright villainy, calling for drastic remedies. He accordingly issued an edict, dealing with all commodities in the greatest detail and fixing a maximum price for each. We hear – and we are not surprised to hear – that the edict was a failure; prices remained as they were or rose even higher. It is easy to blame Diocletian for his short-sighted folly in thinking that he could enforce by legislation the acceptance of a coinage that could not win respect on its merits. But there is something to be said for his point of view, if not for his method of enforcing it. We know from experience how much room for conscienceless profiteering is provided by a sudden change of money-values. During the whole of the third century the world had seen falling values and soaring prices. The reform of Aurelian had brought only partial relief; prices had again risen, reducing the real, if not the nominal, values of the coins. We may well believe that it was partly a matter of bad habit and deliberate fraud, if the well-judged reform of 296 was at once followed by a new rise in prices. Lactantius, indeed, accuses Diocletian of causing dear prices himself by 'various unfair measures'; but, in the absence of more exact information, we cannot determine what weight to attach to this charge.[1] All we can say is that the reform of 296 appears to have provided a possibility of financial stability.

The collection of taxes was another matter calling for continual legislation. It was a particular hardship of the time that the demands were not regular and constant, but that, in addition to fixed charges, there were requisitions to be made, varying from time to time both in quality and in amount.[2] Here too edict after edict was issued, prescribing how payments were to be effected and at what rates payments in one metal might be expressed in terms of another.

8. THE CASTE OF MONEYERS

It is a well-established fact that Roman society from the time of Diocletian came to be organized more and more on a basis of caste. A man was born into a caste or profession and could only with the very greatest difficulty escape from it. It seemed as if nearly everyone was engaged in the sad attempt to escape out of the frying-pan into the

---

[1] If we were right in attributing to Diocletian a reduction of the 'twenty' piece of Aurelian from one sestertius to a half, that measure may have led to a rush to spend the old money before its devaluation, and so to a rise in prices; cp above, p. 195.
[2] Cp. *Cod. Theod.*, XI, 21, 3.

fire. The State was so distrustful of its reserves that it feared to leave any gaps to be filled by natural processes. The caste of mint officials, 'monetales', was no exception to this rule. It became an hereditary profession, recruited from the families of the moneyers; various edicts expressly forbid any moneyer to resign his functions, unless he can provide a substitute. We gather that attempts at evasion were common and infer that the normal emoluments were poor, however tempting might be the prospects of illicit gain to such bold spirits as chose to brave the penalties for forgery.

9. SUCCESS AND FAILURE

To sum up the results of our inquiry, we find that the Government of the period after Diocletian was at least partially successful in overcoming the evils inherited from the third century and in preventing the recurrence of any desperate financial crisis. It established a uniform system of coinage for the Empire and secured a steady supply of good gold and silver. So far we must give it credit for excellent intentions, not so poorly expressed in action. But there is a reverse side to the medal. The needs of the individual were subordinated to those of the State and, in the long run, the State suffered with him. Where abuses occurred the State proceeded by edict, instead of by a careful examination and removal of the causes. The Government aspired to regulate everything and leave nothing to chance. It hindered the free movement of coin and, in so doing, cramped trade. It failed to secure a satisfactory supply of small change and, by its continul experiments, contributed to instability and unsettlement. We are not in a position to estimate exactly the weight of the difficulties with which it had to contend. But, in general, we must admit that a judicious comment which has been made on the general policy of Diocletian and Constantine applies to the coinage as well. The Emperors felt themselves unable to preserve the interests of both individual and State; and, as the lesser of the two evils, they allowed those of the individual to go to the wall. That this meant nothing better than a postponement of the evil day for the State as well, was a misfortune which it lay beyond their power to prevent.

To this chapter, as to the others on coinage in the life of the State, I must append the warning that many of the questions raised still await exact answers, and that there may be other questions of importance, which have not even been raised.

Epilogue

There is no one fixed date which can be taken to mark the end of the Roman Empire. We have here taken the fall of the Western Empire in 476. But the West still acknowledged the supremacy of the Eastern Emperor; it was not until the Western kings began to strike independently that the fall of Rome can be regarded as an accomplished fact. It is obviously impossible for us to follow Byzantium, as the successor of Rome, into the Middle Ages. Byzantium is, of course, a bridge between the ancient and the modern worlds; but it is convenient to treat the later history from the fall of the Western Empire as a separate episode, while never forgetting that there is historical continuity with Rome.

We saw the coinage of Rome beginning as that of a city-state, which gradually rises to supremacy in Italy and then crosses the seas to extend its sway little by little over the whole of the Mediterranean world. The first coinage is indigenous – a coinage of bronze; soon the Greek use of silver is borrowed, later gold is struck in the tradition of Philip and Alexander of Macedon. Rome begins her career as a part of Western barbarism; she develops a civilization under Etruscan and Greek influences and hands it on to the more backward peoples of the West. She wins political, but never cultural, supremacy over the Greek East. Finally she first shares her sway with an Eastern capital, then resigns her sceptre to the 'New Rome' of the East. The West relapses towards barbarism but the memory of Imperial Rome and the example and power of Byzantium save Rome and Italy and even the more Western peoples from a complete submersion in the barbarian night. Let us see how these changes expressed themselves in coinage. Byzantine coinage carries on in direct line the traditions of the late Roman Empire. But there was fresh life awaiting expression that was not Roman and the later developments of Byzantium, interesting as they are, are certainly not Roman in inspiration. It is noteworthy that the full development of the Christian element in coins was reserved for Byzantium. The position of the Emperor changed little, but that was only because Oriental despotism had already won the day over Roman liberty before Rome fell. All that is really characteristic of Rome in coinage steadily declines. The alphabet is more and more infected with Greek forms; and the reform of the money-system by Anastasius made the breach palpable.

We have to look more closely at the course of development in the West.[1] The first stage is that of coinage of the barbarians in imitation of Roman and Byzantine models. The Vandals strike gold only with Roman types, silver and bronze with their own types and legends. The Visigoths in Gaul imitate the coins of Valentinian III; in Spain they develop a coinage of their own on the Roman model, giving name of mint as well as of king. A somewhat similar coinage is attributed to the Suevi in Spain. The Burgundians and Merovingians begin with Byzantine imitations; the Merovingian kings pass on to royal coinage in their own names and thence to the typical coinage of tremisses, with name of town and moneyer. Odoacer and the Ostrogoths copy Byzantine types, then develop silver and bronze of their own. Quasi-independent coinage is issued by Rome herself. The Lombards copy Byzantine coins and only advance slowly to coinage in their own name, both in the North and in their south Italian duchy of Beneventum. Coins of the Gepidae on Byzantine models have only recently been identified. Britain at the Roman retirement was left without a coinage; all that we can place in the dark years between c. 410 and 600 are one or two imitations of Roman solidi with runic legends and, conceivably, some of the 'minimi', tiny bronze coins imitating the radiate heads of the Gallic Emperors and the diademed heads of Constantine I and his successors. Out of this confusion of coinage the feudal coins of the Middle Ages and after them the national issues of the West gradually emerged.

The fact that strikes us most forcibly is the vast prestige of Rome – a prestige so great as to impose itself on the barbarian successors of the Empire. But, by the side of this, another fact becomes prominent; the Roman tradition, potent in the appeal of its great past, is weak and unprogressive in the present. The influence of that great past is slowly forgotten. The Roman tradition is involuntarily and insensibly lost and new independent forms arise. There is no longer sufficient vigour in the remains of Roman life in the West to give a Roman stamp to these new developments. There is very little of Rome, except the language, in the coinage of the later Merovingians and of the Carolingians. However high we assess the debt of the West to Rome, there

[1] Cp. C. F. Keary, *The Coinages of Western Europe*, London, 1879.

is nothing gained by obscuring the fact that the world of the sixth and following centuries found itself unable to develop on Roman lines and was forced to branch off on many new paths of its own. If we look at the last few years of the Western Empire we find this view confirmed. The impulse of Roman civilization had spent itself internally – the Empire was penetrated through and through by barbarian elements, long before its political structure broke. There was an unhappy discord between the brain and the body of the world. The educated and cultured classes lacked strength, the barbarian intruders lacked depth of culture. Italy herself, with her concentrated traditions of political life, was deeply influenced racially by barbarian settlement. Out of the blend of strong unexhausted races and old political and social conditions has risen our modern Europe, redeemed from barbarism by the heritage of the ancient world, but re-invigorated by the new blood of the barbarians who had knocked for so long at the doors of the Empire.

Select Bibliography

It has been essential here to cut references down to a minimum. For fuller lists see MAX BERNHART, *Münzkunde der röm. Kaiserzeit*, Geneva, 1922: S. L. CESANO, *Bibliografia Numismatica per gli anni, 1914–1921*: the B.M. *Catalogues*: R. A. G. CARSON, *A Report on Research in Roman Numismatics*, 1936–1952: a continuation, 1953–1960, by HAROLD and HAROLD B. MATTINGLY, will shortly appear.

GENERAL

Summary references may be given to some famous works of the past. B.M. *Catalogues* (Republic and Empire): BABELON, *Traité and Description of Coins of the Republic*: ECKHEL on *Ancient Coins*: HILL'S *Handbook* and *Historical Roman Coins*: MOMMSEN'S *Römische Münzwezen* (French translation by the DUC DE BLACAS): BAHRFELDT-SAMWER on *Early Roman Coinage*: BAHRFELDT on Roman gold, overstrikes and Antony's Prefects of the Fleet: BARON D'AILLY on *Republican Coins:* HAEBERLIN on *Aes Grave*: WILLERS on *Aes of the Republic*.

BOOK I

ALFÖLDI, A. 'Isiskult und Umsturzbewegung im letzten Jahrhundert der röm. Republik', *Schweiz. Münzbl.* 1954, pp. 25 ff.
'Komplementäre Doppeltypen in der Denarprägung der römischen Republik', *Schweiz. Münzbl.* 1951, pp. 1 ff.
'Studien zur Zeitfolge der Münzprägung der römischen Republik', *Schweiz. Num. Runds.* 1954, pp. 5 ff.
Studien über Caesars Monarchie, 1953.
'Juba I und die Pompeianer in Afrika', *Schweiz. Münzbl.* 1958, pp. 103 ff., and 1959, pp. 1 ff.
Die troianische Urahnen der Römer, 1957.
'Hasta-summa imperii. The spear as embodiment of sovereignty in Roma', *AJA* 1959, pp. 1 ff.

ALTHEIM, F. 'The First Roman Silver Coinage,' *TINC* 1938, pp. 137 ff.

BREGLIA, LAURA. 'La monetazione di Capua e il problema del denario', *Numismatica*, 1948, pp. 11 ff.

'L'oro del giuramento e i denarii Romani ed Italici del 1° secolo', *Numismatica*, 1947, pp. 67 ff.

'Spunti di politica monetale romana in Sicilia ed in Sardegna', *Rendic. dell'Acad. di Arch. di Napoli*, 1949–50, pp. 3 ff.

'La Prima Fase della coniazione romana dell'argento'. (*Collana di Studi Numismatici III*), 1952.

BROUGHTON, T. R. S. *The Magistrates of the Roman Republic*, 1951–2.

BUTTREY, T. V. 'On the retariffing of the Roman denarius', *Am. Num. Soc. Mus. Notes*, 1957, pp. 57 ff.

'The Triumviral Portrait Gold of the Quattuorviri Monetales of 42 B.C.', *Am. Num. Soc.* 1956.

CARSON, R. A. G. 'The Gold Stater of Flamininus', *BMQ* 1955 (March), pp. 66 ff.

CESANO, S. L. 'I Fasti della repubblica romana sulla moneta di Roma', *Studi di Num.* 1942, pp. 5 ff.

'La monete di Cesare', *Rendic. della Pont. Ac. Rom. di Arch.* 1947–9, pp. 103 ff.

'Silla e la sua moneta', *Rendic. della Pont. Ac. Rom. di Arch.* 1945–6, pp. 187 ff.

GAGÉ, J. 'Les Cornelii Lentuli et le "Genius Populi Romani" ', *Congres Int. de Num.; Paris, Actes*, 1957, pp. 219 ff.

GREDGKE, GERHERT. 'Zur röm. campanischen Didrachmen Prägung', *BNZ* 1951, pp. 165 ff.

HAMILTON, J. R. 'T. Didius and the "Villa Publica" ', *NC* 1955, pp. 224 ff.

HERBIG, R. 'Aes Signatum', *Mitth. der d. Arch. Inst. Röm. Abt.* 1956, pp. 1 ff.

HERSH, C. A. 'Overstrikes as evidence for the history of Roman Republican Coinage', *NC* 1953, pp. 53 ff.

'Sequence marks on the denarii of Publius Crepusius', *NC* 1952, pp. 52 ff.

KRAAY, C. M. 'Caesar's Quattuorviri of 44 B.C.', *NC* 1954, pp. 18 ff.

KRAFT, K. 'Der goldene Kranz Caesars', *Jahr. f. Num. u. Geldg.* 1952–3, pp. 7 ff.

KŘIŽEK, F. 'On the Beginnings of Roman Coinage', *Num. Sbornik*, 1956, pp. 5 ff.

KUBITSCHEK, W. *Studien zur Münzen der röm. Republik.* Vienna, 1911.

KUTHMANN, HAROLD. 'Zur röm. campanischen Didrachmen Prägung', *Jahr. f. Num. u. Geld.* 1958, pp. 87 ff.

LAFFRANCHI, L. 'Alcuni Problemi di Geografia num. nella monetazione Neopompeiana d'Hispania', *RIN* 1950–1, pp. 91 ff.

LIEGLE, J. 'Ein Münzbild des Sextus Pompeius', *TINC* 1938, pp. 211 ff.

MATTINGLY, HAROLD. 'The Romano-Campanian coinage and the Pyrrhic war', *NC* 1924, pp. 181 ff.

'The Roman "serrati" ', *NC* 1924, pp. 31 ff.

'Aes and Pecunia: records of Roman currency down to 269 B.C.', *NC* 1943, pp. 21 ff.

'The Diana-Victory didrachms and the decadrachms of Arsinoe', *NC* 1946, pp. 63 ff.

'Dives Anagnia', *NC* 1946, pp. 91 ff.

'Eid. Mar.', *Antiquité Classique*, 1948, XVII, pp. 445 ff.

'The First age of Roman coinage', *JRS* 1945, XXXV, pp. 65 ff.

'The little talents of Sicily and the West', *NC* 1943, pp. 14 ff.

'Nummus und As', *Schweiz. Num. Runds.* 1947, XXXIII, pp. 5 ff.

'The Romano-Campanian coinage: an old problem from a new angle', *Journal of the Warburg Inst.* 1947, Vol. I, pp. 197 ff.

'Various styles of the Roman Republican coinage', *NC* 1949, pp. 57 ff.

'Nomentanus', *Proc. Cam. Phil. Soc.* 1950–1, pp. 12 ff.

'Tribuni Aerarii', *Proc. Cam. Phil. Soc.* 1950–1, pp. 27 ff.

'Some new studies of the Roman Republican coinage', *Proc. Brit. Acad.* XXXIX (1954), pp. 239 ff.

MATTINGLY, H. B. 'The Denarius of Sufenas and the "Ludi Victoriae" ', *NC* 1956, pp. 159 ff.

'The Victoriate', *NC* 1957, pp. 97 ff.

MILNE, J. G. ' "Aes Grave" of Central Italy', *JRS* 1942, pp. 27 ff.

'Bigati', *JRS* 1944, pp. 49 ff.

'The Problem of Early Roman Coinage', *JRS* 1946, pp. 91 ff.

NEATBY, L. H. 'The "Bigatus" ', *AJA* 1951, pp. 241 ff.

PINK, K. 'The Triumviri monetales and the Structure of the Coinage of the Roman Republic', *Am. Num. Soc. Studies*, No. 7, 1952.

ROBINSON, E. S. G. 'Punic Coins of Spain and their Bearing on the Roman Republican Series', *Essays presented to Harold Mattingly*, 1956, pp. 34 ff.

SELTMAN, C. 'Argentum oscense and bigati', *NC* 1944, pp. 77 ff.

STAZIO, A. 'Bigati e argentum oscense', *Numismatica*, 1947, pp. 11 ff.

'Nummus in Plauto', *Numismatica*, 1948, pp. 11 ff.

Select Bibliography

'Primi elementi per lo studio della circolazione argenti della rep. rom. nell'Italia meridionale,' *Congrès Int. de Num.; Paris, Actes,* 1957, pp. 205 ff.
'Progressimo e conservatorismo negli studi sulla piu antica monetazione antica', *Annali,* 1955, pp. 233 ff.
SYDENHAM, E. A. *Aes Grave,* London, 1926.
The Coinage of the Roman Republic, London, 1952.
'Ornamental detail as a guide to the classification of Republican denarii', *NC* 1941, pp. 117 ff.
'Problems of the Early Roman denarius', *TINC* 1938, pp. 262 ff.
THOMSEN, RUDI. *Early Roman Coinage,* Vol. I, *The Evidence.* Copenhagen, 1957.
VOLKMAN, H. 'Caesars letzte Pläne im Spiegel der Münzen', *Gymnasion,* 1957, pp. 299 ff.

BOOK II

ALFÖLDI, A. 'Die Hauptereignisse der Jahre 253–61 n. Chr. im Orient', *Berytus,* 1937, pp. 41 ff.
'Klein Mittheilungen aus der Münzstatte Siscia', *Bl. f. Mzfr.* 1923, pp. 9 ff.
'Regnal years and victories of Gallienus and Valerian', *JRS* 1945, pp. 11 ff.
'Die römische Münzpragung und die historischen Ereignisse im Osten zwischen 260 and 270 n. chr.', *Berytus,* 1938, pp. 47 ff.
ALFÖLDI, MARIA. 'The Consecration Coins of the third century', *Acta Arch. Hung.* 1955, pp. 57 ff.
BAHRFELDT, M. 'Contremarken Vespasian auf römischen Familien denaren', *Z.f.N.* 1876, pp. 354 ff.
CARSON, R. A. G. 'The British Empire of Carausius', *History Today,* Nov. 1954, pp. 734 ff.
'The Coinage and Chronology of A.D. 238', *Am. Num. Soc. Centennial Vol.* 1959, pp. 18 ff.
'Internuntius Deorum', *Congrès Int. de Num.; Paris, Actes,* 1957, pp. 259 ff.
'The Mints and Coinage of Carausius and Allectus', *Journ. Brit. Arch. Assoc.* 1958, pp. 33 ff.
DELBRUECK, R. 'Die Münzbildnisse von Maximinus bis Carinus', *Das Röm. Herrescherbild,* III abt. Band 2, Berlin, 1940.
'Uranius of Emesa', *NC* 1948, pp. 11 ff.

262

DODD, C. H. 'On Coins of Antoninus Pius to Commodus', *NC* 1911–14.

ELMER, GEORGE. 'Eugenius: eine historisch-numismatische Studie', *NZ* 1936, pp. 29 ff.

'Die Kupfergeldreform unter Julianus Philosophus', *NZ* 1937, pp. 25 ff.

'Die Münzprägung der gallischen Kaiser in Köln, Trier und Mailand', *Bonner Jahrbuch*, 1941, pp. 108 ff.

GAGÉ, J. 'Saceculum Novum', *TINC* 1938, pp. 179 ff.

GÖBL, R. 'Der Aufbau der römischen Münzprägung in der Kaiserzeit: V/1, Valerianus und Gallienus (253–260)', *NZ* 1951, pp. 8–45.

'Continuation: Gallienus als Alleinherrscher', *NZ* 1953, pp. 5 ff.

GRANT, MICHAEL. 'Complex Symbolism and new mints, c. 14 B.C.', *NC* 1949, pp. 22 ff.

'Constantiae Augusti', *NC* 1950, pp. 23 ff.

From Imperium to Auctoritas: a historical study of aes *coinage in the Roman Empire*, 49 B.C.–A.D. 14, Cambridge, 1946.

'The Mint of Rome in Gold and Silver in the early Principate', *NC* 1955, pp. 39 ff.

Roman History from Coins, 1955.

Roman Imperial Money, 1954.

The Six main 'Aes' coinages of Augustus, 1953.

'Some Aspects of the Principate of Tiberius', *Am. Num. Soc. Notes & Mon.* 116, 1950.

'A Step towards World Coinage: 19 B.C.', *Studies in Honour of A. C. Johnson*, 1951, pp. 88 ff.

HAMMOND, M. 'The Tribunician day during the early Empire', *Mem. of the Am. Acad. in Rome*, 1938, pp. 23 ff.

'The Tribunician day from Domitian through Antoninus: a re-examination', *Mem. of the Am. Acad. in Rome*, 1948–9, pp. 35 ff.

HERZFELDER, H. 'The Cistophori of Hadrian', *NC* 1936, pp. 1 ff.

KRAAY, C. M. 'The "Aes" Coinage of Galba', *Am. Num. Soc.* (N.N.M. 133), 1954.

'The Behaviour of Early Imperial Countermarks', *Essays presented to Harold Mattingly*, 1956.

'The Coinage of Vindex and Galba', *NC* 1949, pp. 129 ff.

'Revolt and Subversion: the so-called "military" coinage of A.D. 69 re-examined', *NC* 1952, pp. 75 ff.

KRAFT, K. 'Die Datierung der röm. Münzmeisterprägung unter Augustus', *Mainzer Zeits.* 1951–2.

Select Bibliography

'Zu den Schlagmarken des Tiberius und Germanicus', *Jahr. f. Num. u. Geldg.* 1958–9, pp. 21 ff.

KUBITSCHEK, W. 'Die Münzen der Ara Pacis', *Deut. Jahrb.* 1902, pp. 153 ff.

'Valerianus iunior und Saloninus', *NZ* 1905, pp. 109 ff.

Zur Abfolge der Prägungen der Kaisers Marcus und Verus, Vienna & Leipzig, 1932.

'Nervas romischr Münzen', *Anz. der Akad. der Wissen in Wien, Philos-Hist. Klasse*, 1933.

LAFFRANCHI, L. 'La cronologia delle monete di Adriana', *RIN* 1906, pp. 329 ff.

'I diversi stile nella monetaxione romana', *RIN* 1907–10.

'Un centenario numismatico nell'antichita', *RIN* 1911.

La monetazione di Augusto, Milan, 1919.

'La monete legionarie dell' imperatore Gallieno', *TINC* 1938, pp. 211 ff.

'L'usurpazione di Domitio Allessandro', *Numismatica* 1947, pp. 1 ff.

'La monetazione imperatoria e senatoria di Claudio 1° durante il quadriennio 41–44 d. Cr.' *RIN* 1949, pp. 41 ff.

'Sulla numismatica del Flavii', *RIN* 1915, pp. 139 ff.

LE GENTILHOMME, P. 'Le Désastre d'Autun en 269', *Revue des Études Anciennes*, XLV, pp. 233 ff.

MABBOTT, T. O. 'A Newly Found Coin of Bonosus', *Numismatist*, 1955, pp. 1078 ff.

'Pescennius Niger', *Num. Review*, 1946, pp. 145 ff.

MACDOWALL, D. W. 'The *Aes* coinage of Nero, etc.' (shortly to appear).

MARKL, A. 'Die Reichsmünzstätten unter der Regierung Claudius II Gothicus und ihre Emissionen', *NZ* 1884, pp. 370 ff.

MATTINGLY, HAROLD. 'Coinage of the Civil Wars of A.D. 68–69', *NC* 1914, pp. 190 ff. 'The Restored Coins of Titus, Domitian and Nerva', *NC* 1920, pp. 179 ff. 'The Mints of Vespasian', *NC* 1921, pp. 187 ff. 'Posthumous issues of Galba', *NC* 1922, pp. 186 ff. 'The restored coins of Trajan', *NC* 1926, pp. 232 ff. 'The reigns of Trebonianus Gallus and Volusian, and of Aemilian', *NC* 1946, pp. 36 ff. 'Coins of the "Divi" issued by Trajan Decius', *NC* 1949, pp. 78 ff. 'The coinage of Macrian II and Quietus', *NC* 1954, pp. 53 ff. 'Virginius at Lugdunum?', *NC* 1954, pp. 32 ff. 'The "Military" class in the coinage of the Civil Wars of A.D. 68–69', *NC* 1952, pp. 6 ff.

'The Clash of the Coinages, circa 270–296', *Studies in Honour of A. C. Johnson*, 1951, pp. 275 ff.

'The Consecration of Faustina the Elder and her daughter', *Harv. Theol. Rev.* 1943, pp. 147 ff.

'The Legionary Coins of Victorinus', *TINC* 1938, pp. 214 ff.

MENADIER, K. *Die Münzen und das Münzwesen bei den 'Scriptores Historiae Augustae'*, Berlin, 1913.

MERLIN, A. *Les revers monétaires de l'empereur Nerva*, Paris, 1906.

MISSONG, A. 'Gleichartig systemisirte Münzreihen unter Kaiser Probus', *NZ* 1873, pp. 102 ff.

MOWAT, R. 'Bronzes remarquables de Tibère, de son fils, de ses petits-fils, et de Caligula', *RN* 1911, pp. 335 ff.

'Le Bureau de l'Equité et les ateliers de la monnaie imperiale à Rome', *NZ* 1909, pp. 87 ff.

'Le Monnayage de Clodius Macer', *RIN* 1902, pp. 168 ff.

OMAN, SIR CHARLES. 'Coins of Severus and Gallienus commemorating the Roman Legions', *NC* 1918, pp. 80 ff.

'The Decline and Fall of the Denarius in the 3rd century', *NC* 1916, pp. 37 ff.

'The Legionary Coins of Victorinus and Carausius', *NC* 1924, pp. 53 ff.

PICK, B. 'Zur Titulatur der Flavier', *Z.f.N.* 1885, pp. 190 ff, 355 ff.

PINK, K. 'Der Aufbau der römischen Münzprägung in der Kaiserseit', *NZ* 1937, pp. 10 ff.

'Die Triumviri monetales unter Augustus', *NZ* 1946, pp. 113 ff.

REGLING, K. 'Nochmals die Söhne des Gallenus', *NZ* 1908, pp. 115 ff.

ROHDE, TH. *Die Münzen des Kaisers Aurelianus*, Miskolcz, 1881.

ROSTOVTZEFF, M. 'Res Gestae Divi Saporis and Dura', *Berytus*, VIII, 1943, pp. 17 ff.

SMITH, H. R. W. *Problems historical and numismatic in the reign of Augustus*, Los Angeles, 1951.

STRACK, P. L. *Untersuchungen zur römischen Reichsprägung des zweiten Jahrhunderts*, Teil III: Die Reichsprägung zur Zeit des Antoninus Pius, Stuttgart, 1937.

SUTHERLAND, C. H. V. 'Claudius and the Senatorial Mint', *JRS* 1941, Vol. XXI, pp. 70 ff.

Coinage and Currency in Roman Britain, London, 1937.

Coinage in Roman Imperial Policy, 31 B.C.–A.D. 68, London, 1951.

'The date and significance of the candelabrum coins of Augustus', *Classical Review*, Vol. 54, 1944, pp. 46 ff.

'Divus Augustus Pater – a study in the *aes* coinage of Tiberius', *NC* 1941, pp. 97 ff.

'The Symbolism of a unique *aes* coin of Tiberius', *NC* 1950, pp. 290 ff.

SYDENHAM, E. A. 'The Coinages of Augustus', *NC* 1920, pp. 17 ff.

'Divus Augustus', *NC* 1937, pp. 258 ff.

'The Mint of Lugdunum', *NC* 1918, pp. 53 ff.

The Coinage of Nero, 1920.

VERMEULE, C. *Some Notes on Ancient Dies and Coining Methods*, London, 1954.

VOETTER, OTTO. 'Die Munzen des Kaisers Gallienus and Seiner Familie', *NZ* 1900, pp. 117 ff.; 1901, pp. 70 ff.

'Die römischen Münzen des Kaisers Gordianus III', *NZ* 1894, pp. 388 ff.

WEBB, PERCY. 'The Coinage of Allectus', *NC* 1906, pp. 127 ff.

'The Reform of Aurelian', *NC* 1919, pp. 234 ff.

The Reign and Coinage of Carausius, 1908.

'Third Century Roman Mints and Marks', *NC* 1921, pp. 226 ff.

WOODWARD, A. M. 'The Coinage of Pertinax', *NC* 1957, pp. 8 ff.

'Notes on the Augustan Cistophori', *NC* 1952, pp. 19 ff.

BOOK III

ALFÖLDI, A. *The Conversion of Constantine and Pagan Rome*, 1948.

'A Festival of Isis in Rome under the Christian Emperors of the IVth Century', *Dissertationes Pannonicae*, Ser. II, 7, 1937.

'The Initials of Christ on the Helmet of Constantine', *Studies in Honour of A. C. Johnson*, 1951, pp. 303 ff.

Kampfgegen das Christliche Kaisertum, 1942–3.

'Das Kreuz-szepter Konstantins des Grossen', *Schweiz. Münzbl.* 1954, pp. 81 ff.

BOYCE, A. A. 'Eudoxia, Eudocia, Eudoxia, dated solidi of the fifth century', *Am. Num. Soc. Mus. Notes*, VI, pp. 131 ff.

BRUCK, G. 'Die Verwendung Christlicher Symbole auf Münzen von Constantin I bis Magnentius', *NZ* 1955, pp. 26 ff.

BRUUN, P. 'The Constantinian Coinage of Arelate', *Finska Fornminnesföreningens Tidskrift*, 1953, pp. 1 ff.

'Constantinian mint policy and the imperial "vota"', *Nordisk Num. Årsscrift.* 1954, pp. 1 ff.

CARSON, R. A. G. 'The Geneva Forgeries', *NC* 1958, pp. 47 ff.

Select Bibliography

CARSON, R. A. G. and KENT, J. P. C. 'Constantinian Hoards and other studies in the late Roman Bronze Coinage', *NC* 1956, pp. 83 ff.

CARSON, R. A. G., HILL, P. V. and KENT, J. P. C. *Late Roman Bronze Coinage*, 1960.

ELMER, GEORGE. 'Eugenius: eine historisch-numismatische Studie', *NZ* 1936, pp. 29 ff.

'Die Kupfergeldreform unter Julianus Philosophus', *NZ* 1937, pp. 25 ff.

EVANS, SIR ARTHUR. 'Notes on the Coinage and Silver Currency in Roman Britain from Valentinian I to Constantine III', *NC* 1915, pp. 433 ff.

GOODACRE, HUGH. *The Bronze Coinage of the Late Roman Empire*, 1929.

KENT, J. P. C. 'Arelate or Constantinople?', *NC* 1959, coll. 13 ff.

'Notes on Some Fourth Century Coin Types', *NC* 1954, pp. 20 ff.

'The Pattern of Bronze Coinage under Constantine', *NC* 1957, pp. 161 ff.

'Carausius II: Fact or Fiction?', *NC* 1958, pp. 75 ff.

KRAFT, K. 'Die Taten der Kaiser Constans und Constantin II', *Jahr. f. Num. u. Geld.* 1958, pp. 141 ff.

LAFAURIE, J. 'La chronologie des monnaies de Constantin III et de Constant II', *RN* 1953, pp. 37 ff.

LAFFRANCHI, L. 'Commento numismatico alla storia dell' imperatore Magnenzio e del suo tempo', *Atti e memorie*, 1930, pp. 134–205.

MADDEN, F. W. 'Christian Emblems on the Coins of Constantine the Great, his family and his successors', *NC* 1877, pp. 242 ff., and 1878, pp. 169 ff.

MATTINGLY, HAROLD. 'Monetary system of the Roman Empire from Diocletian to Theodosius I', *NC* 1946, pp. 111 ff.

'Fel. Temp. Reparatio', *NC* 1933, pp. 182 ff.

MAURICE, JULES. *Numismatique Constantinienne* (3 vols.), 1908–12.

MAYREDER, F. 'Die Halben Centionales mit Vota-Legenden zur Zeit des Theodosius', *NZ* 1936, pp. 52 ff.

PEARCE, J. W. E. 'Eugenius', *NC* 1944, pp. 48 ff.

'Eugenius and his Eastern Colleagues', *NC* 1940, pp. 1 ff.

'Gold Coinage of the Reign of Theodosius I', *NC* 1939, pp. 205 ff.

'Issues of the Solidi "Victoria Augg." from Treveri', *NC* 1937, pp. 138 ff.

'Lugdunum Siliqua coinage of Valentinian II and Eugenius', *NC* 1944, pp. 45 ff.

'The Reign of Theodosius I', *TINC* pp. 227 ff.

PINK, KARL. 'Die Silberprägung der Diocletianische Tetrarchie', *NZ* 1930, pp. 9 ff.

'Die Goldprägung des Diocletianus und seiner Mitregenten (284 bis 305)', *NZ* 1931, pp. 1 ff.

SEECK, OTTO. 'Die Münzpolitik Diocletians und Seiner Nachfolger', *Z.f.N.* 1890, pp. 86 ff., 113 ff.

STEVENS, C. E. 'Marcus, Gratian, Constantine', *Athenaeum*, 1957, pp. 316 ff.

'Some thoughts on "Second Carausius" ', *NC* 1956, pp. 34 ff.

SUTHERLAND, C. H. V. 'Diocletian as "Aeternus Augustus" ', *Am. Num. Soc. Mus. Notes*, VII, 1957, pp. 7 ff.

'Flexibility in the Reformed Coinage of Diocletian', *Essays presented to Harold Mattingly*, 1956, pp. 174 ff.

'The Folles of Cyzicus down to A.D. 306', *NC* 1955, pp. 70 ff.

'The Folles of Ticinum, 305–307', *NC* 1954, pp. 68 ff.

TOYNBEE, J. M. C. 'Roma and Constantinopolis in late antique art from 312 to 365', *JRS* 1947, pp. 135 ff.

ULRICH-BANSA, O. 'Monete d'oro del V e VI secolo rinvenute a Sebatum (S. Lorenzo di Pusteria)', *Notizie degli scavi.* 1939, pp. 150 ff.

Moneta Mediolanensis, 352–498, Milan, 1947.

'Note sulla zecca di Aquileia Romana', *Aquil. Nostra*, 1936–8, 1947.

Note sulla zecca di Aquileia Romana. I multipli dei Solidi d'oro, Udine, 1936.

VOETTER, OTTO. 'The Coinage of Diocletian, etc.', *NZ* 1899, pp. 1 ff. and 223 ff.; 1911, pp. 171 ff.; 1918, pp. 11 ff.; 1919, pp. 181 ff.; 1920, pp. 101 ff.

'Die Münzen der römischen Kaiser, Kaiserinnen und Caesaren von Diocletianus bis Romulus', *Katalog Paul Gerin*, 1921.

WEBB, PERCY. 'The Coinage of the Reign of Julian the Philosopher', *NC* 1910, pp. 238 ff.

WILLERS, H. 'Römische Silberbarren', *NZ* 1898, pp. 211 ff.; 1829, pp. 38 ff.

There is only room for very summary reference to works on some special subjects: on *barbarous imitations*, works by HILL, SUTHERLAND and others: on *economics*, works by STURE BOLIN, A. H. M. JONES, HAROLD MATTINGLY, GUNNAR MICKWITZ, L. WEST, etc.: on *medallions* the famous old 'Corpus' of GNECCHI and more recent works by

ALFÖLDI, PINK and PROFESSOR TOYNBEE. Among *general* works we may mention MICHAEL GRANT on Anniversaries and other subjects, MATTINGLY on imperial VOWS and VERMEULE on Roman art in several aspects. *Coinages outside Rome* and *Hoards* receive brief independent treatment.

HOARDS

Hoards that have been found since the first edition may be traced in such periodicals as the *Numismatic Chronicle*, *Revue Numismatique*, *Revue Belge de Numismatique*, *Revue Suisse*, *Annali*, etc. Important finds include the following:

Republic

Three hoards of victoriates. A. STAZIO, 'Ripostigli di vittoriati nel Museo Nationale de Napoli', *Annali*, 1957, pp. 67 ff.

Early Empire

Aurei from Julius Caesar to Claudius. R. A. G. CARSON, 'The Bredgar Treasure of Roman Coins', *NC* 1959, pp. 17 ff.

Denarii and antoniniana from Nero to Trajan Decius. N. A. MOUCHMOV, *Le trésor numismatique de Rēka-Devnia*, Sofia, 1934.

Aurei from Nero to Aurelian. P. LE GENTILHOMME, 'Les aurei du trésor découvert a Rennes en 1774', *RN* 1943, pp. 11 ff.

Aurei (including multiples) from Gallienus to Aurelian. J. LAFAURIE, 'Trésor d'un navire romain trouvé en Méditerranée', *RN* 1958, pp. 79 ff.

Denarii and antoniniani from Julia Domna to Valerian II. H. MATTINGLY, 'The Great Dorchester hoard', *NC* 1939, pp. 21 ff.

Antoniniani of Macrian and Quietus. H. MATTINGLY, 'The Coinage of Macrianus II and Quietus', *NC* 1954, pp. 53 ff.

Denarii and antoniniani from Clodius Albinus to Saloninus. P. LE GENTILHOMME, *RN* 1946, pp. 15 ff.

Late Empire

Folles from Diocletian to Constantine Caesar. E. T. LEEDS, *A Hoard of Roman Folles found at Fyfield, Berks*, Oxford, 1946.

Folles from Diocletian to Maxentius. N. LEWIS, 'A hoard of folles from Seltz (Alsace)', *Am. Num. Soc. Notes & Mon.* 79 (1937).

Folles from Diocletian to Constantine II. R. A. G. CARSON and J. P. C. KENT, 'Constantinian hoards and other studies', *NC* 1956, pp. 83 ff.

Aurei and solidi from Diocletian to Constantine I. A. BALDWIN BRETT, 'Aurei and solidi of the Arras hoard', *NC* 1933, pp. 268 ff.

Silver coins from Trajan to Julian II. H. A. GRUEBER, 'The Southsea find of fourth-century silver coins', *NC* 1936, pp. 292 ff.

Bronze coins from Constans to Constantius Gallus. H. MATTINGLY, 'A fourth-century hoard from Egypt', *NC* 1950, pp. 179 ff.

Bronze coins from Valentinian II to Arcadius-Honorius. F. S. SALISBURY, 'Weymouth Bay Hoard', *NC* 1931, pp. 14 ff.

Gold and silver coins from Constantius II to Arcadius-Honorius. B. H. ST. J. O'NEIL, 'The Terling Treasure', *NC* 1933, pp. 157 ff.

Silver coins (including multiples) from Constantius II to Arcadius. O. ULRICH BANSA, 'Ripostiglio di monete d'argento del IV secolo d. Cr. (S. Genesio, Pavia)', *Atti dell' Acc. Naz. dei Lincei*, VIII (1954), pp. 166 ff.

COINAGES OUTSIDE ROME

Out of the large material which has been accumulating I select the following as typical but by no means exhaustive.

Spain

M. GRANT. 'Decline and fall of City-coinages in Spain', *NC* 1949, pp. 93 ff.

A. SCHULTALN. *Numantia*, Vol. IV (1929). (Coin finds described by Haeberlin.)

J. NAVASCUES. 'En torno a las series hispanicas imperialos', *Num. Hisp.* 1–2, pp. 33 ff.

J. AMOROS. 'Argentum Oscense', *Num. Hisp.* 11, pp. 51 ff.

C. SELTMAN. 'Argentum oscense and bigati', *NC* 1944, pp. 77 ff.

A. BELTRAN. '*Las monedas latinas di Cartagena*, 1949. 'Monuments on Hispano-roman coins', *AEA* 1953.

O. GIL FARRES. 'La ceca de la colonia Augusta Emerita', *AEA* 1946, pp. 209 ff. 'La ceca de la colonia Caesarea Augusta', *Ampurias*, XIII, pp. 65 ff.

G. F. HILL. 'The ancient coinage of Hispania Citerior', *ANS NNM* 50, 1931.

Select Bibliography

Africa

J. MAZARD. *Corpus nummorum Numidiae Mauretaniaeque*, 1955.
J. G. MILNE. *Catalogue of the Alexandrian Coins in the Ashmolean Museum*, 1933.

Gaul

C. M. KRAAY. The Chronology of Colonia Nemausus. *NC* 1955, pp. 75 ff.

Greece

K. M. EDWARDS. *Corinth*, Vol. VI, 1933.
M. THOMPSON. *Agora Coin Finds*, 1954.

Asia Minor

J. BABELON. 'La pénétration romain en Asie Mineure d'après les documents numismatiques', *RN* 1939, pp. 1 ff., 149 ff.
L. ROBERT. *Étude de numismatique grecque* (chap. I: Monnaies et villes de Troade), 1951.
    Villes d'Asie Mineure, 1935.
J. G. MILES. 'Colophon', *ANS NNM* 96, 1941.
    'Antioch in Pisidia', *NC* 1947, pp. 97 ff.
    'Notes on the Oxford Collections (Asia Minor)', *NC* 1935 annually to 1940.
A. R. BELLINGER. 'Late bronze of Alexandria Troas', *ANS MN* VIII, pp. 25 ff.
K. REGLING. *Priene Münzen*, 1927.
B. TRELL. 'The Temple of Artemis at Ephesus', *ANS NNM* 107.
D. H. COX. 'A Tarsus Coin Collection in the Adana Museum', *ANS NNM* 92.
    'The Coins' (from H. GOLDMAN, *Excavations at 'Gözlü' Kuli, Tarsus*, Vol. I, 1950).
    'Coins from the Excavations at Curium', *ANS NNM* 145.
Sylloge Nummorum Graecorum, Sammlung von Aulock (Berlin, 1957–   ), in progress.

Syria, Palestine, Mesopotamia

A. R. BELLINGER. 'Syrian tetradrachms of Caracalla and Macrinus', *ANS Num. Studies*, 3.
    Dura Final Report VI; The Coins, 1949.

D. B. WAAGE. *Antioch on the Orontes*. Vol. IV, part 2 (Greek, Roman, Byzantine and Crusader's Coins), 1952.

H. SEYRIG. 'Sur les éres de quelque villes de Syrie', *Syria*, 27, 1950.
'Les trouvailles de monnaies peloponnesiennes', *Syria*, 17; *Syria*, 34.
'Monnaies Contremarquées en Syrie', *Syria*, 35, 1958.

L. KADMAN. *Aelia Capitolina*, 1956.
Caesarea Maritima, 1957.

K. CASTELIN. 'Rhesaena', *ANS NNM* 108.

General

Sylloge Nummorum Graecorum: Copenhagen (now complete as far as Syria), 1942–.

L. LACROIX. *Les Reproductions de statues sur les monnaies Grecques*, 1949.

Abbreviations

AR	Silver
A͵	Gold
Abh. d. Kais. Ak. d. Wiss., etc.	*Abhandlungen der Kaiserlichen Akademie der Wissenschaften, Vienna, Philologisch-Historische Klasse*
Atti e Mem. Ist. It.	*Atti e memorie dell'Istituto Italiano di Numismatica* (Rome)
B.M.C.	*British Museum Catalogue*
Berl. M͵bl.	*Berliner Münͻblätter* (Berlin)
Bl. f. M͵fr.	*Blätter für Münͻ freunde* (Leipzig & Dresden)
Brit. Mus. Quart.	*British Museum Quarterly*
Bull. Soc. Num. Rom.	*Bulletino della Societa Numismatica Romana* (Rome)
C.I.L.	Corpus Inscriptionum Latinarum
Cl. R.	*Classical Review* (London)
Cod. Just.	*Codex Justinianus*
Cod. Theod.	*Codex Theodosianus*
De Verb. Sig.	*De verborum significatione* (Festus)
Epit.	*Epitome* of Livy
Gr.	Grains
Grm.	Grammes
J.R.S.	*Journal of Roman Studies* (London)
M.N.	*Mélanges Numismatiques* (Le Mans & Paris)
Mitth. f. Münͻsammler	*Mittheilungen für Münͻsammler*
N.d.S.	*Notiͻie degli Scavi*
N.Z.	*Numismatische Zeitschrift* (Vienna)
Nat. Hist.	*Naturalis Historia* (Pliny the Elder)
Num. Chron.	*Numismatic Chronicle*
Num. Notes & Monographs	*Numismatic Notes and Monographs* (New York)
Pl.	Plate
Proc. Brit. Acad.	*Proceedings of the British Academy* (London)
R.I.C.	*Roman Imperial Coinage*
RN	*Revue Numismatique* (Paris)
Rass. Num.	*Rassegna Numismatica* (Orbetello & Rome)
Rev. Arch.	*Revue Archéologique* (Paris)
Riv. It.	*Rivista Italiana di Numismatica* (Milan)
Röm. Münͻwesen	*Römisches Münͻwesen* (Mommsen)
Sitͻ. d. k. pr. Ak.	*Sitͻungsberichte der königlichen preussischen Akademie* (Berlin)
T.I.N.C.	*Transactions of the International Numismatic Congress* (London)
Z.f.N.	*Zeitschrift für Numismatik* (Berlin)

Index

276

Key to the Plates

Key to the Plates

PLATE VI (pp. 16 ff., 26 ff.)

1. Dextans, c. 170 B.C.
2. Quincunx, c. 170 B.C.
3. Sextans (local issue), c. 160 B.C.
4. Triens (M. FABRINI.), c. 130 B.C.
5. Quadrans (P. MAE. ANT.), c. 125 B.C.
6. Dodrans (C. CASSI.), c. 121 B.C.
7. Bes (C. CASSI.), c. 121 B.C.
8. As (M. FONTEI. C. F. – semuncial standard), c. 87 B.C.
9. Quinarius (Anonymous), c. 105 B.C.
10. Quinarius (L. PISO), c. 90 B.C.
11. Sestertius (A. LICINIVS MACER.), c. 47 B.C.
12. Aureus (Sulla), c. 83 B.C.
13. Aureus (Julius Caesar), c. 45 B.C.
14. As (Julius Caesar – Q. OPPIVS), c. 45 B.C.
15. Cistophoric tetradrachm (= 3 denarii, Mark Antony), c. 37 B.C.

PLATE VII (pp. 28 ff.)

1. Denarius (VAR.), c. 165 B.C.
2. Denarius (L. PORCI. LICI., L. LIC. CN. DOM.), c. 118 B.C.
3. Denarius (M. CALID. Q. METE. CN. FL.), c. 122 B.C.
4. Quadrans (M. SILA. Q. CVRT.), c. 120 B.C.
5. Denarius (M. SERGIVS. SILVS Q. EX S.C.), c. 106 B.C.
6. Denarius (A. ALB. S. F. L. METEL. C. MALL.), c. 100 B.C.
7. Denarius (C. VAL. FLA. IMPERAT. EX S.C.), c. 82 B.C.
8. Denarius (M. FAN. L. CRIT. AED. PL.), c. 87 B.C.
9. Denarius (Q. ANTO. BALB. S.C.), c. 82 B.C.
10. Denarius (P. GALB. AED. CVR. S.C.), c. 68 B.C.
11. Denarius (M. PLAETORIVS CESTIANVS AED. CVR. EX S.C.), c. 68 B.C.
12. Denarius (L. FVRI. CN. F. BROCCHI IIIVIR), c. 55 B.C.
13. Denarius (T. CARISIVS – MONETA), c. 45 B.C.
14. Aureus (L. PLANC. PRAEF. VRB. – C. CAES. DIC. TER.), c. 45 B.C.
15. Denarius (L. FLAMINI. CHILO IIIIVIR PRI(mus) FL(avit)), 44 B.C. (?)
16. Denarius (Q. SICINIVS IIIVIR – C. COPONIVS PR. S.C.), c. 49 B.C.
17. Denarius (METEL. PIVS SCIP. IMP. – CRASSVS IVN. LEG. PRO PR.), c. 46 B.C.
18. Denarius (M. ANTON. COS. IMP. – M. LEPID. C OS. IMP.), c. 43 B.C.
19. Aureus (L. MUSSIDIVS T. F. LONGVS IIIIVIR A.P.F. – C. CAESAR IIIVIR R.P.C.), c. 42 B.C.
20. Denarius (C. CAESAR IMP. S.C.), c. 43 B.C.

PLATE VIII (pp. 34 ff., 82 ff.)

1. Denarius (LENT. MAR. F. P.E.S.C.), c. 99 B.C.
2. Triens (L.P.D.P.P.), c. 89 B.C.
3. Denarius (EX A.P. – anonymous – types of L. IVLI. BVRSIO), c. 85 B.C.
4. Denarius (M. LVCILI. RVF. PV.), c. 100 B.C.
5. Denarius (M. VOLTEI. M.F. S.C.D.T.), c. 80 B.C.
6. Denarius (L. SATVRN. – C.), c. 100 B.C.
7. Denarius (L. PISO FRVG.), c. 90 B.C.
8. Denarius (M. SERVEILI. C.F. – ω – A.), c. 100 B.C.
9. Denarius (C. FVNDAN. Q. – A.), c. 100 B.C.
10. Denarius (L. IVLI. BVRSIÓ – Anchor), c. 87 B.C.
11. Denarius (C. MALLE. C. F., L. LIC. CN. DOM. – serrate), c. 118 B.C.
12. Denarius (L. COT. – O – serrate), c. 102 B.C.

13. Denarius (L. PAPI. – pulley with hook, rope – serrate), c. 75 B.C.
14. Denarius (L. VOLT. L. F. STRABO. – serrate), c. 81 B.C.
15. Denarius (C. HOSIDI. C. F. GETA IIIVIR – serrate), c. 70 B.C.
16. Denarius (M. PLAETORIVS CEST. S.C.), c. 64 B.C.
17. Denarius (M. PLAETORI. CEST. S.C.), c. 64 B.C.
18. Denarius (M. PISO M. F. FRVGI), c. 70 B.C.
19. Denarius (CN. PLANCIVS AED. CVR. S.C.), c. 54 B.C.
20. Denarius (L. PLAVTIVS PLANCVS), c. 47 B.C.

PLATE IX (pp. 36 ff.)

1. Denarius (no mint-mark), c. 170 B.C.
2. Denarius (caduceus), c. 170 B.C.
3. Denarius (palm), c. 160 B.C.
4. Denarius (M.A.), c. 160 B.C. (?)
5. Denarius (C.), c. 160 B.C. (?)
6. Denarius (caduceus), c. 160 B.C.
7. Denarius (knife), c. 170 B.C.
8. Denarius (D.), c. 160 B.C.
9. Denarius (GR.), c. 160 B.C.
10. Denarius (Q.L.C.), c. 190 B.C.
11. Victoriate (CROT.), c. 170 B.C.
12. Quinarius (H.), c. 180 B.C.
13. Victoriate (MP. ?), c. 180 B.C.
14. Victoriate (MT. ?), c. 180 B.C.
15. Victoriate (Q.), c. 180 B.C.
16. Victoriate (VIB.), c. 190 B.C.
17. Denarius (SX. Q.), c. 150 B.C.
18. Denarius (fly), c. 145 B.C.
19. Denarius (PVR.), c. 145 B.C.
20. Denarius (C. MAIANI.), c. 140 B.C.

NOTE: *The date at the foot of the plate should read c. 170-135 B.C.*

PLATE X (pp. 36 ff.)

1. Denarius (P. CALP.), c. 123 B.C.
2. Denarius (CARB.), c. 122 B.C.
3. Denarius (C.F.L.R.Q.M.), c. 118 B.C.
4. Denarius (CN. DOMIT.), c. 120 B.C.
5. Denarius (M. CIPI. M.F.), c. 105 B.C.
6. Denarius (L. CAESI.), c. 110 B.C.
7. Denarius (L. IVLI L.F.), c. 105 B.C.
8. Denarius (C. MALL.), c. 99 B.C.
9. Aureus (L. MANLI. PROQ. – L. SVLLA IMP.), c. 81 B.C.
10. Aureus (L. SVLLA IMPER. ITERV.), c. 86 B.C.
11. Denarius (Q.), c. 81 B.C.
12. Denarius (C. ANNI. T.F.T.N. PRO COS. EX S.C. – L. FABI. L. F. HISP. Q.), c. 81 B.C.
13. Denarius (L. TORQUAT. IIIVIR), c. 66 B.C.
14. Denarius (Q. SICINIVS IIIVIR), c. 49 B.C.
15. Denarius (Q. METELL. PIVS SCIPIO IMP.), c. 46 B.C.
16. Denarius (MAG. PIVS IMP. ITER. – PRAEF. CLAS. ET ORAE MARIT. EX S.C.), c. 38 B.C.
17. Denarius (C. ANTONIVS M. F. PROCOS.), c. 43 B.C.
18. Aureus (C. CASSI. IMP. – LENTVLVSSPINT.), c. 43 B.C.

19. Denarius (C. CAESAR IIIVIR R.P.C. – Q. SALVIVS IMP. COS. DESG.), c. 40 B.C.
20. Denarius (M. ANTONIVS AVG. IMP. IIII. COS. TERT. IIIVIR R.P.C. – D. TVR.),
    c. 31 B.C.
    NOTE: *The date at the foot of the plate should read c. 123–31 B.C.*

PLATE XI (pp. 54 ff.)

1. Denarius (Victory crowning Dioscuri), c. 170 B.C.
2. Denarius (Dioscuri – griffin), c. 160 B.C.
3. Denarius (Diana in biga – AV.), c. 145 B.C.
4. Denarius (Dioscuri – Victory crowning Roma), c. 145 B.C.
5. Denarius (Victory in biga – S. AFRA.), c. 145 B.C.
6. Denarius (Victory in biga – C. TAL.), c. 145 B.C.
7. Denarius (Juno in biga of goats – C. RENI.), c. 124 B.C.
8. Denarius (Juno (?) in quadriga – C. CVR. TRIGE.), c. 124 B.C.
9. Denarius (Hercules in biga of centaurs – M. AVRELI. COTA), c. 124 B.C.
10. Denarius (Dioscuri – L. IVLI. – XVI), c. 123 B.C.
11. Denarius (Victory in biga – C. VAL. C. F. FLAC. – XVI), c. 123 B.C.
12. Denarius (Corn-monument and statues – C. AVG.), c. 125 B.C.
13. Denarius (Apollo in quadriga – CN. BAEBI. Q.F. TAMPIL.), c. 126 B.C.
14. Denarius (Juno (?) in quadriga – C. CVR. F. TRIGE.), c. 124 B.C.
15. Denarius (Jupiter in quadriga – L. ANTES. GRAG.), c. 122 B.C.
16. Denarius (Sol in quadriga – M. ABVRI. M. F. GEM.), c. 119 B.C.
17. Denarius (Venus, crowned by Cupid, in biga – SEX. IVLI. L. F. CAESAR),
    c. 120 B.C.
18. Denarius (Victory in biga – corn-ear – T. CLOVLI.), c. 124 B.C.
19. Denarius (Pax in biga – elephant's head), c. 121 B.C.
20. Denarius (Corn-monument and statues – TI. MINVCI. C. F. AVGVRINI.),
    c. 119 B.C.
    NOTE: *The date at the foot of the plate should read c. 169–119 B.C.*

PLATE XII (pp. 51 ff.)

1. Sextans (Uncial standard – Victory above prow), c. 145 B.C.
2. As (Uncial standard – Victory crowning trophy – CN. BLASIO CN. F.),
   c. 105 B.C.
3. Quadrans (Uncial standard – Club in wreath – L. OPEIMI.), c. 121 B.C.
4. As (Semuncial standard – Victory on prow – L. PISO FRVGI.), c. 90 B.C.
5. As (Semuncial standard – Numa Pompilius and Ancus Marcius – prows and
   column – C. CENSO.), c. 88 B.C.
6. As (Semuncial standard – triple prow – C. PANSA), c. 87 B.C.
7. Quadrans (Semuncial standard – rudder and anchor – L. PISO), c. 90 B.C.
8. Dupondius (?), (Crocodile – rostrum – CRAS.), c. 31 B.C.
9. As (?), (Apollo – fasces – CRA.), c. 31 B.C.

PLATE XIII (pp. 58 ff.)

1. Denarius (Apollo – C. PISO L. F. FRVGI), c. 66 B.C.
2. Denarius (Apollo – M. METELLVS Q.F.), c. 81 B.C.
3. Denarius (Bacchus (Liber) – Libera – L. CASSI. Q.F.), c. 80 B.C.
4. Denarius (Ceres – L. CASSI. CAEICIAN.), c. 98 B.C.
5. Denarius (Cybele – C. FABI. C.F.), c. 103 B.C.
6. Aureus (Cybele – C. NORBANVS L. CESTIVS), c. 44 B.C.
7. Denarius (Diana – TI. CLAVD. TI. F. AP. N.), c. 78 B.C.
8. Denarius (Diana – C. POSTVMI. TA.), c. 75 B.C.
9. Denarius (Diana – C. HOSIDI. C. F. GETA IIIVIR.), c. 70 B.C.

10. Denarius (Dioscuri – M. FONTEI.) c. 106 B.C.
11. Denarius (Dioscuri – M. CORDIVS RVFVS), c. 46 B.C.
12. Denarius (Juno – L. RVBRI. DOS.), c. 88 B.C.
13. Denarius (Juno Sospita – L. THORIVS BALBVS), c. 105 B.C.
14. Denarius (Juno Sospita – L. ROSCI. FABATI), c. 57 B.C.
15. Denarius (Juno Moneta – L. PLAETORI. L.F.Q.S.C.), c. 75 B.C.
16. Victoriate (Jupiter – MAT.), c. 180 B.C.
17. Denarius (Jupiter – L. PROCILI. F.), c. 81 B.C.
18. Denarius (Jupiter – Q. POMPONI. RVFVS), c. 74 B.C.
19. Denarius (Jupiter – VALERIVS ACISCVLVS), c. 45 B.C.
20. Denarius (Jupiter (Veiovis) – GAR. VER. OGVL.), c. 84 B.C.

PLATE XIV (pp. 60 ff.)

1. Didrachm (Mars – club), c. 235 B.C.
2. Denarius (Mars – CN. LENTVL.), c. 87 B.C.
3. Denarius (Mars – P. SATRIENVS), c. 75 B.C.
4. Denarius (Mars – L. AXSIVS L. F. NASO S.C.), c. 75 B.C.
5. Denarius (Mars – ALBINVS BRVTI F.), c. 49 B.C.
6. Denarius (Medusa – L. COSSVTI. C. F. SABVLA), c. 73 B.C.
7. Denarius (Minerva (on rev.) – C. VIBIVS C. F.), c. 88 B.C.
8. Denarius (Neptune – L. LVCRETI. TRIO), c. 75 B.C.
9. Denarius (Silenus – D. SILANVS L. F.), c. 90 B.C.
10. Denarius (Pan-Silenus – C. VIBIVS C. F. PANSA), c. 89 B.C.
11. Denarius (Pan – C. VIBIVS C. F. PANSA), c. 49 B.C.
12. Denarius (Priapus – Q. TITI.), c. 87 B.C.
13. Denarius (Roma – C. SCR.), c. 145 B.C.
14. Denarius (Roma – C. CVR. F. TRIGE.), c. 125 B.C.
15. Denarius (Roma – L. POST. ALB.), c. 120 B.C.
16. Denarius (Roma – C. POBLICI. Q.F.), c. 78 B.C.
17. Aureus (Roma – C. VIBIVS VARVS), c. 43 B.C.
18. Denarius (Sol – M′. AQVIL.), c. 108 B.C.
19. Denarius (Venus – L. CENSORIN. P. CREPVS. C. LIMETAN.), c. 85 B.C.
20. Denarius (Vesta – Q. CASSIVS), c. 52 B.C.

PLATE XV (pp. 65 ff.)

1. Denarius (Bonus Eventus – LIBO), c. 55 B.C.
2. Denarius (Concordia – L. M VSSIDIVS LONGVS), c. 42 B.C.
3. Quinarius (Felicitas – PALIKANVS), c. 46 B.C.
4. Denarius (Genius P.R. – CN. LENT. Q. EX S.C.), c. 75 B.C.
5. Denarius (Libertas – Q. CASSIVS), c. 52 B.C.
6. Denarius (Fides – A. LICINIVS MACER), c. 48 B.C.
7. Aureus (Fortuna (rev.) – TI. SEMPRON. GRACCVS IIIIVIR Q.D.), c. 41 B.C.
8. Denarius (Honos et Virtus – KALENI – CORDI.), c. 59 B.C.
9. Denarius (Honos – PALIKANVS), c. 46 B.C.
10. Quinarius (Pax(s) – L. AEMILIVS BVCA IIIIVIR), c. 44 B.C.
11. Denarius (Pietas – M. HERENNI.), c. 106 B.C.
12. Denarius (Salus – D. SILANVS L.F.), c. 90 B.C.
13. Denarius (Triumpus – L. PAPIVS CELSVS IIIVIR), c. 46 B.C.
14. Denarius (Victory (rev.) – M. CATO), c. 100 B.C.
15. Denarius (Victory – L. VALERI. FLACCI), c. 108 B.C.
16. Aureus (Victory – L. PLANC. PR. VRB.), c. 45 B.C.
17. Aureus (Victory – C. NVMONIVS VAALA), c. 43 B.C.

Key to the Plates

PLATE XVI (pp. 70 ff.)

1. Denarius ('Scipio Africanus' – CN. BLASIO CN. F.), c. 104 B.C.
2. Denarius (Philip V of Macedon – L. PHILIPPVS), c. 104 B.C.
3. Denarius (Jugurtha – FAVSTVS), c. 61 B.C.
4. Denarius (C. Coelius Caldus, consul – CALDVS), c. 61 B.C.
5. Denarius (Brutus – Ahala – BRVTVS ?), c. 50 B.C.
6. Denarius (Marcellus – MARCELLINVS), c. 45 B.C. (?).
7. Denarius (Numonius Vaala (?) – C. NVMONIVS VAALA), c. 43 B.C.
8. Aureus (Sex. Pompey, Cn. Pompeius Magnus and Cn. Pompeius iun. MAG. PIVS IMP. ITER, etc.), c. 38 B.C.
9. Denarius (Cn. Pompeius Magnus – M. MINAT. SABIN. PR. Q.), c. 46 B.C.
10. Denarius (L. Regulus the praetor – L. REGVLVS), c. 42 B.C.
11. Denarius (Dog – C. ANTESTI.), c. 140 B.C.
12. Denarius (Faustulus, she-wolf and twins – SEX. POMP. FOSTLVS.), c. 125 B.C.
13. Denarius (Macedonian shield – T.Q.), c. 122 B.C.
14. Denarius (Mars and Nerio – CN. GEL.), c. 125 B.C.
15. Denarius (Macedonian shield – M. METELLVS Q.F.), c. 121 B.C.
16. Denarius (Perseus of Macedon (?) – Q. PHILIPVS), c. 121 B.C.
17. Denarius (Quirinus – N. FABI. PICTOR), c. 121 B.C.
18. Denarius (Ulysses and dog Argos – C. MAMIL. LIMETAN.), c. 83 B.C.
19. Denarius (Acca Larentia (?) – P. ACCOLEIVS LARISCOLVS), c. 43 B.C. (?).
20. Aureus (Venus Victrix – C. VIBIVS VARVS), c. 42 B.C.

PLATE XVII (pp. 69 ff., 82 ff.)

1. Denarius (Roma, she-wolf and twins, birds – Anonymous), c. 105 B.C.
2. Denarius (Quirinus – Games of Ceres – C. MEMMI. C.F.), c. 61 B.C.
3. Denarius (Numa Pompilius and Ancus Marcius – C. CENSO.), c. 87 B.C.
4. Denarius (Titius Tatius – Rape of Sabines – L. TITVRI. SABINI), c. 88 B.C.
5. Denarius (Purification after Sabine War – L. MVSSIDIVS LONGVS), 42 B.C.
6. Aureus (Brutus the first consul – M. BRVTVS – COSTA LEG.), c. 42 B.C.
7. Denarius (Brutus the first consul – BRVTVS), c. 50 B.C.
8. Aureus (Tusculum – L. SERVIVS RVFVS), c. 43 B.C.
9. Denarius (Lepidus, guardian of Ptolemy V – M. LEPIDVS), c. 70 B.C.
10. Denarius (Perseus and his sons – PAVLLVS LEPIDVS), c. 55 B.C.
11. Denarius (M. Lepidus, the warrior of fifteen – M. LEPIDVS), c. 70 B.C.
12. Denarius (Games of Flora – Gladiators – C. SERVEIL. C.F.), c. 64 B.C.
13. Denarius (M'. Aquillius, restorer of Sicily – M. AQVIL. M'.F.M.'N. IIIVIR), c. 59 B.C.
14. Denarius (Bocchus surrendering Jugurtha to Sulla – FAVSTVS), c. 61 B.C.
15. Denarius (Trophies of Cn. Pompeius Magnus – FAVSTVS), c. 58 B.C.
16. Denarius (Games of Victory founded – SEX. NONI. SVFENAS.), c. 63 B.C.
17. Denarius (Oath-Scene – C. SVLPICI. C.F.), c. 101 B.C.
18. Denarius ('Provocatio' – P. LAECA), c. 106 B.C.
19. Denarius (Voting-scene – P. NERVA), c. 108 B.C.
20. Aureus (Vestal Virgin – C. CLODIVS VESTALIS), c. 43 B.C.

PLATE XVIII (pp. 73 ff.)

1. Denarius (Ahala and Sp. Maelius – Gaius Gracchus – C. SERVEIL.), c. 121 B.C.
2. Denarius (Ahala and Sp. Maelius – Gaius Gracchus – C. SERVEIL.), c. 81 B.C.
3. Denarius (War against Bituitus – CN. DOM.), c. 120 B.C.
4. Denarius (Cn. Domitius in Gaul – C. METELLVS.), c. 119 B.C.
5. Denarius (C. SERVEILI. M.F.), c. 120 B.C.

Key to the Plates

6. Denarius (Victories in Illyricum (?) – M. FOVRI. L. F. PHILI), c. 108 B.C.
7. Denarius (War in Gaul (?) – L. TORQVA. EX S.C.), c. 105 B.C.
8. Denarius (Cimbrian War – Q. THERM. M.F.), c. 105 B.C.
9 Denarius (Triumph of Marius – LENT. MAR. F.), c. 100 B.C.
10. Denarius (Social War – Rebels – ITALIA.), c. 89 B.C.
11. Denarius (Social War – Rebels – VITELLIV), c. 89 B.C.
12. Denarius (Social War – Rebels – C. PAAPIVS C. F. MVTILVS.), c. 89 B.C.
13. Denarius (Social War – Despatch-rider – L. PISO L. F. FRVGI), c. 90 B.C.
14. Denarius (Largesse of curule aedile – P. FOVRIVS CRASSIPES AED. CVR.), c. 87 B.C.
15. Denarius (C. EGNATIVS CN. F. CN. N.), c. 75 B.C.
16. Denarius (C. EGNATIVS CN. F. CN. N.), c. 75 B.C.
17. Denarius (L. FARSVLEI. MENSOR.), c. 75 B.C.
18. Denarius (War in Spain – A. POST. A.F.S.N. ALBIN.), c. 72 B.C.
19. Denarius (War in Spain – A. POST. A.F.S.N. ALBIN.), c. 72 B.C.
20. Denarius (Q. CREPER. M. F. ROCVS), c. 70 B.C.

PLATE XIX (pp. 76 ff.)

1. Denarius (Sale of slaves – Pirates – SER. SVLP.), c. 51 B.C.
2. Denarius (Surrender of Aretas – Capture of Privernum – M. SCAVR. AED. CVR. EX S.C. – P. HYPSAEVS AED. CVR.), c. 58 B.C.
3. Denarius (Bacchius Iudaeus – A. PLAVTIVS AED. CVR. S.C.), c. 54 B.C.
4. Denarius (Consulship of Messalla – MESSAL. F.), c. 53 B.C.
5. Denarius (Pompeians in Africa – L. LENTVLVS MAR. COS.), c. 48 B.C.
6. Denarius (Caesar's 52nd birthday – CAESAR.), c. 49 B.C.
7. Aureus (Caesar's 4th year as dictator – CAES. DIC. QVAR. COS. QVINC.), 44 B.C.
8. Denarius (Cato at Utica – M. CATO PRO PR.), c. 46 B.C.
9. Denarius (Julius Caesar – P. SEPVLLIVS MACER.), 44 B.C.
10. Denarius (Julius Caesar dictator for life – L. BVCA.), 44 B.C.
11. Denarius (Cn. Pompeius jun. welcomed in Spain – M. MINAT. SABIN. PR. Q.), c. 45 B.C.
12. Denarius (Sex. Pompeius in Spain – SEX. MAGNVS IMP. (SAL.)), c. 45 B.C.
13. Denarius (Dream of Sulla – L. BVCA.), 44 B.C.
14. Aureus (M. Lepidus – L. MVSSIDIVS LONGVS), 42 B.C.
15. Denarius (Julius Caesar – L. MVSSIDIVS LONGVS), 42 B.C.
16. Denarius (Battle of Philippi – L. MVSSIDIVS LONGVS), 42 B.C.
17. Aureus (Brutus in the East – Q. CAEPIO BRVTVS IMP. – M. SERVEILIVS LEG.), c. 42 B.C.
18. Aureus (Cassius in the East – C. CASSEI. IMP. – M. SERVEILIVS LEG.), c. 42 B.C.
19. Denarius (Murcus in Asia – MVRCVS IMP.), c. 42 B.C.
20. Denarius (Q. Labienus and the Parthians – Q. LABIENVS PARTHICVS), c. 40 B.C.

PLATE XX (pp. 78 ff.)

1. Denarius (Antony in Gaul – M. ANTO. IMP.), c. 43 B.C.
2. Denarius (Octavian in Italy – C. CAESAR IIIVIR R.P.C.), c. 43 B.C.
3. Denarius (Antony in the East – M. ANTONIVS IIIVIR R.P.C.), c. 41 B.C.
4. Denarius (Q. Cornuficius in Africa – Q. CORNVFICI. AVGVR IMP.), c. 43 B.C.
5. Denarius (P. Ventidius Bassus in Italy – P. VENTIDI. PONT. IMP. – M. ANT. IIIV. R.P.C.), 41 B.C.
6. Denarius (Antony and Octavian – M. ANT. IMP., etc. – M. BARBAT. Q.P.), 41 B.C.

7. Denarius (Antony and L. Antonius – M. ANT. IMP., etc. – P. NERVA PROQ.P.), 41 B.C.
8. Denarius (L. Antonius; 'Pietas' – ANT. AVG. IMP., etc. – PIETAS COS.), 41 B.C.
9. Denarius (Octavian in Gaul – M. AGRIPPA COS. DESIG.), c. 38 B.C.
10. Denarius (Victory of Sex. Pompeius – Q. NASIDIVS), c. 36 B.C.
11. Denarius (Triumph of Metellus in Spain – P. LENT. P.F.L.N.), c. 77 B.C.
12. Aureus (Antony and Octavia – M. ANTONIVS M.F.M.N. AVGVR, etc.), c. 37 B.C.
13. Denarius (Antony's Armenian triumph – ANTONIVS AVGVR COS. DES. ITER. ET. TERT), c. 35 B.C.
14. Denarius (Antony's Armenian triumph (?) – ANT. AVGVR IIIVIR R.P.C.), c. 35 B.C.
15. Aureus (Antony and Antyllus – M. ANTONI. M.F.M.N. AVG., etc.), c. 34 B.C.
16. Denarius (Antony and Cleopatra – ANTONI. ARMENIA DEVICTA, etc.), c. 32 B.C.
17. Denarius (Actium (fleet and army) – praetorian cohorts – ANT. AVG. IIIVIR R.P.C.), c. 32 B.C.
18. Denarius (Actium (fleet and army) – Leg. XVIII Libyca – ANT. AVG. IIIVIR R.P.C.), c. 32 B.C.
19. Denarius (Actium (fleet and army) – Cohorts speculatorum – ANT. AVG. IIIVIR. R.P.C.), c. 32 B.C.
20. Denarius (Scarpus in Cyrene (?) – Leg. VIII. – SCARPVS IMP.), c. 31 B.C.

PLATE XXI (pp. 80 ff.)

1. Denarius (Thunderbolt and cornucopiae – Q. MAX.), c. 121 B.C.
2. Denarius (Marsyas – L. CENSOR.), c. 86 B.C.
3. Denarius (Corn-ears, fasces, caduceus – C. NORBANVS), c. 84 B.C.
4. Denarius (Knife, simpulum, axe – P. GALB. AED. CVR. S.C.), c. 68 B.C.
5. Denarius (Curule chair, etc. – Q. POMPEI. RVF.), c. 57 B.C.
6. Denarius (Curule chair – C. CONSIDIVS PAETVS), c. 45 B.C.
7. Aureus (Crescent and five stars – P. CLODIVS M.F.), 42 B.C.
8. Denarius (Wreath, sceptre and *sella castrensis* – M. ARRIVS SECVNDVS), c. 43 B.C.
9. Aureus (Clasped hands – C. VIBIVS VAARVS), 42 B.C.
10. Denarius (Curule chair and fasces – L. LIVINEIVS REGVLVS), 42 B.C.
11. Denarius (Caduceus and cornucopiae on globe – M. ANT. IMP. IIIVIR R.P.C.), c. 38 B.C.
12. Aureus (Star and prow – ANT. IMP. – CN. DOMIT. AHENOBARBVS IMP.), c. 40 B.C.
13. Quinarius (Clasped hands holding caduceus – M. ANTON. C. CAESAR IIIVIR R.P.C.), c. 40 B.C.
14. Denarius (Lituus, jug – thunderbolt, jug, caduceus – M. ANTON. IMP. . . . L. PLANCVS PROCOS.), c. 40 B.C.
15. Denarius (Temple of Jupiter Capitolinus – M. VOLTEI. M.F.), c. 80 B.C.
16. Denarius (Basilica Aemilia – M. LEPIDVS AIMILIA REF. S.C.), c. 70 B.C.
17. Denarius (Temple of Venus Erycina – C. CONSIDI NONIANI), c. 60 B.C.
18. Denarius (Villa Publica – P. FONTEIVS IIIVIR – T. DIDI. IMP. VIL. PVB.), c. 70 B.C.
19. Denarius (Rostra – PALIKANVS), c. 46 B.C.
20. Denarius (Temple of Jupiter Capitolinus – PETILLIVS CAPITOLINVS), c. 40 B.C. (?).

PLATE XXII (Introduction, p. xi f, and n., pp. 91 ff.)

1. Tetradrachm (Syracuse – Agathocles), c. 310–306 B.C.
2. Tetradrachm (Syracuse), c. 287–278 B.C.
3. Didrachm (Syracuse – Hiero (Gelo.)), c. 240 B.C.
4. Tetradrachm (Carthage), c. 330 B.C. (?).
5. Electrum stater (Carthage), 330–264 B.C.
6. Drachm (Massalia), c. 250 B.C.
7. Drachm (Rhoda), c. 200 B.C.
8. Drachm (Emporiae), c. 200 B.C.
9. Silver piece of five units (Etruria), c. 400 B.C.
10. Silver piece of five units (Etruria), c. 260 B.C.
11. Silver piece of twenty units (Etruria), c. 205 B.C.
12. Silver piece of ten units (Etruria), c. 205 B.C.
13. Silver piece of five units (Etruria), c. 260 B.C.
14. Silver piece of two and a half units (Etruria), c. 260 B.C.

PLATE XXIII (pp. 91 ff.)

1. Didrachm (Metapontum), c. 310 B.C.
2. Drachm (?) (Bruttium), c. 275 B.C.
3. Hemidrachm (Bruttium), c. 275 B.C.
4. 'Corinthian' stater (Syracuse), c. 275 B.C. (?).
5. Didrachm (Arpi), c. 215 B.C.
6. Didrachm (Cales), c. 235 B.C.
7. Didrachm (Naples), c. 260 B.C.
8. Didrachm (Nuceria), c. 270 B.C.
9. Didrachm (Suessa), c. 235 B.C.
10. Didrachm (Tarentum), c. 275 B.C.
11. Didrachm (Tarentum – 'Campanian' coinage), c. 250 B.C.
12. Copper (Beneventum), c. 268 B.C.
13. Didrachm (Tarentum – reduced weight), c. 272 B.C.
14. Didrachm (Syracuse), c. 212 B.C.

PLATE XXIV (pp. 91 ff.)

1. Sextans (Capua), c. 215 B.C.
2. Copper (Canusium), c. 100 B.C. (?).
3. Gold drachm (Capua), c. 215 B.C.
4. Semis (Syracuse), 2nd century B.C.
5. Semis (Panormus), 2nd–1st century B.C.
6. Denarius (Oscan money), 2nd century B.C.
7. As (?) (Valentia), c. 135 B.C.
8. As (?) (Saguntum), c. 135 B.C.
9. As (?) (Sardinia), c. 58 B.C. (or later).
10. Victoriate (Massalia), 2nd century B.C.
11. Quinarius (Cabellio), c. 40 B.C.
12. Quinarius (Lugdunum), 43 B.C.
13. Quinarius (Nemausus), c. 40 B.C.
14. Victoriate (Apollonia Illyrici), 2nd century B.C.
15. Denarius (Corcyra), 2nd–1st century B.C.

PLATE XXV (pp. 94 ff.)

1. Tetradrachm (Perseus of Macedon), c. 175 B.C.
2. Tetradrachm (Macedonia – first division), c. 160 B.C.

3. Tetradrachm (Macedonia – AESILLAS Q.), c. 93–92 B.C.
4. Gold stater (Philip III. of Macedon), c. 340 B.C.
5. Copper (Macedonia – Brutus ?), c. 42 B.C.
6. Tetradrachm, Cistophoric (Q. METELLVS PIVS.), c. 49–48 B.C.
7. Tetradrachm (Philip Epiphanes of Syria), 92–85 B.C.
8. Tetradrachm (Tyre), 63 B.C.
9. Tetradrachm (Athens), 2nd century B.C.
10. Drachm (Rhodes), 3rd–2nd century B.C.

PLATE XXVI (pp. 120 ff.)

1. Aureus (Augustus), c. A.D. 8.
2. Gold quinarius (Augustus), c. 6 B.C.
3. Silver quinarius (Augustus), c. 27 B.C.
4. Denarius (Tiberius), c. A.D. 24.
5. Aureus (Nero), c. A.D. 66.
6. Denarius (Nero), c. A.D. 66.
7. Silver quinarius (Galba, struck by Vespasian ?), c. A.D. 71.
8. Double aureus (Caracalla), A.D. 216.
9. Aureus (Caracalla), A.D. 217.
10. Antoninianus (Double denarius) (Caracalla), A.D. 217
11. Antoninianus (Double denarius) (Balbinus), A.D. 238.
12. Denarius (Gordian III) c. A.D. 242.
13. Aureus (Trajan Decius), c. A.D. 250.
14. Gold triens (Saloninus), c. A.D. 257.
15. Silver quinarius (Trajan Decius), c. A.D. 250.

PLATE XXVII (pp. 120 ff.)

1. Antoninianus (Double denarius) (Gallienus), c. A.D. 261.
2. Antoninianus (Double denarius) (Gallienus), c. A.D. 267.
3. Aureus (Postumus), c. A.D. 260.
4. Aureus (Aurelian), A.D. 270–275.
5. Sestertius (Aurelian), A.D. 270–275.
6. Denarius (Aurelian), A.D. 270–275.
7. Half-denarius (Probus), A.D. 270–275.
8. Aureus ($\frac{1}{70}$th lb.) (Diocletian), c. A.D. 286.
9. Eight-denarius piece (Domitian), A.D. 85.
10. Seven-denarius piece (?) (Hadrian), c. A.D. 119.
11. Five-aureus piece (Gallienus), c. A.D. 265.

PLATE XXVIII (pp. 120 ff.)

1. Sestertius (Augustus), c. 22 B.C.
2. 'Triumphal' Coin (Augustus), c. 7 B.C.
3. As (Tiberius), A.D. 22–23.
4. Quadrans (Augustus), c. 11 B.C.
5. As (orichalcum) (Nero), c. A.D. 65.
6. Semis (copper) (Nero), c. A.D. 65.
7. Semis (orichalcum) (Nero), c. A.D. 65.
8. Quadrans (orichalcum) (Nero), c. A.D. 65.
9. Semis (Trajan Decius), c. A.D. 250.
10. As (Probus), A.D. 276–282.
11. Quadrans (?) (Probus), A.D. 276–282.

Key to the Plates

PLATE XXIX (pp. 126 ff.)

1. Double sestertius (Trajan Decius), c. A.D. 250.
2. Dupondius (?) (Aurelian), A.D. 270–275
3. Dupondius (Trajan Decius), c. A.D. 250.
4. Sestertius (?), A.D. 274.
5. Sestertius (Postumus), c. A.D. 260.
6. Billon 'medallion' (Probus), A.D. 276–282.

PLATE XXX (pp. 101 ff.)

1. Aureus (Augustus – Rome), 18 B.C.
2. Denarius (Augustus – Emerita Lusitaniae), c. 23 B.C.
3. Denarius (Augustus – Emerita Lusitaniae?), c. 22 B.C.
4. Denarius (Augustus – Caesaraugusta Tarraconensis?), c. 18 B.C.
5. Aureus (Augustus – Colonia Patricia Baeticae?), c. 18 B.C.
6. Denarius (Augustus – Asia), c. 30 B.C.
7. Aureus (Augustus – Pergamum), c. 28 B.C.
8. Denarius (Augustus – Samos?), c. 21 B.C.
9. Aureus (Caligula – Lugdunum), A.D. 37–38.
10. Aureus (Caligula – Rome), A.D. 37–38.
11. Aureus (Nero – Rome), A.D. 56.
12. Denarius (Clodius Macer – Africa), A.D. 68.
13. Denarius (Civil Wars – Spain), A.D. 68.
14. Denarius (Civil Wars – Gaul), A.D. 68.
15. Denarius (Civil Wars – Upper Germany), A.D. 68 (end).
16. Aureus (Galba – Tarraco), A.D. 68.
17. Denarius (Galba – Narbo?), A.D. 68.
18. Aureus (Vitellius – Tarraco), A.D. 69.

PLATE XXXI (pp. 110 ff.)

1. Aureus (Vespasian – Tarraco), A.D. 69.
2. Aureus (Vespasian – Lugdunum), A.D. 72.
3. Denarius (Vespasian – Aquileia?), A.D. 69.
4. Denarius (Vespasian – Ephesus), A.D. 71.
5. Aureus (Titus – Tyre?), A.D. 69.
6. Aureus (Vespasian and Titus – Antioch), A.D. 69.
7. Aureus (Vespasian – Cyprus?), A.D. 72.
8. Denarius (Domitian – O mint – Lycia?), A.D. 76.
9. Aureus (Trajan – East?), A.D. 117.
10. Denarius (Hadrian – Antioch?), c. A.D. 121.
11. Denarius (Hadrian – Asia), A.D. 128.
12. Aureus (L. Verus – Rome), A.D. 164.
13. Denarius (Pescennius Niger – Antioch), A.D. 193.
14. Aureus (Septimius Severus – Syria), A.D. 194.
15. Aureus (Septimius Severus – Antioch), A.D. 202.
16. Denarius (Albinus – Lugdunum), A.D. 195–196.
17. Aureus (Elagabalus – Nicomedia), A.D. 218.
18. Antoninianus (Double denarius) (Gordian III – Antioch?), c. A.D. 244.
19. Antoninianus (Double denarius) (Philip I – Antioch?), A.D. 244–249.

PLATE XXXII (pp. 115 ff.)

1. Antoninianus (Double denarius) (Philip I – Antioch), A.D. 247.
2. Antoninianus (Double denarius) (Pacatian – Viminacium), A.D. 248–249.
3. Antoninianus (Double denarius) (Jotapian – Syria), c. A.D. 248.

4. Antoninianus (Double denarius) (Trebonianus Gallus – East), A.D. 251–253.
5. Antoninianus (Double denarius) (Valerian I – Lugdunum), c. A.D. 256.
6. Antoninianus (Double denarius) (Valerian I – Antioch ?), c. A.D. 256.
7. Antoninianus (Double denarius) (Gallienus – Mediolanum), c. A.D. 265.
8. Antoninianus (Double denarius) (Gallienus – Rome), c. A.D. 261.
9. Antoninianus (Double denarius) (Gallienus – Asia ?), A.D. 266
10. Antoninianus (Double denarius) (Quietus – East), A.D. 259–260.
11. Antoninianus (Double denarius) (Regalian – Carnuntum), c. A.D. 259.
12. Aureus (Postumus – Lugdunum), c. A.D. 259.
13. Antoninianus (Double denarius) (Postumus – Colonia Agrippina), c. A.D. 266.
14. Aureus (Victorinus – Mogontiacum ?), A.D. 268.
15. Aureus (Tetricus I – Lugdunum ?), A.D. 270–273.
16. Antoninianus (Double denarius) (Claudius II – Cyzicus), A.D. 268–270.

PLATE XXXIII (pp. 105 ff., 118 ff.)

1. Double sestertius (Aurelian – Ticinum), c. A.D. 274.
2. Double sestertius (Aurelian – Serdica), c. A.D. 270.
3. Double sestertius (Florian – Ticinum), A.D. 276.
4. Double sestertius (Probus – Rome), A.D. 276–282.
5. Aureus (Probus – Siscia), A.D. 276–282.
6. Aureus (Probus – Antioch), A.D. 276–282.
7. Double sestertius (Julian – Siscia), c. A.D. 283.
8. Double sestertius (Probus – Cyzicus), A.D. 276–282.
9. Double sestertius (Carus – Lugdunum), A.D. 282–283.
10. Double sestertius (Carausius – Boulogne ?), c. A.D. 287.
12. Double sestertius (Carausius – Clausentum ?), c. A.D. 289.
13. Quadrans (Augustus – Rome), c. 11 B.C.
14. Sestertius (Nero – Lugdunum), c. A.D. 66.

PLATE XXXIV (pp. 106 ff.)

1. Dupondius (Augustus – Lugdunum), c. A.D. 11.
2. Dupondius (Claudius I – Western imitation), c. A.D. 50.
3. Dupondius (Tiberius – Commagene), A.D. 20–21.
4. As (Vitellius – Tarraco), A.D. 69.
5. Sestertius (Vespasian – Rome ?), A.D. 71.
6. Dupondius (Vespasian – Commagene), A.D. 74.
7. Dupondius (Vespasian – Lugdunum), A.D. 77–78.
8. Sestertius (Domitian – Western Mint), A.D. 81.

PLATE XXXV (pp. 144 ff.)

1. Denarius (Augustus – quadriga-insignia), c. 17 B.C.
2. Aureus (Augustus – doorway, laurels and oak-wreath), c. 12 B.C.
3. Aureus (Augustus – M. Agrippa), c. 13 B.C.
4. Aureus (Galba – oak-wreath), A.D. 68–69.
5. Denarius (Hadrian – adoption), A.D. 118.
6. Sestertius (Titus – 'Pietas' group), A.D. 80.
7. Sestertius (Titus – 'Providentia' group), A.D. 80.
8. Aureus (Hadrian – 'rector orbis'), A.D. 121.
9. Aureus (Hadrian – 'vota publica'), c. A.D. 135.
10. Aureus (Hadrian – Emperor and Senate), A.D. 138.
11. Aureus (Septimius Severus – Julia Domna and sons), c. A.D. 202.

12. Aureus (Julia Domna – 'Mater Augg, etc.'), c. A.D. 202.
13. Denarius (Plautilla – 'Concordia'), c. A.D. 202.
14. Denarius (Diadumenian – 'Princeps Iuventutis'), A.D. 217–218.
15. Antoninianus (Double denarius) (Philip I – Emperor with orb and sceptre), A.D. 245.
16. Aureus (Philip II – 'Princeps Iuventutis'), c. A.D. 245.
17. Aureus (Postumus – 'Aeternitas Aug.'), c. A.D. 263.

PLATE XXXVI (pp. 146 ff.)

1. Denarius (Augustus – 'sidus Iulium'), c. 17 B.C.
2. Denarius (Augustus – 'consecration' of Agrippa ?), 12 B.C.
3. Aureus (Domitia – 'divus Caesar'), c. A.D. 83.
4. Aureus (Vespasian, restored by Trajan – Jupiter, Mercury and star), c. A.D. 107.
5. Aureus (Nerva, restored by Trajan – biga of elephants), c. A.D. 107.
6. As (Augustus, restored by Titus – altar), A.D. 80.
7. Aureus (Hadrian – 'divis parentibus'), c. A.D. 138.
8. Aureus (Sabina – Empress borne aloft by eagle), A.D. 138 (?).
9. Aureus (Faustina I – AETERNITAS, Fortuna), c. A.D. 141.
10. Aureus (Antoninus Pius – pyre), A.D. 161.
11. Antoninianus (Double sestertius) (Divus Augustus, struck by Trajan Decius), c. A.D. 251.
12. Antoninianus (Double sestertius) (Divus Marcus – struck by Trajan Decius), c. A.D. 251.
13. Aureus (Vespasian – Triumph), A.D. 71.
14. Aureus (Septimius Severus – 'adventus'), A.D. 195–196.
15. Denarius (Caracalla – 'adventus'), c. A.D. 202.
16. As (Hadrian – galley, FELICITATI AVG.), c. A.D. 132.
17. Aureus (Trajan – 'profectio'), c. A.D. 114.

PLATE XXXVII (pp. 148 ff.)

1. Sestertius (Nero – 'congiarium'), c. A.D. 66.
2. Denarius (Hadrian – 'liberalitas'), A.D. 121.
3. Sestertius (Galba, struck by Vespasian – 'libertas restituta'), c. A.D. 71.
4. Sestertius (Trajan – Emperor as colonizer), c. A.D. 111.
5. Aureus (Civil Wars – 'Genius P.R.'), A.D. 68.
6. Sestertius (Galba, struck by Vespasian – 'Senatus Pietati Augusti'), c. A.D. 71.
7. Dupondius (Antoninus Pius – 'Genio Senatus'), A.D. 140–144.
8. As (Antoninus Pius – 'vota suscepta dec. III'), A.D. 157–158.
9. As (Antoninus Pius – 'primi decennales'), A.D. 147–148.

PLATE XXXVIII (pp. 150 ff.)

1. Denarius (Galba – 'Tres Galliae'), A.D. 68.
2. Aureus (Vespasian – 'Iudaea'), A.D. 70.
3. Aureus (Domitian – 'Germania Capta'), A.D. 86.
4. Denarius (Trajan – 'Danuvius'), c. A.D. 107.
5. Denarius (Trajan – 'Via Traiana'), c. A.D. 111.
6. Aureus (Hadrian – 'Africa'), c. A.D. 134.
7. Denarius (Hadrian – 'Asia'), c. A.D. 134.
8. Denarius (Hadrian – 'Germania'), c. A.D. 134.
9. Aureus (Hadrian – 'Hispania'), c. A.D. 134.
10. Aureus (Hadrian – 'Nilus'), c. A.D. 134.
11. Aureus (Hadrian – 'Tiberis'), c. A.D. 121.

12. Antoninianus (Double sestertius) (Trajan Decius – 'Pannoniae'), c. A.D. 250.
13. Antoninianus (Double sestertius) (Trajan Decius – 'Gen(ius) Illyrici'), c. A.D. 250.
14. Sestertius (Vespasian – Roma of the Seven Hills), A.D. 71.
15. As (Hadrian – Antioch ?), c. A.D. 126.
16. Sestertius (Hadrian – 'Adventus Aug. Iudaeae'), c. A.D. 134.
17. Sestertius (Hadrian – 'Britannia'), c. A.D. 134.
18. Sestertius (Hadrian – 'Cappadocia'), c. A.D. 134.
19. Sestertius (L. Aelius Caesar – 'Pannonia'), c. A.D. 137.

PLATE XXXIX (pp. 152 ff.)

1. Aureus (Claudius I – 'praetor. recept.'), A.D. 41–42.
2. Denarius (Clodius Macer – 'leg. III. Aug.'), A.D. 68.
3. Denarius (Civil Wars – 'fides exercituum'), A.D. 68 (end).
4. Aureus (Nerva – 'concordia exercituum'), A.D. 97.
5. Aureus (Hadrian – 'disciplina Aug.'), c. A.D. 135.
6. Aureus (Hadrian – Emperor in the field), c. A.D. 135.
7. Aureus (Commodus – 'concordia militum'), A.D. 186.
8. Aureus (Septimius Severus – 'leg. VIII Aug.'), A.D. 193.
9. Antoninianus (Double sestertius) (Gallienus – 'leg. III Ital.'), c. A.D. 261.
10. Antoninianus (Double sestertius) (Gallienus – 'leg. XI Cl.'), c. A.D. 261.
11. Aureus (Victorinus – 'leg. IIII Flavia p.f.'), c. A.D. 268.
12. Double sestertius (Carausius – 'leg. I. Min.'), c. A.D. 287.
13. Sestertius (Nero – 'decursio'), c. A.D. 66.
14. Sestertius (Domitian – the 'sacramentum'), A.D. 85.
15. Sestertius (Hadrian – address to British Army), c. A.D. 134
16. Sestertius (Hadrian – address to Spanish Army), c. A.D. 134.
17. Sestertius (Geta – Princes in the field), A.D. 210.

PLATE XL (pp. 155 ff.)

1. Denarius (Augustus – youthful Jupiter), c. 29 B.C.
2. Denarius (Augustus – Mars), c. 16 B.C.
3. Denarius (Augustus – Tarpeia), 18 B.C.
4. As (Nero – Apollo Citharoedus), c. A.D. 66.
5. Aureus (Vespasian – Neptune), A.D. 72.
6. Aureus (Titus – Venus Victrix), A.D. 80.
7. Aureus (Domitian – *pulvinar* of Jupiter), A.D. 81.
8. Aureus (Titus – *pulvinar* of Venus and the Divi ?), A.D. 86.
9. Aureus (Domitian – Minerva), A.D. 83.
10. Aureus (Domitian – Minerva), A.D. 92.
11. Aureus (Trajan – Jupiter protecting Emperor), A.D. 118.
12. Aureus (Hadrian – Hercules Gaditanus), A.D. 119.
13. Aureus (Hadrian – Roma Aeterna), c. A.D. 135.
14. Aureus (Hadrian – Jupiter Victor), c. A.D. 136.
15. Aureus (Sabina – Ceres), c. A.D. 138.
16. Aureus (Faustina II – Juno Lucina), c. A.D. 164.
17. Aureus (Commodus – Hercules Commodianus), A.D. 191.

PLATE XLI (pp. 155 ff., 159 ff.)

1. Denarius (Albinus – Minerva Pacifera), A.D. 194.
2. Aureus (Julia Domna – Cybele), c. A.D. 204.
3. Antoninianus (Double denarius) (Caracalla – Serapis), A.D. 216.

Key to the Plates

4. Aureus (Elagabalus – sacred stone of Emesa), c. A.D. 220.
5. Antoninianus (Double denarius) (Volusian – Apollo), A.D. 251–253.
6. Antoninianus (Double denarius) (Salonina – 'Aug. in Pace'), c. A.D. 265.
7. Denarius (Postumus – Hercules), c. A.D. 266.
8. Denarius (Postumus – Hercules), c. A.D. 266.
9. Aureus (Probus – Sol.), A.D. 278–282.
10. As (Vespasian – Aequitas), A.D. 72.
11. Sestertius (Titus – Annona), A.D. 80.
12. Aureus (Faustina I – Aeternitas?), c. A.D. 141.
13. Aureus (Vitellius – Clementia), A.D. 69.
14. Aureus (Vitellius – Concordia), A.D. 69.
15. Aureus (Claudius I – Constantia), A.D. 41.
16. Denarius (Julia Maesa – Fecunditas), A.D. 218–222.
17. Aureus (Laelian – Felicitas Temporum), c. A.D. 268.
18. Denarius (Titus – Bonus Eventus), c. A.D. 80.
19. Aureus (Marius – Sae(culi) Felicitas), c. A.D. 268.

PLATE XLII (pp. 159 ff.)

1. Denarius (Hadrian – Fides), c. A.D. 135.
2. Aureus (Hadrian – Fortuna – Spes), A.D. 137.
3. Aureus (Didia Clara – Hilaritas Temporum), A.D. 193.
4. Aureus (Augustus – M. Durmius – Honos), 18 B.C.
5. Denarius (Hadrian – Indulgentia), A.D. 132–134.
6. Denarius (Hadrian – Iustitia), A.D. 132–134.
7. Double sestertius (Tacitus – Laetitia), A.D. 274–276.
8. Denarius (Commodus – Liberalitas), A.D. 186.
9. Denarius (Galba – Libertas), A.D. 68.
10. Antoninianus (Double denarius) (Philip I – Nobilitas), A.D. 248–249.
11. Denarius (Hadrian – Patientia), A.D. 128.
12. Denarius (Albinus – Pax), A.D. 195–196.
13. Denarius (Vespasian – Pax?), A.D. 72.
14. Denarius (Hadrian – Pax Victrix), c. A.D. 119.
15. Denarius (Domitia – Pietas), c. A.D. 81.
16. Aureus (Antoninus Pius – Pietas), A.D. 138.
17. Antoninianus (Double denarius) (Claudius II – Providentia), A.D. 268–270.
18. Antoninianus (Double denarius) (Herennia Etruscilla – Pudicitia), c. A.D. 250.
19. Denarius (Severus Alexander – Salus), A.D. 222–235.
20. Antoninianus (Double denarius) (Gordian III – Securitas), A.D. 238–244.
21. Denarius (Hadrian – Tranquillitas), c. A.D. 132–134.
22. Antoninianus (Double denarius) (Trajan Decius – Ubertas), c. A.D. 250.
23. Denarius (Augustus – Victoria), c. 29 B.C.
24. Aureus (Otho – Victoria), A.D. 69.
25. Denarius (Hadrian – Victoria – Nemesis), c. A.D. 135.
26. As (Domitian – Virtus), A.D. 95–96.

PLATE XLIII (pp. 164 ff.)

1. Aureus (Augustus – Conquest of Rhaetia), c. 14 B.C.
2. Aureus (Augustus – Conquest of Armenia), c. 19 B.C.
3. Aureus (Augustus – Conquest of Egypt), c. 28 B.C.
4. Aureus (Augustus – Recovery of captives and standards from Parthia), c. 16 B.C.
5. Denarius (Augustus – German returning standards), c. 12 B.C.

6. Didrachm (Caligula – Germanicus crowning Artaxias), c. A.D. 38.
7. Aureus (Claudius – Conquest of Britain), A.D. 46.
8. Didrachm (Nero – Armenian victories), c. A.D. 60.
9. Aureus (Vespasian – Vespasian as restorer), A.D. 72.
10. Denarius (Civil Wars – Gaul and Spain allied), A.D. 68.
11. Aureus (Domitian – Victory over Chatti), A.D. 85.
12. Aureus (Trajan – Trajan presenting Dacian to Senate), c. A.D. 106.
13. Aureus (Trajan – Assignment of kingdoms in East), A.D. 116.
14. Sestertius (Antoninus Pius – King given to Armenia), c. A.D. 143.

PLATE XLIV (pp. 169 ff.)

1. Aureus (L. Verus – Armenian victory), A.D. 163.
2. Aureus (Marcus Aurelius – Sarmatian victory), A.D. 175.
3. Aureus (Septimius Severus – Victories in Parthia, Arabia and Adiabene), c. A.D. 195.
4. Aureus (Septimius Severus – British victory), c. A.D. 211.
5. Denarius (Maximin I – German victory), c. A.D. 137.
6. Antoninianus (Double denarius) (Philip I – Carpic victory), c. A.D. 247.
7. Antoninianus (Double denarius) (Philip I – Peace established with Persia), c. A.D. 244.
8. Antoninianus (Double denarius) (Trajan Decius – German victory), c. A.D. 251.
9. Antoninianus (Double denarius) (Gallienus – 'Gallienus and his army to Jupiter Victor'), c. A.D. 257.
10. Aureus (Gallienus – 'Universal Peace'), c. A.D. 268.
11. Antoninianus (Double denarius) (Claudius II – Gothic victory), c. A.D. 269.
12. Aureus (Probus – 'Pacator orbis'), A.D. 276–282.
13. Double sestertius (Probus – German victory), A.D. 276–282.
14. Silver coin (Carausius – Carausius welcomed in Britain), c. A.D. 287.

PLATE XLV (pp. 164 ff.)

1. Aureus (Augustus – Saecular Games), 16 B.C.
2. Aureus (Augustus – Saecular Games), c. 17 B.C.
3. Quadrans (Caligula – 'remissa ducentesima'), A.D. 39–40.
4. As (Domitian – Saecular Games), A.D. 88.
5. Denarius (Domitian – Saecular Games), A.D. 88.
6. As (Domitian – Saecular Games), A.D. 88.
7. Sestertius (Domitian – Saecular Games), A.D. 88.
8. Sestertius (Nerva – 'vehiculatione Italiae remissa'), A.D. 96–98.
9. Aureus (Trajan – 'alimenta Italiae'), c. A.D. 107.
10. Sestertius (Hadrian – 'libertas restituta'), A.D. 119.
11. Aureus (Hadrian – 'Golden Age'), c. A.D. 121.
12. Aureus (Hadrian – 'Natalia Urbis'), A.D. 121.
13. Sestertius (Hadrian – Burning of old bonds), A.D. 119–120.
14. Aureus (Faustina I – 'Puellae Faustinianae'), c. A.D. 144.
15. Denarius (Septimius Severus – Saecular Games), A.D. 204.

PLATE XLVI (pp. 170 ff.)

1. Aureus (Augustus – capricorn), c. 20 B.C.
2. Aureus (Augustus – cow), c. 19 B.C.
3. Aureus (Augustus – bull), c. 8 B.C.
4. Quadrans (Domitian – rhinoceros), c. A.D. 85.
5. Aureus (Julia Titi – peacock), c. A.D. 89.

Key to the Plates

6. Aureus (Divus Traianus – phoenix), A.D. 118.
7. Aureus (Hadrian – she-wolf and twins), c. A.D. 126.
8. As (Hadrian – griffin), c. A.D. 126.
9. Aureus (Faustina II – dove), c. A.D. 164.
10. Antoninianus (Double denarius) (Otacilia Severa – hippopotamus), A.D. 248.
11. Antoninianus (Double denarius) (Philip I – lion), A.D. 248.
12. Aureus (Postumus – lion), c. A.D. 258.
13. Denarius (Augustus – tiara, bow-case and quiver), c. 20 B.C.
14. As (Tiberius – rudder on globe), A.D. 36–37.
15. Aureus (Nero Drusus – vexillum, shields, spears), c. A.D. 42.
16. As (Galba, struck by Vespasian(?) – aquila and standards on prows), c. A.D. 70.
17. Semis (Nero – table of games), c. A.D. 65.
18. Denarius (Civil Wars – clasped hands), A.D. 68.
19. Aureus (Vitellius – tripod, dolphin and raven), A.D. 69.
20. Aureus (Domitian – cornucopiae), A.D. 76.
21. Aureus (Vespasian – statue on rostral column), A.D. 79.
22. Aureus (Antoninus Pius – twins in cornucopiae), c. A.D. 150.
23. Aureus (Caracalla – sacrificial implements), c. A.D. 197.
24. Antoninianus (Double denarius) (Herennius Etruscus – sacrificial implements), c. A.D. 250.
25. Antoninianus (Double denarius) (Philip I – column), A.D. 248.

PLATE XLVII (pp. 172 ff.)

1. Aureus (Augustus – temple of Mars Ultor), c. 18 B.C.
2. Aureus (Claudius I – praetorian camp), A.D. 41–42.
3. Aureus (Vespasian – temple of Vesta), c. A.D. 73.
4. Denarius (Domitian – temple of Cybele), c. A.D. 95.
5. Denarius (Domitian – temple of Serapis), c. A.D. 95.
6. Denarius (Domitian – temple of Jupiter), c. A.D. 95.
7. Aureus (Trajan – forum of Trajan), c. A.D. 112.
8. Sestertius (Nero – harbour of Ostia), c. A.D. 66.
9. As (Nero – altar of Peace), c. A.D. 66.
10. Sestertius (Nero – closed temple of Janus), c. A.D. 66.
11. Sestertius (Vespasian – temple of Jupiter Capitolinus restored), A.D. 78.
12. Tetradrachms, cistophoric (Domitian – temple of Jupiter Capitolinus restored), c. A.D. 85.
13. Sestertius (Titus – the Colosseum), A.D. 80.
14. Sestertius (Trajan – the Circus Maximus), c. A.D. 111.
15. Sestertius (Trajan – temple of Jupiter), c. A.D. 111.
16. Sestertius (Trajan – bridge), c. A.D. 111.

PLATE XLVIII (pp. 188 ff.)

1. *Aes* (Augustus – Emerita), c. 20 B.C.
2. *Aes* (Caligula – Caesaraugusta), c. A.D. 37.
3. *Aes* (Augustus and Agrippa – Nemausus), c. 20 B.C.
4. *Aes* (Tiberius – Paestum), c. A.D. 20
5. *Aes* (Divus Augustus – Panormus), c. A.D. 20.
6. *Aes* (Nero – Buthrotum), c. A.D. 65.
7. Drachm (Juba II – Mauretania), 25 B.C.–A.D. 23.
8. Tetadrachm, cistophoric (Augustus – Asia), c. 25 B.C.
9. Tetradrachm, cistophoric (Claudius I – Asia), c. A.D. 50.
10. Tetradrachm, cistophoric (Hadrian – Asia), c. A.D. 136.

11. Drachm (Antoninus Pius – Nicopolis), A.D. 138–161.
12. Drachm (Hadrian – Amisus), c. A.D. 131.

PLATE XLIX (pp. 190 ff.)

1. Drachm (Rhescuporis I and Tiberius – Pontus), A.D. 28.
2. Didrachm (Divus Augustus – Byzantium), c. A.D. 45.
3. Tetradrachm (Claudius I – Crete), c. A.D. 45.
4. Drachm (Tiberius – Hierapytna), A.D. 14–37.
5. Drachm (Trajan – Lycia), A.D. 98–117.
6. Tetradrachm (Hadrian – Tarsus), A.D. 117–138.
7. Tetradrachm (Vespasian – Cyprus), A.D. 69–79.
8. Drachm (Trajan – Cyrene ?), A.D. 98–117.
9. Didrachm (Nero – Caesarea Cappadociae), A.D. 54–68.
10. Tetradrachm (Trajan – Caesarea Cappadociae), A.D. 98–117.
11. Drachm (Septimius Severus – Caesarea Cappadociae), A.D. 193–211.
12. Tetradrachm (Nero – Antioch), A.D. 54–68.
13. Tetradrachm (Trajan – Tyre), A.D. 98–117.

PLATE L (pp. 188 ff.)

1. Tetradrachm (Caracalla – Heliopolis), A.D. 211–217.
2. Tetradrachm (Philip I – Antioch), A.D. 244–249.
3. Tetradrachm (Nero – Alexandria), A.D. 54–68.
4. *Aes* (Augustus – Antioch) 27 B.C.–A.D. 14.
5. *Aes* (Antoninus Pius – Alexandria), A.D. 144–145.
6. *Aes* (Hadrian – Macedon), A.D. 117–138, c. A.D. 65.
7. *Aes* (Vespasian – Bithynia), A.D. 69–79.
8. *Aes* (Hostilian – Viminacium), c. A.D. 251.
9. *Aes* (Philip I – Dacia), A.D. 248–249.

PLATE LI (pp. 196 ff.)

1. *Aes* (Erythrae – *ΙΕΡΑ ΣΥΓΚΛΗΤΟΣ*), 1st century A.D.
2. *Aes* (Chios – Homer), 1st century A.D.
3. *Aes* (Mytilene – Sappho), 1st century A.D.
4. *Aes* (Magnesia Lydiae – Cicero), 27 B.C.
5. *Aes* (Mytilene – Pancratidas and Dada), 1st century A.D.
6. *Aes* (Septimius Severus – Mylasa – Zeus Labrandeus), A.D. 193–211.
7. *Aes* (Otacilia Severa – Mastaura – the triple Hekate), A.D. 244–249.
8. *Aes* (Gordian III – Alia Phrygiae – Mên), A.D. 238–244.
9. *Aes* (Uncertain mint – C.P. – Divus Marcus Aurelius), c. A.D. 250 (?).
10. *Aes* (Philip I – Philippopolis Arabiae – Divus Marinus), A.D. 244–249.
11. *Aes* (Caracalla – Sestos – Hero and Leander), A.D. 211–217.
12. *Aes* (Trebonianus Gallus – Tyre – Dido building Carthage), A.D. 251–253.

PLATE LII (pp. 196 ff.)

1. *Aes* (Septimius Severus – Ilium – Hector and Patroclus), A.D. 193–211.
2. *Aes* (Philip I – Smyrna – dream of Alexander), A.D. 244–249.
3. *Aes* (Antoninus Pius – Aboniteichus – sacred snake), A.D. 138–161.
4. *Aes* (Claudius I – Philippi – Julius Caesar and Augustus), A.D. 42–54.
5. *Aes* (Trajan – Ephesus – 'Parthia capta'), A.D. 98–117.
6. *Aes* (Gordian III – Edessa – Gordian III and Abgar X), A.D. 244–249.
7. *Aes* (Julia Domna – Tomi – shrine of legionary eagle), A.D. 193–211.
8. *Aes* (Commodus – Nicaea – group of athletes), A.D. 186–192.

PLATE LIII (pp. 196 ff.)

1. *Aes* (Gallienus – Synnada – wild-beast fight in arena), A.D. 253–268.
2. *Aes* (Augustus – Cnossus – labyrinth), 27 B.C.–A.D. 14.
3. *Aes* (Macrinus – Neapolis Samariae – Mt Gerizim), A.D. 217–218.
4. *Aes* (Septimius Severus – Nicopolis Moesiae – city gates), A.D. 193–211.
5. *Aes* (Athens – theatre of Dionysus), 1st century A.D.
6. *Aes* (Septimius Severus – Corinth – temple of Aphrodite on Acropolis), A.D. 193–211.
7. *Aes* (Augustus – Italica – 'Genius populi Romani'), c. 20 B.C.
8. *Aes* (Tiberius – Bilbilis – wreath and magistrates' names), A.D. 14–37.
9. *Aes* (Tiberius – Romula – Divus Augustus – 'Iulia Augusta genetrix orbis'), c. A.D. 20.
10. *Aes* (Tiberius – Tarraco – temple of 'deus Augustus'), c. A.D. 20.

PLATE LIV (pp. 215 ff.)

1. Aureus (60 to lb.) (Diocletian – Thessalonica), c. A.D. 296.
2. Aureus (60 to lb.) (Galerius – Nicomedia), c. A.D. 308.
3. Tremissis ($\frac{1}{8}$ aureus) (Licinius I – Treveri), c. A.D. 315.
4. Double solidus (Constantine I – Ticinum), c. A.D. 320.
5. Solidus (Constantine I – Treveri), c. A.D. 320.
6. Semissis (half-solidus) (Crispus – Treveri), c. A.D. 320.
7. Solidus (Constantius II – Antioch), c. A.D. 353.
8. Five-solidus piece (Honorius – Rome), c. A.D. 400.
9. Double solidus (Eugenius – Treveri), c. A.D. 393.
10. Semissis (Honoria – Rome), c. A.D. 430.
11. Tremissis (Julius Nepos – Rome), c. A.D. 473.
12. Solidus (Valentinian III – Rome), c. A.D. 450.

PLATE LV (pp. 215 ff.)

1. Argenteus (96 to lb.) (Diocletian – Rome), c. A.D. 296.
2. Half-argenteus (Constantine I – Treveri), c. A.D. 308.
3. Argenteus (Constantius II – Treveri), c. A.D. 340.
4. Miliarense (Constantius II – Sirmium), c. A.D. 340.
5. Miliarense (Valentinian I – Treveri), A.D. 364–375.
6. Four-argenteus piece (Constantine II – Siscia), c. A.D. 337.
7. Siliqua (Theodosius I – Treveri), A.D. 378–395.
8. Follis (Sestertius of two denarii) (Constantius I – Siscia), A.D. 305–306.
9. Follis (Sestertius of two denarii) (Diocletian – Treveri), A.D. 296–305.
10. Follis (Sestertius of two denarii) (Galerius – Nicomedia), c. A.D. 308.
11. Follis (Sestertius of two denarii (Maximinus II – Treveri), c. A.D. 308.
12. Half-sestertius-denarius (Maximian – Alexandria), A.D. 296–305.

PLATE LVI (pp. 215 ff.)

1. Follis (Sestertius of two denarii) (Constantine I – Lugdunum), c. A.D. 308.
2. Small bronze (Diocletian – Rome), A.D. 296–305.
3. Small bronze (Maximian (after death) – Rome), c. A.D. 312.
4. Small bronze (Maxentius – Rome), c. A.D. 308.
5. Small bronze (Constantius I Chlorus (after death) – Rome), c. A.D. 324.
6. Small bronze (Constantine I – Rome), c. A.D. 320.
7. Follis (Sestertius of two denarii) (Constantine I – Treveri), c. A.D. 312.
8. Follis (Sestertius of two denarii) (Constantine I – Treveri), c. A.D. 315.

9. Small bronze (Licinius I – Nicomedia), c. A.D. 317.
10. Small bronze (Constantine I – Treveri), c. A.D. 317.
11. Small bronze (Constantine I – Treveri), c. A.D. 330.
12. Small bronze (Constantine I – Treveri), c. A.D. 335.
13. Centenionalis (Constantius II – Treveri), c. A.D. 345.
14. Pecunia Maiorina (?) (Magnentius – Ambianum), A.D. 350–353.

PLATE LVII (pp. 211 ff., 220 ff.)

1. Centenionalis (Constantius Gallus – Aquileia), A.D. 351–354.
2. Centenionalis (reduced) (Constantius Gallus – Aquileia), A.D. 351–354.
3. 'Pecunia Maiorina' (Jovian – Antioch), A.D. 363–364.
4. 'Pecunia Maiorina' (Julian II – Antioch), c. A.D. 361.
5. Centenionalis (Gratian – Antioch), c. A.D. 378.
6. 3 Æ piece (?) (Valens – Rome), A.D. 364–378.
7. 3 Æ piece (?) (Theodosius I – Antioch), A.D. 378–395.
8. 4 Æ piece (?) (Theodosius I – Antioch), A.D. 378–395.
9. Solidus (Magnus Maximus – Londinium – Augusta), A.D. 383–388.
10. Aureus (Galerius – Treveri), c. A.D. 308.
11. Centenionalis (Magnentius – Ambianum), A.D. 350–353.
12. Sestertius of two denarii (Constantine I – Arles), c. A.D. 312.

PLATE LVIII (pp. 211 ff.)

1. Follis (Sestertius of two denarii) (Maxentius – Ostia), c. A.D. 308.
2. Solidus (Petronius Maximus – Ravenna), c. A.D. 456.
3. Solidus (Priscus Attalus – Rome), c. A.D. 410.
4. Solidus (Anthemius – Mediolanum), c. A.D. 468.
5. 3 Æ (Licinius I – Aquileia), c. A.D. 320.
6. Miliarense (Julian II – Sirmium), c. A.D. 361.
7. Argenteus (Maximian – Serdica), A.D. 296–305.
8. 3 Æ (Theodosius I – Thessalonica), A.D. 378–395.
9. 3 Æ (Constantine I – Constantinopolis), c. A.D. 330.
10. Aureus (Licinius I – Nicomedia), c. A.D. 312.
11. Follis (Sestertius of two denarii) (Alexander – Carthage), c. A.D. 308.
12. Follis (Sestertius of two denarii) (Domitius Domitianus – Alexandria), A.D. 296.
13. 3 Æ (?) (Anonymous – Antioch), c. A.D. 317 (?).

PLATE LIX (pp. 234 ff.)

1. Aureus (Severus – Serdica – 'princeps iuventutis'), A.D. 305–306.
2. Follis (Sestertius of two denarii) (Maxentius – Rome – 'Conservatores urbis suae'), c. A.D. 308.
3. Follis (Sestertius of two denarii) (Maxentius – Rome – 'Fel. process. cons. III Aug.'), c. A.D. 308.
4. Follis (Sestertius of two denarii) (Constantine I – Lugdunum – 'bono reipublicae natus'), c. A.D. 307.
5. Solidus and a half (Constantine I – Nicomedia – 'Eques Romanus'), c. A.D. 320.
6. Follis (Sestertius of two denarii) (Constantine I – Rome – 'Liberatio orbis'), c. A.D. 313.
7. Solidus (Constantine I – Treveri – 'Felicitas reipublicae'), c. A.D. 320.
8. Solidus (Constantine I – Treveri – 'Restitutor libertatis'), c. A.D. 320.
9. 3 Æ (Fausta – Alexandria – 'Spes reipublicae'), c. A.D. 324.
10. Solidus (Crispus – Aquileia – 'Princeps iuventutis'), c. A.D. 320.

11. Centenionalis (Constans – Treveri – 'Fel. temp. reparatio'), c. A.D. 345.
12. Centenionalis (Constans – Lugdunum – 'Fel. temp. reparatio'), c. A.D. 345.
13. Centenionalis (Constantius II – Rome – 'Fel. temp. reparatio'), c. A.D. 345.
14. Solidus (Constantius II – Antioch – largesse), c. A.D. 350.
15. Miliarense (Constantius II – Sirmium – 'Felicitas Romanorum'), c. A.D. 340.

PLATE LX (pp. 234 ff.)

1. Argenteus (Constantius II – Treveri – 'pax Augustorum'), c. A.D. 340.
2. 3 Æ (Constantius II – Thessalonica – 'Spes reipublicae'), c. A.D. 340.
3. Solidus (Vetranio – Siscia – 'Salvator reipublicae'), A.D. 350.
4. Solidus (Procopius – Constantinople – 'Securitas reipub.'), A.D. 365.
5. Siliqua (Valentinian I – Arelate – 'Restitutor orbis'), A.D. 364–375.
6. Solidus (Valentinian I – Thessalonica – 'Restitutor reipublicae'), A.D. 364–375.
7. Miliarense (Valens – Siscia – 'Gloria Romanorum'), A.D. 364–378.
8. Solidus (Valens – Antioch – 'Salus reip.'), A.D. 364–375.
9. Solidus (Gratian – Antioch – 'Spes r.p.'), c. A.D. 368.
10. Solidus (Theodosius I – Antioch – 'Victoria Augg.'), A.D. 378–395.
11. 2 Æ (Theodosius I – Sirmium – 'Gloria Romanorum'), A.D. 378–395.
12. 3 Æ (?) (Theodosius I – Cyzicus – 'Gloria Romanorum'), A.D. 378–395.
13. Solidus (Honorius – Ravenna – 'Victoria Augg.'), c. A.D. 405.
14. 4 Æ (?) (Honorius – Constantinople – 'Gloria Romanorum'), c. A.D. 406.
15. 2 Æ (Honorius – Nicomedia – 'Gloria Romanorum'), c. A.D. 405.
16. 4 Æ piece (?) (Honorius – Antioch – 'Gloria Romanorum'), c. A.D. 405.
17. Solidus (Eudoxia – Rome – 'Salus reipublicae'), c. A.D. 437.
18. Aureus (Constantine I – Antioch – 'Votis V. Multis X'), c. A.D. 311.

PLATE LXI (pp. 234 ff.)

1. Sestertius of two denarii (Crispus – Arelate – 'Vot. X.'), c. A.D. 325.
2. Siliqua (Constantius II – Arelate – 'Votis XXX Multis XXXX'), c. A.D. 353.
3. Solidus (Honorius – Mediolanum – 'Vota publica'), c. A.D. 400.
4. Solidus (Galla Placidia – Ravenna – 'Vot. XX mult. XXX'), c. A.D. 427.
5. Solidus (Valentian III – Rome – 'Vot. XXX Mult. XXXX'), c. A.D. 455.
6. Follis (Sestertius of two denarii) (Maximian – Carthage – 'salvis Augg. et Caess. fel. Kart.'), A.D. 296–305.
7. Argenteus (Constantius I – Carthage – Africa), c. A.D. 305.
8. Solidus (Constantine I – Treveri – Alamannia), c. A.D. 324.
9. 3 Æ (Hannibalianus – Constantinople – Bosphorus), c. A.D. 337.
10. Aureus (Maximian – Rome – 'comitatus Augg.'), A.D. 296–305.
11. 3 Æ (Constantine I – Constantinople – 'Constantiniana Dafne'), c. A.D. 330.
12. Follis (Sestertius of two denarii) (Galerius – Aquileia – 'Virtus Augg. et Caess. nn.'), A.D. 296–305.
13. 3 Æ (Constantine I – Thessalonica – 'Virt. exerc.'), c. A.D. 330.
14. 3 Æ (Constantine I – Siscia – 'Virtus exercit.'), c. A.D. 324.
15. Solidus (Julian II – Antioch – 'Virtus exercitus Romanorum'), c. A.D. 363.
16. Miliarense (Constantius II – Arelate – standards), c. A.D. 340.

PLATE LXII (pp. 238 ff.)

1. Aureus (Constantine I – Aquileia – Dioscuri), c. A.D. 308.
2. Follis (Sestertius of two denarii) (Maxentius – Ostia – Dioscuri, she-wolf and twins), c. A.D. 308.

3. Aureus (Maximian – Treveri – Hercules and hydra), A.D. 296–305.
4. Follis (Sestertius of two denarii) (Constantius I – Siscia – Hercules), c. A.D. 305.
5. 3 Æ (Licinius I – Treveri – Jupiter on eagle's back), c. A.D. 320.
6. Aureus (Galerius – Siscia – Mars propugnator), c. A.D. 308.
7. Solidus (Constantine II – Treveri – Virtus exercitus Gall.), c. A.D. 337.
8. Follis (Sestertius of two denarii) (Constantine I – Treveri – Mars Conservator), c. A.D. 321.
9. Follis (Sestertius of two denarii) (Constantine I – Rome – Roma Aeterna), c. A.D. 312.
10. Siliqua (Valentinian II – Treveri – Urbs Roma), c. A.D. 380.
11. 'Pecunia Maior.' (Valentinian II – Rome – Urbs Roma), c. A.D. 380.
12. Siliqua (Constantine III – Arles – Urbs Roma), c. A.D. 411.
13. 3 Æ (?) (Maximin II – Treveri – Sol Invictus Comes), c. A.D. 312.
14. Follis (Sestertius of two denarii) (Maximin II – Alexandria – Sol Invictus), c. A.D. 310
15. Follis (Sestertius of two denarii) (Valeria – Alexandria – Venus Victrix), c. A.D. 308.
16. 3 Æ (Rome – Isis Faria-Anubis), c. A.D. 400.
17. 3 Æ (Rome – Deus Sarapis-Isis), c. A.D. 400.

PLATE LXIII (pp. 238 ff.)

1. Follis (Sestertius of two denarii) (Constantius I, posthumous – Ticinum – altar), c. A.D. 306.
2. Follis (Sestertius of two denarii) (Romulus, posthumous – Rome – temple), c. A.D. 310.
3. 3 Æ (?) (Maximian, posthumous – Rome – lion), c. A.D. 312.
4. 3 Æ (?) (Maximian, posthumous – Rome – eagle), c. A.D. 312.
5. 3 Æ (Constantine I, posthumous – Antioch – veiled figure), c. A.D. 337.
6. 3 Æ (Constantine I, posthumous – Constantinople – chariot), c. A.D. 337.
7. 3 Æ (Constantine I – Constantinople – labarum on serpent), c. A.D. 333.
8. Siliqua (Julian II – Arelate – star in wreath), c. A.D. 361.
9. Semissis (Valentinian III – Roma – ☧, Salus reipublicae), A.D. 425–455.
10. Half-siliqua (Anthemius – Mediolanum – ☧ in wreath), A.D. 467–472.
11. 4 Æ (Honorius – Cyzicus – +, Concordia Augg.), c. A.D. 400.
12. Solidus (Olybrius – Rome – Cross, SALVS MVNDI), A.D. 472.
13. Solidus (Valentinian II – Mediolanum – Roma), c. A.D. 390.
14. Follis (Sestertius of two denarii) (Maximin II – Alexandria – Concordia), c. A.D. 308.
15. Aureus (Diocletian – Rome – Fata Victricia), A.D. 296–305.
16. Follis (Sestertius of two denarii) (Galerius – Ticinum – Fides militum), A.D. 296–305.
17. Miliarense (Constantius II – Thessalonica – Gloria Exercitus), c. A.D. 340.
18. Follis (Sestertius of two denarii) (Maximian – Treveri – Fortuna Redux), c. A.D. 296–305.

PLATE LXIV (pp. 241 ff.)

1. 3 Æ (Constantine I (?) – Constantinople – Populus Romanus), c. A.D. 335.
2. Solidus (Constantine I – Ticinum – Liberalitas XI), c. A.D. 324.
3. Aureus (Diocletian – Treveri – Pietas), A.D. 296–305.
4. Follis (Sestertius of two denarii) (Diocletian – Ticinum – Sacra Moneta), A.D. 296–305.

5. Follis (Sestertius of two denarii) (Diocletian – Ticinum – Providentia Deorum), A.D. 296–305.
6. Solidus (Helena – Ticinum – Securitas Reipublicae), c. A.D. 324.
7. Solidus (Constantine I – Treveri – Victory), c. A.D. 315.
8. 3 Æ (Constantine I – Londinium – two Victories), c. A.D. 324.
9. 3 Æ (Constantine I – Constantinople – Libertas Publica), c. A.D. 330.
10. Solidus (Constantius II – Thessalonica – two Victories), c. A.D. 340.
11. Solidus (Magnentius – Arelate – Victory and Libertas), A.D. 350–353.
12. Centenionalis (Magnentius – Lugdunum – two Victories), A.D. 350–353.
13. Solidus (Aelia Flaccilla – Constantinople – Salus Reipublicae), c. A.D. 390.
14. Solidus (Romulus Augustulus – Rome – Victory), A.D. 475–476.
15. Aureus (Maxentius – Ostia – she-wolf and twins), c. A.D. 308.
16. Half centenionalis (Constantius II – Siscia – phoenix), c. A.D. 345.
17. 4 Æ (?) (Magnus Maximus – Arelate – gateway), A.D. 383–388.
18. 3 Æ (Theodosius I – Thessalonica – gateway), A.D. 378–395.
19. 4 Æ (?) (Valentinian III – Rome – gateway), A.D. 425–455.

PLATE I

DENOMINATIONS · ROMANO · CAMPANIAN · COINAGE

PLATE II

DENOMINATIONS - ROMANO - CAMPANIAN - COINAGE (1, 2),
EARLY REPUBLICAN
A∕, AR, Æ (3-15)

PLATE III

I

DENOMINATIONS - LIBRAL AS

PLATE IV

1

2

3

DENOMINATIONS - SEMIS, TRIENS, QUADRANS

PLATE V

1

2

DENOMINATIONS - DUPONDIUS, SEMIS

PLATE VI

DENOMINATIONS - Æ (1-8, 14), DEXTANS, etc.,
Æ (9-11, 15), A/ (12, 13)

PLATE VII

MINT-OFFICIALS

PLATE VIII

MARKS OF CONTROL, etc. (1-10), FABRIC (11-15), ART (16-20)

PLATE IX

MINTS - c. 268-180 B. C.

PLATE X

MINTS - c. 130-31 B. C

PLATE XI

TYPES - SILVER - c. 242-123 B.C.

PLATE XII

TYPES - VARIATIONS OF TYPES ON AES

PLATE XIII

TYPES · RELIGIOUS · APOLLO · JUPITER

PLATE XIV

TYPES - RELIGIOUS - MARS - VESTA

PLATE XV

VIRTUES - BONUS EVENTUS - VICTORY

PLATE XVI

PORTRAITURE (1-10), FAMILY HISTORY (11-20)

PLATE XVII

TRADITIONAL HISTORY OF ROME (1-17)
PROVOCATIO (18), VOTING (19), VESTAL VIRGIN (20)

PLATE XVIII

CONTEMPORARY HISTORY - c. 133-75 B. C.

PLATE XIX

CONTEMPORARY HISTORY - c. 66-40 B. C.

PLATE XX

CONTEMPORARY HISTORY - c. 42-31 B. C.

PLATE XXI

INANIMATE OBJECTS (1-14), BUILDINGS (15-20)

PLATE XXII

CURRENCIES OF THE WEST IN RELATION TO THE EARLY ROMAN

PLATE XXIII

CURRENCIES OF ITALY AND SICILY - 3ᴿᴰ TO 2ᴺᴰ CENTURIES B.C.

PLATE XXIV

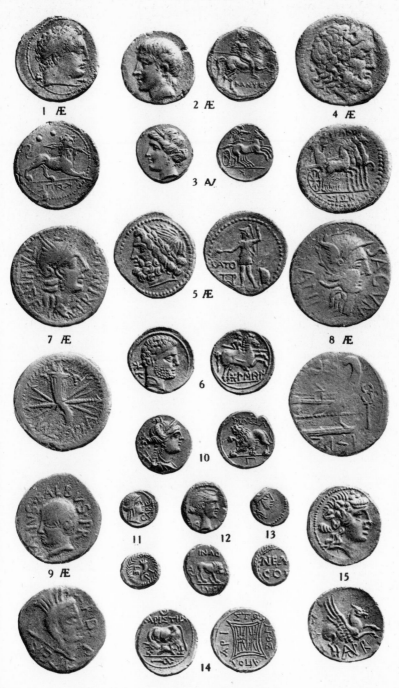

1 Æ

2 Æ

3 A/

4 Æ

5 Æ

6

7 Æ

8 Æ

9 Æ

10

11

12

13

14

15

CURRENCIES OF ITALY, THE WEST, etc.
3ʀᴅ TO 1ˢᵀ CENTURIES B. C.

PLATE XXV

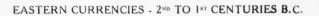

PLATE XXVI

DENOMINATIONS - A/, Æ

PLATE XXVII

1   2   3 A/   4 A/

5   6   7   8 A/

9   11 A/

10

DENOMINATIONS - A/, Æ

PLATE XXVIII

DENOMINATIONS · AES

PLATE XXIX

PLATE XXX

MINTS - AUGUSTUS TO VITELLIUS

PLATE XXXI

PLATE XXXII

MINTS · PHILIP I · CLAUDIUS II

PLATE XXXIII

NTS · AURELIAN · CARAUSIUS (A/, Æ) · AUGUSTUS · NERO (AES)

PLATE XXXIV

MINTS · AUGUSTUS · DOMITIAN (AES)

PLATE XXXV

TYPES - EMPEROR AND FAMILY

PLATE XXXVI

TYPES - EMPERORS - CONSECRATION, TRIUMPH, TRAVELS

PLATE XXXVII

TYPES - EMPERORS - LIBERALITIES, THE STATE, VOWS

PLATE XXXVIII

TYPES - PROVINCES, etc.

PLATE XXXIX

TYPES - EMPEROR AND ARMY

PLATE XL

TYPES - RELIGIOUS - AUGUSTUS - COMMODUS

PLATE XLI

TYPES - RELIGIOUS - ALBINUS - PROBUS
PERSONIFICATIONS - AEQUITAS - FELICITAS

PLATE XLII

TYPES - PERSONIFICATIONS - FIDES - VIRTVS

PLATE XLIII

TYPES · HISTORICAL · AUGUSTUS · TRAJAN

PLATE XLIV

TYPES - HISTORICAL - L. VERUS - CARAUSIUS

PLATE XLV

PLATE XLVI

TYPES - ANIMATE & INANIMATE

PLATE XLVII

TYPES - BUILDINGS

PLATE XLVIII

LOCAL AND PROVINCIAL COINAGE

PLATE XLIX

LOCAL AND PROVINCIAL COINAGE

PLATE L

LOCAL AND PROVINCIAL COINAGE

PLATE LI

LOCAL AND PROVINCIAL COINAGE - TYPES

PLATE LII

LOCAL AND PROVINCIAL COINAGE - TYPES

PLATE LIII

LOCAL AND PROVINCIAL COINAGE - TYPES

PLATE LIV

DENOMINATIONS - A/

PLATE LV

DENOMINATIONS

PLATE LVI

DENOMINATIONS - SILVERED BRONZE

PLATE LVII

DENOMINATIONS - SILVERED BRONZE - MINTS

PLATE LVIII

PLATE LIX

TYPES RELATING TO EMPEROR

PLATE LX

1   Æ   2   3   Æ   4   Æ   5   Æ

6   Æ   7   Æ   8   Æ   9   Æ

10   Æ   11   12   13   Æ   14

15   16   17   Æ   18   Æ

TYPES RELATING TO EMPEROR

PLATE LXI

TYPES RELATING TO EMPEROR, PROVINCES, ARMY

PLATE LXII

RELIGIOUS TYPES

PLATE LXIII

RELIGIOUS TYPES, PERSONIFICATIONS

PLATE LXIV

TYPES - PERSONIFICATIONS, VARIOUS